The Transformation of EU Treaty Making

Treaty making is a site of struggle between those who claim the authority to speak and act on the international stage. The European Union (EU) is an important test case in this respect because the manner in which the EU and its member states make treaties has shifted significantly over the last six decades. Drawing insights from EU law, comparative constitutionalism and international relations, this book shows how and why parliaments, the people and courts have entered a domain once dominated by governments. It presents qualitative and quantitative evidence on the importance of public trust and political tactics in explaining this transformation of EU treaty making and challenges the idea that EU treaties are too rigid. Analysing legal developments in the EU and each of its member states, this will be essential reading for those who wish to understand the EU's controversial experiment in treaty making and its wider significance.

Dermot Hodson is reader in political economy at Birkbeck College, University of London, and Visiting Professor at the College of Europe, Bruges. He has published extensively on European integration and governance and his books include *Governing the Euro Area in Good Times and Bad* (2011), *The New Intergovernmentalism: States and Supranational Actors in the Post-Maastricht Period* (2015, edited with Christopher Bickerton and Uwe Puetter) and *The Institutions of the European Union*, 4th edition (2017, edited with John Peterson). He is a member of the editorial board of the *Journal of European Public Policy*.

Imelda Maher is the Sutherland Full Professor of European Law, University College Dublin. She has published extensively in EU law and her books include *Asian Capitalism and the Regulation of Competition: Towards a Regulatory Geography of Global Competition Law* (Cambridge University Press, 2013, edited with M. Dowdle and J. Gillespie). She was general editor of *Legal Studies* (2012–2017) and is a member of the editorial boards of the *European Law Journal* and the *Irish Yearbook of International Law*. She is a member of the Royal Irish Academy and served as president of the Society of Legal Scholars in 2017.

Cambridge Studies in European Law and Policy

This series aims to produce original works which contain a critical analysis of the state of the law in particular areas of European law and to set out different perspectives and suggestions for its future development. It also aims to encourage a range of work on law, legal institutions and legal phenomena in Europe, including 'law in context' approaches. The titles in the series will be of interest to academics; policymakers, especially those who are interested in European legal, commercial and political affairs; practising lawyers, including the judiciary; and advanced law students and researchers.

Joint Editors

Professor Dr Laurence Gormley
University of Groningen
Professor Jo Shaw
University of Edinburgh

Editorial advisory board

Professor Kenneth Armstrong, *University of Cambridge*
Professor Catherine Barnard, *University of Cambridge*
Professor Richard Bellamy, *University College London*
Professor Marise Cremona, *European University Institute, Florence*
Professor Michael Dougan, *University of Liverpool*
Professor Dr Jacqueline Dutheil de la Rochère, *University of Paris II Pantheon-Assas,*
Director of the Centre for European Law, Paris
Professor Daniel Halberstam, *University of Michigan*
Professor Dora Kostakopoulou, *University of Warwick*
Professor Dr Ingolf Pernice, *Director of the Walter Hallstein Institute, Humboldt University of Berlin*
Judge Sinisa Rodin, *Court of Justice of the European Union*
Professor Eleanor Spaventa, *Durham University*
Professor Neil Walker, *University of Edinburgh*
Professor Stephen Weatherill, *University of Oxford*

Books in the Series

Redefining European Economic Integration
Dariusz Adamski

Human Rights in the Council of Europe and the European Union: Achievements, Trends and Challenges
Steven Greer, Janneke Gerards and Rosie Slowe

Core Socio-Economic Rights and the European Court of Human Rights
Ingrid Leijten

Green Trade and Fair Trade in and with the EU: Process-based Measures within the EU Legal Order
Laurens Ankersmit

New Labour Laws in Old Member States: Trade Union Responses to European Enlargement
Rebecca Zahn

The Governance of EU Fundamental Rights
Mark Dawson

The International Responsibility of the European Union: From Competence to Normative Control
Andrés Delgado Casteleiro

Frontex and Non-Refoulement: The International Responsibility of the EU
Roberta Mungianu

Gendering European Working Time Regimes: The Working Time Directive and the Case of Poland
Ania Zbyszewska

EU Renewable Electricity Law and Policy: From National Targets to a Common Market
Tim Maxian Rusche

European Constitutionalism
Kaarlo Tuori

Brokering Europe: Euro-Lawyers and the Making of a Transnational Polity
Antoine Vauchez

Services Liberalization in the EU and the WTO: Concepts, Standards and Regulatory Approaches
Marcus Klamert

Referendums and the European Union: A Comparative Enquiry
Fernando Mendez, Mario Mendez and Vasiliki Triga

The Allocation of Regulatory Competence in the EU Emissions Trading Scheme
Josephine Van Zeben

The Eurozone Crisis: A Constitutional Analysis
Kaarlo Tuori and Klaus Tuori

International Trade Disputes and EU Liability
Anne Thies

The Limits of Legal Reasoning and the European Court of Justice
Gerard Conway

New Governance and the Transformation of European Law: Coordinating EU Social Law and Policy
Mark Dawson

The Lisbon Treaty: A Legal and Political Analysis
Jean-Claude Piris

The European Union's Fight against Corruption: The Evolving Policy towards Member States and Candidate Countries
Patrycja Szarek-Mason

The Ethos of Europe: Values, Law and Justice in the EU
Andrew Williams

State and Market in European Union Law: The Public and Private Spheres of the Internal Market before the EU Courts
Wolf Sauter and Harm Schepel

The European Civil Code: The Way Forward
Hugh Collins

Ethical Dimensions of the Foreign Policy of the European Union: A Legal Appraisal
Urfan Khaliq

Implementing EU Pollution Control: Law and Integration
Bettina Lange

European Broadcasting Law and Policy
Jackie Harrison and Lorna Woods

The Transformation of Citizenship in the European Union: Electoral Rights and the Restructuring of Political Space
Jo Shaw

The Constitution for Europe: A Legal Analysis
Jean-Claude Piris

The European Convention on Human Rights: Achievements, Problems and Prospects
Steven Greer

Social Rights and Market Freedom in the European Constitution: A Labour Law Perspective
Stefano Giubboni

EU Enlargement and the Constitutions of Central and Eastern Europe
Anneli Albi

The Transformation of EU Treaty Making
The Rise of Parliaments, Referendums and Courts since 1950

Dermot Hodson
Birkbeck College, University of London

Imelda Maher
University College Dublin

CAMBRIDGE
UNIVERSITY PRESS

University Printing House, Cambridge CB2 8BS, United Kingdom

One Liberty Plaza, 20th Floor, New York, NY 10006, USA

477 Williamstown Road, Port Melbourne, VIC 3207, Australia

314-321, 3rd Floor, Plot 3, Splendor Forum, Jasola District Centre, New Delhi - 110025, India

79 Anson Road, #06-04/06, Singapore 079906

Cambridge University Press is part of the University of Cambridge.

It furthers the University's mission by disseminating knowledge in the pursuit of education, learning and research at the highest international levels of excellence.

www.cambridge.org
Information on this title: www.cambridge.org/9781107112155
DOI: 10.1017/9781316282557

© Dermot Hodson and Imelda Maher 2018

This publication is in copyright. Subject to statutory exception and to the provisions of relevant collective licensing agreements, no reproduction of any part may take place without the written permission of Cambridge University Press.

First published 2018

A catalogue record for this publication is available from the British Library

Library of Congress Cataloging in Publication data
Names: Hodson, Dermot, author. | Maher, Imelda, author.
Title: The transformation of EU treaty making : the rise of parliaments,
    referendums and courts since 1950 / Dermot Hodson, Birkbeck College,
    University of London and Imelda Maher, University College Dublin.
Description: Cambridge, United Kingdom ; New York, NY, USA : Cambridge
    University Press, [2018] | Series: Cambridge studies in European law and policy
Identifiers: LCCN 2018010119 | ISBN 9781107112155 (hardback) |
    ISBN 9781107531062 (pbk.)
Subjects: LCSH: Constitutional law–European Union countries. | European Union
    countries–Foreign relations–Treaties. | European Union–Constitution. |
    European Union countries–Politics and government.
Classification: LCC KJE4445 .H635 2018 | DDC 341.3/7094–dc23
    LC record available at https://lccn.loc.gov/2018010119

ISBN 978-1-107-11215-5 Hardback
ISBN 978-1-107-53106-2 Paperback

Cambridge University Press has no responsibility for the persistence or accuracy of URLs for external or third-party internet websites referred to in this publication, and does not guarantee that any content on such websites is, or will remain, accurate or appropriate.

For Emma, William and Hugh
and
Colin, Clodagh and Declan

Contents

List of Figures	*page* xii
List of Tables	xiii
Series Editors' Preface	xv
Acknowledgements	xvii
List of Abbreviations	xix

1 The Transformation of EU Treaty Making 1
  A Brief History of Treaty Making, 1416–2016 5
  Approach and Methods 11
  Central Argument 16
  The Plan of This Book 19
  Appendix 1.1   A Closer Look at EU Treaties 21

2 Two-Level Games, Two-Level Legitimacy and EU Treaties 34
  Tying Hands in Two-Level Games 36
  Normative Perspectives on Two-Level Games 39
  The Two-Level Legitimacy Approach 42
  Responding to Ratification Crises 47
  Conclusion 49

Part I The Negotiation Stage

3 EU Treaty Making and the Partial Eclipse of the IGC 57
  EU Treaty Negotiations from Paris to Post-Lisbon 58
  Tactics, Trust and the Transformation of EU Treaty Making 65
  Conclusion 79

ix

CONTENTS

Part II The Consent Stage

4 The Rise of Parliaments in EU Treaty Making — 87
Classifying the Role of Parliaments — 88
Changing Rules and Norms in the EU-28 — 90
Conclusion — 118
Appendix 4.1   Parliaments Scales — 120

5 The Rise of Referendums in EU Treaty Making — 133
Classifying Referendums — 134
Changing Rules and Norms in the EU-28 — 137
Conclusion — 158
Appendix 5.1   Referendums Scales — 160

6 The Rise of Higher Courts in EU Treaty Making — 170
Classifying the Role of Higher Courts — 171
Changing Rules and Norms in the EU-28 — 175
Conclusion — 193
Appendix 6.1   Courts Scales — 194

7 Explaining the Transformation of EU Treaty Making 205
Dependent Variables — 206
Independent Variables — 208
Data — 211
Regression Results — 211
Conclusion — 215
Appendix 7.1   Data Sources — 217

Part III The Practice of EU Treaty Making

8 How Changing Rules and Norms Have Shaped EU Treaty Making — 221
The Amendment Rate for EU Treaties — 222
Ratification Crises — 227
The Turn to International Law Treaties — 234
Conclusion — 240

9 Eight Ideas for Reforming EU Treaty Making — 246
Upholding the Unanimity Requirement — 248
Regulating Referendums — 250
A Pan-European Referendum — 253
Time Locks on Treaty Reform — 255
Citizen-Led Treaty Making — 258

	Judicial and Parliamentary Oversight	260
	A European Convention on the Law of Treaties	263
	Allowing Treaties to Fail	265
	Conclusion	267
10	**The Future of Treaty Making**	273
	The End of EU Treaties?	276
	Consentification	278
	Wider Implications	282
	References	287
	Index	321

Figures

4.1	Parliaments scale (average, 1951–2016)	*page* 119
4.2	Parliaments scales (by member state, 1951–2016)	120
5.1	Referendums scale (average, 1951–2016)	159
5.2	Referendums scales (by member state, 1951–2016)	160
6.1	Courts scale (average, by member state, 1951–2016)	193
6.2	Courts scales (by member state, 1951–2016)	194
8.1	Treaty amendment rate (by treaty, 1952–2016)	223
8.2	Treaty amendment rate (article by article, 1952–2016)	224

Tables

1.1	List of EU treaties	*page*	21
4.1	Parliaments scale		89
5.1	Referendums scale		136
6.1	Courts scale		174
7.1	Re-cap of ratification scales		207
7.2	Descriptive statistics: dependent and independent variables		212
7.3	Determinants of ratification scales		214
7.4	Data sources		217
8.1	Drivers of EU treaty amendment		226

Series Editors' Preface

National referendums, parliaments and indeed the courts have come to play an important part in the treaty-making process in the European Union. This applies not merely to the treaties by which the European Communities (there is still one, EURATOM), and now the European Union have been established and adapted, but also to treaties concluded between them and third countries. This study examines this process, noting rightly that treaty making is not merely a technocratic exercise. Indeed, as the various treaties establishing the Communities and the Union have created rights and obligations for legal and natural persons, not merely for the member states, which have become characterized as part of their legal heritage, it is unsurprising that there is more and more pressure for sub-state-level or even individual interest involvement in the treaty-making process. That may be inimical to a logical system of allocation of powers between states, sub-state actors, and international organisations that are created by treaties, but it has become very much a political and legal reality in the context of national pressures for regional involvement, or even popular involvement outside an election framework. People have begun to feel left out, and the perceived or real distance between the treaties and those who are affected by them is all too easily exploited for mischievous ends by populists and other purveyors of illusionary immaculate misconceptions. The need to involve and inform people, in securing the achievements of integration, while addressing their concerns, has never been more evident.

This work is a fascinating discussion of the problems and the requirements made in the legal systems of the member states, but it also offers eight positive suggestions for reforming EU treaty making. These suggestions deserve serious consideration; they should be of interest to lawyers and policymakers, as well as to policy-influencers, on the one hand, and to those involved in the academic debate, on the other hand, given that the discussion is conducted in the light of significant theoretical approaches and considerations.

In short, it is a pleasure for us to welcome this work as a most appropriate and stimulating addition to the *Cambridge Studies in European Law and Policy* series.

Laurence Gormley
Jo Shaw

Acknowledgements

This book spans political and legal developments in the EU and twenty-eight states over a six-decade period. For this reason, we have been even more dependent than usual on the generosity and insights of academic colleagues. The series editor Jo Shaw deserves special thanks for her encouragement to take on this book and we thank Kim Hughes, Finola O'Sullivan, Gemma Smith and their colleagues at Cambridge University Press for their patience and professionalism. Yassar Arafat Abdulnasser, Stephanie Sakson and Robert Swanson ensured that the book went to print in record time. Legal scholars from all EU member states reviewed our manuscript and offered their advice and constructive criticism. Particular thanks go to Marko Baretic, Gavin Barrett, Martin Belov, Celine Braumann, Arnis Buka, Judge Eugène Buttigieg, Tamara Capeta, Bruno De Witte, Tomas Dumbrovsky, Thomas Evans, Kathrin Hamenstädt, H.G. Hoogers, Maria Kendrick, Sune Klinge, Rui Tavares Lanceiro, Peter Lysina, Elisabeth Margue, Marek Martyniszyn, Tamas Molnar, Joakim Nergelius, John O'Dowd, Anestis Papdopoulos, Marie Luce Paris, Philippe-Emmanuel Partsch, Janis Pleps, Lehte Roots, Janne Salminen, Ivan Sammut, Maria Esther Seijas Villadangos, Luca Siliquini-Cinelli, Nikos Skoutaris and Oana Stefan. Several legal academics and practitioners gave us helpful referrals as we searched for relevant expertise. We would like to thank Kenneth Armstrong, Marise Cremona, Miguel Sousa Ferro, Laurence Gormley, András Jakab, Ulla Neergaard, Brian O'Gorman, Philippe-Emmanuel Partsch, Jukka Snell and Christiane Wendehorst. Thanks to Michael Breen, Michele Cini, Richard Collins, Marie-Pierre Granger, Joseph McMahon, Mario Mendez, Simona Piattoni, Uwe Puetter and Kim Lane Scheppele, for commenting on specific chapters either bilaterally or through their role as discussants at conferences and workshops. Discussions with Bob Hancké and

xvii

xviii ACKNOWLEDGEMENTS

Joni Lovenduski inspired specific lines of inquiry for which we are grateful. All errors that remain are our own.

Three institutions helped to support the research behind this book. First, the University of Illinois at Urbana–Champaign's European Union Center hosted Dermot Hodson as EU Scholar in Residence, where he presented early ideas about EU treaty making. Thanks to Sebnem Ozkan, Matt Rosenstein and Kim Rice from making this visit happen and to Robert Pahre for a brief but informative talk about two-level games and treaties over tacos. Second, Birkbeck College provided research leave, a vibrant intellectual environment and stimulating discussions with students. A full draft of this book was presented at the Birkbeck Book Lab in April 2017. Thanks to Luca Andriani, Monica Claes, Alex Colas, Jason Edwards, Deborah Mabbett, Abby Semple, Christine Reh and Ben Worthy for comments that inspired many months of additional work. Third, University College Dublin provided research support and a great collegiate environment in which to work. Particular thanks to Francis McNamara, Kate Moloney and Ronan Riordan, who provided able research assistance at various points in the project. Support of a different kind was provided by our friends and family. Dermot would like to thank Andrea, who contributed more to this manuscript than she realises; Mark for raising spirits; Róisín, Samuel and Aidan for asking great questions; and Noreen and Kevin for their insatiable interest in politics. Above all, he thanks Emma for providing the initial spark for this book and much support thereafter, and William and Hugh, whose love of learning is an inspiration. Imelda would most of all like to thank Dermot, who is the inspiration and driving force behind this book and who showed endless patience as it jostled for attention with the other demands on her time. She also wants to thank Anne, Ramel, Kathleen, Niamh and Siobhan for their support; Colin for his commitment to scholarship and family and Clodagh and Declan for their curiosity, companionship and resilience.

Abbreviations

CDU	Christian Democratic Union
CETA	Comprehensive Economic and Trade Agreement
COSAC	Conference of Parliamentary Committees for Union Affairs of Parliaments of the European Union
ECB	European Central Bank
ECI	European Citizens' Initiative
ECOSOC	Economic and Social Council
ECSC	European Coal and Steel Community
EDC	European Defence Community
EEC	European Economic Community
EURATOM	European Atomic Energy Community
EMU	Economic and Monetary Union
EU	European Union
G20	Group of Twenty
ICBL	International Campaign to Ban Landmines
ICJ	International Court of Justice
IGC	Intergovernmental Conference
ILC	International Law Commission
IMF	International Monetary Fund
MEP	Member of the European Parliament
NATO	North Atlantic Treaty Organisation
NGO	Non-governmental organisation
ÖVP	Austrian People's Party
SDP	Social Democratic Party
SPÖ	Social Democratic Party of Austria

TEU	Treaty on European Union
TFEU	Treaty on the Functioning of the European Union
TTIP	Transatlantic Trade and Investment Partnership
UN	United Nations

1 The Transformation of EU Treaty Making

Treaties are written agreements under which states and other actors bind themselves in law to act in a particular way or to create certain relations between themselves.[1] From the Peace of Westphalia[2] to the Treaty of Versailles,[3] from the Covenant of the League of Nations[4] to the Charter of the United Nations (UN),[5] from the Ottawa Treaty[6] to the Paris Agreement,[7] the history of the international system is punctuated by treaties. The United Nations Treaty Series records more than 250,000 treaties or treaty actions since 1946.[8] *Pacta sunt servanda* – whereby every treaty in force is binding upon the parties to it and must be performed by them in good faith[9] – is not only a founding principle of international law. It is, for some scholars, akin to an ethical rule or a self-evident truth.[10]

Treaty making is not simply a technocratic exercise. It is – and has long been – a site of struggle for those who claim authority to speak and act on international matters. Treaty making is, in this sense, about the exercise and control of power. Being closely connected to questions of war and peace, the power to make treaties in the medieval period lay to a large extent in the hands of monarchs.[11] Today, treaties are negotiated by states, although not exclusively so. International organisations can and do conclude treaties with states and with one another.[12] Regions, territories, indigenous people, insurgent groups and, sometimes, private actors are involved in the processes through which treaties are made.[13] The principle of consultation with non-governmental organisations (NGOs) in treaty making has been championed by the UN.[14] In negotiations over the UN Framework Convention on Climate Change at the Rio Earth Summit in 1992, more than 1,400 NGOs were invited to attend as observers and to make oral and written statements.[15] The Paris Climate Change Conference in 2015 had 25,000 official delegates

THE TRANSFORMATION OF EU TREATY MAKING

and a dedicated 'village' to accommodate a further 25,000 participants from NGOs and civil society.[16]

Who makes treaties and how such actors are held to account in doing so is a recurring concern in the study of international law.[17] Treaty making begins with the negotiation and conclusion stages, in which agreement on a final text is sought and secured. Negotiation typically takes place in a diplomatic conference,[18] while conclusion includes the production of full powers and the adoption, authentication and signature of the treaty.[19] Before a treaty can enter into force, it must pass through what we call the consent stage. Consent is sometimes equated with ratification, but ratification is just one of several means through which states can give their consent to be bound by a treaty.[20] Other means include signature, the exchange of instruments constituting a treaty, acceptance, approval or accession or any other agreed means.[21] Ratification also has internal and external faces. It refers to an internal act of approval under domestic constitutional law and the international procedure that brings the treaty into force, e.g. the depositing by states of instruments of ratification.[22]

The consent of states to be bound remains a classic principle of treaty making that is closely connected to the idea of state sovereignty.[23] The Vienna Convention on the Law of Treaties – which codifies international treaty making law – allows states to agree on the means through which they express their consent to be bound but it requires an expression of some sort.[24] Multilateral treaties sometimes include provisions that allow for treaty amendment without the consent of all parties.[25] For instance, three-fifths of International Monetary Fund (IMF) members can amend aspects of the Fund's Articles of Agreement.[26] However, the Vienna Convention makes clear that a treaty amendment cannot bind a state unless the state is party to this amendment.[27] Treaty making practices sometimes diverge from this provision, as in the Rome Statute's provision that amendments of an exclusively institutional nature can be adopted by a reinforced majority vote by state parties.[28] However, such practices arguably rework rather than reject the need for states to express their consent to be bound.[29]

The consent stage of treaty making is, to a large extent, a matter for domestic law, usually governed by state constitutions. Whether and what checks and balances should be placed on treaty-making power is a matter of debate among constitutional theorists. John Locke saw treaty making as an instance of federative rather than executive power and argued that the former should be 'left to the prudence and wisdom of those who have the power to exercise it for the public good'.[30] Alexander Hamilton disagreed on the grounds that 'the operation of treaties as laws, pleads strongly for the participation of the whole or a portion of the legislative body in the office of making them'.[31] Today, treaty making is most commonly an executive function, but other actors play a role. Parliaments participate in the consent stage of treaty making in most democracies, thus providing democratic oversight of executives' treaty-making powers.[32] This does not prevent executives from taking steps to curtail such checks and balances. Had the Paris Agreement (2016) been a treaty, it would have required the advice and consent of the US Senate by a two-thirds majority of its members.[33] By avoiding the 'T' word and relying on existing legal authority, President Barack Obama circumvented the need for congressional approval.[34] This move was merely the latest attempt by the executive branch to work around treaty-making powers that have, Oona Hathaway argues, been 'overtaken by actual political practice'.[35]

The European Union – the subject of this book – is fertile ground for students of treaty making. This is so because EU treaties – a term that encompasses Community treaties – are in flux. The EU was established by the Maastricht Treaty (1992),[36] which in turn was built on a triumvirate of treaties that formed the European Communities: the Treaty of Paris (1951),[37] the Rome Treaty (1957)[38] and the EURATOM Treaty (1957).[39] These founding treaties have been amended fifteen times since 1951 (see Appendix 1.1). The most important EU treaty amendments have taken place since the mid-1980s. The Single European Act (1986)[40] was the first full-scale revision of the treaties, and there have been four further amendments since then: Maastricht (1992), the Amsterdam Treaty (1997),[41] the Nice Treaty (2000)[42] and the Lisbon Treaty (2007).[43] The European Constitution[44] was a more ambitious project that would have replaced this patchwork of treaties with a single legal text, but it never entered into force. Lisbon was supposed to draw a line under this intense period of treaty change, but there have been several amendments since, the most significant of which was the Article 136 TFEU amendment, which allowed for the creation of a stability mechanism for the eurozone.[45]

EU treaty making is also the site of a pronounced, public struggle between competing actors over who has the right to negotiate treaties. In 1950, the representatives of six sovereign states met in a tightly sealed intergovernmental conference (IGC) initiated by the French government to negotiate the Treaty of Paris.[46] The European Parliament has long sought a role in EU treaty negotiations, and today it has the authority, alongside the European Commission and individual member states, to initiate treaty amendments.[47] For major treaty changes, member states are expected to hold a Convention – a forum including representatives of national parliaments, the European Parliament, the European Commission and EU heads of state or government – to consider treaty changes prior to an IGC.[48] In this respect, the EU is in the vanguard of participatory approaches to treaty making.

The increased involvement of parliaments, the people and courts over time in the consent stage of EU treaty making is also striking. The Treaty of Paris was approved by national parliaments on the basis of a simple majority.[49] Today, most member state parliaments require a reinforced majority in one or more chamber, and the number of chambers involved has increased with each enlargement of the EU.[50] In Belgium, subnational parliaments are routinely given a say on EU treaties.[51] Referendums on treaties are rare worldwide but they have become routine in relation to EU treaties.[52] In February 1986, Denmark became the first member state to hold a referendum on an EU treaty amendment; EU member states have held fifteen such referendums since. No less than ten member states announced referendums on the European Constitution.[53] National higher courts are also now routinely involved in EU treaty making. The Article 136 TFEU amendment led to constitutional challenges in six member states[54] and a preliminary reference to the Court of Justice of the EU.[55] Through its landmark judgments on Maastricht[56] and the Lisbon[57] treaties, Germany's Federal Constitutional Court is a prominent actor in the process through which EU treaties are changed.[58]

Few other instances of treaty making can match the EU for intensity or controversy. During the period 2010–2011 alone, EU member states launched a combined 105 national ratification procedures connected to treaty amendments.[59] Once thought of as epoch-making events, treaty amendments are now part of the 'everyday politics' of the EU, argues Thomas Christiansen.[60] And yet treaties are no less controversial for this. The troubled passage of the Maastricht Treaty, which was rejected by Danish voters in a referendum and only narrowly endorsed by their French counterparts, intensified popular concerns over EU treaty change.[61] Thirteen years later, referendums on the European Constitution in France and the Netherlands produced a popular backlash against a treaty that was designed to bring the EU closer to its people.[62] The United Kingdom had planned to hold a referendum on this treaty, but its failure to do so on earlier or later agreements goes some way towards explaining why Prime Minister David Cameron called and lost a referendum in 2016 on the United Kingdom's continued membership of the EU.

This book seeks to understand the transformation of EU treaty making over the period 1950–2016. Our overarching aim is to discover how and why parliaments, the people and courts came to play a role in a domain once dominated by national governments and what the consequences of this shift are. We consider how the European Parliament, national parliaments and – to a lesser extent – the Court of Justice of the EU became part of the process through which the EU negotiates treaty amendments. We investigate changing constitutional laws and practices in each of the EU's member states to understand how parliaments, the people and courts acquired a greater say in the process through which such treaty amendments are accepted. We consider what effect such changes had on the rate of EU treaty amendment and examine the case for reforming EU treaty making yet further. In the light of these findings, students of international law and international relations can learn about the increasing frequency and complexity of EU treaty making.

In this introductory chapter, we set the scene for what follows by situating this six-decade study of EU treaty making in a wider historical context in the first section before discussing the theoretical and methodological approach of our study in the second section. The third section introduces our central argument. The fourth presents a plan of what follows.

A Brief History of Treaty Making, 1416–2016

The treaty-making powers of monarchs in the medieval period were sweeping but by no means absolute. Treaties at this time were essentially private contracts between rulers rather than the territories they ruled,[63] although these agreements frequently imposed obligations on the latter.[64] For this reason, the consent of nobles, prelates and towns for treaties was periodically sought, this process of 'co-ratification' serving as a precursor to parliamentary involvement in the consent stage of treaty making.[65] In fact, parliaments occasionally participated in medieval treaty making, albeit on an ad hoc basis.[66] In England, for instance, the Treaty of Canterbury (1416) was approved by parliament after being read aloud in both its houses.[67] In France, Assemblies of Estates played a comparable role on occasion.[68] Treaties were otherwise ratified by rulers through solemn oaths, the exchange of hostages, the

6 THE TRANSFORMATION OF EU TREATY MAKING

kiss of peace and written texts.[69] Confirmation by an oath in a religious ceremony was the most common way of ratifying a treaty, a process that gave the pope and papal courts an important, indirect role in the legitimation of treaties.[70]

The Peace of Westphalia (1646–1648) did not, it is now widely recognised, found the international state system.[71] Nevertheless, Westphalia was a significant episode in the history of treaty making, which reflected the gradual secularisation of the treaty ratification process while foreshadowing the emergence of diplomatic conferences in the nineteenth and twentieth centuries. The ratification of treaties via religious oaths died out after the Reformation, as did references to canon law, with treaties being ratified instead by rulers.[72] The norm by this point was that rulers were obliged to ratify agreements negotiated by their representatives unless these representatives had exceeded their full powers. Today, full powers designate the authority of individuals to negotiate and sign treaties on behalf of a state, but then they came with detailed instructions from rulers and 'wide authority to negotiate and a promise to accept as binding anything signed as a result of these negotiations'.[73] For this reason, verifying full powers was a critical and, at times, laborious part of treaty making. At Westphalia, it took several months of diplomatic exchanges before Spain's full powers, which had initially been vested in a double delegation, were revised to the satisfaction of other parties.[74]

The obligation to ratify in early modern treaty making jarred with the emerging domestic constitutional requirements for treaty ratification. For example, the Peace of Münster (1648)[75] – an agreement negotiated at Westphalia – was put to the Estates General of the Dutch Republic.[76] The Treaty of Münster (1648), another Westphalian agreement, gave the 'Emperor, the most Christian King, the Electors of the Sacred Roman Empire, the Princes and States' eight weeks to prepare and present solemn Acts of Ratification at Munster.[77] The Treaty also provided for the transposition of its provisions into the 'other fundamental Laws and Constitutions of the Empire in the Acts of the next Diet of the Empire', an early example of constitutional amendment being linked to treaty making.[78]

Westphalia prefigured the modern treaty conference by bringing together the representatives of rulers in a treaty-making congress to which interested parties were invited.[79] This was not a gathering of the victors of war or even its victims but an assembly of those with a stake in the future of Europe. The delegations at Westphalia included noblemen and jurists and other experts,[80] accompanied by a coterie of 'noble companions, guards, pages, lackeys, grooms, cooks [and] tailors'.[81] All told, the negotiations lasted five years.[82] In contrast to today's treaty-making forums, the delegates never met in plenary, but the interaction between them was intensive, sustained and structured. Venice and a papal nuncio acted as mediators in Münster, while negotiations took place without mediation in Osnabrück.[83]

The negotiation of treaties by the plenipotentiaries of heads of state or government became the norm in the eighteenth and nineteenth centuries, although the inclusivity of treaty-making conferences varied. The Treaty of Paris (1814) invited 'all the powers engaged on either side' of the War of the Sixth Coalition to send plenipotentiaries to Vienna.[84] Although there were 216 states represented at the Congress of Vienna (1814–1815), its deliberations were dominated by the great powers. 'The Congress never formally opened', as Genevieve Peterson notes; 'credentials were never officially verified, and there was no plenary session'.[85] 'The Congress dances', said Prince de Ligne of the lavish entertainment offered to him and his fellow delegates, 'but it doesn't advance'.[86]

The first Hague Peace Conference (1899) demonstrated a clearer commitment to the equality of states in treaty negotiations after Tsar Nicholas II invited fifty-nine of the world's sovereign states to discuss 'the most efficacious means for assuring to all peoples the blessing of real and lasting peace'.[87] Twenty-six nations small and large participated in the decision-making structures of the conference, with the appointment of Auguste Beernaerts, a Belgian, as chair of one of the conference's three commissions, reinforcing this point. The presence of delegates from Brazil, China, Japan, Persia, the United States and Siam embodied a less Eurocentric vision of multilateral treaty making, albeit one in which European states remained firmly in the majority. Forty-three states participated in the second Hague Peace Conference (1907), which was convened, in part, due to the efforts of the American Peace Society. This society was kept away from the conference, which nonetheless marked the beginning of systematic efforts by NGOs to shape the course of treaty negotiations.[88]

The Paris Peace Conference (1919) harkened back to an earlier period of treaty making as well as ushering in a new one. The participation of Australia, Canada, India and South Africa as delegates showed the increasing influence of smaller powers.[89] As at Vienna a century earlier, however, the most important negotiations played out in the margins of the conference among the most powerful states. Germany and other Central Powers, meanwhile, were entirely excluded until the Treaty of

Versailles and related agreements had been negotiated. In spite of its secretive working methods, the Paris Peace Conference was committed to a new era of transparent treaty making. The Covenant of the League of Nations (1919) required all treaties or international engagements entered into by League members to be registered with the League's secretariat.[90] A response to the role played by secret treaties in the run-up to the First World War, this provision spoke to Leon Trotsky's vision of 'democratic foreign policy'[91] as much as to Woodrow Wilson's aim of 'open covenants of peace, openly arrived at'.[92]

So long as the traditional doctrine of full powers prevailed, instances of non-ratification were rare. The Dutch Republic's failure to ratify the Treaty of Elbing (1656) after the United Provinces objected was treated not as a constitutional right but, in the words of Dutch diplomat Abraham de Wicquefort, as an act that ridiculed the power of ambassadors.[93] A failure to ratify was, as one scholar put it, treated as an unfriendly act.[94] The American and French Revolutions were turning points in this respect, the US constitution (1789), as noted above, making the US president's treaty-making powers subject to the advice and consent of the Senate,[95] and the French constitution (1793) giving the power to authorise treaties to the legislature.[96] Thereafter, it gradually came to be accepted that states had discretion over whether and how to give their consent to be bound to treaties. The Treaty of Frankfurt (1871), for example, recognised the need for its approval by the French Assembly and Chief Executive of the French Republic.[97]

By the twentieth century, parliamentary involvement in the consent stage of treaty making was commonplace. Even in the United Kingdom, where treaty making fell, and still falls, under the royal prerogative, the government agreed in 1924 to lay treaties before both houses of parliament so as to provide an opportunity for discussion.[98] The inter-war period also saw the first modern European referendum on treaty making, when the people of Luxembourg voted in 1919 against economic union with Belgium.[99] In a harbinger of controversy to come, the Belgium–Luxembourg Economic Union went ahead regardless. In 1921, the Swiss constitution was amended to allow citizens to petition for a referendum on treaties of an unspecified duration or which could not be renounced, this amendment coming one year after Switzerland held a referendum on joining the League of Nations.[100] To this day, Switzerland remains one of the few non-EU states in which treaty-related referendums are a regular occurrence, although a significant share of these are related to the state's relationship with the EU.

The involvement of higher courts in treaty making is more tentative, with treaty making being widely seen as a matter for the executive. In 1858, a controversy over whether a Latin American border treaty was compatible with Nicaragua's constitution was settled not in the Nicaraguan courts but by US President Grover Cleveland, acting as an arbiter.[101] The US Supreme Court itself has treaded cautiously in relation to treaties. Although it made clear in 1870 that 'a treaty cannot change the Constitution or be held valid if it be in violation of that instrument',[102] the Supreme Court had yet to strike down a treaty as unconstitutional at the time of writing.[103] National constitutions that expressly provide for the constitutional review of treaties are an altogether more recent phenomenon. The introduction of constitutional reviews in France's constitution of 1958, Mendez suggests, encouraged constitution makers in Europe, Latin America and Africa to introduce similar provisions from the 1970s onwards.[104]

States dominate modern treaty making, but they have faced competition from new actors since the late nineteenth century. From the Treaty of Bern (1874) onwards, treaties began to create international organisations and some of these organisations eventually acquired a treaty-making role. The Universal Postal Union created at Bern can enact changes to the Postal Convention in plenary sessions of its congress before its members have submitted their instruments of ratification.[105] The League of Nations was a tentative participant in treaty making, but an early success was the Åland convention (1921), which ensured the non-fortification and non-militarisation of Finland's autonomous Swedish-speaking region. The treaty was negotiated between Sweden, Finland and six other states, but these states met at the request of the League, responded to its recommendations and signed the final agreement in Geneva.[106] Also significant was the League's development of the first rules of procedure for treaty-making, rules that continue to shape the conduct of treaty-making conferences today.[107]

The United Nations Charter (1945) gave little indication of the UN's prolific role to come in treaty making.[108] The Charter invited the General Assembly to initiate studies and make recommendations 'for the purpose of promoting international co-operation in the political field and encouraging the progressive development of international law and its codification'.[109] To this end, the General Assembly created the International Law Commission (ILC), which in 1949 began preparatory work on codifying the law of the sea. Following this work, the General Assembly sponsored a convention of eighty-six states in Geneva, which agreed

10 THE TRANSFORMATION OF EU TREATY MAKING

on four treaties that entered into force once twenty-two states had deposited their instruments of ratification. This model of treaty making, one of several followed by the General Assembly, produced twenty-one other treaties in this way over the next forty-eight years, including the Vienna Convention on the Law of Treaties (1969) and the Rome Statute of the International Criminal Court (1998).

By 2015, more than 560 multilateral treaties had been negotiated under the auspices of the UN.[110] In most of these cases, the UN served as an initiator and enabler of negotiations rather than an actor in negotiations themselves. The final text of UN-sponsored multilateral treaties is typically signed by representatives of states, which alone give their consent to be bound by such agreements. A rare exception in this regard is the Vienna Convention on the Law of Treaties between States and International Organizations or between International Organizations, which was signed and subject to an act of formal confirmation by the UN and other international organisations.[111]

As the title of this last convention suggests, international organisations can be parties to treaties in their own right. Although this convention has not yet entered into force,[112] its recognition that 'international organizations possess the capacity to conclude treaties, which is necessary for the exercise of their functions and the fulfilment of their purpose',[113] reflects international customary law.[114] The World Health Organization (WHO), for example, was party to nearly 800 treaties by 2009.[115] And yet the treaty-making powers of international organisations fall well short of those enjoyed by states. The International Court of Justice (ICJ) has noted that international organisations do not possess the 'general competence' enjoyed by states in international law. They can participate in treaty making, the Court concluded, but only if they act in accordance with 'common interests whose promotion those States entrust to them'.[116]

Since the Second World War, NGOs have made significant inroads into treaty making. An early indication of this trend was the Congress of Europe (1948), organised by the International Committee for Movements for European Unity. This umbrella group of pro-European pressure groups gathered in The Hague to discuss plans for post-war European unity. The Congress of Europe produced a political resolution rather than a draft treaty, but its ideas for a European Assembly, a Charter for Human Rights and a Supreme Court were taken up in the Treaty of London (1949), which created the Council of Europe. The Congress of Europe reconvened in The Hague in 1953 but was less influential. This experiment in NGO-led treaty making had run its course.

NGOs found a more long-lasting route into treaty making via the UN. Under the UN Charter, the Economic and Social Council (ECOSOC) is authorised both to convene international conferences[117] and to consult with NGOs.[118] By using these powers in tandem, the ECOSOC ensured that NGOs were widely consulted in UN treaty making. The Ottawa Treaty (1997) provides a paradigmatic example in this respect, with more than 600 NGOs from 40 states working together through the International Campaign to Ban Landmines (ICBL) to influence treaty negotiations.[119] Members of the ICBL were present in the review conferences that preceded these negotiations, allowing NGOs to table proposals, present papers and take the floor.[120] Whether NGOs herald a new age of democratic treaty making or privilege certain voices is a matter of heated debate among students of international law and international relations.[121]

Approach and Methods

This book explores how the EU and its member states have transformed EU treaty making. Our focus is on EU treaty making since the Treaty of Paris (1951). Treaties between the EU and non-member states, for example, the EU–Canada Comprehensive Economic and Trade Agreement and treaties of accession are put to one side in this study, although they work their way back into the closing stages of our argument.[122] This is not a book about Brexit, although it has much to say about the contested process through which the United Kingdom gave its consent to be bound by EU treaties and what British withdrawal from the Union tells us about treaty making in the United Kingdom and the EU. International law treaties negotiated between some or all EU member states, as in the Fiscal Compact (2012)[123] are explored in later chapters of the book.

Our emphasis in this study is on major treaty-making episodes. The Treaty on European Union (1992) counts as major by our reckoning, whereas the Treaty Amending Certain Provisions of the Protocol on the Statute of the European Investment Bank (1975) does not. Beyond extremes of this sort, it is difficult to rank treaties according to their significance. While there is a plausible case to be made for the Lisbon Treaty being more significant than the Amsterdam Treaty, for example, not all member states agree. Denmark's Ministry of Justice saw Amsterdam as entailing a transfer of sovereignty but not Lisbon.[124] As a result, a referendum was held on the former but not the latter. The Treaty of

Lisbon complicated rather than clarified matters by introducing ordinary and simplified revision procedures for amending EU treaties.[125] The ordinary revision procedure is aimed at amendments that increase or reduce the competences conferred on the EU by treaties, although not exclusively so.[126] The simplified revision procedure cannot be used to increase the competences of the EU and it is limited to revisions concerning certain aspects of the Treaty on the Functioning of the European Union (TFEU).[127] Simplified does not necessarily mean insignificant, however, as EU leaders demonstrated when they used this procedure to create a €500 billion rescue fund during the euro crisis.[128]

In undertaking this research, we are mindful that EU treaties are arguably the most studied international agreements in history.[129] And yet – aside from a flurry of interest in the European Convention in the 2000s[130] – much less has been written on the process through which EU treaties are made. Bruno de Witte is one of the few legal scholars to have written extensively about EU treaty amendment.[131] He highlights the tension between the 'internationalist' rules governing EU treaty amendment and the 'constitutionalist' character of the EU's legal order.[132] EU law goes well beyond conventional international law, de Witte accepts, but the EU's approach to treaty making, by relying on the unanimous consent of all member states, is 'more respectful of national sovereignty than the amendment procedures of many other multilateral treaties'.[133] De Witte has also written about what he calls 'the national constitutional dimension of European treaty revision'.[134] He suggests that the growing influence in national ratification procedures of national parliamentarians, sub-state governments and assemblies, constitutional courts and the public casts an increasingly visible shadow over treaty negotiations.

Monica Claes's seminal study of national courts' role in the EU legal order offers a wealth of detail on the judicial dimension of EU treaty making. In particular, she offers the most comprehensive comparative constitutional analysis to date of how the prior constitutional review of EU treaties emerged in France, Spain, Germany, Ireland and the United Kingdom.[135] Claes's book also deals extensively with the question of how a posteriori reviews of EU treaties fared in Germany, Belgium, Denmark, France, Ireland and the Netherlands.[136] Claes extends this analysis in her 'bird's eye view' of the role played by national constitutions in EU law.[137] Here Claes traces the 'shaky constitutional foundations' of EU treaty making in the EU-15 and their eventual resort to constitutional amendments and so-called Europe provisions.[138] The Maastricht Treaty was a turning point in this regard, she argues, because of the ambition of this treaty and because constitutional amendments in one member state prompted similar changes in others.[139]

Among political scientists, Finn Laursen's fine-grained studies of the Maastricht,[140] Amsterdam,[141] Nice[142] and Lisbon[143] treaties and the European Constitution shed considerable light on EU treaty making.[144] So too does his edited collection on EU treaty making from Paris to Lisbon, which draws together key findings and provides an invaluable resource on lesser-known EU treaties such as the Merger Treaties (1965) and the Budget Treaties (1970 and 1975).[145] Thomas Christiansen and Christine Reh have written the most extensive account to date of treaty negotiation in the EU, identifying key actors at the various stages of treaty reform and conceptualising their role in the 'continuous consti-tutionalization' of the EU since the 1950s.[146] Carlos Closa breaks new ground in his comparative study of national ratification processes in relation to EU treaty making. This important work shows how the roles played by national actors, including parliaments, presidents, higher courts and the people, have changed since the EU's founding treaties and sheds light on the multifarious reasons why referendums were called on for specific treaties and for ratification failure and success. Fernando Mendez, Mario Mendez and Vasiliki Triga offer an excellent interdisciplinary analysis of referendums on European integration.[147] Although this study is not limited to treaty making, it has much to say about the turn to direct democracy in this domain and the case for reforming the EU's treaty-making methods.

Although we draw extensively on this literature, we also go beyond it in seeking to understand the puzzle at the heart of this book. The methods we employ are historical and comparative as well as qualitative and quantitative. In analysing changes to the negotiation stage, we retrace the history of EU treaty conferences from the Schuman Plan Conference in 1950 to post-Lisbon treaty amendments within the European Council. This historical study shows how and when norms surrounding EU treaty making shifted to empower the European Parliament, national parlia-ments and the Court of Justice of the EU and identifies the key drivers behind this shift. Our analysis of the consent stage takes the form of a comparative constitutional analysis of changing treaty-making rules and norms in the EU's twenty-eight member states based on an analysis of constitutional laws, case law before higher courts and particular treaty-making episodes. To compare rules and norms in a systematic way, we construct a set of ratification scales, which we use to code for the relative prominence of parliaments, the people and courts for treaty revision in EU member states over time. These scales form the dependent variables in an ordinal regression analysis through which we test competing explanations of the factors driving the transformation of EU treaty making.

The emphasis on both constitutional rules and norms in this study is deliberate. That constitutional norms matter can be seen, for example, in the case of Ireland. Although the literature sometimes suggests otherwise, referendums on EU treaties in Ireland are not mandatory.[148] A referendum is required to amend the Irish constitution,[149] but the constitution does not require a constitutional amendment to incorporate major EU treaty amendments. Such amendments have been routinely undertaken since the Irish government lost a court challenge against its decision to ratify the Single European Act by parliamentary channels alone.[150] Hence referendums on EU treaties are not a constitutional rule as their prevalence would suggest. They have become a constitutional norm in the sense that the organisational practice surrounding the ratification of EU treaties in Ireland has been given a broad and inclusive meaning leaning towards referendums.

Constitutional norms have been extensively studied by both legal scholars and political scientists. For Antje Wiener, a key scholar of constitutional norms in a European context, such norms capture the 'historically and culturally contingent' character of constitutions and involve three key elements: limited government, the rule of law and the protection of human rights.[151] They derive validity not only from legal frameworks, she suggests, but also via their appropriateness to specific groups and cultural validity.[152] Norms have a stable dimension as a social institution – constitutional norms in particular being at the heart of the state. There is also a dynamic dimension, where norms are a flexible social construct. Wiener points to the importance of this dynamic dimension where contestation is a focus.[153] It is through contestation that legal norms secure their (democratic) legitimacy, and such contestation also points to the evolutionary nature of norms whose meaning can change over time.[154]

Within the legal literature, A.V. Dicey was among the first to observe the 'understandings, habits, or practices' that drive constitutional law, and scholars continue to study such conventions, which are inherent within the constitution even if recognised but not enforceable in court.[155] Following Jennings, constitutional norms can be understood as more than 'mere practice'.[156] They refer to precedents that actors respect not because they are compelled to do so under constitutional rules but because they are deemed appropriate. Waldron goes further and argues that those norms practiced by the powerful in society are part of the legal system and are more than just accepted moral norms.[157] Constitutional norms may be formally articulated in foundational documents of the state – to a greater or lesser degree. There may be binding norms, enforceable before the courts, or constitutional conventions may emerge that are based on generally articulated foundational norms with practice giving meaning to those norms, and that meaning changing over time reflecting their evolutionary and dynamic nature.

To be clear, our focus in this volume is not on the central role played by the Court of Justice of the EU in interpreting the treaties and, through that process, building a community of law.[158] Rather, we are interested in how the contestation and dynamic nature of constitutional norms encourage policymakers to choose one path of treaty formation over another. This concerns both treaty formation, as in the decision to involve observers from the European Parliament in treaty negotiation, and the practice of routinely amending national constitutions in the context of treaty ratification (or not). We use the term 'constitutional norm' to encapsulate principles and values[159] and to encompass the customary, moral and political quality of dynamic and contestable constitutional norms.[160]

The comparison of constitutional rules and norms governing EU treaty making across EU member states presented in this book is influenced by Beth Simmons's pioneering work on treaty making in the field of human rights.[161] As part of this study, Simmons coded constitutional provisions on treaty making in 125 states. This was achieved with reference to a scale that classified the role played by chief executives, cabinets, legislatures and referendums in ratification and made clear the author's assumptions about what constituted a higher hurdle for treaty ratification. While readers might differ on how high to set the hurdle, the methodology is clear, reproducible and, as we show, revisable. Elements of this approach can be seen in Simon Hug and Thomas König's analysis of ratification constraints relating to the Amsterdam Treaty.[162] But the authors devote more energy to codifying political constraints. Also, their index, like Simmons's, provides a snapshot of treaty making at a given point in time rather than a moving image of how it has evolved.

Treaty making, especially in the EU context, is a close cousin of constitutional design. The comparative turn in constitutional law since the

1990s – or comparative constitutionalism as Ran Hirschl calls it – has opened up new research agendas that we draw on in this book.[163] Tom Ginsburg and Mila Versteeg's study of constitutional review in 204 states over the period 1781–2011 shows the scope and promise of this research agenda.[164] Gabriel L. Negretto's analysis of constitutional choice in Latin America between 1900 and 2008 also breaks new ground.[165] We do not match these studies in terms of scope or methodological sophistication, but we draw inspiration from them nonetheless. Specifically, our empirical ambition is not only to compare the constitutional rules and norms governing EU treaty change but also to explain the variation that we see over time and across member states.

Comparative constitutionalism also influences our analysis of how rules and norms have shaped treaty making. A seminal contribution to this literature is Donald Lutz's study of the rules governing constitutional amendment across countries and US states. Lutz's methodology has been questioned[166] but has inspired new and more sophisticated approaches to comparing constitutions. Inspired by this literature, we use linear regression techniques to investigate the impact of treaty-making rules and norms on the rate of EU treaty amendment. The comparative method also underpins our discussion of reform ideas. In discussing whether EU treaty making should be more or less flexible, we consider how other international organisations amend treaties. We also draw inspiration from different modes of constitutional amendment in other political systems.

Central Argument

By means of the approach and methods outlined above, this book charts the transformation of EU treaty making since 1950. The evidence and analysis presented within show that the constitutional rules and norms underpinning the negotiation and consent stages have shifted to provide a more prominent role to parliaments, the people and courts. But how do we explain this development and evaluate its consequences? Our central argument is that this shift is a product of trust as well as tactics. This explanation emerges from two theoretical lines of inquiry. The first, which follows Robert Pahre's classic theory of two-level games, sees governments as involving the people, parliaments and courts in treaty making to boost their bargaining position in EU treaty negotiations.[167] The second offers a normative twist on the theory of two-level games. The two-level legitimacy approach, as we call it, sees the involvement of new actors in EU treaty making as a response to the problem of declining trust in the EU and member state governments.

Putnam's archetypal account of diplomacy and domestic politics is stylised and its shortcomings are widely recognised,[168] but it sheds some light, we contend, on how and why national governments have complicated EU treaty making. Governments prefer to keep room for manoeuvre in the domestic arena when entering international negotiations, Putnam suggests, but they may, on occasion, use more stringent ratification rules at home to drive a harder bargain abroad. Our findings suggest that EU member states' decision to involve new actors in the consent stage of treaty making is consistent with this strategy of tying hands, as Andrew Moravcsik calls it.[169] In contrast, the two-level game struggles to explain why such national governments appear to have tied their hands at the negotiation stage, although it helps us to understand why the involvement of the European Parliament and national parliaments has been balanced by a greater role for EU heads of state or government. The latter's decision to send personal representatives to EU treaty-making conventions and the European Council's dominant role in the simplified revision procedure are just two ways in which EU leaders have strengthened their grip on the negotiation stage at the same time as making it more inclusive. Above all, we argue, the two-level game approach explains why governments have consistently responded to the risk of involuntary defection in relation to EU treaty making by untying their hands. Involuntary defection refers to a situation in which governments negotiate and conclude a treaty but are unable to ratify it. Where the risk of involuntary defection emerges in relation to EU treaties, national governments tend to untie hands, we noted, by seeking to rerun referendums after 'no' votes against EU treaties and by making treaties under international rather than EU law.

Putnam accepted that a 'testable two-level theory of international negotiations must be rooted in a theory of domestic politics, that is a theory about the power and preferences of the major actors at Level II'.[170] For all his insights into the interplay between international diplomacy and domestic politics, Putnam does not claim to offer such a theory and, instead, sees his two-level game approach as being compatible with 'such diverse perspectives as Marxism, interest group pluralism, bureaucratic politics, and neo-corporatism'.[171] The two-level legitimacy approach is based on an understanding of domestic politics – and, indeed, European politics – in which a crisis of legitimacy has taken hold. It sees the rise of the people, parliaments and courts in EU treaty making as a response, in particular, to the persistent problems of trust facing the EU and its member states since the 1990s. In keeping with this approach, we find that member states in which there are low levels of trust in national governments tend to give parliaments a greater say over EU treaties. Those in which trust in the EU is low tend to adopt constitutional rules that make referendums more likely and that give a more prominent role to courts. Our findings also suggest that the increased role of parliaments in the negotiation stage owes more to governments' attempts to address the problems of trust and legitimacy facing the EU than the efforts of parliaments themselves. The European Parliament has staked a claim for treaty-making powers, we find, but its involvement and that of national parliaments is the product of a choice by national governments in response to the problems of legitimacy facing the EU. More puzzling from a two-level legitimacy perspective is national governments' determination to press ahead with treaty amendments after ratification difficulties have been encountered. This determination, we argue, suggests that tactics rather than trust wins out in such cases, although legitimacy concerns were not entirety absent. The EU's frequent recourse to treaty making in the 1990s and 2000s can be understood, we suggest, as a sincere but misguided attempt to address legitimacy concerns highlighted by earlier rounds of treaty amendment.

A recurring theme in the literature on EU treaty making is that the constitutional rules and norms underpinning the negotiation and consent stages are too rigid. The evidence presented in this book challenges such claims. The rate of treaty amendment has slowed as parliaments and the people have assumed a greater role in treaty making, we find, although the annual rate of treaty amendments has increased since the mid-1980s rather than decelerated (Chapter 8). Treaty-making rules and norms impede treaty amendment, in other words, but the former have not produced deadlock. Whereas greater flexibility would nonetheless be welcome from a two-level game perspective so as to minimise the risk of involuntary defection, the two-level legitimacy approach offers a dissenting view. Attempts to circumvent the role of parliaments, the people and courts in EU treaty making, it suggests, could further inflame the problems of legitimacy facing the EU. Drawing on these competing theoretical perspectives, this book interrogates a range of ideas for reforming EU treaties. It debates arguments for a reinforced majority of EU members to approve treaty amendments, the regulation of referendums and the case for a pan-European referendum. It explores the case for citizen-led treaty making, greater judicial and parliamentary oversight of EU treaty making and ways to limit EU member states' ability to conclude international treaties with one another. It asks whether EU treaties that encounter problems at the consent stage should ultimately be allowed to fail.

The Plan of This Book

The remainder of this book is divided into nine chapters and three parts. It begins by describing in more detail the theories that motivate our study (Chapter 2). This chapter situates the idea of tying hands within Putnam's two-level game approach and the wider literature he inspired. It considers the normative underpinning of two-level games and develops the two-level legitimacy approach as an alternative way of conceptualising, explaining and evaluating the transformation of EU treaty making. The normative assumptions underpinning Putnam's approach and ours are compared.

Part I of the book looks at the negotiation stage of EU treaty making. It explores the origins and evolution of the IGC as a forum for negotiating treaties since the Schuman Plan Conference of 1950. This historical analysis charts the role played by parliamentarians in the negotiation stage from the work of the Ad Hoc Assembly in 1952 and 1953 to the Convention Method codified by the Lisbon Treaty. At the same time, it explores the rise of the European Council as a forum for EU treaty making in relation to IGCs and through the Lisbon Treaty's simplified revision procedure. This chapter asks whether the partial eclipse of the IGC can be understood in two-level game terms or as a response to the problems of two-level legitimacy facing the EU.

Part II turns to the consent stage of treaty making. It begins by tracing the evolution of the constitutional rules and norms governing the role of parliaments (Chapter 4), the people (Chapter 5) and courts (Chapter 6) in the process through which EU member states give their consent to be bound by EU treaties. Covering the 28 EU member states over a period of six decades, the results of this comparative constitutional analysis are summarised by means of ratification scales, which facilitate a comparison of EU treaty-making rules and norms across member states and over time. Using probit regression analysis, we ask whether the evolution of these scales can be explained by variables associated with the two-level game or two-level legitimacy approaches (Chapter 7).

Part III considers the consequences of the changing constitutional rules and norms governing EU treaty making. It asks whether the rise of the people, parliaments and courts had a significant impact on the rate of treaty amendment between 1950 and 2016 before considering how EU member states have responded to such constraints (Chapter 8). Examining the history of EU ratification crises, it shows how national governments tend to untie their hands when faced with the prospect that a treaty might fail by rerunning referendums and pursuing international law treaties. This tendency is in line with the two-level game approach, it is noted, although concerns over legitimacy are not entirely absent from ratification crises. Building on this analysis, we consider the case for reforming EU treaty making as viewed from the two-level game and two-level legitimacy approaches (Chapter 9). In line with the first of these perspectives, we explore ideas for making treaty making more flexible. In line with the second, we ask how parliaments, the people and courts could be given an even more prominent role in this domain.

The book concludes by summarising the key findings of this study and considering their wider significance (Chapter 10). It asks whether the era of EU treaty making is over or whether there is a new age of treaty amendment and considers the dispersal of EU treaty-making rules and norms to other domains of EU decision making. It considers what students of international law and international relations can learn from the EU experience of treaty making.

Appendix 1.1 A Closer Look at EU Treaties

Table 1.1 List of EU treaties

Title of treaty	Also known as	Signed	Entered into force	Type of treaty
Treaty establishing the European Coal and Steel Community	Treaty of Paris	18-Apr-51	23-Jul-52, terminated 23-Jul-02	EU
Treaty Constituting the European Defence Community	EDC Treaty	27-May-52	Never entered into force	EU
Treaty embodying the Statute of the European Community		Not signed	Never entered into force	EU
Treaty amending the Treaty establishing the European Coal and Steel Community	Saar Treaty	27-Oct-56	01-Jan-57	EU
Treaty establishing the European Economic Community	Treaty of Rome	25-Mar-57	01-Jan-58	EU
Treaty establishing the European Atomic Energy Community	EURATOM Treaty	25-Mar-57	01-Jan-58	EU
Convention on certain institutions common to the European Communities		25-Mar-57	01-Jan-58, terminated 01-Jan-99	EU

Table 1.1 (*cont.*)

Title of treaty	Also known as	Signed	Entered into force	Type of treaty
Convention amending the Treaty establishing the European Economic Community, with a view to making applicable to the Netherlands Antilles the special regime of association defined in part IV of the said Treaty	Netherlands Antilles Convention	13-Nov-62	01-Oct-64	EU
Convention drawn up on the basis of Article K.3 of the Treaty on European Union, on mutual assistance and cooperation between customs administrations	Naples II Convention	07-Apr-65	18-Dec-97	International law
Treaty establishing a Single Council and a Single Commission of the European Communities	Merger Treaty	08-Apr-65	01-Jul-67	EU
Convention on mutual assistance between customs administrations	Naples Convention	07-Sep-67	07-Sep-67	International law
Convention on jurisdiction and the enforcement of judgments	Brussels Convention	27-Sep-68	01-Feb-73	International law
Convention on the Mutual Recognition of Companies and Bodies Corporate		29-Feb-68	Never entered into force	International law

Treaty amending Certain Budgetary Provisions of the Treaties establishing the European Communities and of the Treaty establishing a Single Council and a Single Commission of the European Communities	First Budgetary Treaty	22-Apr-70	01-Jan-71	EU
Treaty concerning the accession of the Kingdom of Denmark, Ireland, the Kingdom of Norway and the United Kingdom of Great Britain and Northern Ireland to the European Economic Community and to the European Atomic Energy Community	Treaty of Accession 1972	22-Jan-72	01-Jan-73	Accession
Treaty amending Certain Budgetary Provisions of the Treaties establishing the European Communities and of the Treaty establishing a Single Council and a Single Commission of the European Communities	Second Budgetary Treaty	22-Jul-75	01-Jun-77	EU
Treaty amending certain provisions of the Protocol on the Statute of the European Investment Bank		10-Jul-75	01-Oct-77	EU
Council agreement on establishment of TREVI		02-Dec-75	29-Jun-76	International law
Convention for the European patent for the common market		15-Dec-75	Never entered into force	International law

Table 1.1 (cont.)

Title of treaty	Also known as	Signed	Entered into force	Type of treaty
Treaty concerning the accession of the Hellenic Republic to the European Economic Community and to the European Atomic Energy Community	Treaty of Accession 1979	28-May-79	01-Jan-81	Accession
Rome Convention on Contractual Obligations		19-Jun-80	01-Apr-91	International law
Treaty amending, with regard to Greenland, the Treaties establishing the European Communities	Greenland Treaty	13-Mar-84	01-Jan-85	EU
Treaty concerning the accession of the Kingdom of Spain and the Portuguese Republic to the European Economic Community and to the European Atomic Energy Community	Treaty of Accession 1985	12-Jun-85	01-Jan-86	Accession
Agreement between the Governments of the States of the Benelux Economic Union, the Federal Republic of Germany and the French Republic on the gradual abolition of checks at their common borders	Schengen Agreement	14-Jun-85	15-Jun-85	International law
Single European Act	Single European Act	28-Feb-86	01-Jul-87	EU
Agreement relating to Community patents		15-Dec-89	Never entered into force	International law treaty

Convention implementing the Schengen Agreement of 14 June 1985 between the Governments of the States of the Benelux Economic Union, the Federal Republic of Germany and the French Republic on the gradual abolition of checks at their common borders	Schengen Convention	19-Jun-90	01-Sep-93	International law
Treaty on European Union	Treaty of Maastricht	07-Feb-92	01-Nov-93	EU
Act amending the Protocol on the Statute of the European Investment Bank empowering the Board of Governors to establish a European Investment Fund		25-Mar-93	01-May-95	EU
Treaty concerning the accession of the Republic of Austria, the Kingdom of Sweden, the Republic of Finland and the Kingdom of Norway to the European Union	Treaty of Accession 1994	24-Jun-94	01-Jan-95	Accession
Treaty of Amsterdam amending the Treaty on European Union, the Treaties establishing the European Communities and certain related acts	Treaty of Amsterdam	02-Oct-97	01-May-99	EU
Treaty of Nice amending the Treaty on European Union, the Treaties establishing the European Communities and certain related acts	Treaty of Nice	26-Feb-01	01-Feb-03	EU

Table 1.1 (*cont.*)

Title of treaty	Also known as	Signed	Entered into force	Type of treaty
Treaty concerning the accession of the Czech Republic, the Republic of Estonia, the Republic of Cyprus, the Republic of Latvia, the Republic of Lithuania, the Republic of Hungary, the Republic of Malta, the Republic of Poland, the Republic of Slovenia and the Slovak Republic to the European Union	Treaty of Accession 2003	16-Apr-03	01-May-04	Accession
Treaty establishing a Constitution for Europe	European Constitution	17-Jun-04	Never entered into force	EU
Treaty concerning the accession of the Republic of Bulgaria and Romania to the European Union	Treaty of Accession 2005	25-Apr-05	01-Jan-07	Accession
Treaty of Lisbon amending the Treaty on European Union and the Treaty establishing the European Community	Treaty of Lisbon	13-Dec-07	01-Dec-09	EU
Amending the protocol on transitional provisions annexed to the Treaty on European Union, to the Treaty on the Functioning of the European Union and to the Treaty Establishing the European Atomic Energy Community	Protocol on European Parliament seats	23-Jun-10	01-Dec-11	EU

Treaty on the Functioning of the European Union Article 136 amendment	Amended Protocol 136 TFEU ESM amendment	25-Mar-11	01-May-13	EU
Treaty concerning the accession of the Republic of Croatia to the European Union	Treaty of Accession 2011 source text	09-Dec-11	01-Jul-13	Accession
Treaty on Stability, Coordination and Governance in the Economic and Monetary Union	Fiscal Compact	02-Mar-12	01-Jan-13	International law
Treaty Establishing the European Stability Mechanism		02-Feb-12	27-Sep-12	International law
Protocol on the concerns of the Irish people on the Treaty of Lisbon	Irish protocol on the Lisbon Treaty	16 May 2012 – 13 June 2012	01-Dec-14	EU
Agreement on a Unified Patent Court		19-Feb-13	Not yet entered into force	International law
Agreement on the transfer and mutualisation of contributions to the Single Resolution fund	Single Resolution Fund Agreement	15-Jul-14	19-Aug-14	International law
Convention on the stepping up of cross-border cooperation, particularly in combating terrorism, cross-border crime and illegal migration	Prüm Convention	27-May-05	01-Nov-06	International law

Notes

1 Shaw (2014), pp. 66–9. McNair (1961) is the classic work on treaty making. Hollis (2012) is a modern classic. See also Article 2(1), United Nations, Vienna Convention on the Law of Treaties, 23 May 1969, 1115 UNTS, 331.
2 Treaty of Peace between Sweden and the Empire, (24) October 1648, 1 CTS 119 and Treaty of Peace between France and the Empire, 14(24) October 1648, 1 CTS 271.
3 Treaty of Peace between the Allied and Associated Powers and Germany, 28 June, 225 CTS 188.
4 Covenant of the League of Nations, 28 June 1919, 225 CTS 18.
5 United Nations, Charter of the United Nations, 24 October 1945, 1 UNTS XVI.
6 United Nations, Convention on the Prohibition of the Use, Stockpiling, Production and Transfer of Anti-Personnel Mines and on Their Destruction, 18 September 1997, 2056 UNTS, 211.
7 United Nations Framework Convention on Climate Change, Paris Agreement, 16 February 2016, C.N.63.2016.TREATIES-XXVII.7.d.
8 Source: https://treaties.un.org/Pages/Overview.aspx?path=overview/overview/page1_en.xml.
9 Article 26, Vienna Convention on the Law of Treaties.
10 See Hyland (1993), p. 406.
11 Meron (1995), p. 20.
12 Article 1, United Nations, Vienna Convention on the Law of Treaties between States and International Organizations or between International Organizations, 12 March 1986, Document A/CONF.129/15.
13 Grant (2012).
14 Article 71, Charter of the United Nations and ECOSOC Resolution 1996/31.
15 Soares (1998), p. 133.
16 Source: www.cop21paris.org/about/cop21.
17 Finch (1954); McNair (1961); Wildhaber (1971); Lobel (1985); Kumm and Comella (2005); Hathaway (2009).
18 Korontzis (2012), pp. 179–84.
19 Korontzis (2012), pp. 184–95.
20 Korontzis (2012), pp. 195–201.
21 Article 11, Vienna Convention on the Law of Treaties.
22 Crawford (2012), p. 372.
23 Brand (1994).
24 Article 11, Vienna Convention on the Law of Treaties.
25 Pergantis (2017), p. 99.
26 XXVIII, IMF Article of Agreement, 22 July 1944, 2 UNTS 39. Such members must also account for 85 per cent of voting with the Fund.
27 Article 40(4), Vienna Convention on the Law of Treaties.
28 Article 121, UN General Assembly, Rome Statute of the International Criminal Court, 17 July 1998, 2187 UNTS 3.

29 Fitzmaurice (2005), p. 505.
30 Locke (2016) [1689], chapter 12, para. 47.
31 Hamilton, Federalist Paper No. 75, in Hamilton (2010) [1788].
32 Korontzis (2012), p. 198.
33 Article II, Section 2(2), US Constitution (1789).
34 Wirth (2016), p. 14.
35 Hathaway (2009), p. 1250.
36 Treaty on European Union, 7 February 1992, 1992 O.J. (C191) 1, 31 I.L.M. 253.
37 Treaty Establishing the European Coal and Steel Community, 18 April 1951, 261 UNTS, 140. This treaty expired in 2002.
38 Treaty Establishing the European Economic Community, 25 March 1957, 298 UNTS, 3, 4 Eur. Y.B. 412.
39 The Treaty Establishing the European Atomic Energy Community, 25 March 1957, 298 UNTS, 259, 5 Eur. Y.B. 454.
40 Single European Act, 17 February 1986, 1987 O.J. (L 169) 1, 25 I.L.M. 506.
41 Treaty of Amsterdam Amending the TEU, the Treaties Establishing the European Communities and Certain Related Acts, 2 October 1997, 1997 O.J. (C340) 1, 37 I.L.M. 253.
42 Treaty of Nice Amending the TEU, the Treaties Establishing the European Communities and Certain Related Acts, 26 February 2001, 2001 O.J. (C80) 1.
43 Treaty of Lisbon Amending the Treaty on European Union and the Treaty Establishing the European Community, 13 December 2007, 2007 O.J. (C306) 1.
44 Treaty Establishing a Constitution for Europe, Rome, 29 October 2004, 2004 O.J. (C310) 1.
45 European Council Decision of 25 March 2011 amending Article 136 of the Treaty on the Functioning of the European Union with regard to a stability mechanism for Member States whose currency is the euro, *Official Journal* 91, 6.4.2011, pp. 1–2. See C-370/12 *Pringle* v. *Government of Ireland and Others* [2012] ECLI: EU:C:2012:756.
46 Glockner and Rittberger (2012).
47 Article 48(2) and (6), Treaty on European Union (1992, amended to 2016), Official Journal of the European Union, C 202, 7 June 2016.
48 Article 48(3), Treaty on European Union (1992, amended to 2016).
49 This is not to suggest that the Treaty of Paris was politically uncontroversial. A sizable minority of parliamentarians voted against the agreement in both France and Germany (McGowan 2010, p. 84).
50 Closa (2013a), p. 45.
51 Closa (2013a), p. 62.
52 Mendez, Mendez and Triga (2014).
53 DeHousse (2006).
54 These states are Austria, Estonia, Germany, Hungary, Ireland and Poland (Reestman 2017).

THE TRANSFORMATION OF EU TREATY MAKING

55 de Witte and Beukers (2013). Court of Justice of the EU, C-370/12 *Pringle v. Government of Ireland and Others* [2012] ECLI: EU:C:2012:756.

56 *Brunner v. European Union Treaty* 12 October 1993, BVerfGE 89, 155, 207; [1994] CMLR 57.

57 Judgment on 30 June 2009, BVerfG, 2 BvE 2/08.

58 See, for example, Kumm (1999) and Grosser (2009).

59 Four treaty revisions were launched using the Simplified Revision Procedure during this period. They concerned: (1) transitional arrangements on the number of Members of the European Parliament, (2) the revision to Article 136 TFEU to allow the creation of a stability mechanism for the eurozone, (3) the accession of Croatia to the EU, and (4) Ireland's Lisbon protocols. A treaty change concerning the Czech Republic's 'opt out' out from the Charter on Fundamental Rights – an eleventh-hour concession secured by President Václav Klaus in December 2009 before he agreed to sign the Lisbon Treaty – was postponed as a result of domestic wrangling.

60 Christiansen (2015), p. 95.

61 Franklin, Marsh and McClaren (1994).

62 Qvortrup (2006).

63 Lesaffer (2000), p. 182.

64 Meron (1995), p. 2.

65 Lesaffer (2004), p. 19.

66 Meron (1995), p. 2.

67 Meron (1995), p. 4.

68 Meron (1995), p. 2.

69 Vollrath (2004), pp. 162–3.

70 Lesaffer (2004), pp. 23–4.

71 Osiander (2001).

72 Lesaffer (2004), pp. 24–5.

73 Jones (1946), p. 3.

74 Jones (1946), pp. 7–8.

75 Treaty of Peace between Spain and the Netherlands, 30 January 1648, 1 CTS 1.

76 Coxton (2013), p. 213.

77 Article CXIX, Treaty of Peace between France and the Empire.

78 Article CXX, Treaty of Peace between France and the Empire.

79 Duchhardt (2004), p. 51.

80 Duchhardt (2004), p. 51.

81 Croxton (2013), p. 146.

82 Croxton (2013), p. 16.

83 Croxton (2013), p. 185.

84 Definitive Treaty of Peace and Amity between Austria, Great Britain, Portugal, Prussia, Russia and Sweden, and France, 30 May 1814, 63 CTS 171.

85 Peterson (1945), p. 551.

86 Vick (2014), p. 51.

THE TRANSFORMATION OF EU TREATY MAKING 31

87 Division of International Law of the Carnegie Endowment for International Peace (1920), p. 17.
88 Raustiala (2012), p. 153.
89 Fitzhardinge (1968).
90 Article 18, Covenant of the League of Nations.
91 See Bunyan and Fisher (1961), pp. 243–4.
92 Wilson (1918).
93 Jones (1946), p. 67.
94 Steiger (2004), pp. 78–9.
95 Article II, Section 2(2), US Constitution (1789).
96 Article 55, French Republic Constitution of 1793.
97 Article XVIII, the Frankfurt Peace Treaty, 10 May 1871, 143 CTS 163.
98 Templeman (1991), p. 65 (the Ponsonby rule).
99 Hunter (1991).
100 Article 89, Swiss Constitution (1874, amended to 1921). See Brooks (1921).
101 Jones (1946), pp. 140–1.
102 US Supreme Court, The Cherokee Tobacco, 78 U.S. (11 Wall) 616, 620–1 (1870); Levin and Chenn (2012), p. 773.
103 Levin and Chen (2012).
104 Mendez (2017).
105 Alvarez (2005), p. 335.
106 Alvarez (2005), p. 336.
107 Alvarez (2005), p. 303. See also Sabel (2006).
108 The Preamble to the Charter of the United Nations pledged 'to establish conditions under which justice and respect for the obligations arising from treaties and other sources of international law can be maintained'.
109 Article 13, Charter of the United Nations.
110 United Nations (2015), p. iii.
111 Article 82(c), Vienna Convention on the Law of Treaties between States and International Organizations or between International Organizations (1986).
112 Under Article 85(1), 35 states must ratify for it to enter into force. The 39 bodies that have ratified include several international organisations, so the 35-state threshold has not yet been reached.
113 Preamble, Vienna Convention on the Law of Treaties between States and International Organizations or between International Organizations.
114 Elias (2012), p. 91.
115 Brölmann (2011), p. 289.
116 International Court of Justice, Legality of the Threat or Use of Nuclear Weapons, Advisory Opinion, I.C.J. Reports 1996, p. 226, International Court of Justice (ICJ), 8 July 1996.
117 Article 62(3–4), Charter of the United Nations.
118 Article 71, Charter of the United Nations.
119 Raustiala (2012), p. 158.

THE TRANSFORMATION OF EU TREATY MAKING

120 Raustiala (2012), p. 158.

121 Raustiala (2012), pp. 169–72; Anderson (2000).

122 Nor does our study encompass the Treaty's flexibility or passerelle clauses. The former allows the Council, on the basis of a Commission proposal and with the consent of the European Parliament, to adopt appropriate measures to 'attain one of the objectives set out in the Treaties' where 'the Treaties have not provided the necessary powers' (Article 352, Consolidated version of the Treaty on the Functioning of the European Union, 26 October 2012, OJ L. 326/47–326/390; 26.10.2012). This provision is considered by some scholars as a form of informal treaty amendment (Schütze 2015: 80–1), although the Court of Justice of the EU has made clear that this provision cannot be used 'as a basis for the adoption of provisions whose effect would, in substance, be to amend the Treaty without following the procedure which the Treaty provides for that purpose' (Opinion 2/94 of 28 March 1996, ECR, EU:C:1996:140, para. 30). The Lisbon Treaty's simplified revision procedure includes a general passerelle clause, whereby the European Council can deviate under certain conditions from some of the Treaty's legislative procedures (Article 48(7) Treaty on the Functioning of the European Union). The consent of the European Parliament is required for such purposes and national parliaments can exercise a veto, making it an interesting case for this book, but this passerelle clause had yet to be used at the time of writing. The Treaty also contains more long-standing specific passerelle clauses, but these have been used sparingly (Barrett 2008: 21–2).

123 Treaty on Stability, Coordination and Governance in the Economic and Monetary Union of 2 March 2012. It is not published in the Official Journal. Full text available at: http://eur-lex.europa.eu/legal-content/EN/TXT/?uri=LEG ISSUM:1403_3.

124 See Chapter 4.

125 Article 48(1) Treaty on European Union (1992, amended to 2016).

126 Article 48(2–5) Treaty on European Union (1992, amended to 2016).

127 Article 48(6) Treaty on European Union (1992, amended to 2016).

128 de Witte (2011).

129 Moravcsik (1998) remains the most ambitious study of the politics of EU treaty negotiations. See Dyson and Featherstone (1999) for a comprehensive account of negotiations on – and leading up to – the Maastricht Treaty. Piris (2010) offers a comprehensive account of the Lisbon Treaty.

130 Maurer (2003); Shaw (2003); Magnette and Nicolaïdis (2004).

131 Peers (2012) offers an in-depth account of treaty amendment after the Lisbon Treaty.

132 de Witte (1994), p. 332.

133 de Witte (1994), pp. 331–2.

134 de Witte (2004), p. 1.

135 Claes (2006), chapter 15.

136 Claes (2006), chapter 16.
137 Claes (2007).
138 Claes (2007), p. 21.
139 Claes (2007), p. 21.
140 Laursen and Vanhoonacker (1992); Laursen (1994).
141 Laursen (2002).
142 Laursen (2005a).
143 Laursen (2012a).
144 Laursen (2008).
145 Laursen (2012b).
146 Christiansen and Reh (2009), p. 2.
147 Mendez, Mendez and Triga (2014).
148 Finke (2009), p. 501.
149 Article 47, Constitution of Ireland (1937, amended to 2015).
150 Supreme Court of Ireland, *Crotty* v. *An Taoiseach* [1987] IR 713 (April 1987). See Chapters 4–6 for further details.
151 Wiener (2007), p. 2.
152 Wiener (2007), p. 5.
153 Wiener (2007), p. 6.
154 Wiener (2007), p. 5.
155 Dicey (2013), p. 20.
156 Jennings (1967) quoted in Albert (2015).
157 Waldron (2006–7).
158 Albert (2015).
159 Waluchow (2009).
160 Grey (1979).
161 Simmons (2009a).
162 Hug and König (2002).
163 Hirschl (2014).
164 Ginsburg and Versteeg (2014).
165 Negretto (2013).
166 See, for example, Ferejohn (1997).
167 For a more sophisticated treatment, see Mo (1995), Milner and Rosendorff (1997) and Pahre (1997).
168 See, for example, Evans, Jacobson and Putnam (1993), Schoppa (1993), Jacobson (1996) and Keck and Sikkink (1998).
169 Moravcsik (1993a), p. 156.
170 Putnam (1988), p. 442.
171 Putnam (1988), p. 442.

2 Two-Level Games, Two-Level Legitimacy and EU Treaties

The idea of tying hands in a two-level game was influenced by Thomas Schelling's seminal study of rationalist bargaining, the *Strategy of Conflict*.[1] If an executive has free rein in treaty making, he argued, then it might end up conceding controversial points rather than terminating negotiations. Where it 'negotiates under legislative authority, with its position constrained by law, and it is evident that Congress will not be reconvened to change the law within the necessary time period', suggested Schelling, 'then the executive branch has a firm position that is visible to its negotiating partners', while recognising that such a strategy could be counterproductive if it creates an 'immovable position' in which other parties are unable to concede and negotiations stall or collapse.[2]

The paradox of weakness – or the Schelling conjecture, as it is sometimes known – was more of a metaphor than a model.[3] It fell to Robert Putnam to explore, in a more systematic way, how and why governments choose to tie their hands in treaty making so as to confer bargaining advantages.[4] Typically, governments will prefer to enter negotiations with as large a 'win set' as possible, Putnam accepts, because, all other things being equal, this will maximise the chances of successful negotiations.[5] Simply put, a win set refers to the set of all agreements that can conceivably be concluded by a government in the negotiation stage and accepted by relevant constituencies in the consent stage.[6] The size of a win set will be determined, inter alia, by the rules that shape treaty making, with a requirement that a parliament approve an agreement on the basis of a super majority vote, for example, producing a larger win set than a simple majority rule.[7] Governments may occasionally prefer more stringent rules, Putnam suggests, so as to narrow the range of agreements that can be concluded in the negotiation stage, as when US President Jimmy

34

Carter used the need for Senate approval of the Panama Canal Treaty to secure concessions from Panama's leader, Omar Torrijos.[8]

At first glance, the transformation of EU treaty making looks like a straightforward case of tying hands in a two-level game. Indeed, it has been sold as such by some politicians. 'Can [David Cameron] see the attraction of passing into law in this parliament a binding commitment to a referendum in the following parliament? And that may well strengthen his negotiating hand if he is able to look his fellow heads of government in the eye and know that any deal he negotiates will have to be put to the British people', asked a British Member of Parliament in 2012.[9] We have already done so, the Prime Minister reportedly replied.[10] Referendum pledges, Kai Opperman argues, 'serve to build up firewalls shielding governments from attempts of other actors on the European level to push the integration agenda beyond their red lines and keeping inconvenient issues off the agenda in the first place'.[11] Direct democracy, as Matt Qvortrup puts it, has gone from being 'the rarest of all political procedures to Europeans' bargaining chip of choice'.[12] And yet, for all the potential advantages of tighter ratification constraints in treaty negotiations, there is limited evidence to suggest that national governments in the EU would choose to make international diplomacy any more difficult than it already is. The two-level game approach is also less capable of explaining why national governments would seek to involve other actors in the negotiation stage through the convention method.

Treaty making is not only about tactics for Schelling; it also embodies concerns over trust. Establishing trust where it is hitherto absent is a key challenge for treaty makers, he argues, with the medieval practices of negotiating in public forums and ratifying agreements through the exchange of hostages all designed to foster trust.[13] By negotiating in public, the two sides addressed concerns that one side would slaughter the other, while the exchange of hostages ensured that both parties had a stake in sticking to the terms of the treaty. The two-level legitimacy approach introduced in the preceding chapter considers treaty making as being about trust *in* and *between* political elites. Thought of in these terms, the involvement of parliaments, the people and courts in EU treaty making is not simply an attempt to exert leverage but also a response to the problems of legitimacy facing the EU and member governments.

This chapter sets out in more detail these alternative theoretical perspectives on the puzzle at the heart of this book. The first section considers the conditions under which national governments would be

36 THE TRANSFORMATION OF EU TREATY MAKING

expected to engage in a strategy of hand tying. The second explores the neglected normative assumptions underpinning Putnam's work. The third sets out a two-level legitimacy perspective on the transformation of EU treaty making. The fourth section considers how governments might respond to ratification crises from two-level game and two-level legitimacy perspectives.

Tying Hands in Two-Level Games

Putnam sees Level 1, in which treaties are negotiated, and Level 2, in which such agreements are approved by domestic constituents, as distinct but related political arenas. The 'need for Level 2 ratification', he contends, 'is certain to affect Level 1 bargaining'.[14] Ratification constraints can be formal, as in the voting procedures followed by parliament to approve a treaty, or informal, as in the power of interest groups to determine whether an international agreement is enforced.[15] A government will typically prefer as broad a win set as possible so as to maximise its chances of ratifying international agreements, and yet this may not always be the case, Putnam contends. Large win sets bring a risk of being 'pushed around' in Level 1, such that increasing domestic constraints can be a useful way for a chief negotiator to steer negotiations in a direction that they consider to be preferable. Andrew Moravcsik refers to this strategy as 'tying hands' and contrasts it with a policy of 'cutting slack', where the government seeks to expand their win set so as to win support for an international agreement that would be otherwise rejected.[16]

Whether – and under what circumstances – chief negotiators might tie their hands is the subject of ongoing debate in the literature on two-level games. Jongryn Mo, who helped to pioneer game-theoretic representations of two-level games, found that governments will almost always gain from delegating powers over ratification to a third party, such as a parliament or electorate, providing the preferences of the latter do not deviate too much from that of the government.[17] Helen Milner gives grounds for scepticism, however, by noting that foreign governments will typically exploit domestic divisions.[18] A 'united home front', she concludes, is usually the best way to drive a hard bargain abroad. Tarar casts further doubt on tying hands when he finds that two-sided constraints – i.e. a situation in which home and foreign governments tie their hands in international negotiations – can lead to an outcome in which both sides are worse off.[19]

Although there is a rich theoretical literature on tying hands, there have been few documented cases of governments consciously choosing tighter ratification constraints for tactical reasons. For all of the theoretical advantages of a smaller win set, as Peter Evans notes, 'governments generally prefer to come to a negotiating table with as large a win set as possible or arrive with constraints that are not of their own choosing'.[20] One exception, Bahar Leventoglu and Ahmer Tarar show, concerns the use of public statements by politicians during Level 1 negotiations as a way to reduce room for manoeuvre in Level 2, but this example is about the audience costs of political rhetoric (i.e. the consequences of saying one thing as a politician and doing another) rather than tangible changes to the legal rules and norms governing ratification in the domestic arena.[21]

Seen through the lens of this two-level game literature, can the rise of parliaments (Chapter 4), the people (Chapter 5) and courts (Chapter 6) in EU treaty making be seen as a rare instance of hand tying? Several scholars suggest as much but few deal with this issue systematically. A noticeable exception is a sizable body of work by Simon Hug and Thomas König that shows in a convincing way how EU member states exploit ratification constraints in treaty negotiations. In their analysis of the Amsterdam Treaty, Hug and König show that domestic ratification constraints shaped negotiations over this agreement, with governments better able to defend the status quo on specific issue areas when pivotal actors in the ratification process shared their preferences.[22] Similarly, Hug and Schulz find that that member states that called referendums on the European Constitution before the conclusion of the Intergovernmental Conference (IGC) yielded negotiating gains in cases where the electorates in question had a significant share of Eurosceptic voters.[23] Calling referendums in this case was not entirely about bolstering bargaining positions, Finke and König observe. Governments expecting limited gains from negotiations over the European Constitution and those that sought to separate referendums from electoral campaigns were more likely to give the people a say on this treaty.[24]

Path breaking though these studies of EU treaty-making are, they focus on the question of whether member states exploit constraints rather than why and where such constraints emerge. As such, they shed limited light on the particular puzzle at the heart of this book. Most students of two-level games treat domestic ratification constraints as exogenous, which is problematic as Mo notes, because if tying hands is an advantage in some cases, it makes little sense for governments to allow such constraints to be determined beyond their control.[25] Robert Pahre is one of few scholars to endogenise domestic institutions in a two-level game, and so his contribution is of central importance to our study.[26] Pahre offers two variations on the two-level game approach to explain why domestic ratification rules might be more stringent in some EU member states than others: the divided government model and the minority government model. The first assumes that a government will cede control over ratifying the results of EU negotiation to domestic actors, such as a parliament, only when this actor has stronger preferences for maintaining the status quo than the government. The intuition behind this model is that such a constraint would not tie the government's hands in a meaningful way if parliament, for example, was more enthusiastic about negotiating a new treaty with other EU member states. The minority government model assumes that governments that lack a parliamentary majority are more likely to embrace tight ratification rules. One rationale for this result is that majority government cannot credibly tie its own hands since it would have sufficient support in parliament to loosen such constraints.

The two-level game approach also struggles to explain why governments would involve parliaments and courts in the negotiation as well as the consent stages of treaty making. Although Putnam allows for the possibility that chief negotiators might consult with Level 2 constituents before Level 1 negotiations are concluded, he does not foresee a situation in which such constituents join the negotiating table as players.[27] Giving other actors a role in the negotiation stage 'effectively makes the ratifier the agenda setter', Pahre suggests, making it harder for governments to 'exploit the domestic constraint'.[28] König and Slapin are more open-minded in this regard. The European Parliament played an informal agenda-setting role in the IGC on the Amsterdam Treaty, they suggest, by gathering valuable information on the preferences of conference participants.[29] This informational advantage, they suggest, allowed the European Parliament to put forward integrationist proposals that were in line with member states' win sets and to exploit member states' concerns about how the EU legislature would respond to its empowerment through treaty reforms.[30] And yet König and Slapin find no definitive evidence that the European Parliament brought such leverage to bear at Amsterdam.[31] The role of Members of the European Parliament (MEPs) in the IGC may, they accept, have reflected member states' desire to imbue negotiations with greater legitimacy by involving the EU's only directly elected institution.[32]

König and Slapin are more radical in their reading of the European Convention, which they see as an attempt to break the status-quo bias in IGCs by coopting reform-minded actors such as the European Parliament into the negotiation stage.[33] Key to the Convention Method, they argue, is that its negotiations play out prior to an IGC and so at one remove from domestic ratification constraints.[34] The Convention, in other words, is an attempt not to tie hands but to untie them. Domestic constraints mattered less in the context of the European Convention than in the IGCs, the authors' findings suggest, which might explain why the European Constitution eventually fell foul of voters in France and the Netherlands.[35] Magnette and Nicolaïdis note the different degrees of enthusiasm for the convention among the member states, but the twin factors of the idea that the major enlargement of the EU required radical methods and the need to democratise in the context of the relative failures of the Amsterdam and Nice IGCs provided the impetus needed for the convention.[36]

Normative Perspectives on Two-Level Games

To look for legitimacy and the role of law in two-level games will strike some readers as ontologically odd. The two-level approach is a canonical work of rational choice institutionalism[37] and, as such, it tends to privilege interests over norms and explanation over evaluation. We are not, however, the first to offer a normative reworking of Putnam. Albert Weale, in a pair of papers with Deborah Savage[38] and Richard Bellamy,[39] incorporates insights from social contract theory and constructivism to explore the normative logic of two-level games.[40] This approach posits a link between the pursuit of credibility in Level 1 negotiations and legitimacy in Level 2 ratification, with Bellamy and Weale arguing that governments can strike a deal in Level 1 only if they are 'simultaneously ... responsible and accountable to their domestic populations'.[41] The concepts of responsibility and accountability employed in this approach go beyond the formal ratification of agreements and appeal instead to a more open-ended process of democratic deliberation involving voters rather than technical or judicial bodies.[42] Amadine Crespy and Vivien Schmidt offer a constructivist take on Putnam's two-level game theory in which national governments can strike a deal at Level 1 only if this agreement can be justified to one another and to domestic constituencies using appropriate 'justificatory discourses'.[43] For example, the authors highlight the importance of 'ordo-liberal framing' for Angela Merkel's approach to the euro crisis and Nicolas Sarkozy's reframing of it as France and Germany converged towards a shared view of how to tackle the euro crisis.

'Ratification need not be "democratic" in any normal sense', Putnam admits, citing examples of the role played by the Japanese military in ratifying the London Naval Treaty and, prophetically, the likely role of the Irish Republican Army in any Northern Irish peace settlement.[44] And yet there is a 'normative aspect' to rationalist approaches,[45] and the two-level approach is no exception. Implicit in Putnam's approach is the claim that national governments derive legitimacy in the domestic arena from their involvement in international negotiations. Although he allows for the possibility that chief negotiators could be 'labor or management representatives, or party leaders in a multiparty coalition or ethnic group leaders in a consociational democracy', governments play a central role in two-level games for Putnam.[46] This is because rank matters in international diplomacy; media exposure and mutual support from other leaders help to boost government leaders' standing compared with other domestic political actors, Putnam suggests,[47] as does the fact that government leaders are likely to dispose of more side payments and more 'good will' at home.[48]

Andrew Moravcsik's liberal intergovernmentalism is built, in part, on a reworking of Putnam's two-level game approach for the study of European integration.[49] Like Putnam, Moravcsik sees executives as occupying a 'privileged position' in international diplomacy through their dual role in EU negotiations and in the domestic arena.[50] This privilege is as much about legitimacy as credibility, for Moravcsik, who sees EU member states as employing a 'two-level strategy' that brings not only 'greater domestic agenda-setting power' but also 'greater domestic political legitimacy'.[51] He gives the example of France's efforts to 'employ the legitimacy of the EC to force French firms to modernise – a goal that French governments had been promoting for almost a decade without success'.[52]

Whereas Putnam remained agnostic about questions of democratic accountability, Moravcsik's early work teases out the normative implications of two-level games for debates about the EU's 'democratic deficit'. In an early version of this argument, Moravcsik suggests that the EU's lack of democratic accountability may be a strength because it shields policymakers from voters and interest groups that might otherwise oppose initiatives aimed at European integration.[53] A corollary of this point, he suggests, is that while democratisation may create greater legitimacy in the short-term, a possible but paradoxical consequence in the long-term may be a further erosion of precisely the popular support that democratisation seeks to restore'.[54] A case in point is France's referendum on the ratification of the Maastricht Treaty, which Moravcsik sees as 'an unfortunate experiment' that put complex issues before the people and invited 'dissatisfaction with incumbent governments and economic performance, rather than EC policy'.[55]

Normative concerns feature in Moravcsik's early work but they dominate his more recent scholarship, which is deeply critical of the EU's changing approach to treaty making. Having once described the EU's democratic deficit as a dilemma rather than a problem,[56] he has come to see it as a 'myth'[57] premised on a problematic understanding of how modern democracies and international institutions work. This change is rooted, in part, in a reconsideration of his argument about the EU being shielded from democracy, an argument that he suggests 'is easily exaggerated, particularly by those who tend to overlook the multi-level constraints arising from democratic control over national governments'.[58] The 'most fundamental source of the EU's legitimacy lies in the democratic accountability of member states', Moravcsik suggests.[59] The European Parliament provides a 'robust' mechanism of democratic accountability, he concedes, but more important is 'the democratically elected governments of the Member States, which dominate the still largely territorial and intergovernmental structure of the EU'.[60] Simply put, the EU is accountable to national governments, which in turn are accountable to their electorates.

Seen through the lens of two-level games, this argument reverses Putnam's normative logic by suggesting not that national governments derive their legitimacy from the EU's two-level game but that the EU's two-level game is legitimated by the essential legitimacy of its member state governments. Treaty making links these points, for Moravcsik, who sees the requirement that all member states must agree and ratify treaty revisions as 'an exceptionally high standard for any fundamental act of substantive redirection or institutional delegation'.[61] The corollary to this point, consistent with Moravcsik's earlier critique of France's Maastricht referendum, is that approaches to treaty making that deviate from this intergovernmental modus operandi could be counterproductive from the point of view of legitimacy. As the Convention on the Future of Europe sat, Moravcsik warned that 'referendums, parliamentary elections, or constitutional conventions based on EU issues encourage informationally impoverished and unstructured deliberation, which in turn encourages unstable plebiscitary politics'.[62] He was even more critical when the European Constitution collapsed, suggesting that 'it should come as no surprise that ... the constitutional process so utterly failed to inspire, engage, and educate European publics'.[63]

The Two-Level Legitimacy Approach

The two-level game approach sees the transformation of EU treaty making as an attempt to confer bargaining advantages in treaty negotiations. Underlying this approach, as we have seen, is the idea that governments occupy a privileged position in the EU two-level game both in terms of their access to the negotiation and consent stages and because they are the representatives of sovereign states.[64] The two-level legitimacy approach sees this privilege as being contested because of the problems of legitimacy facing the EU and its member governments. The rise of the people, parliaments and courts is a response to and reflection of these problems, it contends, rather than an attempt by governments to extract concessions in treaty negotiations by emphasising domestic constraints.

Legitimacy can be a protean concept.[65] We define it as the belief that an institution should be carrying out the functions assigned to it.[66] Following Clark, we think of legitimacy as having a dual face inasmuch as it concerns a battle over 'rightful membership' and a debate over 'rightful conduct'.[67] As the legitimacy of the EU and its member state governments is called into question, the two-level legitimacy approach expects other actors to seek some measure of control over EU treaty making at both the negotiation and consent stages. Governments will not cede such power easily but they may turn to these actors to demonstrate an inclusive and accountable approach to treaty making and hence rightful conduct. In this sense, the transformation of EU treaty making could be a choice by governments as well as a constraint imposed on them. A concern for legitimacy is the common denominator in both cases.

'Political legitimacy is too unwieldy and complex a concept to be grappled in a frontal assault', Weatherford writes, 'and virtually all the empirical literature follows the tactic of breaking it into component parts'.[68] Our study focuses on one of the most common components of legitimacy: trust.[69] Thomassen, Andeweg and van Ham remind us that the concept of political trust and legitimacy are closely intertwined, with legitimacy implying a normative judgment as to the holding and exercise of political power, while trust implies an instrumental judgment on the performance of a regime over a long period of time.[70] Scharpf notes that legitimacy in western society has come to rely heavily on trust in institutional arrangements.[71] Political scientists approach the concept of trust in different ways, but they typically view it in relational terms, by which is meant a situation in which A puts B in a position to do X, where X can be harmful to A.[72] 'This willingness', Arron Hoffman argues, 'is based on a belief, for which there is some uncertainty, that potential trustees will avoid using their discretion to harm the interests of the first'.[73] Trust can also be understood as a situation in which A trusts the competence of B to do Y, where the act of trusting is the knowledge or belief that the trusted has the incentive to do what they have been engaged to do.[74] This description sits easily with relational forms of trust, but a different form of analysis is required for trust in government, or public trust, where knowledge of the actors is limited or non-existent. Warren identifies five different forms of public trust. First, there is generalised trust among citizens, which leads to a civil society rich in social capital. The other forms of trust are all about the relationship between the citizen and the state, viz. (2) trust in experts and professionals, (3) trust in public office, e.g. agencies and courts, (4) trust in political institutions and (5) trust in individual public representatives. We are most interested in trust in political institutions. Institutions are important for encouraging trust in government as they create incentives to behave in a trustworthy manner and affect social beliefs about trustworthiness through the dissemination of information about expected behaviour.[75] In the partisan environment of political institutions, democracy is important in institutionalising distrust through elections, referendums, and other mechanisms of accountability[76] and transparency[77] that help to ensure the trustworthiness of the political elites[78] and a convergence between their interests and those of the electorate, thereby paradoxically shoring up trust in the regime.[79]

Within the international relations literature, the relationship between trust and treaties is complex. Treaties can be read as a sign that states do not trust each other to uphold commitments, Hoffman suggests, but he also sees them, in two-level game terms, as a mechanism for maintaining the trust of actors not involved in the negotiation of such commitments.[80] In the international arena, where the treaty is negotiated, trust requires a willingness to risk that the other parties will do what they say – assumptions are made about motivation, and where incorrect inferences are drawn about motivation, cooperation fails.[81]

It also requires a judgement to be made about who should negotiate, a process that may involve the delegation of such responsibility to multiple actors. In the national arena, where the treaty is ratified, trust requires a decision about where the responsibility for ratification should rest.

Also of relevance is public trust in the institutions that are created through treaties, especially when it comes to the amendment of such agreements. When trust in such institutions is lacking, governments will face additional pressures to include other actors at different stages of treaty making. Trust is, in this sense, a concept that spans international relations and comparative politics and attempts to link the two.

In thinking about governments' contested privilege in EU treaty making, we are influenced by the work of Peter Mair. Privilege and legitimacy do not always go hand in hand, Mair noted, because political institutions can retain their influence while relinquishing their grip on the traditional levers of legitimacy.[82] Mair observed this trend in relation to political parties in Western Europe, but he came to view it as symptomatic of a more deep-seated problem of political trust.[83] This problem of trust is by no means unique to Europe but the EU is particularly vulnerable to it, Mair argues, because European integration is a project that is premised on trust in elites; once trust was diminished, elites became vulnerable and with that the European project.[84] This means that a major challenge for those elites is how to ensure a convergence between their interests and those of the electorates with the need to effect more democratic moments either through national parliaments or more directly (see Chapter 10).

Ratification crises over the Maastricht Treaty in Denmark, the Nice and Lisbon Treaties in Ireland and the European Constitution in France and the Netherlands are manifestations of the EU's trust deficit, but the EU's problems run deeper than the fraught politics of treaty making. Referendum votes against specific EU policies, low or falling turnout in European Parliament elections, the UK's vote in 2016 to leave the EU and the rise of anti-EU parties in a number of member states reflect a deep divide between EU elites and citizens. Such problems can also be seen in public opinion surveys. According to the Eurobarometer, the percentage of EU citizens who tend to trust the EU fell from 50 per cent in 2004 to 36 per cent in 2016.[85] In Greece, the epicentre of the euro crisis, less than 20 per cent of citizens expressed trust in the EU by 2016.[86]

While large-scale empirical studies are scarce, Staffan Kumlin and Atle Haugsgjerd argue that there is sufficient evidence to support the claim that economic crises hamper political trust, with the combination of major crises and feared or realised retrenchment leaving citizens with more social risks and reduced protection against them.[87] The euro crisis can be seen as a stress test for political trust with Torcal pointing to a diminution in political trust in southern European states and in the western states that suffered most during the crisis.[88] Van der Meer argues that perception of economic performance (along with impartiality and accountability) is strongly related to political trust with citizens having expectations shaped by previous experience rather than having any particular regard to performance in other jurisdictions.[89]

The EU's legitimacy problems have not arisen in isolation. Trust in national governments is lower on average than trust in the EU, with post-communist Europe in particular not having a high level of political trust (although there is some variation between the relevant states).[90] According to the Eurobarometer, the percentage of EU citizens who tend to trust national governments has fallen from 38 per cent in 2004 to 31 per cent in 2016.[91] There is also evidence to suggest that low levels of trust in national governments drive low levels of trust in the EU, which speaks to the idea that citizens form their evaluations about the EU on the basis of cues from national political systems.[92] More trusting citizens could be more likely to trust national governments and the EU just as citizens in countries where national governments are distrusted could be more wary about trusting the EU.[93] That said, trust in national government and the EU do not always move in lock step. In Denmark, for instance, the percentage of citizens who tend to trust national government fell from 63 per cent in 2003 to 46 per cent in 2016.[94] During the same period, citizens trust in the EU increased from 40 per cent to 46 per cent.[95] Such cases are not surprising insofar as the literature suggests that regional institutions tend to engender greater public trust than national institutions, although the picture is more mixed for the EU. Those member states that have higher levels of transparency are also those whose citizens trust their national institutions more than the EU, while those states where corruption is more widespread tend to trust the EU more than their own national parliaments.[96]

The involvement of parliaments, the people and courts in EU treaty making could be a response to the problems of legitimacy facing the EU, but this does not necessarily make it a remedy. These other actors, after all, face questions over their own legitimacy. While trust in national legal systems has remained at 51 per cent between 2004 and 2016 in the EU as a whole, the percentage of people who tend to trust national parliaments fell from 38 per cent to 32 per cent.[97] We see EU referendums as a symptom of, rather than a cure for, the EU's legitimacy crisis. As Bowler, Donavan and Karp show, a preference for direct democracy is linked to low political trust.[98] In addition, too often, EU referendums illustrate Butler and Ranney's arguments against direct democracy by placing significant analytic demands on voters under conditions of imperfect information, imposing results on a disgruntled minority and creating strains in representative democracies.[99] The quality of EU referendum campaigns, moreover, varies according to the players involved and the constitutional rules and norms that govern this debate.[100]

There is an important relationship between trust, mistrust and distrust. For political trust to work, some mistrust (caution, doubt, scepticism or the absence of trust) is required as it fosters vigilance and is facilitated through democracy with elections allowing citizens to exercise their support for politicians and their policies. Distrust (suspicion or the absence of trust) and scepticism, on the other hand, do not facilitate trust as they lead to disengagement and/or abstention.[101] Relationships between control, accountability and trust are complex,[102] but an excess of either accountability or control will diminish trust (leaving aside the question of what constitutes excess). The establishment of control or accountability mechanisms can be symptomatic of low trust,[103] and such mechanisms do not necessarily restore trust. The risk of either too much control or too much accountability is that a culture of distrust is engendered.[104] The paradox is that it is necessary to institutionalise distrust in order to maintain trust in government with the opportunity to signal disagreement – through elections, for example – an important element of this. Where distrust is institutionalised inappropriately, then the fragile dynamic necessary for trustworthiness is rapidly dissipated. Warren suggests that it is necessary to identify the conditions where trust in government is justified (given that the complexity and interdependence of modern societies increase the need for trust while reducing the scope of participation in government) and the institutional arrangements that will support that trust.[105]

In the EU the institutionalisation of (dis)trust is all the more complex as the EU is a multilevel polity.[106] Jennings's research on US government has shown that central government trust is more contingent on performance, with the weakening of the link between the citizen and the level of government increasing the importance of outputs for trustworthiness.[107] And yet Pharr and Putnam show how increasing prosperity has failed to halt a decline in public trust in (most) 'western' democracies.[108] As citizens acquire more information about government, higher and more divergent standards of living make it harder for governments to meet expectations. In this context, the fact that for so long EU legitimacy has been predicated on outputs is salient.[109] The absence of opportunities for disagreement within the EU means that there is a greater tendency to disparage the polity in its entirety when given the opportunity to voice an opinion directly through a referendum rather than simply disagree with a particular policy, leading to general distrust. Research on Switzerland shows that the existence of referendum rights generates political trust as citizens know they can render politicians accountable, but the actual exercise of the right undermines political trust[110] as the citizen is placed in a potentially adversarial relationship with government, leading them to question political trustworthiness.[111] This leaves EU treaty making more susceptible to distrust,[112] especially where referendums are held that relate to changing the fundamental law of the EU and where debate tends towards the polarisation of views.[113]

Applied to the EU, all of this suggests, in keeping with the two-level legitimacy approach, that the involvement of new actors in the negotiation and ratification of treaties reflects the diminution of trust in the processes through which treaties are made. What it does not say is whether such changes to EU treaty making are likely to reduce distrust. Braithwaite notes that the institutionalisation of distrust is essential for the development of a culture of trust.[114] On this basis, recourse to super majorities, referendums and litigation can be seen as institutional mechanisms motivated by a lack of trust. A problem is that the norms that underpin trust are meant to be latent and only mobilised as an ultimate appeal.[115] Another challenge in relation to EU treaty ratification is that treaty reform has arguably become too common,[116] and the stronger ratification rules are not latent but may be overused insofar as their frequency serves to reduce rather than instil trust.

Responding to Ratiflcation Crises

Scholars typically study cases where treaty making succeeds, but attempts to agree and amend treaties can and do fail.[117] The United States, in particular, has a reputation for non-ratification.[118] The Covenant on Economic, Social, and Cultural Rights,[119] the Convention on the Elimination of All Forms of Discrimination against Women[120] and the

48   THE TRANSFORMATION OF EU TREATY MAKING

Convention on the Rights of the Child are among many international agreements signed by the United States but not ratified.[121] Such involuntary defection is closely connected to the rules and norms governing treaty making. US presidents engage in treaty making under conditions of imperfect information about Congress's preferences, argue Guri Bang, Jon Hovi and Detlef F. Sprinz, and yet there can be electoral advantages to supporting multilateral international treaties regardless.[122] The Clinton administration's backing of the Kyoto Protocol without the guarantee of congressional support, they suggest, is a case in point. Such problems are not, of course, unique to the United States. Legislative delay is a common feature of environmental treaty making.[123] States' willingness to ratify human rights treaties, Beth Simmons shows, varies according to value commitment, expectation that other states will approve such agreements and the effect of domestic ratification procedures.[124]

How governments respond to ratification crises is another point on which the two-level game and two-level legitimacy approaches diverge. A government that ties its hands too tightly, Putnam warns, could produce deadlock in negotiations.[125] Such a strategy runs the risk of involuntary defection, whereby parties reach an agreement that one or more of them is unable to ratify.[126] While some domestic constituents might prefer no deal to a bad one, governments have little incentive to walk away from Level 1 once a deal has been concluded between negotiating partners. A corollary to this point is that governments that have their hands too tightly bound have a strong incentive to cut themselves some slack either by changing or circumventing domestic constraints to ratification or through some other means. Other governments are likely to support such efforts and, indeed, may use international bargaining to expand the win sets of those states that face significant domestic constraints.[127]

Reasonable though these arguments appear in Putnam's rationalist world – where international negotiations entail sunk costs and the risk of involuntary defection is potentially fatal for cooperation[128] – things appear differently beyond it. Before seeking slack, it argues, governments must consider why their hands have been tied to begin with. Where new actors have sought rightful membership of treaty-making forums or been included to demonstrate rightful conduct, their exclusion could aggravate problems of legitimacy. For this reason, the two-level legitimacy approach would expect governments to be wary about excluding or circumventing parliaments, the people and courts if faced with a ratification crisis.

The two-level game approach, argues John Kurt Jacobsen, 'makes a fetish of agreements which, no matter what their terms, are deemed good. More agreements imply more international cooperation, which is always good.'[129] The two-level legitimacy approach does not make a fetish of failure. However, it does allow for the possibility of voluntary concession, i.e. the abandoning of a treaty after it has failed to win the support of domestic constituents. Research suggests that legitimacy and political success are interrelated. Voters who support losing candidates in elections tend to be more dissatisfied with political systems, with repeated losses magnifying this loss of trust.[130] Institutions can play a role in mitigating such problems of legitimacy, especially when they allow current losers to be future winners.[131] Extended to the case of treaty making, this line of reasoning warns against the legitimacy backlash that could occur if governments salvage treaties in spite of significant domestic opposition. Allowing a treaty to fail could help to address such problems of trust, although it could, of course, create problems of distrust among those citizens who supported the agreement. Nevertheless, from a two-level legitimacy perspective, we would expect governments to consider the possibility of voluntary concession when faced with a ratification crisis.

Conclusion

How can we explain the rise of parliaments, the people and courts in EU treaty making? This chapter has considered two theoretical lines of inquiry that will guide our empirical analysis. The first sees the transformation of treaty making as a rare instance of tying hands in a two-level game. Governments have involved other actors in EU treaty making, it suggests, to strengthen their bargaining position in EU treaty negotiations. The two-level legitimacy approach interrogates the idea that governments occupy a privileged position in treaty making because of their key role in the negotiation and consent stages. This privilege is under threat, it argues, because of the problems of legitimacy facing the EU, as manifest through declining trust in the Union and member governments. Such problems have encouraged parliaments, the people and courts to seek a role in treaty making as well as encouraging governments to involve such actors. The two theoretical perspectives considered also differ on how EU member states are likely to respond to ratification crises. Where hands have been tied too tightly, the two-level game approach predicts, governments will loosen such constraints

50 THE TRANSFORMATION OF EU TREATY MAKING

rather than running the risk of involuntary defection. Governments will be mindful about cutting slack, the two-level legitimacy approach contends, because of the reasons why such hands have been tied to begin with. Faced with a ratification crisis, governments will be reluctant to circumvent the role played by the people, parliaments and courts and they will consider the possibility of allowing a treaty to fail.

Notes

1 Schelling (1980).
2 Schelling (1980), p. 28.
3 Bailer and Schneider (2006), p. 155.
4 Putnam (1988: 435) did not claim to be offering a model – or even a fully fledged theory – but his approach was intended as a step towards a more analytic understanding of international negotiations.
5 Putnam (1988), p. 437.
6 Putnam (1988), p. 437.
7 Putnam (1988), p. 448.
8 Putnam (1988), p. 440.
9 Watt (2012).
10 Hardman (2012).
11 Oppermann (2013b), p. 690.
12 Qvortrup (2016).
13 Schelling (1980), p. 20.
14 Putnam (1988), p. 436.
15 Putnam (1988), p. 436.
16 Moravcsik (1993a), p. 128.
17 Mo (1995).
18 Milner (1997).
19 Tarar (2005).
20 Evans (1993), pp. 402–3.
21 Leventoglu and Tarar (2005).
22 Hug and König (2002), p. 471.
23 Hug and Schulz (2007), pp. 194–202. See also König and Finke (2007), the results of which confirms the importance of pivotal parliamentary players in realising gains during negotiations over the European Constitution.
24 Finke and König (2009).
25 Mo (1995).
26 Pahre (1997).
27 Putnam (1988: 348) mentions 'kibitzers' as other actors at the table but he does not elaborate.
28 Pahre (1997), p. 150.
29 König and Slapin (2004), p. 373.

30 König and Slapin (2004), p. 373. This argument acknowledges its debt to Simon Hix's analysis of the European Parliament's informal agenda-setting role in the Amsterdam negotiations (Hix 2002).
31 König and Slapin (2004), p. 387.
32 König and Slapin (2004), p. 373.
33 König and Slapin (2006).
34 König and Slapin (2006), p. 435.
35 König and Slapin (2006), p. 439.
36 Magnette and Niolaïdis (2004).
37 Pollack (2001: 238); Abbott (2008).
38 Savage and Weale (2009).
39 Bellamy and Weale (2015).
40 The importance of social contract theory for the authors' normative logic of two-level games can be seen in their appeal to political constitutionalism, which argues that 'the political contract must be subject to ongoing debate among citizens with regard to both the procedures of decision-making and the substance of decisions' (Bellamy and Weale 2015: 268). The constructivism of their approach is implicit in reference to 'the justifiability ... of the reasoning underlying the norms and principles on which the construction of EMU is based' (Bellamy and Weale 2015: 261).
41 Bellamy and Weale (2015), p. 259.
42 Bellamy and Weale (2015), p. 268.
43 Crespy and Schmidt (2014), p. 1098.
44 Putnam (1988), p. 437.
45 Pollack (2006), p. 51n.
46 Putnam (1988), p. 435.
47 Putnam (1988), p. 452.
48 Putnam (1988), p. 435.
49 Pollack (2001), p. 225.
50 Moravcsik (1994), p. 14.
51 Moravcsik (1993b), p. 515.
52 Moravcsik (1993b), p. 516.
53 Moravcsik (1994), pp. 54–5.
54 Moravcsik (1994), pp. 54–6.
55 Moravcsik (1994), p. 55.
56 Moravcsik (1994), p. 55.
57 Moravcsik (2008), p. 331.
58 Moravcsik (2002), p. 611.
59 Moravcsik (2002), p. 619.
60 Moravcsik (2002), p. 612.
61 Moravcsik (2002), p. 609.
62 Moravcsik (2002), p. 201.
63 Moravcsik (2006), p. 228.

64 Putnam (1988), p. 434.

65 Weiler (1997).

66 Hodson and Maher (2002).

67 Clark (2005), p. 5.

68 Weatherford (1992), p. 149.

69 Weatherford (1992), p. 153.

70 Thomassen, Andeweg and van Ham (2017) pp. 509, 511 and 513.

71 Scharpf (2003).

72 Levi and Stoker (2000), p. 476.

73 Hoffman (2002), p. 376.

74 Hardin (1998) p. 12; Levi (1998), p. 78.

75 Farrell and Knight (2003), p. 542; Hardin (1998), pp. 10–12; Kohn (2008), p. 42.

76 Including judicial review. Courts as public bodies have higher trust than partisan political institutions. See Warren (2018), p. 38; Norris, (2017), p. 28 re US Supreme Court.

77 Abazi and Tauschinsky (2015).

78 Levi (1998); Hardin (1998), p. 12; Pettit (1998), p. 297.

79 Warren (2017), p. 35.

80 Hoffman (2002), p. 392.

81 Hoffman (2002); Larson (1997).

82 Mair (1997).

83 Mair (2013), p. 3. Mair treats the problem of trust as being built on a more fundamental crisis of political indifference and disengagement. We see political trust as a phenomenon to be studied in its own right; see van der Meer and Zmerli (2017), p. 6.

84 Mair (2013), p. 114.

85 Eurobarometer (2016), p. 14.

86 Source: Eurobarometer Interactive, http://ec.europa.eu/commfrontoffice/pub licopinion/index.cfm/Chart/getChart/themeKy/18/groupKy/97.

87 Kumlin and Haugsgjerd (2017), p. 291.

88 Torcal (2017).

89 Van der Meer (2017), p. 279.

90 Závecz (2017).

91 Eurobarometer (2016), p. 14.

92 Armingeon and Ceka (2014), p. 99.

93 Muñoz, Torcal and Bonet (2011).

94 Source: Eurobarometer Interactive, http://ec.europa.eu/commfrontoffice/pub licopinion/index.cfm/Chart/getChart/themeKy/18/groupKy/98.

95 Source: Eurobarometer Interactive, http://ec.europa.eu/commfrontoffice/pub licopinion/index.cfm/Chart/getChart/themeKy/18/groupKy/97.

96 Muñoz (2017).

97 Eurobarometer (2016), p. 46.

98 Bowler, Donavan and Karp (2007).

99 Butler and Ranney (1994), pp. 17–21.
100 On the Irish experience, see Barrett (2009).
101 Thomassen, Andeweg and van Ham (2017), p. 515. Van der Meer and Zmerli (2017) see scepticism as a separate category (p. 5), while Thomassen, Andeweg and van Ham (2017) conflate it into distrust.
102 Edelenbos and Eshuis (2012); Maher (2006).
103 Hoffmann (2002), p. 391.
104 O'Neill (2002), p. 57.
105 Warren (1999), p. 3.
106 Maher (2010).
107 Jennings (1998).
108 Pharr and Putnam (2000), p. 20.
109 Scharpf (1999); Maher (2010).
110 Bauer and Fatke (2014).
111 van der Meer (2017), p. 273; Dyck (2009), p. 558.
112 Follesdal and Hix (2006).
113 Moravcsik (2006).
114 Braithwaite (1998).
115 Luhmann (1979), p. 36.
116 Maher (2010).
117 Faure (2012).
118 Bradley (2007), p. 309.
119 Alston (1990).
120 Halberstam (1997).
121 Kilbourne (1996).
122 Bang, Hovi and Sprinz (2012).
123 Fredriksson and Gaston (2000).
124 Simmons (2009a).
125 Putnam (1988), p. 441.
126 Putnam (1988), p. 438.
127 Putnam (1988), p. 451.
128 Putnam (1988), p. 439.
129 Jacobsen (1996), p. 99.
130 Anderson, Blais, Bowler, Donovan and Listhaug (2005), p. 68.
131 Anderson, Blais, Bowler, Donovan and Listhaug (2005), p. 128.

PART I

The Negotiation Stage

3 EU Treaty Making and the Partial Eclipse of the IGC

The Treaty of Paris begins with the words 'The President of the Federal Republic of Germany' and so this formula remains for major EU treaty amendments.[1] This opening appeal to the treaty-making powers of heads of state makes clear that such treaties are made between the sovereign rulers, who have designated representatives as their plenipotentiaries, who have, in turn, 'exchanged their full powers, found in good and due form'.[2] These representatives come exclusively from government, and it is they alone who sign the final text of EU treaties. And yet such continuity gives an incomplete picture of how the negotiation stage has evolved to give a more prominent role to other actors. The clearest manifestation of this trend is the Convention Method pioneered in the drafting of the European Constitution and codified in the Lisbon treaty. Parliamentarians – drawn from the European Parliament and national parliaments – were the single biggest block in the Convention on the Future of Europe (2002–2003), and their participation is guaranteed in future conventions.[3] Aside from Italy's pre-Maastricht referendum in 1989, the people have not appeared in the negotiations stage of treaty making. Held in conjunction with elections for the European Parliament, this referendum saw 80 per cent of Italian voters agree that the European Parliament should be given a mandate to draw up a European Constitution (see Chapter 5). The Court of Justice of the EU has been drawn deeper into the negotiation stage since the 1990s, culminating in the 2012 *Pringle* case, in which it was asked to adjudicate on the legality of the use of particular treaty amendment procedures.[4]

This chapter offers a historical perspective on the EU's changing approach to treaty making from the Schuman Plan Conference in 1950 to early experiences of treaty amendment under the Lisbon Treaty. It charts the means through which the European Parliament, national parliaments and, to a lesser extent, the Court of Justice of the EU acquired a role in the negotiation stage. In explaining the involvement of these actors, we return to the two-level game and two-level legitimacy approaches introduced in Chapter 2. In so doing, we explore the factors driving this transformation of the negotiation stage, drawing on official documentation and historical accounts of EU treaty negotiations.

EU Treaty Negotiations from Paris to Post-Lisbon

In June 1950, representatives of Belgium, France, Germany, Italy, Luxembourg and the Netherlands – the Six – met in Paris to discuss French foreign minister Robert Schuman's proposals for a common market for coal and steel. Nine months later, the European Coal and Steel Community (ECSC), the founding treaty of what would become the EU, was concluded. The so-called Schuman Plan Conference was an IGC in all but name, although some national delegations included experts from industry and academia.[5] Walter Hallstein, a law professor who had written his LLM thesis on the Versailles Treaty,[6] headed the German delegation but he joined the Federal Chancellery once the conference was under way. Other actors sought to exert influence on the conference from the outside, including US diplomats and legal scholars,[7] but the formal negotiations played out between national delegations of the Six chaired by Jean Monnet, Commissioner-General of the French National Planning Board and principal drafter of the Schuman Declaration. The final text of the Treaty was initialed by the heads of national delegations in March 1951 before being signed the following month by foreign ministers. Only one head of government, Konrad Adenauer, signed this Treaty, but he did so in his capacity as Germany's Chancellor and Foreign Minister.

The Treaty of Paris put the IGC at the centre of future treaty amendments, while giving the High Authority (an antecedent of the European Commission) and member states the right to initiate such changes.[8] It was not long before parliamentarians acquired a role too. In May 1951, representatives of the Six signed the European Defence Community (EDC) Treaty following the Paris Conference on the European Army. This IGC agreed to create a directly elected EDC Assembly, which would be invited to consider plans for a 'permanent political organization' as part of a 'federal or confederal structure'.[9] The EDC Treaty had not yet entered into force when the Six agreed four months later to invite members of the ECSC Common Assembly to form an Ad Hoc Assembly to prepare a draft treaty setting up a European Political Community. The Ad Hoc Assembly, to which some members of the Assembly of the Council of Europe were coopted, was given six months to complete its work, after which an IGC on the European Political Community was envisaged.

The Ad Hoc Assembly was not intended to replace the IGC, but it marked a significant departure from the Schuman Plan Conference and the Paris Conference on the European Army by giving parliamentarians a major preparatory role in EU treaty making. But this experiment neither succeeded nor endured. Although the Ad Hoc Assembly delivered a Draft Treaty Embodying the Statute of the European Community on schedule, the IGC on the European Political Community was abandoned after the French National Assembly voted against the EDC Treaty in 1954. Negotiations over the Treaties of Rome reverted to a more traditional IGC format in which the ECSC Common Assembly did not participate.

Although parliamentarians were present in this opening phase of EU treaty making, their involvement was sporadic. At the Messina Conference in June 1955, the Foreign Ministers of the Six delegated responsibility for preparing the Treaty Establishing the European Economic Community (EEC) to the Spaak Committee, which included delegates from each member state (and a UK representative) led by Belgian Foreign Minister Paul Henri Spaak. The ECSC Common Assembly played no formal role in the Spaak Committee or the subsequent IGC, although Spaak kept his former colleagues at the Assembly informed of negotiations.[10] The IGC was led by foreign ministers, but a meeting of Heads of Government and Foreign Ministers was convened in Paris in February 1957 to deal with some thorny issues. This was the first time that the heads of state or government actively intervened in EU treaty negotiations. In recognition of this fact, the treaties were signed by the German Chancellor and the Prime Ministers of Italy and Luxembourg.

The Treaty of Rome and the Euroatom Treaty provided parliamentarians with a formal – if still secondary – role in treaty making. Under the treaties, it fell to the Commission and individual member states to propose treaty amendments to the Council, but, in a departure from the Treaty of Paris, the Council was required to consult the Assembly (as the Common Assembly was renamed) before issuing an opinion on authorising an IGC.[11] EU treaty making between the 1960s and 1980s confirmed just how limited this power was.[12] Although the European Parliament (as the Assembly was renamed in 1962) played an informal role in the Merger Treaty (1965) and Budget Treaties (1970 and 1975), these treaty amendments were formally agreed in IGCs to which Members of the European Parliament (MEPs) were not invited. The Draft Treaty on European Union adopted by the European Parliament in 1984 likewise helped to set the agenda for the Single European Act, but formal negotiations involved no significant new role for the European Parliament. True, the Dooge Committee recommended to the European Council that the European Parliament be 'closely associated' with the next IGC and that the outcome of these negotiations should be 'submitted' to Parliament.[13] But the President of the IGC on the Single European Act agreed only to keep the European Parliament informed of its work.[14] The European Commission, in contrast, invited itself to the IGC without significant objections from the member states and played an active role in its discussions. That the Single European Act was adopted by EEC Foreign Ministers in spite of reservations expressed by MEPs shows how little influence the European Parliament wielded over treaty making at this point.[15]

In 1990, prior to the conference on the Maastricht Treaty, 173 national parliamentarians and 85 Members of the European Parliament attended the so-called Assizes in Rome to discuss the future of the European Union. Hitherto, national parliaments had been involved in the scrutiny of EU treaty making to varying degrees,[16] but they did not seek a collective part in it. This changed with the Assizes, which proposed specific treaty reforms on issues ranging from Economic and Monetary Union (EMU) to fundamental rights and proposed that European parliamentary approval be required after future IGCs. These proposals were forwarded to the IGC on the Maastricht Treaty, the final text of which envisaged further meetings of this 'Conference of Parliaments' and promised to consult the forum 'on the main features of the European Union'.[17] No such conference materialised, but the significance of the Assizes should not be dismissed. 'Never before had a major international negotiation been preceded by a conference of the very parliaments that would later have to approve the outcome of the negotiations', argues Richard Corbett.[18] The Assizes was, with the benefit of hindsight, the forerunner of the Convention Method.

The Maastricht Treaty otherwise preserved the Treaty of Rome's provisions on treaty amendment.[19] One exception concerned the right of the new European Central Bank (ECB) to be consulted on institutional changes relating to monetary policy. This followed the European Council's invitation to the Committee of Central Bank Governors to join the ECOFIN Council and European Commission in preparing the IGC on

EMU, which alongside the IGC on political union prepared the final text of the Maastricht Treaty. The Treaty also allowed certain articles in the Bank's statutes to be amended via a special amendment procedure, with the Council deciding by qualified majority vote if such amendments were proposed by the Bank or by unanimity if proposed by the Commission.[20] In both cases, the assent of the European Parliament was required for such amendments to take effect, thus giving the EU legislature a veto over this very specific category of treaty amendment.[21]

From the 1980s onwards, the European Parliament gradually gained entry to IGCs. During negotiations over the Single European Act, delegates from the European Parliaments met with members of the IGC. In negotiations over Maastricht, member states upgraded these discussions to a more frequent and in-depth interinstitutional preparatory conference.[22] For the IGC on the Amsterdam Treaty, member states went further. The European Council invited two representatives of the European Parliament to participate in the work of the Reflection Group alongside representatives of the foreign ministers and the President of the Commission.[23] In negotiations proper, the President of the European Parliament was invited to hold an exchange of views with foreign ministers in advance of ministerial meetings.[24] Member states went further still in the IGC on the Nice Treaty, with the President of the European Parliament invited to participate in an exchange of views before meetings of the IGC at the level of ministers and heads of state or government and two MEPs invited to participate as observers in the IGC's preparatory group. This did not provide the European Parliament with a full seat at the table, but it ensured the EU legislature's place in the room. The effect can be seen from IGC members' willingness to discuss treaty reforms put forward by the European Parliament.[25]

Another noticeable development in negotiations over the Amsterdam and Nice treaties was the increasingly hands-on role played by EU heads of state or government. Gray and Stubb's suggestion that 'the ministerial level was virtually non-existent' is an overstatement, but their claim that an 'unusually large number of issues' ended up on the European Council's plate is correct.[26] This can be seen in the fact that both IGCs concluded with a late-night summit of heads of state or government, with negotiations proving particularly fraught over Nice. After EU leaders finally reached agreement on the Nice Treaty at 4:30 A.M., UK Prime Minister Tony Blair declared that 'we cannot do business like this in the future'.[27]

In the late 1990s, EU treaty making entered a new and more experimental phase, giving parliaments a more prominent role while also consolidating the dominance of heads of state or government. In 1999, the European Council at Cologne invited members of the European Parliament and national parliaments alongside representatives of the President of the Commission and the Heads of State or Government to join a body to prepare a draft Charter on Fundamental Rights for the European Union. Although this was not an exercise in treaty making, the approach would have lasting consequences for how the EU amended its treaties. The composition of the Convention Responsible for Drafting the Charter of Fundamental Rights, as members of this body chose to call themselves, was strikingly different from that of traditional IGCs. First, one representative of the Commission, sixteen representatives of the European Parliament and two representatives from the national parliaments of the (then) fifteen EU member states were made members of the body, giving them full powers over the negotiation of the charter. Second, there were no national representatives on this body but rather 'representatives of the Heads of State or Government', a form of intergovernmentalism that was quite distinct from traditional IGCs. Third, the Convention was more participatory than such conferences, with two representatives of the Court of Justice and Council of Europe invited to attend as observers and the Economic and Social Committee, Committee of the Regions, Ombudsman and, potentially, other bodies, social groups and experts invited to give their views. The Court's inclusion on this list was striking given its lack of involvement in formal treaty making.

Building on the perceived success of the Charter Convention, the European Council established the Convention on the Future of Europe in December 2001 to consider 'key issues arising for the Union's future development' in advance of the next IGC.[28] A high water mark for parliamentary involvement in EU treaty making, the European Convention included two representatives from each of the member state parliaments and from each accession state parliament, and sixteen MEPs among its 105 members. The participatory character of this exercise was reinforced by the inclusion of observers from the EU's Economic and Social Committee and the Committee of the Regions and Ombudsman and by the invitation extended to the Presidents of the Court of Justice and Court of Auditors to address the Convention. EU heads of state or government once again exerted a grip on the process by sending personal representatives to the European Convention rather than member state representatives. Whereas the Charter Convention appointed a President from among its members, the European Council selected former French President Valéry Giscard d'Estaing to be

President of the European Convention, with Giuliano Amato, former Italian Prime Minister, and Jean-Luc Dehaene, former Belgian Prime Minister, as Vice Presidents.

'The performance of the parliamentary contingent shone by comparison with that of the representatives of the national leaders who, true to IGC form, were unable to agree among themselves when left to their own devices', suggested Andew Duff, an MEP and member of the European Convention.[29] Duff's remarks downplay divisions between MEPs at the European Convention and the sense among some national parliamentarians that they were mere 'visitors to Brussels, invited to meetings and used to endorse the decisions reached by European interest groups',[30] but he is right to recognise the Convention as a 'right of passage' for parliamentarians.[31] National parliaments and the European Parliament had hitherto made their voices heard in EU treaty making, but they had never before played a formal role in treaty negotiation. For some scholars, the Convention Method constituted a 'radical break' from the IGC method,[32] while for others it meshed with 'existing mechanisms'.[33] And yet even those who offer a more conservative reading of the Convention accept that it was 'a new departure in constitutional politics' for the EU.[34]

At Laeken, EU leaders had left open the possibility that the European Convention might settle on 'different options' for reform rather than reaching a consensus. But, thanks in part to the constructive role played by parliamentarians,[35] the European Convention delivered a Draft Treaty Establishing a Constitution for Europe. National parliaments did not participate in the IGC that met to discuss and modify this draft, but the European Parliament was involved to an unprecedented degree. European Parliament President Pat Cox attended all IGC meetings at the level of heads of state or government. MEPs participated in ministerial meetings as representatives of the European Parliament rather than observers. Officials from the European Parliament participated in IGC working groups.[36] The European Parliament was not given a say over the final text of the European Constitution, but it was most certainly present at its creation.

Following 'no' votes by France and the Netherlands against the European Constitution, the European Council reverted to a more conventional IGC, but the results of these negotiations, the Lisbon Treaty, enhanced the role of parliaments in EU treaty making. The European Parliament was given the power to propose treaty amendments and the Council was required for the first time to notify national parliaments of

64   THE TRANSFORMATION OF EU TREATY MAKING

proposed treaty changes.[37] Somewhat surprisingly, given the failure of the European Constitution, Lisbon made the Convention Method the default forum for future major treaty amendments.[38] This guarantees the European Parliament and national parliaments a seat in treaty negotiations alongside representatives of the Heads of State or Government and the European Commission. Where the European Council decides that treaty amendments 'are not of great importance', it can choose not to convene a Convention but only with the consent of the European Parliament.[39]

As parliaments gained ground in the negotiation stage of EU treaty making, EU heads of state or government secured a greater role still. Under the Lisbon Treaty, the Council of Ministers is now relegated to passing proposals for amendment of the Treaties to the European Council, which decides, in consultation with (if calling a convention) or (if not) with the consent of the European Parliament to commence negotiations under the ordinary revision procedure.[40] Most importantly, a new simplified revision procedure allows the European Council to make treaty amendments without recourse to either a Convention or an IGC and after consulting the European Parliament and Commission (and the ECB if relevant to monetary policy). This procedure is limited to issues relating to the internal policies and action of the Union providing such proposals do not increase the EU's competence.[41] The result is that the European Council has become not only an actor that participates in EU treaty making but one that can decide certain categories of treaty amendments. A further special revision procedure that addresses changes to voting in Council and legislative procedures gives the European Council the power to decide to make the change, having secured the consent of the European Parliament and having notified national parliaments, any of which can exercise a veto.[42]

At the time of writing, the Convention Method had been employed only once. In June 2010, the European Council agreed that an IGC should examine a treaty amendment on transitional arrangements concerning the number of MEPs. EU heads of state or government chose to do so without convening a Convention but only after receiving the consent of the European Parliament and notifying national parliaments.[43] Altogether more significant was the European Council's decision in December 2010 to amend Article 136 TFEU to provide for the creation of a stability mechanism for the eurozone. EU heads of state or government did so through the simplified revision procedure, abrogating the need for a Convention or an IGC. However, the amendment did not come into effect for two years, leading to the adoption of the European Stability Mechanism through an intergovernmental treaty rather than as a part of EU law.

The Article 136 amendment also confirmed the EU Court of Justice's emerging role in EU treaty amendment. Hitherto, the Court's involvement in this domain was sporadic and low key, the indirect influence of its judgments on treaty revisions notwithstanding.[44] In 1995, the Court of Justice submitted its views to the Westendorp Group, which laid the groundwork for the Amsterdam Treaty.[45] At Laeken, as noted above, the President of the European Court of Justice was invited to appear before the European Convention. The Court was drawn considerably deeper into EU-related treaty making in April 2012 when Thomas Pringle, a member of the Irish parliament, launched a legal challenge against the European Stability Mechanism in the country's High Court that ultimately ended up before the EU Court of Justice through the preliminary reference procedure.[46] This challenge hinged, in part, on the question of how the treaty amendment was and should have been ratified under Irish constitutional law, but the defendant also claimed that the European Council's decision to amend Article 136 by means of the simplified revision procedure was contrary to EU law because it involved an alteration of the competences of the EU. In this sense, *Pringle* was about how the treaty is amended. The Court of Justice of the EU held that it had jurisdiction to hear the case even though the Treaty confers power only to interpret but not to decide on the validity of the treaties. However, because the European Council must make a decision to trigger the use of the simplified revision procedure, that decision is within the jurisdiction of the Court. As such, the Court now decides whether the adoption of the simplified revision procedure is legally correct and hence has acquired an important role in the negotiation stage of EU treaty making.

Tactics, Trust and the Transformation of EU Treaty Making

IGCs retain an important place in the negotiation stage of EU treaty making, but it is not quite the privileged position of old. As the preceding section showed, the European Parliament's foothold in IGCs and influential role alongside national parliaments in the Convention Method mean that the traditional IGC has been partially eclipsed. The Court of Justice has not been involved to the same degree in EU treaty making, but it has featured in the preparatory phases of EU treaty negotiations since the 1990s and acquired an important role in relation to the Lisbon Treaty's

66   THE TRANSFORMATION OF EU TREATY MAKING

treaty revision procedure. This section seeks to explain these developments with reference to the two-level game and two-level legitimacy approaches outlined in Chapter 2.

Two-Level Games and EU Treaty Negotiations

For Kal Raustiala, the involvement of actors other than governments in international treaty making can be seen as an attempt to 'bridge' the two-level game so as to reduce ratification risk.[47] Such actors can play a bridging role, he suggests, by bringing expertise and through their influence on domestic actors that are formally empowered in the consent stage. This argument might explain the cooption of central bankers in Maastricht negotiations since plans for the EMU would have been hard to realise without the technical and political support of national monetary authorities, but this line of reasoning fits well with the involvement of national and European parliamentarians.[48] The European Parliament has no formal role in the consent stage of EU treaty making, and while its members are often adept at interinstitutional politics, they typically possess no special technical expertise on EU policies. MEPs may be adept at gathering information on national governments, as Simon Hix finds,[49] but such evidence may also be available through other channels. The Council Secretariat, in particular, is an invaluable source of information in IGCs.[50]

More plausible from a two-level game perspective is the idea that national parliaments could help to reduce ratification risk by virtue of their role in approving EU treaties. But such a role would require a much larger representation of national parliamentarians than seen in the European Convention. Although national legislators were the single largest group in the European Convention, the individual chambers of national parliaments were represented by at most two individuals. In the case of France, for instance, it was decided to send the Presidents of the Delegations for European Affairs of the National Assembly and the Senate, two important players in the parliamentary oversight of EU affairs in France, but just two of the country's 925 members of parliament. The United Kingdom sent two relatively junior members of the House of Commons and none from the House of Lords. Romano Prodi's suggestion in 2001 that national parliaments should give their tacit prior consent to certain categories of treaty reform gives a clearer indication of what would be required to reduce ratification risk, while illustrating just how far removed the European Convention was from such a scheme.[51]

Treaties suffer from problems of global collective action, the need for a group response to address a common problem and the challenge of securing that response among many actors.[52] Governments may respond to such problems by delegating certain responsibilities over treaty negotiation to third parties as a means of increasing consensus. This explanation fits with the Six's willingness to give the High Authority the power to initiate treaty reform, subsequently extended to the Commission and, more recently, the European Parliament. However, delegation brings a risk of drift, which could be especially costly in a high-stakes setting such as an IGC. This explains, Mark Pollack argues, why agenda setting by the European Parliament at the IGC on the Amsterdam Treaty was both encouraged by member states but also heavily constrained. The European Parliament secured access to the conference, he argues, by renouncing 'grandiose federalist proposals' of earlier times.[53] And yet national governments afforded MEPs few opportunities to alter the course of the Amsterdam treaty negotiations, Pollack argues, with the European Parliament advancing only those issues that were close to the prevailing consensus among other conference delegates.[54] Persuasive though Pollack's rational choice reading of the Amsterdam IGC is, it reinforces rather than resolves the puzzle of why governments turned to parliaments in the Convention Method, which was introduced later in the treaty-making history of the EU. Participation of parliaments was increased through this method, but the overall size of the Convention on the Future of Europe and the limit of only two delegates from each parliament were a constraint on them.

For some scholars, the involvement of other actors in EU treaty negotiations can be seen as a way to oil the wheels of two-level diplomacy. Maurer makes this point succinctly when he describes the Convention Method as 'an alternative way for steering system change and fundamental reform of the European Union, because it features participative and inclusive forms of open deliberation, it respects and integrates the relative importance of minority positions, it offers open fora for parliamentary discourse and helps to include national parliaments at an early stage of system building, and it is conditioned by the method of consensus-building'.[55] The European Convention certainly styled itself as a deliberative forum through its 'listening phase', in which soundings were taken from a range of civil society groups, and through its working groups, which focused on specific policy or institutional questions. But did governments view the Convention Method in this way? The answer, it would seem, is: only partly so. Speaking at the inaugural meeting of the European Convention on behalf of the European Council, Spanish Prime Minister José María Aznar expressed EU heads of state or governments' commitment to 'new forms of operation and deliberation in order to continue to create "more Europe"'.[56] And yet Aznar made clear the limits of this commitment when he noted that it would be the European Council rather than the Convention that would be 'responsible for taking the definitive decisions on the reform of the treaties'.[57] In this sense, as Paul Magnette and Kalypso Nicolaïdis argue, the Convention took place 'under the shadow of the IGC'.[58]

The Convention was not the first time that heads of state or government employed deliberative methods as a precursor to hard bargaining. From the Spaak Committee to the Westendorp Group, national governments have shown a preference for prefiguring political negotiations over treaties with preparatory discussions among 'experts'. In practice, these discussions tend to be more political than technocratic, but they help to foster an image of deliberation and informed debate before the hard bargaining of IGCs begins. As Moravcsik notes, those involved in the Spaak Committee were 'selected by, and in most cases employed by, the member states; though some were sometimes given autonomy, their views tended to track those of governments'.[59] The same could be said of the Westendorp Group, which helped to prepare the IGC on the Amsterdam Treaty. Billed by the European Council as a 'Reflection Group', this ad hoc body included two academics and one Commission official but was otherwise composed of national politicians and officials. The Westendorp Group, as Christiansen and Reh note, 'remained split along national lines, and, despite its detail and breadth, it neither shifted member states' basic positions nor served as a basis for the IGC itself'.[60] Where technical expertise is genuinely required, as in legal expertise, national governments have been much less willing to empower other actors. This explains why the Commission's legal service, though it contributes to IGCs, plays a secondary role to the Council Secretariat's Legal Service.[61]

The issue of legal expertise raises the question of how the Court of Justice came to play a role in the negotiation stage of EU treaty making. Member states' decision to involve the Court in the Westendorp Group and the Convention of Europe was a low-cost one. It can be understood as an act of courtesy to the Court, given the likely impact of these treaties on the Court's powers, and an information-gathering exercise. In the case of the Westendorp Group, for example, the Court, like the other institutions, was asked to and submitted a report on the functioning of the Maastricht Treaty, the Reflection Group having the task of examining measures deemed necessary for the effective operation of institutions post-enlargement.[62] The involvement of the Court of Justice in the Article 136 amendment to the Treaty on the Functioning of the European Union (TFEU) was a different matter, with the Court assuming jurisdiction on the basis of the decision of the Council to trigger the amendment, opening the way for it to review whether the amendment was within the limits set by the treaty. A situation in which the Court overrules an attempt by the European Council to amend the treaties through the simplified procedure and hence without recourse to either a convention or an IGC would be a costly one to member states since it would require the renegotiation of a treaty amendment or the abandonment thereof. For that reason, Stanislas Adam and Francisco Javier Mena Parras argue, the Court of Justice faces political constraints when it comes to the exercise of ex-post scrutiny over treaty negotiation.[63] In 2012, it was certainly hard to imagine the Court of Justice ruling against the European Council's approach to the Article 136 amendment, as to do so would have created severe tensions with the member states and significantly complicated attempts to contain the euro crisis.

The two-level game approach, while it puzzles over the rise of new actors in the negotiation stage of EU treaty making, offers a more convincing account of heads of state or governments' increasing involvement. This involvement chimes with Putnam's conception of international negotiations as a process led from a 'chief negotiator' from each state.[64] Chief negotiators do delegate to aides, but such delegation will be smoother, he suggests, when the negotiators do not have independent preferences.[65] Once this assumption is relaxed, negotiators serve no longer as a conduit for their constituents but as autonomous actors with distinct aims. Putnam gives the example of US participation in the Paris Peace Conference, which, he claims, saw Woodrow Wilson veto a deal that would have been acceptable to 'perhaps 80 percent of the American public *and* of the Senate'.[66] Applied to EU treaty making, the heads of state or governments' increased role within IGCs and through the Convention Method and simplified revision procedure can be seen as a way of protecting their individual and collective interests not from constituents, who play no formal role in treaty making, but from colleagues in national government who may approach negotiations with different priorities.

Tensions between officials, ministers and the heads of state or government in EU policymaking are well documented. Coreper has long faced accusations that its members 'go native' in Brussels, although such claims are contested.[67] The relationship between foreign ministers and heads of state or government can be strained at times. A well-known example is the tension between Margaret Thatcher and her Foreign Secretary, Douglas Hurd, over the United Kingdom's approach to the Maastricht Treaty negotiations.[68] More generally, the fact that foreign ministers routinely come from coalition partners in a number of member states can make the European Council wary of delegating decisions to the General Affairs Council.[69] Even if officials, foreign ministers and heads of state or government have similar preferences, there are other reasons why the European Council would seek a greater role in the negotiation stage. One is that foreign ministers have struggled to play their traditional role in relation to treaty negotiations as their day-to-day responsibilities in relation to EU foreign policy have increased.[70] The heads of state of government are no less busy, of course, but their involvement in the negotiation stage, as in other EU matters, tends to increase when the Council fails to reach agreement.[71]

That EU heads of state or government have increased their role in EU treaty making as other actors have acquired a more prominent position is no coincidence from a two-level game perspective. By securing a place for their personal representatives in conventions, the heads of state or government countered parliaments' new role in the negotiation stage with a layer of intergovernmental oversight. The Lisbon Treaty also allowed governments to circumvent the Convention Method if a simple majority of member states agree, albeit with the consent of the European Parliament.[72] Most importantly, the treaty permitted governments to circumvent the need for a convention without the approval of the European Parliament or national parliaments for certain categories of treaty amendment.[73] Beneficial though the Lisbon Treaty's bifurcated revision procedures are for governments seeking to retain control, they come at a cost. By codifying the conditions under which the ordinary and simplified revision procedures can be used, the Lisbon Treaty increased the role of the Court of Justice of the EU in the negotiation stage. It seems doubtful that national governments overlooked this possibility when negotiating the treaty, but they can be in no doubt about it following *Pringle*.[74]

Two-Level Legitimacy and EU Treaty Negotiations

The theory of two-level games can only partly explain the evolution of the negotiation stage, it would seem. What about the two-level legitimacy approach? As discussed in Chapter 2, the latter sees the privileged position of heads of state or government in two-level negotiations as being under threat. A battle over rightful membership is driving changing approaches to EU treaty making, it conjectures, alongside a debate over rightful conduct. Applied to the puzzle at the heart of this chapter, the two-level legitimacy approach suggests two explanations for the tussle between national governments and other actors over EU treaty making. The first emphasises the long-standing challenge to heads of state or governments' authority in this domain from parliamentarians. The other sees national governments' turn to parliaments as a response to the former's concern in the post-Maastricht period over the EU's legitimacy.

Parliamentarians sought a rightful place at the treaty-making table from the early days of the European Coal and Steel Community. The ECSC Assembly was not in a position to push for the Ad Hoc Assembly; it was on the day of the former's first meeting that it was asked to lead the latter. Instead, it was the Assembly of the Council of Europe that championed the involvement of parliamentarians in this important treaty-making episode. In May 1952, the Assembly of the Council of Europe had adopted a resolution calling for itself or the embryonic ECSC Assembly 'to draft the statute of a Political Community' as envisaged in the European Defence Community Treaty.[75] The Assembly of the Council of Europe offered its services, in part, because integrationists within and outside the Council of Europe saw its involvement as offering the best chance for deeper political integration between the Six.[76] This arrangement also suited the UK government, which had sought to associate the Council of Europe with the European Defence Community so as to allow the British to exert some influence over the Six's plans for closer cooperation in this sensitive domain.[77]

The collapse of the EDC Treaty, and with it plans for a European Political Community, did not deter parliamentarians from seeking a role in EU treaty making. One month before the Messina conference, the ECSC Assembly adopted a position paper on the future of European integration in which it called for an IGC to be convened.[78] The ECSC Assembly also sought to influence negotiations from the outside, for example, by making the case for the establishment of a unified assembly for the three European Communities.[79] The position papers and resolutions adopted by the ECSC Assembly over the Rome Treaties would become standard operating procedures for future treaty changes and a means for the European Parliament (as it was renamed in 1962) to make its voice heard if not always listened to.

72   THE TRANSFORMATION OF EU TREATY MAKING

The publication of the Kirk-Reay Report in 1978 was a decisive step in this regard because it signaled the European Parliament's willingness to engage, albeit cautiously, in questions of institutional reform.[80] Caution gave way to confidence after the 1979 election, first in the form of reports on institutional questions commissioned by the Political Affairs Committee and later in the Draft Treaty on European Union adopted by the European Parliament in February 1984 at its own initiative and without recourse to the Treaties' formal amendment procedure. Closely associated with the Italian federalist Altiero Spinelli, by then an MEP, the draft treaty was, in fact, backed by a broad coalition of MEPs who sought to shape the constitutional future of the European Community.[81] And yet Spinelli's influence on the project cannot be underestimated. It was the Italian federalist who wrote an open letter to MEPs in 1980, calling for a gathering of those who were 'convinced that the reform of the communitarian institutions is too serious to be left in the hands of statesmen and diplomats'.[82] The result was the creation of the Crocodile Club, an informal group of MEPs that successfully pushed for the establishment of the European Parliament Committee on Institutional Affairs, the body that produced the Draft Treaty on European Union.

Spinelli had long pushed for parliamentarians to play a role in EU treaty making. He had been an influential, if ambivalent, supporter of the Ad Hoc Assembly and played an important role in convincing Alcide De Gasperi of its merits. Writing in 1978, a year before his election as MEP, Spinelli was openly critical of the IGC as a forum for treating what he referred to as the European Community's 'institutional disease'.[83] 'If the drafting of the treaty were put in the hands of an intergovernmental conference', Spinelli argued, 'the inevitable result would be an erosion of the original agreement, a reduction to an acceptable confederal solution – or even less than that'.[84] Only the European Parliament as 'an assembly elected by the people, representing the people, and assuming a constituent role' could assume this responsibility, he suggested, and only then after the direct elections scheduled to take place the following year.[85] That 237 MEPs voted in favour of the Draft Treaty on European Union in 1984, as compared with 31 against and 43 abstaining, showed widespread support for Spinelli's vision of treaty making (if not necessarily his specific views on how the treaties should be amended). The direct elections were decisive in this regard. Whereas the Kirk-Reay Report had been treated with kid gloves, MEPs approached the Draft Treaty with the view that 'those elected by the people have a legitimate right to act on their behalf'.[86]

The European Parliament continued its campaign to play a role in treaty making in the 1990s, but it lacked the political resources to challenge national governments' privileged position. Criticisms of IGCs were raised by the European Parliament but in non-binding resolutions with questionable impact on member states.[87] More daring was the European Parliament's threat to block future enlargements of the EU unless the legislature was satisfied with negotiations over the Amsterdam Treaty.[88] How credible this threat was is debatable,[89] but it might just explain national governments' willingness to grant the European Parliament observer status at the IGC on Nice. However, it hardly accounts for national governments' decision to adopt the Convention Method at Laeken.

Whereas the European Parliament had long sought a formal role in EU treaty making, the Commission was more ambivalent. The Treaties of Rome, as noted above, gave the Commission powers to initiate formal treaty amendments, but it typically allowed member states to take the lead. Instead, the Commission sought an informal role in IGCs, starting with Jacques Delors, who interpreted the Commission's right of initiative in legislative matters as extending to IGCs and tabled more than half of the proposals in the IGC on the Single European Act.[90]

The Commission, although it welcomed the Laeken Declaration, had not consistently argued for it. True, Commission President Romano Prodi had argued two months before Laeken that '[t]raditional State diplomacy alone cannot launch a full European constitutional process in a way which will seem credible in the eyes of the people', but his administration was a late convert to the idea of a Convention.[91] Prodi had hoped that the Amsterdam Treaty would be more ambitious in reforming the EU's institutional architecture, and when this did not happen he convened a wise-person group led by former German President Richard von Weizsäcker. The report was bold in its vision of institutional reform but made no reference to the Convention Method. Instead, it proposed a variation on traditional IGC, in which the Commission would prepare a full draft of treaty amendments before negotiations between conference members began. Similarly, the Commission's White Paper on European Governance, published six months before the Laeken Declaration, wrestled with the problems of legitimacy facing the Union but made no mention of new approaches to treaty making at all.[92]

The Commission, it transpired, had good reason to be ambivalent about the Convention Method. The informal channels that the Commission relied on in IGCs rested uneasily with the Convention's commitment to

74   THE TRANSFORMATION OF EU TREATY MAKING

public debate, and matters were not helped by Convention President's Valery Giscard d'Estaing's intergovernmental vision.[93] The Commission was also hobbled by internal divisions, which came to a head when a draft treaty prepared at the request of the Commission President but not approved by the College, code-named Penelope, was leaked. In its 'official' contribution to the Convention, the Commission put forward no new ideas on treaty making,[94] but Penelope was provocative on this subject. It proposed a modified Convention Method in which the Commission President would play a leading role.[95] Absent from this proposal was any mention of an IGC, with the Commission serving instead as a powerful conduit between the Convention and the European Council. These ideas offered an insight into the role that some inside the Commission aspired to play in treaty making. But these ideas gained limited traction within the Convention or in the IGC that followed.

National parliaments were not, in any straightforward sense, *demandeurs* for the role they eventually acquired in the negotiation stage. Some national parliamentarians sought a place on the European stage, most noticeably Charles-Ferdinand Nothomb, President of France's Chamber of Deputies, who spoke in favour of the Assizes and played a leading role in its discussions in Rome in November 1990.[96] However, Nothomb and his supporters received a lukewarm reaction from many of his counterparts in the British, Danish and Dutch parliaments, who saw European-level cooperation as resting uneasily with national parliamentary sovereignty. The European Parliament also saw the Assizes as a threat to its role in EU policymaking. These tensions are reflected in parliamentarians' reluctance to reconvene even after the Maastricht Treaty's declaration on interparliamentary cooperation encouraged them to do so.[97] The EU's Conference of Parliamentary Committees for Union Affairs of Parliaments of the European Union (COSAC) held periodic discussions about the role of national parliaments in EU treaty making, but no consensus emerged. By mid-2001, COSAC's members remained divided over how national parliamentarians should engage in the debate over the future of Europe, with support for the idea of a Convention emerging only in the run up to the Laeken Declaration.[98]

National governments' privileged position in EU treaty making was, we have seen, openly challenged by the European Parliament from the late 1970s onwards, but the legislature lacked leverage over member states in this domain. National parliaments were more circumspect about seeking a role in EU treaty making and, along with the European Parliament, were agenda-followers rather than agenda-setters when it came to the creation of the Convention Method. From a two-level legitimacy perspective, there is limited evidence that national governments were compelled to open up the process of EU treaty making. Consistent with this approach, however, is the fact that national governments chose to involve these actors to a limited degree in response to the EU's legitimacy crisis. The EU has always faced problems of legitimacy, but these problems, it is commonly recognised, took on a different order of magnitude in the 1990s.[99] Denmark's referendum vote against the Maastricht Treaty in 1992 was a symptom of a more fundamental loss of public trust in the European project.[100] Before this vote, public support for the EU was waning, public protests were increasing and the salience of Europe for political parties was steadily increasing.[101] The permissive consensus that had afforded EU elites a large measure of discretion in how they designed and ran the Union had given way to political dissensus and a new era of politicisation.[102] The European Council made little mention of legitimacy in its conclusions prior to 1990, but such references are commonplace thereafter.[103] It was in this context that governments turned to other actors to play a role in EU treaty making.

Given its timing, the creation of the Ad Hoc Assembly in 1952 is a challenge for our thesis. However, we see limited evidence that normative concerns drove national governments to involve parliaments in plans for the European Political Community. Among the heads of state or government of the Six, Alcide De Gasperi was the driving force behind the European Political Community. The Italian Prime Minister was motivated more by the pursuit of 'political authority which he saw that the responsibility of the EDC demanded'[104] rather than questions of political legitimacy.[105] De Gasperi was, in any case, isolated among the Six, who agreed that the EDC Assembly should study future treaty amendments while ensuring than an IGC had the final say. Once the EDC Treaty was signed, De Gasperi pushed not for parliaments to take the lead on future treaty plans but for an IGC, with other member states insisting that the Ad Hoc Assembly be convened.[106] As an exercise in buying time, the Ad Hoc Assembly was successful. Although it reached agreement on a draft treaty, 32 of its 83 members either formally abstained from voting on the final text or did not register a vote.[107] De Gasperi, meanwhile, had resigned from office before the IGC held its first meeting, to be replaced by the less integrationist Giuseppe Pella.[108]

It was not until the 1990s that national governments explored more radical approaches to treaty negotiations in response to the EU's perceived legitimacy problems. The driving force behind the Assizes was not national parliaments or the European Parliament but French President François Mitterrand, who had called for a conference of parliaments in a speech at the European Parliament in October 1990. '[W]hy should the European Parliament not organize assizes on the future of the Community', he asked MEPs, 'in which, alongside your Assembly, delegations from national parliaments, the Commission and the governments would participate?'[109] As a former delegate to the 1948 Hague Conference, Mitterrand took a personal interest in parliamentary diplomacy, and he would convene a pan-European Assizes in Prague in 1991 as part of his ill-fated plans for a European Confederation after the end of the Cold War.[110]

The mood over European integration darkened yet further after Maastricht.[111] Talk of the EU's democratic deficit, though not new, intensified. It was in this more pessimistic context that support for involving national parliaments in European affairs took hold. Mitterrand's successor, Jacques Chirac, was the leading voice in this debate. In the run-up to the IGC on the Amsterdam Treaty, Chirac openly questioned the European Parliament's ability to bridge the perceived gap between the EU and its citizens. The Parliament's decision-making procedures have become too long and complex, he told a meeting of French ambassadors in Paris in August 1995, while at the same time arguing for national parliaments to become a guarantor of subsidiarity in the EU.[112] Michele Barnier, France's Minister for European Affairs, went further in March of the following year, arguing that the EU must be 'much closer to the national parliaments and the citizens' and proposing a 'high parliamentary council' of national parliamentarians.[113] As France championed the cause of national parliaments, other member states pushed for the European Parliament to play a greater role in EU treaty making. Belgium, the Netherlands, Luxembourg and Italy pushed for the European Parliament to be made permanent observer to the IGC on the Amsterdam Treaty, only for France and the United Kingdom to push back.[114] Member states' invitation to the European Parliament President to hold an exchange of views in advance of the IGC emerged as a compromise in this context.

As concerns over the EU's legitimacy intensified in the 2000s, a consensus emerged among EU member states on involving both national parliaments and the European Parliament in future treaty reforms. Jacques Chirac, once again, led this debate. In May 2000, German Foreign Minister Joscka Fischer triggered the debate over a European Constitution in his speech at the Humbolt University, in which he looked beyond negotiations over the Nice Treaty to a 'constituent treaty' aimed at building a 'European federation'. In so doing, Fischer gave no indication in his intervention that the new treaty should be negotiated through anything other than an IGC. It was Chirac who made the case for the Convention Method in his speech at the Bundestag in 2000. Preparations for a European Constitution 'must be conducted openly, involving our governments and citizens, through their representatives in the European Parliament and the national parliaments', he argued. 'One could imagine a number of possible approaches', the French President suggested, 'from a Committee of Wise Men to a model based on the Convention which is drafting our Charter of Fundamental Rights'. [115]

Chirac's ideas formed the basis for a declaration annexed to the Nice Treaty in which members of the IGC called 'for a deeper and wider debate on the future of the European Union'.[116] The Nice Treaty 'had completed the institutional changes necessary for the accession of new Member States', the declaration insisted, while acknowledging the 'need to improve and to monitor the democratic legitimacy and transparency of the Union and its institutions, in order to bring them closer to the citizens of the Member States'.[117] This normative justification is in keeping with the two-level legitimacy approach, which sees member states as involving new actors in treaty making not only because of tactical reasons but in response to concerns over the legitimacy of the political process.

The Nice Treaty's Declaration did not explicitly call for the creation of a Convention on the Future of Europe, but it set a relatively clear path towards the establishment of this forum. Magnette and Nicolaidis note the different degrees of enthusiasm for the convention among the member states, but the perceived relative failures of the Amsterdam and Nice IGCs helped to overcome such differences.[118] The Swedish and Belgian presidencies – which held office in the first and second half of 2001, respectively – were instructed 'in cooperation with the Commission and involving the European Parliament, [to] encourage wide-ranging discussions with all interested parties: representatives of national parliaments and all those reflecting public opinion'.[119] A declaration concerning the 'continuation of this process' would be decided at the European Council at Laeken in December 2001. Thus Belgian Prime Minister Guy Verhofstadt received a clear mandate to draw up plans for the European Convention, even if some negotiation remained to be done about its mandate and working methods.[120] By November of that year, the leaders of France and Germany were in agreement on the idea of a Convention if not yet over its leadership.[121] UK Prime Minister Tony Blair appears to have been most sceptical about creating a European Constitution by means of a 'single, legally binding document', but after Nice, he was no defender of the traditional IGC.[122] Speaking in Birmingham a month before the Laeken Summit, he praised the idea of a Convention 'as an innovative attempt to involve parliamentarians as well as governments in a wide-ranging debate about Europe's constitutional future'.[123]

The European Convention produced a lively debate on how treaties should be amended, but the question of whether parliaments should be involved in the process was largely uncontroversial. The consensus surrounding this issue can be seen, for example, in the Franco-German submission to the European Convention in January 2003, which called for the involvement of national parliaments in future conventions on the reform of treaties.[124] The draft treaty produced by the European Convention codified the Convention Method, while allowing the European Council to decide by a simple majority and with the consent of the European Parliament to move straight to an IGC.[125] The persistence of this provision in the final versions of the Constitutional Treaty and, later, the Lisbon Treaty could be seen as an instance of path dependence. However, member states did not hesitate to go against the European Convention by introducing the simplified revision procedure. The European Convention had debated but not reached consensus on the need for a way of amending certain elements of the treaty without recourse to an IGC or a convention.[126] However, member states insisted on such a provision in the IGC on the European Constitution and carried over this provision in the Lisbon Treaty. That the Convention Method went unchallenged in this IGC and the one on Lisbon was testament to how the involvement of parliaments in EU treaty making was largely taken for granted by member states at this point.

Although the Convention Method remains the default for major treaty amendments, it had not been redeployed at the time of writing. As a result, the role of parliaments is not quite as prominent as it could have been. Be that as it may, there is limited evidence to suggest that parliaments have been deliberately excluded from EU treaty making. For one thing, the European Parliament has been restrained about using its right of initiative in relation to treaty making. Even the protocol concerning changes to the number of MEPs was proposed by a member state. Furthermore, the European Parliament agreed with the European Council's assessment that the amendments related to the number of European Parliament seats and the Irish protocol to the Lisbon Treaty did not justify the convening of conventions. The European Council's decision to revise Article 136 of the Treaty on the Functioning of European Union via the simplified revision procedure was more controversial, with a number of MEPs arguing that the ordinary revision should have been employed.[127] But the European Parliament as a whole decided otherwise, with 494 votes cast in favour of the European Council's proposed amendment.

Conclusion

This chapter has explored the EU's changing approach to treaty negotiation from the Schuman Plan Conference to the 2010s. The former took the form of an IGC led by foreign ministers, which was intended to serve as a template for future treaty making. But, as we have seen, the EU departed from this template, cautiously at first but definitively in the 1990s by involving national parliaments, the European Parliament and the Court of Justice of the EU in various phases of treaty negotiation. The European Parliament gradually gained a foothold within IGCs before the Convention Method gave it, and national parliaments, a substantive role in drafting major treaty changes prior to the convening of an IGC. The Court was given a consultative role at first, but it assumed a more prominent role in the scrutiny of EU treaty making after the Lisbon Treaty entered into force, at least in relation to the use of the simplified revision procedure. Member states have also departed from the traditional IGC by giving heads of state or government a major say in all phases of treaty negotiation. The heads of state or government are key actors in the Convention Method and the new simplified revision procedure.

That heads of state or government sought to exert a tighter grip on treaty making is consistent with the two-level game approach. But this approach cannot easily account for the increasing prominence of parliaments in this domain. Consistent with the two-level legitimacy approach is the fact that European parliamentarians challenged national governments' privileged position in EU treaty making from the very outset of the European Coal and Steel Community, it was noted, and especially after the first direct elections to the European Parliament. But the European Parliament lacked the means, however, to secure anything other than a heavily constrained role in IGCs, while national parliaments were ambivalent about assuming a role in EU treaty making before and after the Assizes. Member states ultimately involved parliaments in EU treaty making, it was argued, to address the problems of legitimacy confronting the EU. French President François Mitterrand was a key driving force in this regard, as was his successor Jacques Chirac, with other EU leaders warming to their ideas as the EU's legitimacy problems worsened in the 2000s. Contentious though the European Constitution was among EU member states, there was broad support for the means through which it was negotiated. This vision of the Convention Method as a way of encouraging a more open and participatory approach to treaty making survived even as its first incarnation failed.

Notes

1 Preamble, Treaty Establishing the European Coal and Steel Community, 18 April 1951, 261 UNTS, 140.
2 Preamble, Treaty Establishing the European Coal and Steel Community.
3 Article 48(3), Treaty on European Union, 7 February 1992, 1992 O.J. (C191) 1, 31 I.L.M. 253.
4 Court of Justice of the EU, C-370/12 *Thomas Pringle* v. *Government of Ireland and Others* [2012] ECLI: EU:C:2012:756.
5 Laursen (2012c), p. 3.
6 Loth, Wallace and Wessels (1998), p. 3.
7 See Leucht (2010).
8 Article 96, Treaty Establishing the European Coal and Steel Community.
9 Article 38, European Defence Community Treaty, The European Defence Community Treaty, 27 May 1952, British Command Paper, Cmd. 9127 (1954).
10 Spaak served as the first president of the ECSC Common Assembly between 1952 and 1954; see https://europa.eu/european-union/sites/europaeu/files/docs/body/paul-henri_spaak_en.pdf.
11 Article 204, The Treaty Establishing the European Atomic Energy Community, 25 March 1957, 298 UNTS, 259, 5 Eur. Y.B. 454. Article 236, Treaty Establishing the European Economic Community, 25 March 1957, 298 UNTS, 3, 4 Eur. Y.B. 412.
12 de Witte (1994), p. 317.
13 Ad Hoc Committee for Institutional Affairs (1985), p. 32.
14 Corbett (1998), pp. 222–23.
15 Corbett (1998), p. 225.
16 An extreme case of national parliamentary involvement in EU treaty negotiations is Denmark, where the European Affairs Committee on the Folketing gives the government a negotiating mandate. For further details, see Laursen (2005b).
17 Declaration on the Conference of the Parliaments, Treaty on European Union, 7 February 1992, 1992 O.J. (C191) 1, 31 I.L.M. 253.
18 Corbett (1998), p. 296.
19 Article N, Treaty on European Union.
20 Article 41 Protocol on the Statutes of the ECB and the European System of Central Banks, Treaty on European Union.

21 Article 106, Treaty Establishing the European Community (consolidated version 1992). Official Journal C 224, 31.8.1992, pp. 1–130.
22 Corbett (1998), pp. 294–5.
23 European Council (1994).
24 Christiansen and Reh (2009), p. 111.
25 European Parliament (2000).
26 Gray and Stubb (2001), p. 13.
27 Norman (2003), p. 16.
28 European Council (2001).
29 Duff (2005), p. 26.
30 Stuart (2003), p. 18.
31 Duff (2005), p. 26.
32 Hoffmann (2002), p. 10.
33 Christiansen and Reh (2009), pp. 242–3.
34 Christiansen and Reh (2009), pp. 242–3.
35 Duff (2005), p. 26.
36 Duff (2005), p. 28.
37 Articles 48(2) and 48(6), Treaty on European Union (consolidated version 2016), Official Journal C 202, 07.06.2016, pp. 1–405.
38 Article 48(3), Treaty on European Union (consolidated version 2016).
39 Article 48(3), Treaty on European Union (consolidated version 2016).
40 Articles 48(2) and 48(6), Treaty on European Union (consolidated version 2016).
41 Article 48(6), Treaty on European Union (consolidated version 2016).
42 Article 48(7) Treaty on European Union (consolidated version 2016). The provision is limited to the TFEU and Title V TEU (except for military or defence decisions).
43 As required under Article 48(2) Treaty on European Union (consolidated version 2016). For a description of the procedures and the Treaty transitional arrangements notably the Protocol and Declarations nos. 4 and 57, see www.europarl.europa.eu/pdfs/news/expert/background/20100223BKG69359/20100223BKG69359_en.pdf.
44 Christiansen and Reh (2009), p. 114.
45 Pollack (1999), p. 12.
46 Court of Justice of the EU, C-370/12 *Thomas Pringle* v. *Government of Ireland and Others* [2012] ECLI: EU:C:2012:756.
47 Raustiala (2012), p. 168.
48 Kaelberer (2003).
49 Hix (2002). See Chapter 2 on this point.
50 Christian and Reh (2009), p. 109.
51 Prodi (2001).
52 Sandler (2004).
53 Pollack (1999), p. 13.
54 Pollack (1999), pp. 13–14.

55 Maurer (2003), p. 168.
56 The Secretariat of the European Convention (2002).
57 The Secretariat of the European Convention (2002).
58 Magnette and Nicolaidis (2004), p. 381.
59 Moravcsik (1998), p. 143.
60 Christiansen and Reh (2009), p. 162.
61 Beach (2004).
62 Miller, Dodd and Watson (1995), p. 36.
63 Adam and Mena Parras (2014), p. 8.
64 Putnam (1988: 435) does not limit his theoretical approach to heads of state or government, but they are the principal focus of his empirical work on two-level games.
65 Putnam (1988), p. 436n.
66 Putnam (1988), p. 457.
67 Lewis (2017), p. 352.
68 Thompson (1996), p. 182.
69 Hayes Renshaw and Wallace (2006), p. 175.
70 Puetter (2012).
71 De Schoutheete and Wallace (2002), p. 9.
72 Article 48(3), Treaty on European Union (consolidated version 2016).
73 Article 48(6), Treaty on European Union (consolidated version 2016).
74 Court of Justice of the EU, C-370/12 *Thomas Pringle* v. *Government of Ireland and Others* [2012] ECLI: EU:C:2012:756.
75 Consultative Assembly of the Council of Europe Resolution 14 (1952).
76 Jean Monnet and Alterio Spinelli were key advocates in this regard (Pinder 2010: 256).
77 Griffiths (2000), p. 62.
78 Piodi (2007), p. 21.
79 Piodi (2007), p. 35.
80 Cardozo and Corbett (1986), pp. 19–20.
81 Lodge (1984).
82 EPRS (2014).
83 Spinelli (1978), p. 81.
84 Spinelli (1978), p. 87.
85 Spinelli (1978), p. 88.
86 Lodge (1984), pp. 377–8.
87 European Parliament (1987).
88 Christiansen and Reh (2009), p. 113.
89 Maurer (2002), p. 420.
90 Budden (2002), p. 90.
91 In a speech to the European Parliament in October 2000, Prodi (2000) praised the Charter Convention but did not propose to apply it to EU treaty negotiations.

92 European Commission (2001).
93 Dimitrakopoulos and Kassim (2005), p. 189.
94 European Commission (2002).
95 Article 101, Agreement on the Entry into Force of the Treaty on the Constitution of the European Union (European Commission 2002: 87).
96 Westlake (1995), p. 62.
97 Declaration on the Conference of the Parliaments, Treaty on European Union.
98 COSAC Secretariat (2014), p. 19.
99 See Sternberg (2013), chapter 5.
100 Norris (1997), p. 276.
101 Hooghe and Marks (2009), pp. 7–9.
102 Hooghe and Marks (2009), pp. 7–9.
103 The European Council's reference in April 1990 to 'strengthening the democratic legitimacy of the union' is, by our reckoning, the first such reference (European Council 1990: 6).
104 Fursdon (1980), p. 214.
105 Risso (2004), p. 2.
106 Griffiths (2000), p. 66.
107 Griffiths (2000), p. 92.
108 Risso (2004), p. 8n7.
109 Corbett (1998), p. 296.
110 Sutton (1993).
111 Smith (1996).
112 Chirac (1995).
113 House of Commons Library (1996).
114 Maurer (2002).
115 Chirac (2000), p. 6.
116 Declaration on the Future of the Union, Treaty of Nice Amending the TEU, the Treaties Establishing the European Communities and Certain Related Acts, 26 February 2001, 2001 O.J. (C80) 1.
117 Declaration on the Future of the Union.
118 Magnette and Nicolaidis (2004).
119 Declaration on the Future of the Union.
120 Magnette and Nicolaidis (2004), p. 387.
121 Euractiv (2001).
122 Blair (2000).
123 Blair (2001).
124 Chirac and Schroeder (2003).
125 Article IV-7, Draft Treaty Establishing a Constitution for Europe, 18 July 2003, Official Journal C 169, 18.7.2003, pp. 1–150.
126 Miller (2003), pp. 26–7.
127 European Parliament (2011).

PART II

The Consent Stage

4 The Rise of Parliaments in EU Treaty Making

Parliaments, as noted in Chapter 1, acquired a significant role in treaty making from the eighteenth century onwards and especially in the twentieth century. Today, parliamentary involvement in the consent stage of treaty making is commonplace. Around two-thirds of states in Beth Simmon's study of human rights treaties either consulted with legislatures or gave them a say over such agreements.[1] Most democracies involve parliaments in treaty making to some degree, a notable exception being India, where the executive branch has the power to negotiate and approve treaties on behalf of parliament.[2] The parliament of India has no role to play unless there needs to be a change in national law or the implementation of the treaty requires changes in domestic law.[3] Even here, such executive powers are open to question, as evidenced by the political and legal controversy surrounding the government's treaty of accession to the World Trade Organization in spite of a lack of support in the legislature.[4]

Viewed against this backdrop, EU member states are not unusual in granting a role to parliaments in the consent stage of treaty making, but the increased involvement of legislatures since 1950 is striking nonetheless. This chapter offers a systematic comparison of the changing role of national parliaments in EU treaty making to produce the first of our ratification scales. The first section explores different ways of thinking about the role of parliaments in this domain before putting forward the classification on which our analysis is based. The second section compares the changing constitutional rules and norms underpinning the parliamentary approval of EU treaties over the period 1951–2016 on the basis of this classification.

Classifying the Role of Parliaments

Writing in 1958, Gerhard Bebr noted the conflict of laws between the European Coal and Steel Community Treaty and the constitutions of the Six, which fuelled 'prolonged discussions in national parliaments prior to its ratification'.[5] This study marked the beginning of scholarly inquiry into the role played by national parliaments in EU treaty making, but a systematic comparison of ratification rules and norms was slower to materialise. Norton, for instance, broke new ground in his study of national parliaments' involvement in European affairs, but he devoted limited attention to the involvement of these legislatures in treaty making.[6]

Hug and König were among the first to offer a systematic comparison of parliamentary involvement in EU treaty making.[7] Their taxonomy distinguishes between the parliamentary majorities required to approve EU treaties and the number of parliamentary chambers involved. This comparison feeds into a measure of domestic ratification constraints, the aim of which is to identify which political parties were 'pivotal for change' when it came to parliamentary votes on the Amsterdam Treaty. Pivot positions capture the rules governing parliamentary approval and also parties' vote share at the time of ratification. As such, this analysis is drawn to the question of how ratification rules are applied rather than why they were chosen. Nor does this study say whether and how rules change over time.

Carlos Closa offers the most comprehensive treatment of parliaments' role in EU treaty making to date.[8] His study records the procedures by which all major EU treaties were ratified by all member states, encompassing both the decision rules that applied in each parliamentary chamber, the number of chambers involved and those cases in which intervening elections apply. A major contribution of this study is that it captures the link between treaty making and constitutional amendment.[9] This link matters insofar as member states that amend national constitutions in connection with treaty making may find themselves facing a more stringent ratification requirement. This is because constitutional amendments typically require a qualified majority in national parliaments, whereas treaties sometimes require only a simple majority.

In our study we look beyond the EU at the wider literature on both international treaties and constitutional amendment. We are influenced by Beth Simmons's index of ratification rules, which formed part of her seminal study of international human rights treaties.[10] In constructing

Table 4.1 Parliaments scale

Scale	Score
Chamber must be consulted	1
Approval by simple or absolute majority	2
Approval by 3/5 or 2/3 majority	3
Supermajority (greater than 2/3 majority)	4

this index, Simmons starts not with a study of how particular treaties were approved but by identifying the 'hurdles' that treaties are generally required to overcome under national constitutional traditions.[11] The parliamentary component of this index distinguishes between rules that require majority consent in one legislative body and the more stringent stipulation of either a supermajority in one body or a majority in two separate legislative bodies. This distinction is too simplistic for the purpose of studying EU treaty making, but it makes clear its assumptions about what constitutes a more stringent ratification rule without folding this into a discussion of specific treaty-making episodes.

The literature on comparative constitutional amendment also offers useful insights. A foundational contribution is by Donald Lutz, whose 'difficulty' index increases with the majority required for legislative approval.[12] This exercise is repeated for each legislative body involved in constitutional amendment, and an additional score is added when an intervening election is required. Although Lutz's index has been questioned by some scholars,[13] recent studies remain influenced by his methodological approach.[14]

Our parliaments scale tracks the evolution of the constitutional rules and norms governing the involvement of parliaments in the consent stage of EU treaty making (Table 4.1). It assigns a score of 1 when parliament is informed or consulted, 2 when parliamentary approval by a simple or absolute majority is required, 3 when this requirement rises to a threshold of a three-fifths or a two-thirds majority and 4 when a supermajority of greater than two-thirds is required. We repeat this exercise for each national and subnational parliamentary chamber involved in the consent stage, adding scores together to form an aggregate scale. Faced with multiple paths to treaty approval under formal constitutional rules, we seek to identify which one would be expected to apply under prevailing constitutional norms. Where alternative approaches appear equally likely, we split the difference rather than choose one over the other.[15]

Exercises of this sort necessarily rely on simplifying assumptions. Like Simmons and Lutz, we assume that higher legislative hurdles give greater opportunities for parliaments in treaty making. A supermajority gives parliament a greater say in treaty making than a two-thirds majority vote, according to our taxonomy, just as a two-thirds majority does in relation to a simple or absolute majority. In practice, of course, a simple majority could be more onerous in a state that is deeply divided on a treaty than a two-thirds majority is in a state where there is strong support for the agreement. Hug and König's aforementioned measure of ratification constraints is superior in this respect because it combines information on domestic institutions and the domestic preferences of ratifying actors.[16] We keep these dimensions separate, leaving it to later chapters to investigate empirically whether 'divided' member states are more or less likely to choose higher parliamentary thresholds (Chapter 7) and what the impact of the constitutional rules and norms on treaty amendment is (Chapter 8).

Changing Rules and Norms in the EU-28

In this section, we compare the evolution of constitutional rules and norms governing the role of national and subnational parliaments in the consent stage of EU treaty making on the basis of the criteria developed in the previous section. This analysis covers the EU-28 from the year member states join the EU (or the European Communities) to 2016. Appendix 4.1 graphs these scores over our sample period.

Austria

The Federal President is in charge of concluding international treaties. To exercise this power, however, they first require the federal government's proposal.[17] The President may also delegate their powers to conclude treaties to the federal government, which is common practice.[18] After 1988, such powers were shared with the Länder, insofar as the treaty in question concerns the competences of the latter. The Länder were also given treaty-making powers within their own autonomous sphere of competences, as regards agreements with each other and with states and regions bordering Austria.[19] Where such competences are affected, the federal government is required to consult with the Länder, which, if they act in concert, can force the federal government to take account of their comments, unless there are compelling foreign policy reasons to do otherwise.[20] At the Federation level, treaty making is the responsibility of the executive branch, but certain 'political state treaties' or others that are law amending or law supplementing require the approval of the National Council (*Nationalrat*) prior to their ratification.[21] An absolute majority vote applies in such cases.[22] Undefined by the constitution, the term 'state treaty' encompasses all international agreements to which Austria is a party, be it with states or international organisations.[23] A political state treaty commonly refers to an agreement that 'substantially affects Austria's status in international affairs'.[24] The approval of the upper house, the Federal Council (*Bundesrat*), is also required for state treaties that touch upon the competences of the Länder.[25] For political treaties that do not concern the competences of the Länder, the Federal Council is empowered to issue a reasoned objection, which can delay, but not block, the ratification of a treaty.[26]

The Federal Constitutional Act on the Accession of Austria to the European Union provided for its own entry into force on the basis of a qualified majority vote by both the National Council and Federal Council.[27] This practice of approving treaties by means of a Constitutional Act was employed in relation to the Amsterdam and Nice treaties.[28] A constitutional amendment in 2008[29] introduced a provision specifically for treaties modifying 'the contractual bases' of the Union, a two-thirds majority being required in the National Council and Federal Council for such purposes, notwithstanding the need for a referendum (see Chapter 5).[30]

Under the constitution, specific federal competences can be transferred to intergovernmental organisations by means of a law or treaty.[31] Prior to 2008, treaties modifying constitutional law were treated as 'constitutionally modifying' i.e. analogous to a constitutional amendment.[32] This provision was removed in 2008, with the result that an explicit constitutional amendment is now required in cases where a treaty is at odds with the constitution. Partial revisions to Austria's constitution require a two-thirds majority in the National Council and, where such amendments restrict the competence of the Länder, the Federal Council.[33] A total revision of the constitution requires a referendum (see Chapter 5). [34]

Belgium

When it comes to the increasing involvement of parliaments in EU treaty making, Belgium is an extreme case. Under the Constitution of the Kingdom of Belgium (1831), the King was required to obtain the approval of commercial treaties and other agreements that might impinge on his subjects.[35] A similar arrangement lives on in the current constitution, with the King being responsible for the conclusion of treaties subject to parliamentary approval.[36] An absolute majority of votes cast is required for such approval.[37] Prior to a constitutional amendment in 2014, the approval of both the Chamber of Representatives (Chambre des Représentants/Kamer van Volksvertegenwoordigers) and the Senate (Sénat/Senaat) was required.[38] Thereafter, the power to approve treaties – at the federal level – was invested in the Chamber of Representatives, an example of the rules governing the parliamentary approval of treaties becoming less rather than more inclusive.[39] In contradistinction to the Senate's disappearance is the increasingly visible role of subnational parliaments in Belgian treaty making.

Belgium's transition from a unitary state to a federal one, which began in 1970, forged the principle *in foro interno, in foro externo*, whereby subnational tiers of governments assumed treaty-making powers by virtue of their domestic competences.[40] In 1978, a Special Majority Act required the approval of the French Cultural Community and Dutch Cultural Community for treaties that were relevant for cultural cooperation in cultural or education matters.[41] The second state reform created the Flemish, French and German-Speaking Communities, and under the third state reform in 1988, the approval of these communities was required for treaties falling in their sphere of competence.[42] The fourth state reform, in 1993, extended these treaty-making powers to the Walloon Parliament and the Parliament of the Brussels-Capital Region.[43] As a consequence of these constitutional amendments, subnational parliaments have been routinely involved in EU treaty making since the early 1990s. A cooperation agreement between the federal government, the communities and the regions sets out the modalities for this multilevel approach to treaty making.[44] Under this agreement, it falls to a working group of the Inter-Ministerial Conference for Foreign Policy to decide on whether a treaty is 'mixed', in which case the agreement is forwarded by the Minister of Foreign Affairs to the regions and committees for their approval. In practice, most treaties are treated as mixed because they touch upon the competences of all tiers of government.[45] All major EU treaty amendments since Amsterdam have been approved by the federal parliament (*federale Parlement van België/ parlement fédéral de la Belgique*), the Flemish parliament (*Vlaams Parlement*), the Parliament of the Walloon Region (*Parlement de Wallonie*), the Parliament of the Federation Wallonia-Brussels (*Parlement de la Fédération Wallonie-Bruxelles*), the Parliament of the German-Speaking Community (*Parlament der Deutschsprachigen Gemeinschaft*) and the Parliament of the Brussels-Capital Region (*Brussels Hoofdstedelijk Parlement/ Parlement de la Région de Bruxelles-Capitale*).[46] As a consequence, the constitutional norm is that all five subnational legislative bodies play a role in EU treaty making. A simple or absolute majority is the preferred decision rule in each case.[47]

Constitutional amendments in Belgium can be proposed by the Belgian parliament but approved only after an intervening election for both the Chamber of Representatives and the Senate.[48] These amendments can be approved only if they enjoy the backing of two-thirds of members of each chamber under the assumption that two-thirds of members are present.[49] Constitutional amendment in connection with EU treaties is rare. Belgium joined the European Communities without a specific constitutional provision for transferring sovereignty to international bodies and in spite of doubts about the constitutionality of such a move.[50] It was not until 1970 that a constitutional amendment permitted such a transfer. It would also be several years after the ratification of the Maastricht Treaty before Belgium introduced constitutional amendments necessitated by this agreement in spite of reservations expressed at the time of ratification by the Council of State.[51] As in Luxembourg, there has been discussion in Belgium about introducing a fast track procedure for constitutional amendment linked to EU treaty making, but proposals to this end have not been taken up.[52] On this basis, parliamentary approval without recourse to constitutional amendment remains the norm in Belgium.

Bulgaria

Bulgaria's unicameral National Assembly (*Narodno sabranie*) is responsible for approving treaties of a political or military nature and treaties that concern the state's participation in international organisations.[53] A simple majority vote applies in such cases.[54] The National Assembly is also responsible for approving treaties that confer powers emanating from the Constitution to the European Union,[55] with a two-thirds majority of all members of the parliament required for this purpose.[56] Treaties that require a constitutional amendment cannot be approved before the

94 THE TRANSFORMATION OF EU TREATY MAKING

passage of this amendment.[57] Constitutional amendment, unless it falls within the prerogatives of the Grand National Assembly (*Veliko narodno sybranie*) – an ad hoc constitutional body made up of 400 elected members – requires a three-quarters majority among all members of the National Assembly in three ballots on three separate days.[58] The adoption of a new constitution, the amendment of certain constitutional provisions and changes to the state's territory resulting from the ratification of an international treaty must be passed by two-thirds of all members of the Grand National Assembly on three different days.[59] In practice, Bulgaria has not sought to amend its constitution in connection with EU treaty amendment. Nor has it tended to view treaties as entailing a conferring of constitutional powers on the EU. As such, a simple majority vote is the norm for EU treaty making, although a two-thirds majority of all deputies passed both the Accession Treaty and the Lisbon Treaty.[60] Under the Bulgarian constitution, bills should be discussed and voted on twice in different sessions, but the Assembly can, by way of an exception, hold both votes in a single session. The National Assembly has typically done so in relation to EU treaties, thus expediting the process of treaty ratification.[61] A two-thirds majority of all deputies passed both the Accession Treaty and the Lisbon Treaty.[62] On this basis, we consider a two-thirds majority to be the norm in Bulgaria.

Croatia

Croatia's constitution states that the conclusion of international agreements is a matter for the President, the government and the state's unicameral parliament (*Sabor*).[63] International agreements that entail the passage or amendment of laws, are of a military or political nature or commit Croatia financially require approval by the Sabor, on the basis of a simple majority vote.[64] International agreements that delegate powers derived from the constitution to an international organisation or alliance require approval by two-thirds of all members of parliament.[65] The same threshold applies for Croatia's association into alliances with other states, with approval via referendum also required in such cases. [66]

International agreements must be concluded in the manner specified by the constitution.[67] Should a constitutional amendment be required, it must be approved by a two-thirds majority of all members of the Sabor,[68] unless the parliament calls a referendum, although the constitutional court in very recent case law is developing constitutional doctrine that is reducing the scope of referendums.[69] A constitutional amendment enacted in 2010 introduced a new title on the European Union, which committed Croatia to 'participate in the creation of European unity in order to ensure, together with other European states, lasting peace, liberty, security and prosperity, and to attain other common objectives in keeping with the founding principles and values of the European Union'[70] but included no separate provisions on EU treaty approval.[71] The Accession Treaty was ratified by a two-thirds majority in the Sabor. And if any future amendment of the treaties bestows new powers on the EU, then a two-thirds majority will be required. However, it is possible that treaty amendments that do not increase powers of the EU may require only a simple majority in the parliament. At the time of writing, Croatia had not yet ratified a major treaty amendment, so it was difficult to identify the prevailing constitutional rules or norms. Our working assumption, however, is that a two-thirds majority would be required in line with the constitution's provisions on the delegation of powers to international organisations.[72]

Cyprus

Treaty-making powers are fragmented under the Cypriot constitution. Agreements with international organisations relating to 'commercial matters, economic co-operation (including payments and credit) and modus vivendi' are concluded on the basis of a decision of the Council of Ministers, the executive branch of government.[73] But any other treaty, convention or international agreement requires approval by a law made by the House of Representatives (Βουλή των Αντιπροσώπων), Cyprus's unicameral legislature, before it can be operative or binding.[74] A simple majority vote applies in such cases.[75] The President and the Vice President of the Republic[76] – acting separately or in tandem – can exercise a final right of veto on laws concerning foreign affairs,[77] including those concerning international treaties, conventions and agreements.[78]

The House of Representatives cannot pass a law that is 'repugnant to, or inconsistent with, the Constitution'.[79] A constitutional amendment enacted in 2006 extended this provision to include 'any obligation imposed on the Republic as a result of its participation as a member state of the European Union',[80] and at the same time prohibited the constitution from annulling laws, acts or measures arising from the state's obligations as an EU member state.[81] This makes it unlikely that a constitutional amendment would ever be required prior to the ratification of

96   THE TRANSFORMATION OF EU TREATY MAKING

an EU treaty since treaties effectively become part of the constitution.[82] Such an amendment would require the backing of at least two-thirds of the total number of the representatives belonging to the Greek Community and at least two-thirds of the total number of the representatives belonging to the Turkish Community, although since the division of Cyprus there are no Turkish MPs.[83]

The constitutional norm is that Cyprus gives its consent to be bound by EU treaties by submitting a bill for consideration to the Council of Ministers before sending it to the House of Representatives. To date, the constitution has not been amended prior to the ratification of treaties. This is because the written constitution is very different from the functional constitution after the 1974 division. Amendment is difficult due to the absence of Turkish Cypriots from constitutional life and is rendered possible only by a judge-made doctrine of necessity.[84] Thus, Cyprus was unusual among member states that joined the EU since the 1990s in not amending its constitution to enable accession.[85] This was a controversial decision that played out against the backdrop of negotiations over the Annan Plan, with the Attorney General indicating that constitutional amendment was required prior to accession before his successor advised that such changes could be implemented after Cyprus joined the EU.[86] The Office of the Vice President, which is reserved for a Turkish Cypriot, has not been occupied since 1974, making a vice-presidential veto of treaties impossible at present. To date, the President has not sought to veto EU treaty amendments, and we consider the use of such powers to be unlikely. A simple majority vote is the norm for parliamentary involvement in EU treaty making, a situation that has remain unchanged since Cyprus joined the EU in 2004.

Czech Republic

The Czech constitution gives the President the authority to negotiate and ratify international treaties.[87] However, the assent of both chambers of the parliament is required for treaties affecting the rights or duties of persons, treaties of peace or alliance, treaties of a political or general economic nature, treaties by which the state becomes a member of an international organisation and treaties concerning additional measures by statute.[88] A simple majority of all members of the Chamber of Deputies (*Poslanecká sněmovna*) and the Senate (*Senát*) is required to give parliamentary assent in this context,[89] although an absolute majority of all deputies and an absolute majority of all senators is required for participation in the defensive systems of an international organisation.[90] Under a constitutional amendment introduced in 2001, the consent of parliament is also required for treaties that transfer certain powers of the Czech Republic to an international organisation or institution unless a constitutional act provides for a referendum.[91] For such a treaty, the constitution requires that three-fifths of all deputies and three-fifths of senators present give their backing.[92] The same requirement holds for the adoption of a constitutional act.[93]

The ratification of EU treaties is a fraught subject in the Czech Republic, which has given rise to ratification delays and legal challenges. However, such controversy does not revolve around the parliamentary threshold for approving treaties per se. The constitution was amended in 2001 in anticipation of accession to the EU. Article 10a (which does not mention the EU) was introduced in order to allow accession to the EU and other international treaties that would indirectly amend the constitution (hence the same majority for Article 10a treaties and a constitutional change). Since the Czech Republic joined the EU in 2004, it has been taken largely for granted that treaty amendments fall under Article 10a rather than Article 49 of the constitution, the former requiring a three-fifths majority in both houses rather than a simple majority under the latter. This was true of the European Constitution and the Lisbon Treaty and also with respect to the Article 136 TFEU amendment, which arguably could have fallen under Article 49 but instead was approved under Article 10a to 'build and declare broader consensus'.[94] Whether treaties require a constitutional amendment is a more contentious issue but it is one that makes little difference to the parliamentary threshold for treaty approval, which, as noted above, is the same for constitutional amendments and the approval of treaty amendments under Article 10a.

A more serious constitutional sticking point concerns the role of the President in the consent stage of EU treaty making. A vocal critic of the Lisbon Treaty,[95] President Vaclav Klaus delayed ratification of this agreement pending two constitutional challenges (see Chapter 6). Although he seemed likely to sign the law approving the treaty if these challenges failed, Klaus raised additional concerns that the Czech Republic could be liable under the EU Charter of Fundamental Rights to legal challenges over the Beneš Decrees (1940–5).[96] The Czech government did not share such concerns, but to assuage Klaus, it brokered an agreement with EU partners whereby a Czech opt-out from the EU Charter of Fundamental Rights to the Czech Republic would be attached to treaties at the time of the next accession treaty.[97] However, this never happened as the Czech

98   THE TRANSFORMATION OF EU TREATY MAKING

government did not ask for it when Croatia acceded, Klaus no longer being in power. Klaus eventually signed the Lisbon Treaty, but he provoked a second and in some senses more fundamental ratification crisis over the Article 136 TFEU amendment in 2012. Criticising the EU's attempt to create a permanent rescue fund as 'monstrous, senseless and ... absurd',[98] the President refused to allow the ratification of the treaty amendment even though the Czech parliament had voted in favour and in the absence of a constitutional challenge. The Senate responded by filing (among others) a constitutional charge for 'high treason' against the President before the Constitutional Court,[99] which was dismissed by the Court on procedural grounds, the President's term of office having ended. This was an unprecedented step in the history of the Czech Republic and, indeed, EU treaty making, albeit one that petered out after Miloš Zeman succeeded Klaus as President in 2013 and signed the 136 TFEU amendment. Significant though Klaus's interventions were, we interpret them not as a shift in EU treaty-making norms but as an illustration of how contested his attempts to change them were.

Denmark

Under the Constitutional Act of Denmark of 1953, the government shall not enter into any obligation in the domain of foreign affairs without the consent of the Danish parliament (*Folketing*), this provision covering instances in which the approval of the parliament is formally required and cases that are otherwise of 'major importance'.[100] Treaties that do not transfer sovereignty – or more accurately that do not delegate powers 'vested in the authorities of the Realm under this Constitution' – are passed by a simple majority. Treaties entailing such a transfer can be approved by parliamentary channels alone by five-sixths of the members of the Folketing (see Chapter 5 for provisions on a referendum).[101] Constitutional amendments must be passed twice by parliament by a simple majority after an intervening election before being subject to a referendum.[102]

The constitutional norm in Denmark is that EU treaties do not trigger a constitutional amendment. This is, perhaps, because the Constitutional Act of Denmark of 1953 foresaw the state's efforts to promote international rules of law and cooperation.[103] It could also be because constitutional amendments are rare, with roughly two-thirds of the 1849 constitution remaining intact.[104] Denmark's accession to the

European Communities in 1973 did not entail a change to the country's constitution, and no subsequent treaty set in motion a constitutional amendment. By convention, it falls to the Ministry of Justice to decide on whether a treaty involves the delegation of powers.[105] It decides on a case-by-case basis, with the Maastricht and Amsterdam treaties seen to involve a delegation but not so in the case of the Single European Act or the Nice and Lisbon treaties. On this basis, we see a simple majority and supermajority on EU treaties as being equally likely in Denmark.[106]

Estonia

Estonia's unicameral parliament (*Riigikogu*) is constitutionally responsible for ratifying international treaties.[107] This responsibility relates to treaties that (1) alter state borders; (2) entail the passage, amendment or repeal of Estonian laws (3) by which the state joins international organisations or unions; (4) give rise to military or proprietary obligations and (5) in which ratification is prescribed.[108] The Riigikogu Rules of Procedure and Internal Rules Act specify that bills concerning international agreements are deliberated in two readings unless the lead committee moves to conduct a third reading and that the final vote on the bill is conducted at the second reading after the amendment motions have been voted.[109] A simple majority vote applies in such cases.[110] Should a treaty necessitate a constitutional amendment, two successive compositions of the Riigikogu are required to approve this amendment by a three-fifths majority.[111] The question of whether treaty amendments would ever necessitate constitutional amendment is a matter of debate, but to date, the government has ratified treaties without recourse to such amendments and thus on the basis of a simple majority vote.[112]

Finland

A two-thirds majority vote in the state's unicameral legislature (*Eduskunta*) is the constitutional norm in Finland when it comes to approving treaties. Finland's Constitutional Act of 1919, as amended in 1995, required the approval of the Eduskunta for treaties that 'contain provisions within the legislative sphere or if the consent of the Eduskunta is otherwise required by the constitution'.[113] Finland's new constitution, which entered into force in 2000, contains more detailed treaty-making provisions, creating a two-step process. First, it requires the acceptance of treaties by the parliament. These treaties are divided into two categories. Treaties that concern the constitution, national borders or the transfer of authority to the EU or an international body of significance to Finnish sovereignty must be approved by a two-thirds majority.[114] Outside these significant situations, only a simple majority is required.[115] The second step in the process is that once the treaty has been approved, its provisions and other international obligations are brought into force by statute if the provisions are of a legislative nature, otherwise they can be brought into force by decree.[116] The government bill for the bringing into force of an international obligation is considered in accordance with the ordinary legislative procedure pertaining to an act. However, if the proposal concerns the constitution or a change to the national territory, or such transfer of authority to the European Union, an international organisation or an international body that is of significance with regard to Finland's sovereignty, parliament shall adopt it, without leaving it in abeyance, by a decision supported by at least two-thirds of the votes cast.

Should a constitutional amendment be required, it must be approved by a majority of votes cast and then, following a parliamentary election, by two-thirds of the votes cast. If five-sixths agree that constitutional amendment is urgent, the Eduskunta can adopt this amendment without the need for an intervening election and a second vote, provided the proposal is supported by a two-thirds majority.[117]

Finland has generally approved EU treaties by means of a two-thirds majority vote, with the country's treaty of accession the only one that also saw a referendum (see Chapter 5). Treaties do not, under prevailing constitutional norms, tend to trigger a formal amendment to Finland's constitution. Prior to the 2011 amendment, EU treaties that gave rise to constitutional inconsistencies were dealt with by means of exceptive enactments, which were approved by a two-thirds majority by the Eduskunta without recourse to an intervening election.[118] This was true, for example, of Finland's Treaty of Accession to the EU, with an exceptive enactment being used to square the constitution's idea of Finland as a sovereign republic with the transfer of sovereignty entailed by EU membership.[119] For exceptive enactments, the Constitutional Law Committee (*Perustuslakivaliokunta*) decided on whether treaty amendments were compatible with the constitution and existing exceptive enactments. The Committee decided that constitutional revision was required for the Amsterdam and Lisbon treaties but not the Nice Treaty.[120] After 2012, there is now a special procedure for treaties significant with regard to sovereignty, requiring a two-thirds majority of votes cast.[121]

An added complication when it comes to the ratification process for EU treaties in Finland concerns the role of its autonomous, demilitarised, Swedish-speaking region, the Åland Islands. Under the Act of Autonomy of Åland treaties that fall under the competences of Åland require the consent of the Åland parliament (*Lagting*).[122] Where the treaty in question is contrary to this Act, then consent is given by means of a two-thirds majority vote rather than a simple majority.[123] In practice, the Åland parliament has routinely sought to give its consent to major treaty amendments, including the Treaty of Accession and the Amsterdam and Nice treaties.[124] The approval of this regional parliament is required only for an EU treaty to take effect in the Åland Islands, and the consent of the Åland Islands is not required before Finland can give its consent to be bound to an EU treaty. This constitutional norm can be seen from the passage of the Lisbon Treaty, which saw the President of Finland sign the treaty after the Eduskunta had approved it but before the Åland parliament had given its consent.[125] The Constitutional Law Committee (see Chapter 6) confirmed this norm when it decided that Finland could ratify the Lisbon Treaty without the approval of the Åland parliament.[126]

France

Although it is seen by some scholars as one of 'the weakest legislatures in any modern democracy',[127] France's parliament has assumed a more muscular role in EU treaty making over time. France joined the European Communities under the Constitution of the Fourth Republic, which required approval by means of a law of treaties concerning international organisations.[128] An absolute majority was required in the National Assembly (*Assemblée nationale*) and the Council of the Republic (*Conseil de la République*) for this purpose.[129] France did not amend its constitution in connection with these treaties, an amendment that would have required an absolute majority in both chambers on two successive readings, with a referendum being required if a three-fifths majority was not achieved in the second reading.[130] The Constitution of the Fifth Republic, which entered into force in October 1958, brought an end to the 'golden age of parliamentarisation' but has maintained an important role for parliament in treaty making.[131] Under the new constitution, 'treaties or agreements relating to international organizations', 'those that modify provisions which are matters for statute', those relating to the status of persons and those involving the ceding, exchanging or acquiring of territory require an act of parliament approved by a single majority in the National Assembly and Senate (*Sénat*)[132] An absolute majority of votes cast is the norm in such cases.[133] A simple majority vote on an identical motion in both the Assembly and the Senate can block treaty amendments under the Treaty on European Union's Simplified Revision Procedure, as a result of a constitutional amendment introduced in 2008.[134]

A higher threshold will apply if a treaty triggers a constitutional amendment. Under the constitution, it falls to the Constitutional Council (*Conseil constitutionnel*) to decide, on a referral from either the President of the Republic, the Prime Minister or the president of the Senate or of the National Assembly, on whether an international agreement is contrary to the constitution, a revision to the constitution being a prerequisite for treaty ratification in such circumstances.[135] An amendment to this provision in 1992 allowed sixty members of either house to make such a referral.[136] Constitutional amendments, the initiative for which belongs concurrently to the President of the Republic on a proposal or the Prime Minister and to Members of Parliament, require a simple majority vote in both houses followed by a referendum.[137] However, the President can decide to submit the amendment proposed by the Executive to the 'Parliament convened in Congress' – the Senate and National Assembly sitting as one house – where it will be adopted if it wins the backing of a three-fifths majority.[138]

Although the constitutional rules concerning the parliamentary approval of EU treaties have remained fairly constant, constitutional norms have shifted. Until the 1990s, parliament's role in treaty making was seen as 'extremely slight'.[139] This was because EU treaties were not routinely referred to the Constitutional Council, which in any case was reluctant to challenge the constitutionality of a treaty negotiated by the executive.[140] Although the constitutionality of the Single European Act was a matter of controversy, President François Mitterrand chose not to refer the Single European Act to the Constitutional Council and Members of Parliament gave their approval.[141] With the exception of the Nice Treaty, which was negotiated under time pressure and with the French government at the helm,[142] the President has routinely referred EU treaties to the Constitutional Council since Maastricht.[143] In its review of the Maastricht, Amsterdam and Lisbon treaties, the Constitutional Council ruled that constitutional amendments were required.[144] On this basis, we consider a three-fifths majority requirement among the combined membership of the National Assembly and Senate to be the prevailing constitutional norm for majority treaty amendments since 1992.

Germany

The Basic Law of the Federal Republic of Germany, which entered into force in 1949, allowed the Federation to transfer sovereign powers to international institutions by means of a law[145] and in its Preamble refers to the state as seeking to promote world peace as an equal partner in a united Europe.[146] It originally fell to 'the bodies competent at the time for federal legislation' to approve treaties regulating the relations of the Federation or referring to matters of federal regulation.[147] A simple majority vote in the federal parliament (*Bundestag*) was the norm in such cases.[148] In its original form, the Basic Law explicitly required consultation with the Länder only in relation to treaties affecting the special conditions of a Land.[149] Otherwise, the federal government was under a general obligation to keep the federal Council (*Bundesrat*) informed of federal policy.[150] Bundesrat involvement in the consent stage of treaty making was guaranteed only in cases where constitutional amendments were necessary, with such amendments requiring two-thirds majority backing in both the Bundestag and the Bundesrat.[151]

Germany did not seek to amend the Basic Law when it joined the European Economic and Atomic Energy Communities, although a constitutional amendment was envisaged in relation to the failed European Defence Community Treaty.[152] The Treaties of Paris and Rome were consequently approved by the Bundestag on the basis of a simple majority vote and without formally consulting the Bundesrat.[153] The constitutional rules and norms surrounding the parliamentary approval of EU treaties in Germany began to shift in the 1980s. In 1986, the Ratification Act for the Single European Act required consultation with the Bundesrat in relation to this treaty and on all matters of relevance to the Länder,[154] although the government refused, at this point, to accept the Bundesrat's plea for treaty-making powers equal to those of the Bundestag.[155] Maastricht's triggering of an amendment to the Basic Law provided the Bundesrat with a hitherto unprecedented role in EU treaty making, although constitutional amendment did not become the norm in future treaty revisions. The Bundesrat nonetheless used its temporary seat at Maastricht to secure a permanent role in the consent stage. In 1992, a constitutional amendment[156] authorised the Federation to transfer sovereign powers to the EU by law, the approval of which required the consent of the Bundesrat.[157] This amendment also stipulated that the establishment of the European Union at Maastricht

104   THE TRANSFORMATION OF EU TREATY MAKING

'as well as changes in its treaty foundations and comparable regulations that amend or supplement this Basic Law, or make such amendments or supplements possible' would be subject to the same requirements as constitutional amendments.[158] This entails a two-thirds majority requirement in both the Bundestag and Bundesrat. [159]

Since Maastricht, the constitutional norm is that all major EU treaties are approved on the basis of a two-thirds majority in both houses even in cases where the constitution is not amended.[160] As such, rules governing the parliamentary approval of EU treaties in Germany are effectively on a par with those for constitutional amendment. Under the Responsibility for Integration Act (2009), treaty amendments under the Simplified Revision Procedure will be approved according to the same constitutional rules as traditional EU treaty amendments.[161] This leaves open the question of whether such revisions would require simple or two-thirds majorities in both chambers, with the Article 136 TFEU amendment approved by a simple majority vote in both chambers.

Greece

Under Greece's constitution, the President of the Hellenic Republic is empowered to 'conclude treaties of peace, alliance, economic co-operation and participation in international organisations or unions, and announce the same to Parliament with the necessary clarifications, if the interests and security of the state so permit'.[162] However, certain categories of treaty – including those concerning participation in international organisations or unions – must be approved by a 'formal law'.[163] The constitution distinguishes here between laws that 'limit the exercise of national sovereignty', which require an absolute majority of the total number of deputies in the unicameral Hellenic parliament (Βουλή των Ελλήνων),[164] and the vesting of powers in international organisations, which entail a three-fifths majority.[165]

The parliamentary procedures for the approval of constitutional amendments in Greece are stricter than those that apply to treaties. Proposals for constitutional amendments must be tabled by at least fifty members of parliament approved by a three-fifths majority in two votes held at least one month apart.[166] Then, in the opening session of the next parliament the amendments must be approved by an absolute majority of members.[167] The voting requirements can be reversed if the proposals for amendment are approved by absolute majorities; then the vote for adoption in the new parliament can be by three-fifths majority.[168]

Once the constitution has been revised, it cannot be revised again until a period of five years has passed.[169]

The distinction made in Article 28 of Greece's constitution between limiting sovereignty and vesting powers in international organisations is a confusing one.[170] The country's accession to the European Communities was conceived of as a limitation of sovereignty and hence the subject of an absolute majority, but all treaty amendments have been treated as vesting power in an international organisation and hence the subject of a three-fifths majority vote.[171] The introduction of an 'interpretive clause' in 2001 confirmed that Article 28 of the Greek constitution constituted 'the foundation for the participation of the Country in the European integration process', although it made little practical difference to the constitutional norms surrounding treaty making.[172] Constitutional amendment linked to the approval of treaties in Greece is a possibility but not a norm. Indeed, the constitution has been amended only three times since 1975 on issues not directly connected to EU treaties. This makes a three-fifths majority the constitutional norm for the parliamentary approval of EU treaties since the state became a member.

Hungary

Hungary's unicameral National Assembly (*Országgyűlés*) is responsible for authorising international treaties that fall within its functions and powers.[173] The constitutional rule is that the National Assembly takes decisions on the basis of a simple majority unless the Fundamental Law or parliamentary rules of procedure state otherwise.[174] Treaties through which Hungary exercises 'some of its competences set out in the Fundamental Law jointly with other Member States through the institutions of the European Union' require the backing of two-thirds of members.[175] The EU Charter of Fundamental Rights (unusually, with its Explanations) was approved by the parliament and promulgated in Hungarian law through legislation, even though the Charter is not a treaty sensu stricto but an interinstitutional text at the level of EU primary law.[176] It was treated on equal footing with the Lisbon Treaty, hence the Charter's domestic incorporation also required a two-thirds majority. Should a treaty necessitate constitutional amendments, the same parliamentary threshold is required.[177] The only EU Treaty that required constitutional amendment was the Treaty of Lisbon, when the constitutional provisions on *nullum crimen/poena sine lege* (no crime without law) were changed.[178]

106   THE TRANSFORMATION OF EU TREATY MAKING

These changes, triggered by EU law, were made in a separate constitutional amendment that entered into force at the same time as the Lisbon Treaty.[179] After Hungary's EU accession in May 2004, the first EU treaty amendment (the Romanian and Bulgarian accession treaty of 2005) was approved by the parliament with a simple majority, since the legislature considered it had not transferred more competences to the EU and had not altered the allocation of competences between the EU and the member states.[180] To date, EU treaty amendments have not routinely required constitutional amendment, but they have typically been treated as delegating powers to the EU and its institutions. Consequently, qualified majority voting is the norm for EU treaty making in Hungary.

Ireland

Ireland's bicameral parliament (*Oireachtas*) plays a subdued role in treaty making compared with the vocal part played by the people (see Chapter 5). Under the Irish constitution, 'every international agreement to which the state becomes a party must be laid before Dáil Éireann' (the lower house).[181] This provision – an echo of the Ponsonby Rule[182] and the state's roots in the Westminster model – suggests a consultative role for the parliament in treaty making.[183] However, any agreement involving a 'charge upon public funds' requires the Dáil's approval before Ireland can become party to it,[184] save for 'agreements or conventions of a technical and administrative character'.[185] There are no special provisions concerning voting rules for treaties or constitutional amendment. In consequence, such matters are decided by a simple majority.[186]

Ireland's constitution provides no explicit role in treaty making for the upper house, Seanad Éireann, an unusual situation among EU member states with bicameral legislatures. A constitutional norm emerged in 1977 during the passage of the Budget Treaty (1975), which ensured a role for the Seanad. Initially, the Irish considered ratifying this treaty without recourse to domestic legislation at all. However, the Minister of Foreign Affairs, Garrett FitzGerald, decided, after consulting with the Attorney General, that such a course of action would be 'anomalous and illogical'.[187] This decision established a constitutional norm that the approval of EU treaties would require new legislation, meaning that a simple majority vote was henceforth required in both the Seanad and the Dáil.[188]

The Irish constitution does not require a constitutional amendment before treaties can be approved, although the Oireachtas is prohibited from enacting 'any law which is in any respect repugnant to [the] constitution or any provision thereof'.[189] Constitutional amendment became the norm after the Irish Supreme Court's ruling in *Crotty*,[190] as discussed in Chapter 5. This shift did not affect the majority required in parliament to approve treaties. Proposals for amending the Irish constitution require a simple majority in both houses of the Oireachtas before being put to a referendum.[191]

Italy

Italy's constitution permits the state to place limitations on its sovereignty 'that may be necessary for a world order ensuring peace and justice among the Nations' and commits to the promotion and encouragement of international organisations.[192] Although this provision was originally aimed at membership of the United Nations, it has underpinned Italy's involvement in EU treaty making.[193] Italy has consistently given its consent to be bound to EU treaties on the basis of a simple majority vote in both parliamentary chambers. This practice is rooted in both constitutional norms and constitutional rules. Under the Italian constitution, it is the responsibility of the parliament to authorize by law 'the ratification of such international treaties as have a political nature, require arbitration or a legal settlement, entail change of borders, spending or new legislation'.[194] A majority of members of both the Chamber of Deputies (*Camera dei deputati*) and the Senate (*Senato della Repubblica*) must be present for this vote, and a majority must support the treaty in each house.[195] Constitutional amendments require a higher parliamentary threshold, but the constitutional norm since 1951 is that EU treaties do not necessitate changes to the constitution. No such constitutional amendment was undertaken in connection with the Treaties of Paris and Rome, and in a 1973 decision,[196] Italy's Constitutional Court ruled that European obligations have immediate constitutional primacy, marking a change in approach from previous decisions.[197] Thereafter, EU treaties were routinely approved via parliamentary channels without recourse to constitutional amendment.

Latvia

Latvia's constitution requires the approval of the state's unicameral parliament (*Saeima*) for all international agreements that 'settle matters that may be decided by the legislative process'.[198] A simple majority vote

108 THE TRANSFORMATION OF EU TREATY MAKING

after two readings is required for this purpose.[199] Where international agreements delegate 'State institution competencies', or parts thereof, to international institutions, two-thirds of members present must vote in favour of this agreement in a sitting of the Saeima in which two-thirds of all members participate.[200] Substantial changes to Latvia's membership of the EU can be decided by referendum if half of deputies call for such a vote to be held.[201] The constitution can be amended if two-thirds of the members of the Saeima agree in a sitting in which two-thirds of all members are present.[202] A referendum is also required before certain constitutional provisions can be amended (see Chapter 5).[203] Since Latvia joined the EU in 2004, the Saeima has tended to view EU treaty amendments as involving neither the delegation of state institution competences or requiring constitutional amendments, albeit after parliamentary debate in some cases and, as discussed in Chapter 6, unsuccessful court challenges.[204] As such, simple majority voting remains the norm.

Lithuania

Under Lithuania's constitution it is the responsibility of the unicameral parliament (*Seimas*) to approve and denounce international treaties,[205] including participation in universal or regional international organisations and multilateral or long-term economic treaties.[206] Where this is done by means of a law, a majority of members of the Seimas present must support the treaty in question.[207] Once treaties have been approved, they become a constituent part of Lithuania's legal system,[208] although the constitution states that Lithuania shall participate in international organisations provided this is not in conflict with the interests or independence of the state.[209] Should a treaty amendment nonetheless necessitate a constitutional amendment, this would require a referendum in some cases and the approval of the Seimas in all others.[210] In the case of the latter, a constitutional amendment would require the backing of two-thirds of members in two votes held at least three months apart.[211] Controversially, Lithuania did not amend its constitution at the time of joining the EU in 2004,[212] although it did so by means of a Constitutional Amendment Act that came into effect three months after it joined and the Constitutional Court subsequently held that the Act confirmed membership.[213] The Act is now considered a constituent part of the Lithuanian constitution.[214] Its confirmation of membership requires a referendum to amend (see Chapter 5). To date, Lithuania has sought to amend neither its constitution nor the Constitutional Amendment Act, although prior to accession it did amend the constitution on specific issues.[215] As a result, the Seimas has given its approval to treaties on the basis of a simple majority vote. The constitution was amended in 2006 in order to introduce the euro, but the amendment was declared unconstitutional and unnecessary.[216]

Luxembourg

Luxembourg was the first member state to enhance its parliament's role in EU treaty making. Luxembourg's constitution of 1868 entrusted responsibility for treaty making to the Grand Duke, although commercial treaties and those that encumber the state or its citizens required approval by means of a law adopted by the Chamber of Deputies (*Chambre des Députés*)[217] on the basis of a simple majority vote.[218] When it joined the European Coal and Steel Community in 1951, Luxembourg did so without specific constitutional rules concerning the vesting of powers in international organisations, with the government appealing instead to customary constitutional law associated with the state's participation in the Zollverein and the Benelux Union.[219]

Luxembourg's Council of State (*Conseil d'État*) questioned the constitutionality of this move but did not rule against it.[220] A constitutional amendment introduced in 1956 in response to the Council's decision allows Luxembourg to vest powers granted to the executive, legislative and judicial branches under the constitution in 'institutions governed by international law' on a temporary basis.[221] Treaties covered by this provision, the amendment stipulated, must be approved by a two-thirds majority in the Chamber of Deputies.[222] The requirements for constitutional amendment are more stringent still since the Chamber must achieve this two-thirds majority in two votes held at least three months apart, although, as of 2003,[223] a referendum can, under certain circumstances, replace the second of these votes (see Chapter 5).[224] The 2003 amendment to Luxembourg's constitution also abolished the requirement of an intervening election after the first of the Chamber's two votes on a constitutional amendment.[225]

The constitutional norm in Luxembourg is that constitutional amendments required by a treaty come after the treaty has been ratified. As such, constitutional amendment does not routinely feature in the consent stage. As noted above, a constitutional amendment arising from the European Coal and Steel Community Treaty was approved five years after this treaty had entered into force. It took two years after the Maastricht Treaty was ratified before the Chamber of Deputies approved an amendment to Luxembourg's constitution to take account of voting rights for the citizens of other EU member states.[226] An attempt was made in 1994 to introduce a fast-track procedure for constitutional amendment linked to international treaties, but this idea was not taken up.[227] On this basis, the parliamentary approval of EU treaties remains the norm in Luxembourg, the voting threshold increasing from a simple majority to a two-thirds majority in 1956.

Malta

Treaties have played a pivotal role in shaping the sovereign status of Malta, including the Treaty of Amiens (1802), under which the British committed to restore the archipelago to the Knights, and the Treaty of Paris (1814), which placed Malta under the sovereignty of the British monarch.[228] Malta's constitution assigns no role to the state's parliament in the consent stage of EU treaty making. Instead, parliamentary involvement is provided for under the Ratification of Treaties Act (1983), which requires approval via resolution of the House of Representatives for treaties concerning the relationship of Malta with any multinational organisation, agency, association or similar body.[229] An act of parliament is required for treaties that are to become – or be enforceable by – Maltese law, as are treaties that concern the status of Malta under international law and the state's security, sovereignty, independence, unity or territorial integrity.[230] The European Union Act, which provided for Malta's accession to the EU, allows for the approval of a new treaty (or treaty amendment) without recourse to these procedures.[231] Specifically, it allows the Prime Minister to declare by order a new treaty to be 'as one with' the Treaty defined in the European Union Act, after a draft of the treaty has been approved by a resolution of the House of Representatives.[232] A resolution for the approval of the draft must also be submitted for examination to the Committee on Foreign Affairs, after which it reports to the House of Representatives, which must debate and vote on the results of this scrutiny process.[233] An act of parliament requires three readings in the House of Representatives and consultation with stakeholders and committees. Decisions on a resolution or act of parliament in connection with EU treaties are decided, in such cases, by a majority of MPs present and voting, in accordance with the Standing Orders of the House of Representatives.[234] Treaties that trigger constitutional amendments require the support of a simple majority of MPs or a two-thirds majority, depending on the provisions altered.[235]

Since joining the EU in 2004, the approval of treaties via parliamentary resolution in line with the European Union Act (2004) rather than the Ratification of Treaties Act (1983) and without a constitutional amendment is the norm in Malta. This constitutional norm is not uncontested, as evidenced by former Foreign Minister Alex Sceberras Trigona's sharp criticisms concerning the manner in which the European Constitution was ratified.[236] The 'proper way of ratifying' the European Constitution, Trigona, argued, would have been by act of parliament and accompanying amendments to the Maltese constitution. [237] In spite of such criticisms, the Maltese government approached the Lisbon Treaty and subsequent treaty amendments in the same way as it did the European Constitution. Thus, a simple majority vote remains the constitutional norm for the House of Representative's role in EU treaty making.

The Netherlands

The Netherlands – like Italy – has consistently approved EU treaties via a simplified majority vote in both houses of the States General (*Staten-Generaal*). The Senate (*Eerste Kamer der Staten-Generaal*) and the House of Representatives (*Tweede Kamer der Staten-Generaal*) approved the European Coal and Steel Community Treaty in October 1951 and February 1952, respectively. The Treaty was not considered to be in violation of the constitution and, as such, was approved on the basis of a simple majority vote.[238] The constitutional basis for this vote was murky. In 1922, the Constitution of the Netherlands confirmed the States General's role in the approval of treaties, although the government sought to circumvent this requirement by pursuing international agreements from which parliament was kept at arm's length.[239] A royal decree issued in 1950, moreover, allowed foreign ministers to ratify some treaties without parliamentary approval.[240] A constitutional amendment introduced in 1953 requires the prior approval of binding treaties by the States General[241] unless an act of parliament states otherwise.[242] Should a treaty lead to constitutional revision, such revisions require a two-thirds majority of votes cast by the Senate and House of Representatives after an intervening election.[243] However, treaties that conflict with the constitution are permissible provided they are approved by a two-thirds majority in a vote involving both parliamentary chambers.[244] The constitutional norm in the Netherlands is to ratify EU treaties without first

112 THE TRANSFORMATION OF EU TREATY MAKING

amending the constitution or recognising them as incompatible with the constitution.[245] Constitutional amendments, when they occur, tend to follow treaties, as in the amendment of 1953.[246] Assessment as to the prior constitutionality of treaties rests with the government, although it is required to consult with the Council of State, an advisory body that, inter alia, examines treaties in the light of the constitution.[247] With the notable exception of the European Constitution, the Council of State has tended to see EU treaties as compatible with the Dutch constitution.[248]

Poland

Under Poland's constitution, consent by means of a statute is required for treaties concerning peace, alliances, political or military treaties, freedoms, rights or obligations. [249] The same goes for treaties concerning membership in an international organisation and that entail financial responsibilities for the state and concern matters regulated by statute or which must be regulated as such under the constitution.[250] Such an agreement must be approved by means of a simple majority in the *Sejm*, the lower house of Poland's parliament and the Senate (*Senat*), the upper house.[251] Consent to an international agreement that involves the delegation of competences of the organs of the state requires a two-thirds majority in each house.[252] Consent can alternatively be passed by nationwide referendum,[253] but any resolution in relation to the choice of procedure for granting consent must be taken by the Sejm on the basis of an absolute majority vote.[254]

When it comes to ratifying EU treaties, the choice of ratification procedures is the subject of intense domestic debate. Having sought to hold a referendum on the European Constitution[255] before this vote was cancelled, the government sought approval for the Lisbon Treaty via parliament on the basis of a two-thirds majority vote in both chambers.[256] The government's decision to submit the Article 136 TFEU amendment for approval via a simple majority vote[257] led to heated criticisms within the Sejm and the Senate and a constitutional challenge (see Chapter 6).[258] The treaty amendment was ultimately ratified via the procedures proposed by the government, but the affair showed the limited room to approve EU treaty amendments on the basis of a simple majority vote.

Once parliament grants consent by a statute (in the form of a Ratification Act), the president has twenty-one days to sign it, veto it or refer it to the Constitutional Tribunal.[259] Traditionally, presidents have not sought to use this veto, although Lech Kaczyński threatened to do so in relation to the Lisbon Treaty following a stand-off over Poland's proposed opt-out from the EU's Charter of Fundamental Rights. He made common cause on this point with his twin brother, Jaroslaw Kaczyński, leader of the opposition Law and Order Party and Prime Minister during negotiations over the Lisbon Treaty. Donald Tusk, who succeeded Jaroslaw Kaczyński as Prime Minister, was critical of the opt-out, but, otherwise lacking the support for a two-thirds majority and fearing a presidential veto, he brokered a compromise with the President. The opt-out was preserved, and in return, the Sejm and Senate approved the Lisbon Treaty.[260] However, a further delay in ratification occurred when the President refused to sign the statute approving the treaty after Ireland's referendum vote against the agreement. Eventually, one week after the second referendum in Ireland, Lech Kaczyński ratified the treaty.[261] The President refused, once again, to facilitate the ratification of the Article 136 amendment, which was approved by his successor after Kaczyński's untimely death. As in the Czech case, these episodes show the power of a head of state to delay – and even extract concessions over ratification – while ultimately accepting parliament's sovereignty over such matters.

Portugal

Under Portugal's constitution, there are two types of international conventions: treaties and agreements. Treaties are approved by the unicameral Assembly of the Republic (*Assembleia da República*), and then ratified by the President.[262] Agreements, on the other hand, can be approved by government and by the parliament when the government so chooses or where the treaty in question concerns the reserved competences of the Assembly[263] and are signed by the President. Where Portugal's participation in international organisations, peace, defence and the rectification of borders or military affairs are concerned, then the international convention is viewed as a treaty. The EU is viewed as an international organisation, so the stricter constitutional rules on treaties are applied. Approval takes the form of a resolution,[264] which is adopted by a simple majority of members[265] except in cases where the President refers the treaty to the Constitutional Court (*Tribunal Constitucional*) and it declares a rule contained in it to be unconstitutional.[266] The President has never requested a prior constitutional review on an EU treaty.[267] If this did happen, either the offending provision would be removed or the treaty would have to be approved by 'two thirds of all Members present and

114 THE TRANSFORMATION OF EU TREATY MAKING

greater than an absolute majority of all the Members in full exercise of their office'.[268] The constitution thus allows for either a simple or qualified majority vote on EU treaties, but constitutional norms clearly favour the former.[269] This was true, for example, of the country's accession treaty to the European Communities, which was ratified following a simple majority vote. The constitution was revised in advance of the ratification of the accession treaty, but this was an exceptional move so as to ensure it contained no provisions that were unconstitutional.[270] A 'Europe clause' – the scope of which has been expanded by a series of revisions to the constitution – has reinforced this constitutional norm. Anticipating accession, the 1976 constitution committed the country to the reinforcement of European identity and to strengthening European states' action towards peace, economic progress, and justice in the relations among peoples.[271] The third revision of the constitution in 1992 permitted Portugal to enter into agreements for the joint exercise of the powers necessary to establish the European Union subject to certain conditions.[272] The sixth revision in 2004 changed this to powers needed to construct and deepen the European Union and also recognised the primacy of EU law.[273] Overall, we judge that the approval of EU treaties via a simplified majority vote is the prevailing constitutional norm since Portugal joined the European Communities in 1986.

Romania

Under Romania's constitution, the President concludes international treaties on behalf of the state, the government negotiates such agreements and the parliament approves them.[274] Bills and legislative proposals concerning the ratification of treaties are submitted to the Chamber of Deputies (*Camera Deputaților*) for debate and adoption[275] before being sent to the Senate (*Senat*).[276] Treaties approved by ordinary laws are approved by a simple majority vote of members present in each chamber.[277] If a treaty is contrary to the constitution, a constitutional amendment is required before the treaty can be ratified.[278] Constitutional amendments require a two-thirds majority in the Chamber of Deputies and the Senate[279] or, if they fail to reach agreement, a three-fourths majority of a joint session of the two chambers.[280] Constitutional amendments must be approved by a referendum before they take effect.[281] A constitutional amendment introduced in 2003 on the eve of Romania's accession to the EU introduced a new provision on integration into the EU, requiring approval of Romania's accession to the constituent treaties of the EU by two-thirds of deputies and senators in a joint session of both chambers.[282] The same requirement was extended to the accession to the acts amending these constituent treaties.[283] The use of the term 'accession' in the second of these provisions perhaps has led some commentators to see a simple majority vote in both chambers as the constitutional norm for treaty ratification.[284] However, 'accession' is used interchangeably with 'ratification' in this context rather than referring to the process whereby Romania becomes a party to a treaty negotiated by other states. As such, a two-thirds majority in a joint session of the House of Deputies and the Senate is the prevailing constitutional rule and one followed, for example, in relation to the Lisbon Treaty and the Article 136 TFEU amendment.[285]

Slovak Republic

Treaties concerning 'human rights and fundamental freedoms, international political treaties, international treaties of a military character, international treaties from which membership of the Slovak Republic in international organisations arises, international economic treaties of a general character, international treaties for whose exercise a law is necessary and international treaties which directly confer rights or impose duties on natural persons or legal persons' must be approved by Slovakia's unicameral parliament, the National Council of the Slovak Republic (*Národná rada*).[286] The consent of an absolute majority of all Members of Parliament is required for this purpose.[287] The constitution also permits the delegation of part of its powers to the European Community and European Union by means of an international agreement or on the basis of an international agreement.[288] The consent of three-fifths of all Members of Parliament is required in this case, the same threshold that applies for approval of constitutional amendments or constitutional laws.[289] In seeking to amend treaties, the Slovak government has routinely relied on the second of these procedures,[290] with the result that a three-fifths majority can be considered the constitutional norm for EU treaty making in this member state. However, this majority is required only when there is delegation of powers to the EU. Where there is not such delegation, then an absolute majority of all Members of Parliament would be sufficient.

Slovenia

Under Slovenia's constitution it falls to the National Assembly (*Državni zbor*), the lower house of Slovenia's incompletely bicameral parliament, to approve treaties by a majority of the votes cast by deputies present. [291] Constitutional amendment is more difficult. The amending act must first be passed by a two-thirds majority of all deputies, after which at least thirty deputies can call a referendum (see Chapter 5).[292] In 2003, prior to joining the EU, Slovenia amended its constitution, removing the possibility of a referendum on EU treaties and introducing a two-thirds majority requirement for treaties involving the 'transfer of the exercise of part of its sovereign rights to international organisations which are based on respect for human rights and fundamental freedoms, democracy and the principles of the rule of law and may enter into a defensive alliance with states which are based on respect for these values'.[293] Based on the experience of the European Constitution and the Lisbon Treaty, the constitutional norm in Slovenia is that treaties are approved by a two-thirds majority rather than a simple majority vote, although a simple majority vote is a possibility for treaty amendments initiated under the Treaty on European Union's simplified revision procedure provided they do not constitute a transfer of sovereign rights.[294]

Spain

In Spain, it is the constitutional responsibility of the King 'to express the State's assent to international commitments through treaties, in conformity with the Constitution and the laws'.[295] Prior authorisation from parliament (*Cortes Generales*) is required, inter alia for treaties of a political, military or pecuniary nature and those that entail new legislative measures or the modification or repeal of existing laws.[296] Such authorisation is provided by means of a simple majority vote in both houses of parliament, the Congress of Deputies (*Congreso de los Diputados*) and the Senate (*Senado*).[297] A treaty containing 'stipulations contrary to the Constitution' cannot be ratified without a prior constitutional amendment.[298] Partial revisions to the constitution must be approved by a three-fifths majority in both the Congress of Deputies and the Senate.[299] If the proposed amendment is backed by an absolute majority in the Senate but by less than a three-fifths majority, then it can be approved by a two-thirds majority in the Congress of Deputies.[300]

A total revision to the constitution or a partial revision concerning certain elements of the constitution require a two-thirds majority in both houses either side of an intervening election.[301] In practice, Spain has tended not to revise its constitution in connection with major EU treaties. Maastricht was the sole exception here, this amendment being linked to the specific issue of whether foreign voters could participate in municipal elections.[302] As such, a simple majority vote in both chambers remains the constitutional norm in this state.

Sweden

Under the Instrument of Government (*Regeringsformen*), the most important of the country's four fundamental laws, the government must seek the approval of the state's unicameral parliament (*Riksdag*) on binding international agreements that impinge upon the responsibilities of the parliament or are otherwise of 'major significance'.[303] These requirements can be overridden 'if the interest of the Realm so requires' but only with the consent of the Advisory Council on Foreign Affairs, a body that consists of the speaker and nine other members of the Riksdag and which is chaired by the monarch or, in his or her absence, the Prime Minister.[304] Where parliamentary approval is required, the Instrument of Government allows for a simple majority vote unless the amended, abrogated, or new law is one for which a special procedure applies.[305]

A treaty that transfers powers must first be approved by parliament according to the procedures outlined above. The transfer must then be approved by at least three-quarters of Riksdag members, and they can also be approved via the procedure for the enactment of fundamental laws.[306] The enactment of a fundamental law requires approval by the Riksdag by simple majority twice, before and after a general election.[307] A gap of nine months between the submission of a proposal for the enactment of a fundamental law and this intervening election is required unless five-sixths of the Riksdag agree to an exception.[308] Alternatively, the Riksdag can enact a fundamental law by means of a single decision of three-quarters of voting deputies.[309] The constitutional norm in Sweden is that EU treaties are approved by means of a three-fourths majority rather than via a simple majority or by means of a constitutional amendment. Constitutional amendment was required in advance of Sweden's accession as previous provisions allowed for only a limited degree of delegation to international bodies.[310]

United Kingdom

In 1924, Arthur Ponsonby, Under Secretary of State for Foreign Affairs and a noted critic of secret treaties,[311] made an announcement to the

House of Commons during a debate over the Treaty of Lausanne. Henceforth, the government had decided 'Parliament would be allowed an adequate opportunity for the discussion of all treaties before their final ratification ... hitherto there [having] been no constitutional obligation on the government of the day to submit treaties before ratification'.[312] This move did not amount to the 'Americanisation of the British Constitution', as one critic of Ponsonby put it,[313] but it provided an informal check on the government's powers over treaty making under the royal prerogative. Under the Ponsonby rule, most treaties are laid before parliament for a period of twenty-one days, thus affording MPs the possibility of debating treaties. The rule has been codified in statute in 2010 and applies to most treaties.[314] EU treaties are excluded and subject to a separate legislative regime.[315] Treaties that give rise to legislation will require the approval of parliament by means of a simple majority vote in the House of Commons[316] and House of Lords.[317]

As of 2016, the constitutional norm in the United Kingdom was that EU treaties required an accompanying amendment to the European Communities Act (1972), which was enacted at the time of the United Kingdom's accession to the European Economic Community (EEC). The European Parliamentary Elections Act (1978) had to be amended too when an EU treaty transferred further powers to the European Parliament. Subsequent treaties and treaty amendments were added to the list of treaties in the European Communities Act 1972 via a short statute passed by parliament.[318] This constitutional norm became a legislative requirement in 2008.[319] Under this legislation, amendments under the Treaty on European Union's ordinary revision procedure required approval via act of parliament.[320] The European Union Act (2011) extended this requirement to EU treaty amendments made via the ordinary and simplified revision procedures.[321]

Conclusion

This chapter has charted the rise of member state parliaments in EU treaty making (see Figure 4.1). While recognising that there are different ways to classify the role of legislatures in this domain, our approach assumes that parliamentary involvement is enhanced as both the number of chambers involved and the majority required increases.

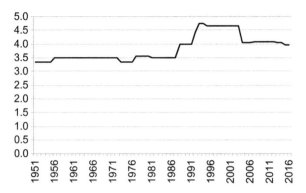

Figure 4.1 Parliaments scale (average, 1951–2016).

Classified in these terms, parliaments, though they were present at the creation of the European Coal and Steel Community, have assumed a more prominent role in EU treaty making over time. Taking the average for EU member states over the period shows that the ratification scale increased sharply in the late 1980s and early 1990s before falling back in the mid-2000s.

The overall trend masks significant changes over time and across member states. Ten parliamentary chambers gave their approval to the Treaty of Paris by means of a simple majority vote. By 2016, an EU treaty had to run the gauntlet before forty-four parliamentary chambers. A three-fifths or two-thirds majority was required in sixteen of these cases and a supermajority in one. Among EU member states, Cyprus, Estonia, Latvia, Lithuania, Malta and Portugal had the lowest parliamentary thresholds concerning EU treaty making. Belgium had the highest thanks to the involvement of its subnational parliaments. Viewed over time, two trends stand out. First, constitutional norms and rules shifted in four of the EU's six founding member states, with only Italy and Netherlands persisting with simple majority voting. Second, enlargement increased the involvement of parliaments in EU treaty making but not uniformly so. The 1981 and 1995 enlargements brought in member states in which a three-fifths majority or higher was the norm. Post-2005 enlargements saw the accession of member states in which a range of parliamentary thresholds applied.

Appendix 4.1 Parliaments Scales

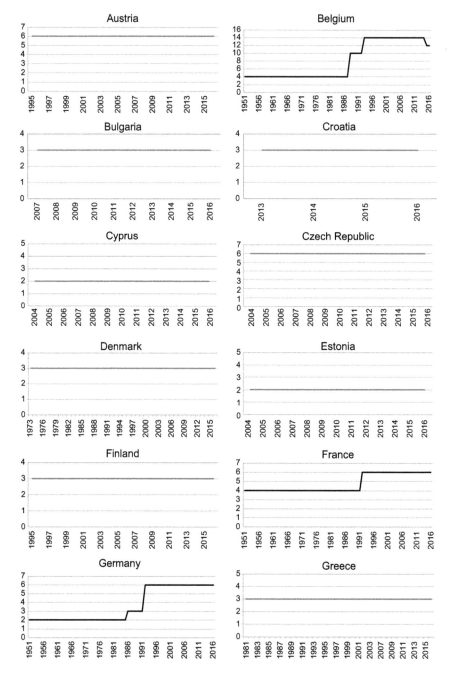

Figure 4.2 Parliaments scales (by member state, 1951–2016).

THE RISE OF PARLIAMENTS IN EU TREATY MAKING 121

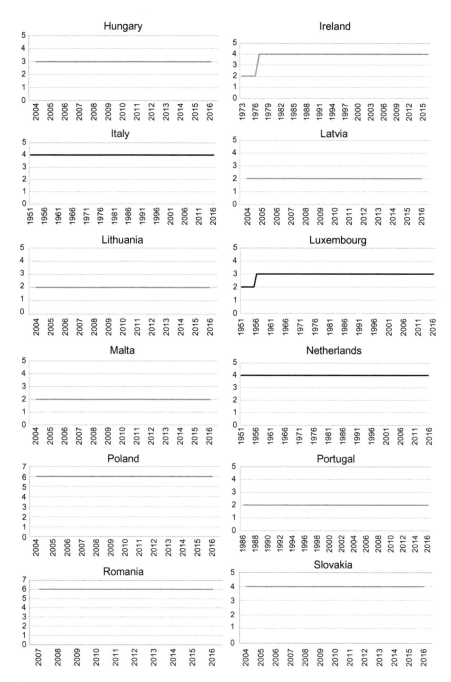

Figure 4.2 (cont.)

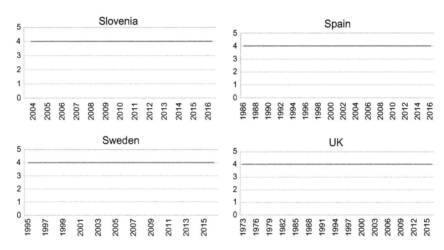

Figure 4.2 (*cont.*)

Notes

1 See Simmons (2009b).
2 Article 73(1b), Indian Constitution (1949, amended to 2012). Saxena (2007), p. 26.
3 Article 253, Indian Constitution (1949, amended to 2012). Ranjan (2009), p. 59.
4 See Jha (2006).
5 Bebr (1958), p. 775.
6 Norton (1996).
7 Hug and König (2002).
8 Closa (2013a).
9 Closa (2013a), pp. 44–6.
10 Simmons (2009a), p. 383. For online appendix, see https://scholar.harvard.edu/files/bsimmons/files/APP_3.2_Ratification_rules.pdf.
11 Simmons (2009b), pp. 68–9.
12 Lutz (1994), p. 360.
13 See, for example, Ferejohn (1997) and Lorenz (2005).
14 Ginsburg and Melton (2015), pp. 694–6.
15 Lijphart (2012), p. xvii.
16 Hug and König (2002), p. 454.
17 Articles 10, 65(1) and 67 Austria Constitution of 1920 (reinstated in 1945 and amended in 2013).
18 Article 66(2), Austria Constitution of 1920 (reinstated in 1945 and amended in 2013).
19 Article 16(1), Austria Constitution of 1920 (reinstated in 1945 and amended in 2013).

20 Article 10(3), Austria Constitution of 1920 (reinstated in 1945 and amended in 2013).

21 Article 50(1), Austria Constitution of 1920 (reinstated in 1945 and amended in 2013).

22 Article 31, Austria Constitution of 1920 (reinstated in 1945 and amended in 2013).

23 Cede and Hafner (1999), p. 6.

24 Cede and Hafner (1999), p. 6.

25 Article 50(2), Austria Constitution of 1920 (reinstated in 1945 and amended in 2013).

26 Article 42, Austria Constitution of 1920 (reinstated in 1945 and amended in 2013).

27 Section II, Federal Constitutional Act on the Accession of Austria to the European Union, StF: BGBl. I Nr. 744/1994.

28 Constitutional Court (Austria), BGBl. I Nr. 76/1998 and BGBl. I Nr. 120/2001. Blanck (2005), p. 22.

29 Constitutional Court (Austria), BGBl. Nr. 2/2008.

30 Article 50(4), Austria Constitution of 1920 (reinstated in 1945 and amended in 2013).

31 Article 9(2), Austria Constitution of 1920 (reinstated in 1945 and amended in 2013).

32 Articles 50(3) and 44, Austria Constitution of 1920 (reinstated in 1945 and amended in 1983).

33 Article 44, Austria Constitution of 1920 (reinstated in 1945 and amended in 2013).

34 Article 44, Austria Constitution of 1920 (reinstated in 1945 and amended in 2013).

35 Article 68, Constitution of Belgium (1831).

36 Article 167(2), Constitution of Belgium (1831, amended to 2014).

37 Article 53, Constitution of Belgium (1831, amended to 2014).

38 See Article 167(2), Constitution of Belgium (1831, amended to 1994).

39 Article 167(1), Constitution of Belgium (1831, amended to 2014).

40 Beyers and Bursens (2006), p. 1072.

41 Alen and Peeters (1998), pp. 123–4.

42 Article 16, Loi spéciale de réformes institutionnelles (1980, amended on 8 August 1988). See also Alen and Peeters (1998), p. 124.

43 Article 167, Constitution of Belgium (1831, amended in 1994). See also Closa (2013a), p. 62.

44 Co-operation agreement concluded on March 8th 1994 between the Federal State, the Communities and the Regions on the further rules for the conclusion of mixed treaties, Belgian Official Gazette, 17 December 1996).

45 Kovziridze (2008), p. 161.

46 De Becker (2011), p. 259.

47 Article 38, Rules of Procedure, Flemish Parliament; Article 68, Règlement du Parlement, le Parlement, le Gouvernement et le Ministère de la Fédération Wallonie-Bruxelles; Article 80, Règlement du Parlement Wallon; Article 50(7), Parlement De La Région De Bruxelles-Capitale Assemblée Réunie de la Commission Communautaire Commune: Règlement; Article 6, Internal Rules of Parliament of the German Speaking Community.

48 Article 195, Constitution of Belgium (1831, amended in 2012).

49 Article 195, Constitution of Belgium (1831, amended in 2012).

50 Claes (2005), p. 86.

51 Claes (2005), p. 97.

52 See Behrendt (2013).

53 Article 85(1–8), Constitution of the Republic of Bulgaria (1991, amended to 2005). This provision also concerns treaties that entail fundamental human rights, envisage corrections to the state's borders or the state's participation in international arbitration or legal proceedings and agreements that impose obligations for the treasury and those that affect the action of the law or require new law to be enforced.

54 Article 81(2), Constitution of the Republic of Bulgaria (1991, amended to 2005).

55 Article 85(9), Constitution of the Republic of Bulgaria (1991, amended to 2005).

56 Article 85(2), Constitution of the Republic of Bulgaria (1991, amended to 2005).

57 Article 85(4), Constitution of the Republic of Bulgaria (1991, amended to 2005).

58 Article 155, Constitution of the Republic of Bulgaria (1991, amended to 2005).

59 Article 161, Constitution of the Republic of Bulgaria (1991, amended to 2005).

60 Besselink et al. (2014), p. 203.

61 Vatsov (2015), p. 52.

62 Besselink et al. (2014), p. 203.

63 Article 139, Constitution of the Republic of Croatia (1991, rev. 2010).

64 Article 140, Constitution of the Republic of Croatia (1991, rev. 2010).

65 Article 140, Constitution of the Republic of Croatia (1991, rev. 2010).

66 Article 142, Constitution of the Republic of Croatia (1991, rev. 2010).

67 Article 139, Constitution of the Republic of Croatia (1991, rev. 2010).

68 Article 149, Constitution of the Republic of Croatia (1991, rev. 2010).

69 Article 87, Constitution of the Republic of Croatia (1991, rev. 2013). See Supreme Court of Croatia, Decisions 1/2013, para. 5; and U-VIIR-164/2014, para. 10; U-VIIR - 1159/2015, para. 33.4

70 Article 143, Constitution of the Republic of Croatia (1991, rev. 2010).

71 Article 143, Constitution of the Republic of Croatia (1991, rev. 2010), although it does refer back to Article 140.

72 Article 140, Constitution of the Republic of Croatia (1991, rev. 2010).

73 Article 169(1), Constitution of the Republic of Cyprus (1960, rev. 2013).

74 Article 169(1), Constitution of the Republic of Cyprus (1960, rev. 2013).

75 Article 78, Constitution of the Republic of Cyprus (1960, rev. 2013).

76 Note that since the division of Cyprus in 1974 there is no Vice-President, that post having been held by a Turkish Cypriot.
77 Article 50(1), Constitution of the Republic of Cyprus (1960, rev. 2013).
78 Article 50 (1) (a) (i)–(ii), Constitution of the Republic of Cyprus (1960, rev. 2013).
79 Article 179(2), Constitution of the Republic of Cyprus (1960, rev. 2013).
80 Article 179(2), Constitution of the Republic of Cyprus (1960, rev. 2013).
81 Article 1 (a), Constitution of the Republic of Cyprus (1960, rev. 2013).
82 Emilianides (2014), p. 236.
83 Article 182(2), Constitution of the Republic of Cyprus (1960, rev. 2013).
84 Supreme Court (Cyprus), *Attorney General* v. *Ibrahim* [1964] CLR 195; Skoutaris (2011), p. 24.
85 Mendez, Mendez and Triga (2014), pp. 227–8.
86 Hoffmeister (2007), p. 68.
87 Article 63, Constitution of the Czech Republic (1993, amended to 2013).
88 Article 49, Constitution of the Czech Republic (1993, amended to 2013).
89 Article 39(2), Constitution of the Czech Republic (1993, amended to 2013).
90 Article 39(3), Constitution of the Czech Republic (1993, amended to 2013).
91 Article 10a, Constitution of the Czech Republic (1993, amended to 2013).
92 Article 39(4), Constitution of the Czech Republic (1993, amended to 2013).
93 Article 39(4), Constitution of the Czech Republic (1993, amended to 2013).
94 Dumbrovsky (2014).
95 Marek and Baun (2010), p. 49.
96 In particular, decree nos. 5/1945 and 12/1945 adopted between April and October 1945. Marek and Baun (2010), p. 50.
97 European Council (2009).
98 Reuters (2012).
99 Article 65(2), Constitution of the Czech Republic (1993, amended to 2013).
100 Section 19, The Constitutional Act of Denmark (1953).
101 Section 20, The Constitutional Act of Denmark (1953).
102 Section 88, The Constitutional Act of Denmark (1953).
103 Section 20, The Constitutional Act of Denmark (1953).
104 Knudsen and Jakobsen (2003), p. 9.
105 Laursen (2006), p. 74.
106 As such, we average the score for simple and supermajority when constructing the parliaments scale for Denmark.
107 §65, Constitution of the Estonian Republic (1992, amended to 2015).
108 §121, Constitution of the Estonian Republic (1992, amended to 2015).
109 §115, Riigikogu Rules of Procedure and Internal Rules Act (2007).
110 §78, Riigikogu Rules of Procedure and Internal Rules Act (2007).
111 §126, Riigikogu Rules of Procedure and Internal Rules Act (2007).
112 Mendez, Mendez and Triga (2014), p. 56.

126   THE TRANSFORMATION OF EU TREATY MAKING

113 Section 33, Constitution of Finland Constitution of Finland (1919, amended to 1995).
114 Section 94, para. 2, Constitution of Finland (1999, amended to 2011). Constitution of Finland Act 1112/2011.
115 Section 94, Constitution of Finland Constitution of Finland (1999, amended to 2011).
116 Article 95 Constitution of Finland, 1112/2011, entry into force 1 March 2012.
117 Section 73, Constitution of Finland (1999, amended to 2011).
118 Section 96, para. 2, Constitution of Finland (1999, amended to 2011).
119 Besselink et al (2014), p. 84.
120 Ojanen (2004), p. 211.
121 Section 94, Constitution of Finland (1999, amended to 2011).
122 Section 58, Act on the Autonomy of Åland (1991/1144).
123 Section 58, Act on the Autonomy of Åland (1991/1144).
124 Ruokola (2007).
125 Hepburn (2014), p. 583.
126 Finland Constitutional Law Committee PeVL 13/2008. See Alilonttinen and Ruà (2008), p. 2.
127 See Kerrouche (2006), p. 79.
128 Article 27, Constitution of the 4th Republic (1946).
129 Article 20, Constitution of the 4th Republic (1946).
130 Article 90, Constitution of the 4th Republic (1946).
131 Auel (2013), p. 7.
132 Article 53, Constitution of 4 October 1958 (amended to 2008).
133 Rule 68, Rules of procedure of the National Assembly (January 2007)
134 Article 88(7), Constitution of 4 October 1958 (amended in 2008).
135 Article 54, Constitution of 4 October 1958 (amended to 2008).
136 Article 54, Constitution of 4 October 1958 (as amended in 1992).
137 Article 89, Constitution of 4 October 1958 (amended to 2008).
138 Article 89, Constitution of 4 October 1958 (amended to 2008).
139 Luchaire (1991), p. 341.
140 Bebr (1958), p. 778.
141 Neuman (2012), p. 291.
142 Neuman (2012), p. 317.
143 Closa (2013a), p. 102. The Nice Treaty was an exception in this regard.
144 French Constitutional Court, Decision 92-308 DC, Treaty on European Union; Decision 97-394 DC, Treaty of Amsterdam amending the Treaty on European Union, the Treaties establishing the European Communities and certain related instruments, Decision 2007–560 DC, Treaty of Lisbon amending the Treaty on European Union and the Treaty establishing the European Community.
145 Article 24, Basic Law of the Federal Republic of Germany (1949).
146 Preamble, Basic Law of the Federal Republic of Germany (1949).

147 Article 59, Basic Law of the Federal Republic of Germany (1949).

148 Article 52(3), Basic Law of the Federal Republic of Germany (1949).

149 Article 32(2), Basic Law of the Federal Republic of Germany (1949).

150 Article 42(1) Basic Law of the Federal Republic of Germany (1949.

151 Article 79(2), Basic Law of the Federal Republic of Germany (1949).

152 Closa (2013a), p. 45.

153 Gunlicks (2003), p. 363.

154 Saalfeld (1995), p. 27.

155 Gunlicks (2003), p. 364.

156 Thirty-Eighth Amendment of the Basic Law, 21 December 1992 (BGBl I, S. 2086).

157 Article 23(1), Basic Law of the Federal Republic of Germany (1949, amended to 2014).

158 Article 23(1), Basic Law of the Federal Republic of Germany (1949, amended to 2014).

159 Article 79(2), Basic Law of the Federal Republic of Germany (1949, amended to 2014).

160 See Closa (2013a), pp. 50 and 59.

161 'Approval by the Federal Republic of Germany of a decision of the European Union within the meaning of Article 48(6), second and third subparagraphs, of the Treaty on European Union shall take the form of a law as defined in Article 23(1) of the Basic Law' (Section 2, The Act on the Exercise by the Bundestag and by the Bundesrat of their Responsibility for Integration in Matters concerning the European Union (Responsibility for Integration Act) from the Federal Republic of Germany of 22 September 2009 (Federal Law Gazette I, p. 3022), last amended by Article 1 of the Act of 1 December 2009 (Federal Law Gazette I, p. 3822).

162 Article 36(1), Constitution of Greece (1975, amended to 2008).

163 Article 36(1), Constitution of Greece (1975, amended to 2008).

164 Article 28(3), Constitution of Greece (1975, amended to 2008).

165 Article 28(2), Constitution of Greece (1975, amended to 2008).

166 Article 110(2), Constitution of Greece (1975, amended to 2008).

167 Article 110(3), Constitution of Greece (1975, amended to 2008).

168 Article 110(4), Constitution of Greece (1975, amended to 2008).

169 104(6), Constitution of Greece (1975, amended to 2008).

170 Claes (2006), p. 92.

171 Spyropoulos and Fortsakis (2009), p. 79.

172 Spyropoulos and Fortsakis (2009), p. 80.

173 Article 1(2) (d), Fundamental Law of Hungary (2011, amended to 2013).

174 Article 5(6), Fundamental Law of Hungary (2011, amended to 2013).

175 Article E(4), Fundamental Law of Hungary (2011, amended to 2013).

176 Hungary: Act of Promulgation of the Lisbon Treaty (Act CLXVIII of 2007).

177 Article S(2), Fundamental Law of Hungary (2011, amended to 2013).

178 Ex-Section 57(4) Fundamental Law of Hungary.
179 Hungary: Act of Promulgation of the Lisbon Treaty (Act CLXVIII of 2007). Priebus (2016), p. 112.
180 Hungary: Act CVII of 2005.
181 Article 29, 5, 1°, Constitution of Ireland (1937, amended to 2018).
182 See discussion of the United Kingdom below.
183 Harrington (2006), p. 142.
184 Article 29, 5, 2°, Constitution of Ireland (1937, amended to 2018).
185 Article 29, 5, 3°, Constitution of Ireland (1937, amended to 2018).
186 Article 11, 1°, Constitution of Ireland (1937, amended to 2018).
187 European Communities (Amendment) Bill, 1977: Second Stage, Wednesday, 23 March 1977, Seanad Éireann Debate, Vol. 86, No. 6.
188 Article 11, 1°, Constitution of Ireland (1937, amended to 2015).
189 Article 15, 4, 1°, Constitution of Ireland (1937, amended to 2015).
190 Supreme Court of Ireland, *Crotty* v. *An Taoiseach* [1987] IR 713 (April 1987).
191 Article 46(2), Constitution of Ireland (1937, amended to 2015).
192 Article 11, Constitution of the Italian Republic.
193 Fontanelli and Martinico (2008), p. 3.
194 Article 80, Constitution of the Italian Republic (1947, amended to 2012).
195 Article 64, Constitution of the Italian Republic (1947, amended to 2012).
196 Constitutional Court of the Italian Republic, judgment No. 183/1973.
197 Fontanelli and Martinico (2008), p. 3.
198 Article 68, Constitution of Latvia of 1922 (reinstated 1991, amended to 2014). See Besselink et al. (2014), p. 232.
199 Article 114(2) (3), Rules of Procedure of the Saeima (1994).
200 Article 68, Constitution of Latvia of 1922 (reinstated 1991, amended to 2014).
201 Article 68, Constitution of Latvia of 1922 (reinstated 1991, amended to 2014).
202 Article 76, the Constitution of Latvia of 1922 (reinstated 1991, amended to 2014).
203 Article 76, the Constitution of Latvia of 1922 (reinstated 1991, amended to 2014).
204 On the Article 136 TFEU amendment, see Rasnača (2013), p. 31. On the European Constitution, see Daimer (2006), p. 149.
205 Article 67, Constitution of the Republic of Lithuania (1992, amended to 2006).
206 Article 138(5), Constitution of the Republic of Lithuania (1992, amended to 2006).
207 Article 69, Constitution of the Republic of Lithuania (1992, amended to 2006). An exception here is international treaties that alter state boundaries, which would require four-fifths backing among all members of the Seimas.
208 Article 138, Constitution of the Republic of Lithuania (1992, amended to 2006).
209 Article 136, Constitution of the Republic of Lithuania (1992, amended to 2006).

210 Article 148, Constitution of the Republic of Lithuania (1992, amended to 2006).

211 Article 148, Constitution of the Republic of Lithuania (1992, amended to 2006).

212 Lithuania had undertaken constitutional amendments in 1996 in preparation for accession negotiations (Van Elsuwege 2008 169).

213 The Constitutional Act 'On Membership of the Republic of Lithuania in the European Union' of 13 July 2004. Hoffmeister (2007), p. 69. Constitutional Court of Lithuania Ruling, 14 March 2006, cited in Martinico and Pollicino (2012), p. 60.

214 Article 150 Constitution of the Republic of Lithuania (1992, amended to 2006).

215 Article 47 and the Constitutional Act (re ownership of land in Lithuania) and Article 119 (participation in municipal elections of non-nationals) were amended.

216 Article 125(1) Constitution of Lithuania, Case 22/2013, 24 January 2014.

217 Article 37, Constitution of Luxembourg (1868).

218 Article 62, Constitution of Luxembourg (1868).

219 Gerkrath (2016).

220 Gerkrath (2016).

221 Acte modificatif, Révision de la Constitution-art 49 bis, 3 November 1956. Article 49bis, the Constitution of Luxembourg (1868, as amended to 2009).

222 Article 37, the Constitution of Luxembourg (1868, as amended to 2009).

223 Loi du 19 décembre 2003 portant révision de l'article 114 de la Constitution.

224 Article 114, the Constitution of Luxembourg (1868, as amended to 2009).

225 Loi du 19 décembre 2003 portant révision de l'article 114 de la Constitution.

226 Loi du 23 décembre 1994 portant révision de l'article 9 de la Constitution.

227 Gerkrath (2016), p. 4.

228 Andò, Aquilina, Scerri-Diacono and Zammit (2012), p. 528.

229 Article 3(1)–(2b), Ratification of Treaties Act (1983).

230 Article 3(2a), Ratification of Treaties Act (1983).

231 European Union Act (Act V of 2003) (Cap. 460).

232 Article 2(2), European Union Act (Act V of 2003) (Cap. 460).

233 Article 2(2), European Union Act (Act V of 2003) (Cap. 460).

234 Article 21, Standing Orders of the House of Representatives (2015).

235 Article 66, Constitution of Malta (1964, amended to 2014).

236 Trigona (2012).

237 Trigona (2012).

238 Article 67(2), Constitution of the Netherlands (1815, amended to 2008).

239 Besselink (2014), p. 1197.

240 Royal Decree, 6 March 1950 (No. 53).

241 Article 60, Constitution of the Netherlands (1815, amended in 1953).

242 Article 91 (1), Constitution of the Netherlands (1815, amended in 1953). Van Dijk and Tahzib (1991), p. 426.

243 Article 137, Constitution of the Kingdom of the Netherlands (1815, amended to 2008).

244 Article 91(3), Constitution of the Kingdom of the Netherlands (1815, amended to 2008).

245 Constitutional amendments, when they do come, tend to follow treaties, as in the amendment of 1953 (Bebr, 1958: 776).

246 Bebr (1958), p. 776.

247 van Dijk and Tahzib (1991), pp. 424–5.

248 Nijeboer (2005), p. 397.

249 Article 89(1), Constitution of the Republic of Poland (1997, amended to 2009).

250 Article 89(1), Constitution of the Republic of Poland (1997, amended to 2009).

251 Articles 120 and 124, Constitution of the Republic of Poland (1997, amended to 2009).

252 Article 90(2) Constitution of the Republic of Poland (1997, amended to 2009).

253 Article 90 (3), Constitution of the Republic of Poland (1997, amended to 2009).

254 Article 90 (4), Constitution of the Republic of Poland (1997, amended to 2009).

255 Article 90(3), Constitution of the Republic of Poland (1997, amended to 2009).

256 Article 90(2), Constitution of the Republic of Poland (1997, amended to 2009).

257 Article 89(1), Constitution of the Republic of Poland (1997, amended to 2009).

258 See also Granat (2014 and 2015).

259 Zwolski (2009), p. 490.

260 Zwolski (2009), p. 492.

261 Zwolski (2009), p.493

262 Article 135b, Constitution of Portugal (2005, 7th Revision).

263 Article 161i, Constitution of Portugal (2005, 7th Revision).

264 Article 166(5), Constitution of Portugal (2005, 7th Revision).

265 Article 116, Constitution of Portugal (2005, 7th Revision).

266 Article 279, Constitution of Portugal (2005, 7th Revision). This is an exclusive right in relation to international treaties. The President shares the powers with other political actors in relation to constitutional review of legislation.

267 Gurrea Martens (2005), p. 256.

268 Article 279(4), Constitution of Portugal (2005, 7th Revision).

269 Provision is made for a referendum on the EU in Article 295, which needs to be read in conjunction with Article 115 (see Chapter 5).

270 Gouveia (2011), p. 22.

271 Article 7(5), Constitution of the Republic of Portugal (1976).

272 Article 7(6), Constitution of the Republic of Portugal (1992, 3rd revision).

273 Articles 7 and 8, Constitution of the Republic of Portugal (2004, 6th revision).

274 Article 91(1), Constitution of Romania (1991, amended to 2003).

275 Article 75(1), Constitution of Romania (1991, amended to 2003).

276 Article 75(3), Constitution of Romania (1991, amended to 2003).
277 Article 76(2), Constitution of Romania (1991, amended to 2003).
278 Article 11(3) and Article 147(3), Constitution of Romania (1991, amended to 2003).
279 Article 151(1), Constitution of Romania (1991, amended to 2003).
280 Article 151(2), Constitution of Romania (1991, amended to 2003).
281 Article 151(3), Constitution of Romania (1991, amended to 2003).
282 Article 148(1), Constitution of Romania (1991, amended to 2003).
283 Article 148(3), Constitution of Romania (1991, amended to 2003).
284 Hageman (2007), p. 5.
285 Vitâ (2014), p. 37.
286 Article 7(4), Constitution of the Slovak Republic (1992, amended to 2017).
287 Article 84(3), Constitution of the Slovak Republic (1992, amended to 2017).
288 Article 7(2), Constitution of the Slovak Republic (1992, amended to 2017).
289 Article 84(4), Constitution of the Slovak Republic (1992, amended to 2017).
290 See O'Neill (2008), p. 367, and Mendez, Mendez and Triga (2014), p. 42.
291 Article 86, Constitution of the Republic of Slovenia (1991, amended 2016).
292 Article 169, Constitution of the Republic of Slovenia (1991, as amended 2016).
293 Article 3a, Constitution of the Republic of Slovenia (1991, amended to 2016).
294 Petrovcic (2015: 23) suggests that the procedure employed by Slovenia to ratify the Article 136(TFEU) was uncertain. Mendez, Mendez and Triga (2014: 55) suggest that a simple majority vote applied in this case. The Slovenian Ministry for Foreign Affairs (2016) has now published a manual on the conclusion of international treaties.
295 Article 63(2), Spanish Constitution of 1978 (as amended up to 2011).
296 Article 94(1), Spanish Constitution of 1978 (as amended up to 2011).
297 Section 79, Standing Order of the Congress of Deputies and Section 93, Standing Orders of the Senate (2017).
298 Article 95(1), Spanish Constitution of 1978 (as amended up to 2011).
299 Article 167(1), Spanish Constitution of 1978 (as amended up to 2011).
300 Article 167(2), Spanish Constitution of 1978 (as amended up to 2011).
301 Article 168, Spanish Constitution of 1978 (as amended up to 2011).
302 See Kumm and Comella (2005), p. 475.
303 Chapter 4, Article 5 and Chapter 10, Article 2, Instrument of Government (1974, amended to 2015).
304 Chapter 10, Article 2, Instrument of Government (1974, amended to 2015).
305 Chapter 10, Article 2, Instrument of Government (1974, amended to 2015).
306 Chapter 10, Article 5, Instrument of Government (1974, amended to 2015).
307 Chapter 8, Article 15.
308 Chapter 8, Article 15.
309 Chapter 8, Article 16.
310 See Claes (2005), pp. 105–6.
311 See Ponsonby (1928) for the MP's views on secret treaties.

312 Quoted in Scott (1924), p. 296.

313 Quoted in Scott (1924), p. 296.

314 Constitutional Reform and Governance Act 2010, Part II.

315 Constitutional Reform and Governance Act 2010, Section 23.

316 Section 37, Standing Orders of the House of Commons – Public Business (2005).

317 Section 56, The Standing Orders of the House of Lords Relating to Public Business (2016).

318 UK Supreme Court, R (Miller) v. Secretary of State for Exiting the EU [2017] UKSC 5 para. 24.

319 European Union (Amendment) Act 2008.

320 Section 5, EU (Amendment) Act 2008.

321 Sections 2 and 3, European Union Act (2011).

5 The Rise of Referendums in EU Treaty Making

Referendums – which Laurence Morel defines as 'a device of direct democracy in which the people are asked to vote directly on an issue or policy' – are possible in most political systems.[1] The International Institute for Democracy and Electoral Assistance lists more than 110 countries as having a legally codified instrument for optional referendums.[2] Referendums are also increasingly common.[3] Altman et al. list 1,149 referendums worldwide between 1795 and 2014, with the most prominent in the small island states of Oceania.[4] Referendums can address a variety of subjects, from constitutional questions over state foundation, constitutional amendment[5] and the devolution of power to more specific policy questions of substantive, moral and symbolic importance.[6] In 2005, Brazil held a referendum on laws governing the sale of firearms and ammunition. In 2015 and 2016, New Zealand held a pair of referendums on whether to choose a new national flag.

The bulk of referendums held worldwide to date concerns questions about national identity and the political system rather than international affairs.[7] Switzerland stands out as a champion of direct democracy in relation to foreign policy, as in other domains. In 1894, it held a referendum on the running costs of the Swiss Embassy in Washington, and since then has held thirty-seven referendums on foreign policy matters.[8] Outside Europe, Bolivia, Brazil, Chad, Costa Rica, Egypt, Gabon, Madagascar, Mauritania, Palau, Panama, Paraguay, the Philippines and Taiwan are among those states to have held referendums on such matters.[9] Palau is the only one of these states in which treaty-related referendums are, in any sense, recurring. It is also a *sui generis* case. The western Pacific state held eight referendums on its relationship with the United States between 1983 and 1994 until the required threshold for approval was finally reached.[10]

None of these cases matches the EU's commitment to direct democracy. Referendums by current or prospective EU member states on EU treaties account for more than a third of foreign policy referendums held worldwide since 1972.[11] How have the people come to play this prominent role in EU treaty making? This chapter offers an in-depth account of the changing constitutional rules and norms underpinning referendums on EU treaty changes during the period 1951–2016. Based on a detailed analysis of national constitutions and changing constitutional traditions in the EU-28, it categorises rules and norms into how likely they make a referendum on EU treaty changes. This exercise picks up on changes within and between EU member states to produce the second of our ratification scales.

Classifying Referendums

Influenced by the initial wave of public votes on EU treaties in the 1970s, Gordon Smith developed an early taxonomy of European referendums.[12] His functional approach distinguishes between pro-hegemonic and anti-hegemonic referendums – the former reinforcing the prevailing political structure and the latter running contrary to it – and controlled or uncontrolled referendums – the former being chosen by governments and the latter being foisted on them. The United Kingdom's 1975 referendum on whether to remain in the Common Market counted as an uncontrolled pro-hegemonic referendum, Smith argued, because Prime Minister Harold Wilson was sympathetic to membership but ultimately pushed into the vote by internal divisions in the Labour Party.[13] Ireland's 1972 referendum on whether to join the European Communities he sees as being controlled and hegemonic because it is something that the state's two major parties, Fianna Fáil and Fine Gael, sought and secured by an overwhelming margin. Smith's functional taxonomy of referendums remains influential but is more concerned with political constraints than constitutional ones. How much control Irish elites had under the Irish constitution to call the 1972 referendum, for instance, is a moot point that Smith himself acknowledges.[14]

Hug offers a systematic cross-country analysis of EU referendums based on a four-fold classification.[15] He distinguishes between required referendums and three non-required alternatives: active referendums on government proposals, active referendums on opposition proposals and passive referendums that allow the government to submit proposals for popular approval. Here, 'active' means the triggering of a referendum by a non-governmental group, while 'passive' covers cases in which the government chooses to have a referendum. Insightful though this taxonomy is, it runs into problems for our purposes. For example, Ireland, Denmark and Finland are all classified by Hug as having held differing categories of referendum, and yet votes in all three countries are counted as having been significant. The distinction between active and passive referendums is also questionable since both are underpinned by constitutional rules and norms, the creation of which involved a central role for government, albeit not necessarily the current government. Hug[16] also discusses the taxonomy offered by Mueller, which distinguishes between (1) the constitutionally mandated referendum, (2) the government-initiated referendum, (3) the citizen-initiated veto and (4) the citizen initiative where Mueller suggests that constitutionally mandated referendums with supra-majority requirements do lend legitimacy to representative democracy – in both two-party and multiparty systems.[17] Gallagher and Uleri also suggest that the most important distinguishing criterion for a referendum is who initiates it, with wide variation found in Europe.[18]

Closa looks much more closely at constitutional context, distinguishing between constitutionally mandated and path-dependent referendums and those motivated by strategic calculation and ideas.[19] Examples of mandated referendums include Denmark and Ireland's referendums on the Single European Act, while the path-dependent ones include public votes held by Spain, Luxembourg and the Netherlands on the European Constitution. This taxonomy is more attuned to member state governments' manifold motivations for calling referendums. Closa has much to say about the importance of constitutional rules and norms for EU treaty making,[20] and his analysis invites a more systematic comparison across member states and over time.

Mendez, Mendez and Triga offer an alternative taxonomy that distinguishes between cases in which referendums are constitutionally provided for and where they are not so provided.[21] Constitutionally regulated referendums are subdivided, in turn, into cases where referendums are (1) non-mandatory or mandatory and (2) only non-mandatory. A puzzle that flows from this taxonomy is how two states that the authors classify as lacking constitutional regulation for referendums held referendums in the period explored under this book. The first was Cyprus, which held a vote in 2004 to reunite the country in a way that would then have allowed all of Cyprus to join the EU.[22] The second was the Netherlands, which held

Table 5.1 Referendums scale

Referendums prohibited	1
Referendums improbable	2
Referendums possible	3
Referendums probable	4

a referendum on the European Constitution in 2005. Although these votes were unusual, they were not widely considered to be unconstitutional and can be seen either as an exception to constitutional life[23] or as potentially creating new constitutional norms.[24]

The focus of our study is not on why referendums on EU treaties are called but on the evolution of the constitutional rules and norms that determine whether they can be called. This distinction is important because the possibility of a referendum can impose constraints on policy-making even if a public vote does not take place.[25] Such constraints are especially salient in a European context, where the 'fear of popular referendums' has come, in part, to define elite approaches to European integration.[26] Our approach, as in the previous chapter, chimes with Lutz's index of the stringency of constitutional amendment procedures, which includes 'referendum threat' for countries in which constitutional referendums are relatively rare,[27] and with Simmons, who asks whether referendums are possible when governments seek approval for international agreements.[28]

Our referendum scale focuses on the likelihood of referendums under prevailing constitutional rules and norms (Table 5.1). We assign a score of 1 for cases in which referendums on EU treaties are prohibited under prevailing constitutional rules and norms, 2 where referendums are improbable, 3 where a referendum is possible and 4 when such a vote is probable. A referendum is prohibited in cases where constitutional rules and norms expressly forbid a public vote on an EU treaty. A referendum is improbable if constitutional rules and norms allow for such a vote but create little expectation that this will happen. A referendum is possible in cases where constitutional rules and norms make a referendum a distinct possibility but by no means a necessity. A referendum is probable in cases where a referendum is routinely expected to take place under constitutional rules and norms governing the consent stage of EU treaty making.

This approach, it should be added, does not distinguish between mandatory and facultative referendums.[29] In so doing, we follow Smith, who writes that a '"mandatory" referendum may give a government considerable leeway in interpretation if the terms of the proposal are suitably vague, whilst a consultative vote which results in a massive majority one way or the other will effectively tie the hands of any regime'.[30] Smith's remarks – written in the mid-1970s – were prescient. Ireland's referendums on the Nice and Lisbon treaties are treated as mandatory, but this did not preclude the holding of second referendums in both cases after initial 'no' votes, just as the Netherlands' consultative referendum on the European Constitution played a part in the EU's eventual decision to abandon this treaty (see Chapter 8).

Changing Rules and Norms in the EU-28

In this section, we compare the evolution of referendum-related constitutional rules and norms in EU member states on the basis of the criteria set out in the previous section. Appendix 5.1 graphs these scores over our sample period, which runs from the year the member state joined the EU (or the European Communities) to 2016.

Austria

Austria's constitution makes treaty-related referendums possible in two ways: binding and non-binding. First, there are two kinds of binding referendum. Such a referendum must be called for the total revision of the constitution. Austria's referendum in 1994 on joining the EU was held on the grounds that membership constituted a total revision to the constitution. Partial revision of the constitution or the submission of any law by the Nationalrat can be submitted to a binding referendum before it is signed by the Federal President.[31] This provision has been invoked on one occasion only, the law in question concerning the opening of a nuclear power plant.[32] Second, the Nationalrat, by its own initiative or at the request of the federal government, can call a non-binding consultation of the people on matters for which the legislature is competent.[33] This provision was used to trigger Austria's 2013 non-binding referendum on conscription.[34] The second form of non-binding referendum is the 'popular initiative' that allows 100,000 voters or one-sixth of the voters in each of three Länder to put forward a motion for discussion in the Nationalrat on matters 'to be settled by Federal law'.[35] The scope of these provisions is a matter of debate, but they have typically been employed with success in relation to domestic rather than international issues. An exception occurred in 2015, when more than 260,000 citizens signed a petition calling for Austria's exit from the EU.[36] Grassroots groups also campaigned for a public vote on the European Constitution, but the main political parties agreed that the treaty should be approved via parliamentary channels alone.[37]

Hence there has been no referendum on EU treaties since accession. Nonetheless, a referendum on EU treaties remains a possibility but is not inevitable. This constitutional norm can be seen, for instance, in the 2008 coalition agreement between the Austrian People's Party (ÖVP) and the Social Democratic Party of Austria (SPÖ), which refused to rule out the possibility of a referendum on future EU treaties and, indeed, agreed that such a vote could be held on the understanding that it would result in the dissolution of the government.

Belgium

Treaty-related referendums are not prohibited in Belgium but are improbable. All powers emanate from 'the Nation' under the Belgian constitution, a provision that is commonly interpreted as being incompatible with the holding of a referendum on any issue.[38] And yet a referendum was held in 1950 on whether King Leopold III should resume his constitutional powers following the Second World War. The constitutionality of this vote was questionable, and the deep divisions it exposed between voters in Flanders and Wallonia reinforced the norm against calling national referendums.[39] For Qvortrup, Belgium seems to be an exceptional case among European countries in not moving towards a greater use of referendums on EU treaties.[40] And yet there has been a debate within Belgium on putting EU treaties to a public vote. In 2004, Belgium Prime Minister Guy Verhofstadt announced that the country would hold a consultative referendum on the European Constitution, but his party's junior coalition partner, the Sociaal-Liberale Partij, subsequently opposed this idea, and plans for the referendum were shelved. Moves by members of the *Groen* and *Ecolo* parties for a referendum on the European Stability Mechanism Treaty fell similarly flat.[41]

Bulgaria

Referendums are rare in Bulgaria, and a referendum related to an EU treaty amendment was improbable until the adoption of the Direct Citizen Participation in State and Local Government Act in 2009.[42] Amendments to Bulgaria's constitution are a matter for the National Assembly or the Grand National Assembly (see Chapter 4).[43] For this reason, Bulgaria amended its constitution in advance of joining the EU without recourse to a referendum.[44] The National Assembly has the authority to pass a resolution on the holding of a national referendum, but it has not used such powers in relations to EU treaty amendments.[45] The Direct Citizen Participation in State and Local Government Act opened the door to a referendum on EU treaties by allowing for the possibility of a referendum on international agreements.[46] Such a vote can be requested by one-fifth of members of the parliament, the President, the Council of Ministers, one-fifth of municipal councils and a petition signed by at least 200,000 citizens who are eligible to vote.[47]

Croatia

Under Croatia's constitution, a referendum is required before the state can be associated with an alliance of states.[48] Prior to an amendment in 2010, the referendum would be passed only if 50 per cent of the entire electorate approved it. This high threshold was reduced in 2010 to 50 per cent of those voting in the referendum to make it easier to pass. It was on this basis that Croatia held a referendum in 2012 on whether to join the EU. There are other possible routes to a treaty-related referendum. The Sabor, Croatia's parliament, can call a binding referendum concerning constitutional amendments or any other issues within its sphere of competence on its own initiative or at the request of 10 per cent of all voters.[49] The President of the Republic can, on a proposal from the government and with the countersignature of the Prime Minister, call a binding referendum on a proposal for the amendment of the constitution or any other issue he or she 'considers to be important for the independence, unity and existence of the Republic of Croatia'.[50] The constitution also allows for a law on referendums, which can also provide for the possibility of consultative referendums; however, that law had not yet been adopted.[51] A referendum on EU treaties is thus possible in Croatia.

Cyprus

In 1950, Makarios II, Archbishop of Cyprus, organised an unofficial referendum on enosis with Greece against the will of the British administration in which more than 95 per cent of voters supported a union with Greece. The 1960 Constitution of the Republic of Cyprus, which affirmed the state's independence, did not provide for referendums and nor have subsequent constitutional amendments. In 1989, the House of Representatives passed a law that permits the parliament to call such a referendum on any important matter of public interest if requested to do so by the Council of Ministers.[52] Of the ten member states that joined the EU in 2004, Cyprus was the only one not to hold a referendum, although a referendum was held on the related issue of the United Nations' Annan Plan, this vote being enabled by a special law adopted by the House of Representatives.[53] In 2008, leaders of the Greek and Turkish communities agreed that any future agreement concerning reunification would be put to simultaneous referendums. This makes a referendum all but inevitable on any future peace treaty. A referendum concerning an EU treaty remains improbable, however.

Czech Republic

In the Czech Republic, treaties that entail the transfer of certain sovereign powers to an international organisation require the consent of parliament (see Chapter 4) unless a constitutional act requires approval by means of a referendum.[54] This creates the possibility of a referendum without setting out the circumstances in which a referendum might be required. A Constitutional Act was adopted in 2002 stating that the decision on the Czech Republic's accession to the EU was to be made solely on the basis of a referendum.[55] In 2002, the government put forward a similar bill to enable a referendum on the European Constitution, but it abandoned this plan following 'no' votes against this treaty in France and the Netherlands.[56] No government has since sought to hold a referendum in connection with an EU treaty, but the constitutional possibility of doing so remains nonetheless.

Denmark

No other EU member state has run more European-related referendums than Denmark, which has held eight public votes since joining the European Communities, covering accession (1972), the Single European

Act (1986), Maastricht (1992 and 1993), Amsterdam (1998), joining the eurozone (2000) and opt-outs in the field of justice and home affairs (2015). Greenland also held a referendum to leave the EU in 1982, following adoption of home rule from Denmark in 1979.[57] A referendum on EU treaties can arise under two different provisions of the 1953 constitution – both of which long predate membership of the EU. Section 20 allows powers to be delegated to international authorities by means of a statute supported by five-sixths of the members of the Folketing.[58] Where the statute wins majority backing but falls short of the five-sixths majority, the government can, if it so choses, hold a referendum. Thus, the calling of a referendum under this provision depends on (1) whether the treaty entails a transfer of sovereignty and (2) whether the government chooses to press ahead with ratification after failing to win sufficient backing from the Folketing. In practice, the government often bypasses the Folketing given the sizable majority required and instead opts to go straight to a referendum.

A referendum can also be requested of the President by one-third of the members of the Folketing on any bill within three weekdays of it receiving parliamentary approval.[59] The bill may then be withdrawn within five weekdays of the request being made. However, bills for the purposes of discharging existing treaty obligations are excluded from this referendum option.[60] Decisions relating to international treaties fall outside this mechanism unless a bill is passed expressly requiring a referendum.[61]

Section 20 was first used for the accession referendum to the European Communities.[62] The Folketing decided that a referendum had to be held on accession in 1973, even if a five-sixths majority was achieved.[63] The Single European Act was not adjudged to entail a transfer of sovereignty, and so neither a five-sixths majority in the Folketing nor a referendum was required.[64] However, the Folketing rejected it, so the minority government led by Poul Schlüter called a consultative referendum, where the people voted in favour and opposition parties then enabled the passage of the Single European Act.[65]

The Maastricht referendum was voted down, and a subsequent second referendum was approved after Denmark secured a set of opt-outs (see Chapter 8).[66] A treaty referendum is thus possible through more than one route under the Danish constitution, but none of these routes makes a public vote more than a possibility. Of critical importance in this respect is whether the treaty entails a delegation of powers, this judgment falling, as noted in Chapter 4, to the Justice Ministry. The Justice

142 THE TRANSFORMATION OF EU TREATY MAKING

Ministry exercises a degree of discretion in such judgment, as evidenced by its decision that the Amsterdam Treaty and European Constitution involved the delegation of powers but that the Nice and Lisbon Treaties did not.[67]

Estonia

Estonia's constitution recognises the right of citizens eligible to vote to express the supreme authority of the people through referendums,[68] and the authority of the Riigikogu to hold referendums[69] on bills or other issues of national importance,[70] but it also expressly forbids issues regarding the ratification and denunciation of treaties from being submitted to a referendum.[71] All constitutional provisions can be amended by referendum,[72] with a referendum mandatory if the bill is to amend general provisions of the constitution.[73] The question of whether an EU treaty amendment triggers a referendum thus hinges, in part, on whether a constitutional amendment is necessary. To date, Estonia has not sought to revise its constitution in connection with EU treaty amendments, so such grounds for a referendum have not arisen. The question of whether a constitutional amendment was required in connection with Estonia's accession to the EU was the subject of debate. In the end, the government opted not to amend the constitution by referendum but to give effect to membership through a Constitutional Act (2003) approved by the Riigikogu and put to the people in a referendum.[74] On this basis, we consider referendums to be improbable in Estonia but not, in spite of the constitutional bar, prohibited.

Finland

Finland's approach to international agreements was fundamentally changed from a formal, narrow concept of sovereignty that rendered most international agreements constitutionally suspect to a more expansive view, culminating with a 2012 amendment that expressly recognises the state's EU membership.[75] Prior to this constitutional change, international agreements were adopted and incorporated into domestic law through two legislative routes: one that simply incorporated the international agreement into the statute through annexing it therein and the other that created a special exception to allow for the international agreement to be incorporated even though it, in effect, amended the constitution.[76] The latter form of legislation was deemed necessary but not sufficient for accession to the EU with a consultative referendum also being held. This referendum was permitted under the constitution, which allows choices to be put to the people by means of an act of the Eduskunta.[77] This 1994 referendum was the first on any issue in this country since 1931, and no treaty-related referendum has been held since. The Åland Islands held a separate advisory referendum on accession.[78] However, for the reasons discussed in Chapter 4, we do not consider the approval of the Åland Islands to be a requirement before Finland can give its consent to be bound to an EU treaty. Following the 2012 amendment of the constitution, there is now no need to resort to the special exception procedure, with even significant amendments of the constitution due to EU membership requiring only parliamentary votes (Chapter 4). The 2012 amendment also introduced a citizens' initiative, which allows a group of at least 50,000 citizens to submit an initiative for the enactment of an act to the parliament.[79] Petitions were signed in 2015 by 53,000 people and in 2016 by 33,600 people on whether Finland should hold a consultative referendum on EMU membership (2015) and on exiting the EU (2016).[80] Even though these referendums did not take place, they illustrate the potential of this new instrument of popular initiative to influence the course of future EU treaty making. Despite the 2012 constitutional reform, which envisages the bringing into force of international obligations of a legislative nature on the basis of either an act or a decree,[81] EU treaty-related referendums remain possible in our judgement.

France

Referendums went from being improbable to possible with France's transition from the Fourth to the Fifth Republic. The Constitution of the Fourth Republic allowed for referendums for constitutional amendment,[82] but, for historical reasons, there was a constitutional aversion to using them.[83] Treaties concerning international organisations were, as noted in Chapter 4, adopted through an act of parliament,[84] in consequence of which France joined the European Communities without consulting the people directly. Treaty-related referendums went from being probable to possible under the Constitution of the Fifth Republic, adopted ten months after France joined the European Economic Community and EURATOM. Like its predecessor, the 1958 constitution provides under Article 89 for a referendum on constitutional amendment. Where the draft amendment initiated by the executive is submitted to the parliament convened at the initiative of the President, this amendment must be adopted by a three-fifths majority.[85] Article 11 of this constitution also allows the President, acting on a proposal from the government or a joint parliamentary motion, to call a referendum to authorise the approval of 'a treaty, that, although not contrary to the Constitution, would affect the functioning of the institutions'.[86] Article 11 has been triggered on three occasions in relation to the approval of EU treaties; the first time was in 1972, when George Pompidou called a referendum on the accession of the United Kingdom, Ireland and Denmark to the European Communities; the second in 1992, when François Mitterrand held a vote on the Maastricht Treaty; and the third in 2005 when Jacques Chirac put the European Constitution to the people.

Article 11 is a controversial constitutional provision, but this controversy relates to its perceived usage by the then President, de Gaulle (and more subtly by his successors Pompidou and Mitterrand), to circumvent Article 89 and the possible opposition of parliament since the proposal of the executive must be voted in identical terms by both assemblies. Although it is now widely accepted that Article 11 should not be used for constitutional amendment, its use in relation to EU treaties is much less controversial. [87] Indeed, the Vedel Committee recommended in 1993 that the scope for ratifying international treaties via Article 11 be extended.[88] Constitutional amendments have been routinely approved via parliament, even in those cases where the EU treaty was subsequently put to a referendum under Article 11.

A third route to a treaty-related referendum was introduced via a constitutional amendment. Under Article 88(5), a referendum was required to authorise an accession treaty unless a three-fifths majority in the National Assembly and Senate decides to approve this agreement via parliamentary channels.[89] Influenced by domestic concerns over the possibility of Turkey's accession to the EU, which would have arguably necessitated the approval of the French people, this article was amended in 2008 to allow for Croatia's accession to the EU without recourse to a referendum.[90]

Germany

'Even if we wanted to have one in Germany, we couldn't', replied German Chancellor Gerhard Schröder when asked in 2004 about the possibility of a referendum on the European Constitution.[91] This statement did not do justice to the constitutional rules surrounding referendums in Germany.[92]

The Basic Law explicitly provides for a referendum on how the federal territory is divided into Länder,[93] and in the final provision it notes that the Basic Law ceases to exist on the day on which 'a constitution freely adopted by the German people takes effect'.[94] The Federation can transfer sovereign powers to the EU with the consent of the Bundesrat even where treaty changes or regulations require amendments or supplements to the Basic Law.[95] The Basic Law implies that such changes will be partial and thus a matter for members of the Bundestag and Bundesrat to decide on.[96] A matter of recurring debate in German politics is whether developments in European integration might necessitate a constitution 'freely adopted by the people' and hence a referendum or a constitutional amendment to allow for a referendum on EU treaties.[97] The Social Democratic Party (SDP) has been at the forefront of this debate, as evidenced by Hans-Joachim Hacker's proposal in 2004 for a referendum lock on future EU treaties and Michael Roth's call in 2011 for a nationwide referendum to be linked to the next amendment to the EU treaties. These proposals have been rejected by the Christian Democratic Union (CDU), although a senior party member, Wolfgang Schäuble, has accepted that a German referendum may one day be necessitated.[98] The Federal Constitutional Court (*Bundesverfassungsgericht*) is a key interlocutor in this debate. In its ruling on the Lisbon Treaty, it acknowledged that 'if however, the threshold were crossed to a federal state and to the giving up of national sovereignty, this would require a free decision of the people in Germany beyond the present applicability of the Basic Law and the democratic requirements to be complied with would have to be fully consistent with the requirements for the democratic legitimation of a union of rule organised by a state'.[99] Although the Court did not explicitly mention the possibility of a referendum, the need and scope for such a vote under such circumstances was implicit. On this basis, we conclude that a referendum in Germany on an EU treaty is improbable rather than prohibited.

Greece

Greece is an archetypical system of representative democracy in which referendums are rare. No referendum was held in connection with Greece's accession to the EU in 1981, and to date, the people have not been directly consulted on a treaty change. Under Greece's constitution, the President of the Republic can call a referendum on 'crucial national matters', with the support of the Cabinet and an absolute majority of members of parliament.[100] The President of the Hellenic Republic is also empowered to call a referendum on bills passed by parliament 'regulating important social matters, with the exception of the fiscal ones'. Again, the deputies need to support this cause. Prior to 2011, the prevailing constitutional norm mitigated against the calling of a referendum related to treaties or on any issue. The relevant articles of the constitution, argue Xenophon Contiades and Alkmene Fotiadou, were 'dormant and disused'.[101] In 1981, Andreas Papandreou, then leader of the opposition, had called for a referendum on Greece's accession to the European Communities, but this call gained little traction.[102] In 2004, PASOK joined other left-wing parties in calling for a referendum on the European Constitution, but it also fell flat.[103] Greece's constitutional taboo on treaty making was broken in 2011 when Prime Minister Papandreou called a referendum on the terms of Greece's loan agreement with the EU and the International Monetary Fund. Although the vote was hastily cancelled, the Greek parliament approved a new law designed to enhance direct and participatory democracy through referendums. This law has yet to be used to trigger a treaty-related referendum. However, it was employed, in conjunction with Article 44 of the constitution, in Greece's controversial bail-out referendum in 2015, the first instance of direct democracy in this state since the Greek Republic Referendum of 1974 (see Chapter 10). The implementation of Article 44 was seen as a measure of last resort[104] – the government had to invoke it to veil a mantle of legitimacy on the bail-out referendum of July 2015 – but we see it as opening the door to treaty-related referendums nonetheless.

Hungary

Hungary's Fundamental Law authorises the National Assembly to call a referendum on any matter falling within its functions and powers[105] including new international treaties and obligations.[106] Referendums on constitutional amendments[107] or obligations arising from existing international treaties[108] are prohibited. The consultative 2003 referendum on EU accession was required by a newly inserted constitutional provision.[109] Hungary ratified the European Constitution and the Lisbon Treaty via parliamentary channels, although citizens sought unsuccessfully to initiate a referendum on both.[110] On this basis, we consider a treaty referendum to be improbable in Hungary but not prohibited.

Ireland

The Irish constitution can be amended only by referendum.[111] It is unlikely, however, that the drafters envisaged the practice of holding a referendum for any major EU treaty revision and the opportunity this constitutional norm provides for dissenting voices. The turning point from referendums being possible to their being probable came with the Single European Act and the *Crotty* case. Raymond Crotty, an agriculture economist and a founding member of the Common Market Defence Committee,[112] was determined to prevent the approval of the act via legislation without consultation of the people.[113] He went to court to try and stop the bill being enacted. When this case was dismissed, he changed solicitor, waited until the bill had been passed and then sought an urgent temporary court order to stop the government taking the final step in the consent stage of depositing the ratification instrument with the Italian government.[114] His attempt to make the order permanent failed initially[115] but was successful in the Supreme Court.[116]

In the *Crotty* case, the Supreme Court took the view that the relevant provision of the Irish constitution, Article 29.4.3°, did not give carte blanche for any further treaty revision without a referendum, but, similarly, it did not mean that every treaty revision required a referendum. This, in effect, meant that the Court had to review the new treaty to decide whether or not a referendum was required, the test being whether the amendments altered 'the essential scope or objectives' of the then Communities.[117] Thus it noted that while the shift from unanimity to qualified majority voting in the Council fell within the constitution and hence did not require a referendum, this did not mean that all future proposals to move away from unanimity could be achieved without a referendum. The Supreme Court thus placed the higher courts as the final arbiters of the relationship between the constitution, the legislature, the Irish voters and EU treaties. This was further underlined by the second part of the case, which concerned European Political Cooperation, Title III of the Single European Act, which was a significant step towards foreign policy cooperation among the member states. As this was a separate international agreement, it did not fall within the constitutional provision on Community membership. The Court considered it separately with a 3:2 division in favour of a referendum on the basis that the restriction on autonomy for the state in foreign policy was a diminution in sovereignty that required popular approval. The Single European Act was put to a referendum in 1987, with 70 per cent voting in favour.[118]

148   THE TRANSFORMATION OF EU TREATY MAKING

Referendums on major treaty revisions became the norm after *Crotty*, with referendums held over the Maastricht, Amsterdam, Nice and Lisbon treaties. This norm stemmed less from the Supreme Court's ruling than the government's response to it. In essence, successive governments erred on the side of holding a referendum on major EU treaty amendments in order to avoid litigation. One reason for the government's risk aversion is that the judiciary clouded rather than clarified the size of the state's win set in relation to treaty changes. The Court was divided over the precise significance of the Single European Act, and its preoccupation with the treaty's intergovernmental provisions on foreign policy coordination can only have added to uncertainty over the constitutional implications of future treaty revisions.[119] Hence, referendums are probable in Ireland, with one caveat: a prohibition was introduced in the constitution at the time of the second Nice referendum in 2002 on the state adopting a decision to establish a common defence policy. This means that a referendum must be held to amend the constitution for Ireland to join an EU common defence policy.[120]

Italy

Nationwide referendums are a regular occurrence in Italy, but not on EU treaties.[121] Italy's constitution allows for two types of referendum: constitutional and general. A constitutional referendum can be called by either one-fifth of the members of either chamber of the Italian Parliament or 500,000 electors but only if the proposed amendment has been approved by each chamber twice and the second of these votes resulted in a majority of less than two-thirds in each chamber.[122] General referendums on the total or partial repeal of a law can be called by either 500,000 voters or five regional Councils.[123] The President of the Italian Republic also is required to call a general referendum when provided for under the constitution.[124] Nevertheless, the scope for a referendum on an EU treaty is substantially curtailed. The constitution prohibits electors or regional Councils from calling a general referendum on international treaties.[125] It also leaves little room for the President to call a referendum on a treaty since they are required to ratify international treaties 'once they are authorised by parliament, provided parliamentary approval is necessary'.[126]

An Italian referendum on an EU treaty would have to be a constitutional one linked to the treaty in question, but such a vote is improbable.

This is because, as noted in Chapter 4, the Italian constitution leaves significant scope for 'limitations of sovereignty where they are necessary to allow for a legal system of peace and justice between nations, provided the principle of equality between states is guaranteed'.[127] In consequence of this provision, Italy has yet to introduce a formal revision to its constitution in connection with the ratification of an EU treaty. The sole referendum to be held in Italy on a European matter to date was an advisory one in 1989, which called for more powers to be granted to the European Parliament in advance of negotiations over the Maastricht Treaty. This non-binding vote was not foreseen in the constitution, being underpinned instead by a constitutional law adopted by the Italian parliament.[128] In our view, a referendum on EU treaties is not prohibited but remains improbable.

Latvia

Latvia's constitution prohibits national referendums on peace treaties and agreements with other nations,[129] but we see referendums on EU treaties to be possible nonetheless. In 2003, on the eve of joining the EU, Latvia introduced a referendum lock for future EU treaty amendments. This constitutional amendment allowed substantial changes to Latvia's membership of the EU to be decided by referendum if half of the members of the Saeima agree on the need for such a vote.[130] This constitutional amendment also established a participation threshold for such a referendum, requiring at least half of the number of electors that turned out in the previous Saeima election to participate in such a referendum.[131] Latvia's constitution requires a referendum when certain constitutional provisions are amended, while also allowing one-tenth of the electorate to put constitutional amendments to a referendum if such amendments are not adopted unchanged by the Saeima.[132] This opens the door to a referendum in cases where EU treaties necessitate constitutional amendment. Half of the electorate must vote in favour of this revision, a higher threshold than applied in the case of a referendum directly concerning an EU treaty amendment.[133] Since joining the EU in 2004, Latvia has not sought to amend its constitution in connection with treaty amendments. Nor has the Saeima sought to trigger a referendum on the grounds of substantial changes to Latvia's membership. Overall, we see a referendum as possible in Latvia under prevailing constitutional norms.

Lithuania

Lithuania's constitution envisages referendums on the 'most significant issues concerning the State and the Nation', with such votes being initiated by the Seimas or by not less than 300,000 citizens.[134] Certain constitutional amendments require a referendum,[135] where they touch on the core values and principles of chapter I of the constitution. The question of whether EU accession required a referendum was much discussed,[136] and ultimately there was a 2002 amendment to the Law on Referendums, which provided for a mandatory referendum concerning the partial transfer of the competences of government bodies to international organisations.[137] The Law on Referendums leaves open the door to a public vote on treaty amendments that entail a significant transfer of competences to the EU. It allows for the possibility of a citizen-initiated referendum if 300,000 people support such a vote, although it remains a moot point as to whether such a referendum would be mandatory or deliberative.[138] There were two unsuccessful referendum initiatives in 2014 related to EU membership: one aimed at restricting the right of foreigners to buy land (it failed as less than the required 50 per cent of the electorate participated) and one in effect seeking to leave EMU by reestablishing the power of the Bank of Lithuania to issue bank notes. No referendum has been sought in relation to an EU treaty amendment to date, but such a vote is, we conclude, a possibility.

Luxembourg

Luxembourg is an example of a country in which the constitutional rules and norms underpinning treaty amendment have shifted. When it joined the European Coal and Steel Community in 1951, a treaty-related referendum was improbable, the Constitution of Luxembourg providing for such a vote neither in relation to a treaty nor, indeed, in connection with constitutional amendment, the latter being a matter for the Chamber of Deputies to decide upon.[139] In 1919, a (vague) consultative referendum procedure had been introduced, facilitating public votes on the form of the Luxembourg state and whether to have an economic union with France or Belgium, but the government did not seek to hold a referendum on the Treaty of Paris. A constitutional amendment in 1956 raised the parliamentary threshold for vesting executive, legislative and judicial powers in institution of international law (see Chapter 4) but made no reference to treaty-related referendums.[140]

In 2003, a constitutional amendment introduced the possibility of a referendum on future constitutional amendments.[141] This opened the door to a referendum in cases where treaties necessitate constitutional amendment, albeit when a quarter of the members of the chamber or 25,000 electors support such a proposal.[142] A further break from the constitutional norms governing EU treaty making occurred in 2005 when Prime Minister Jean-Claude Juncker called a referendum on the European Constitution. Although this referendum was advisory, the Chamber, in the enabling act, made it clear that it felt politically bound to follow the outcome of the referendum with Juncker, saying he would resign if there was a 'no' vote.[143] Luxembourg was undergoing a potentially radical overhaul of its constitution at the time of writing, with constitutional provisions concerning EU membership the subject of debate and constitutional referendums expected.[144]

Malta

Malta's constitution does not envisage a referendum in connection with treaty making, although this would be a possibility if a treaty entailed constitutional amendments, a referendum being a constitutional requirement for amendments to certain constitutional provisions.[145] Malta took a 'minimal' approach to constitutional amendment when it joined the EU,[146] requiring the House of Representatives to make laws in conformity with its treaty of accession.[147] No referendum was required for this purpose, but the government gave the people a say nonetheless. The legal basis for Malta's 2003 referendum on accession was the Referenda Act (1973), which allows the House of Representatives to ask citizens whether they approve of proposals set out in a resolution.[148] Opinion polls suggest that a majority of Maltese citizens wanted a referendum on the European Constitution,[149] but the government instead secured approval via a parliamentary resolution (see Chapter 4). The Referendum Act also allows 10 per cent of registered voters to trigger an 'abrogative referendum',[150] as occurred in the 2015 Spring Hunting Referendum, but this does not apply to legislation giving effect to treaty obligations.[151]

The Netherlands

The Netherlands is another case in which the constitutional norms underpinning EU treaty making have shifted. Debates about the possibility of holding constitutional referendums in the Netherlands are

152   THE TRANSFORMATION OF EU TREATY MAKING

long-standing. In 1985, the Biesheuvel/Prakke Commission, an official study committee established by Royal Decree, put forward proposals for several forms of direct democracy, but they failed to gain support in the short term.[152] In 2002, a Temporary Referendum Act introduced the possibility of a non-binding consultative referendum,[153] although this had expired by the time the Dutch government announced a public vote on the European Constitution.[154] This 2005 referendum, the first to be held in the Netherlands since 1805, was facilitated by means of another temporary law that allowed for a consultative referendum on that treaty.[155] Following the state's rejection of the European Constitution, a group of MPs proposed a Consultative Referendum Law.[156] A revived version of this proposal became law in 2015, allowing 300,000 citizens to trigger a referendum on treaties and other laws after they have been approved but before they have entered into force.[157] EU treaties can be the subject of a referendum petition under this law, thus codifying the constitutional shift that started in 2002 with the introduction of the Temporary Referendum Act.[158] As a result of this shift, the Netherlands went from being a case in which treaty-related referendums were improbable to one in which they are possible. This remains the position despite the proposed repeal of the referendum petition law.

Poland

The 2003 referendum on joining the EU aside, Poland has not held a treaty-related referendum. Such a referendum is possible under prevailing constitutional rules. Under Poland's constitution, consent to an international agreement that involves the delegation of powers to the EU can be granted by means of a referendum.[159] Such a vote can be called by the Sejm following an absolute majority of votes in the presence of at least half of the statutory number of deputies, or by the President of the Republic with the consent of the Senate.[160] The Sejm can also call binding referendums on matters of particular importance to the state if an absolute majority of deputies agree.[161] The Marshal of the Sejm is also authorised to call a confirmatory referendum on the amendment of certain constitutional provisions.[162] There was a broad political consensus in Poland on approving the European Constitution via a referendum. Both Prime Minister Leszek Miller and President Aleksander Kwasniewski supported such a vote, the latter telling reporters that because Poland had a referendum on joining the EU 'it would be difficult not to have one on the European Constitution'.[163] A referendum was duly

THE RISE OF REFERENDUMS IN EU TREATY MAKING   153

called in the days that followed, although the vote was cancelled after the French and Dutch 'no' votes. No referendum was sought in relation to the Lisbon Treaty, although it remained a constitutional possibility.

Portugal

Portugal was – until the fourth revision of its constitution in 1997 – an example of a member state that expressly prohibited referendums on EU treaties. The Constitution of the Portuguese Republic (1976) allowed referendums on matters of 'relevant national interest', facilitating public votes on abortion in 1988 and 2007.[164] But the constitution prohibited referendums on matters relating to the political and legislative powers of the Assembly,[165] including the power to approve treaties involving the state's participation in international organisations.[166] As a result, Portugal joined the European Communities in 1986 without holding a referendum. During the passage of the Maastricht Treaty, opposition politicians proposed a constitutional amendment that would have made a referendum obligatory for certain categories of treaty, but this proposal was rejected by the Ad Hoc Committee of Constitutional Revision.[167]

In 1997, referendums went from being prohibited to possible in Portugal as constitutional rules underpinning the approval of EU treaties shifted. The fourth constitutional revision introduced, for the first time, the possibility of a referendum on 'issues of relevant national interest, which must be the subject of international agreement'.[168] This created a degree of uncertainty as to whether a treaty itself could be the subject of a referendum. A proposal for a public vote on the Amsterdam Treaty was rejected by the Constitutional Court (*Tribunal Constitucional*) because the question proposed did not meet the requirements of clarity and precision established in Article 115(6) of the constitution. The wording made it impossible to determine the significance of the reference to the Treaty.[169] The same reasoning – that the proposed question did not meet the requirements of clarity and formulation of a question calling for a yes/no answer – was adopted by the Constitutional Court in its decision rejecting a referendum on the European constitution.[170] Following this decision, the seventh revision to Portugal's constitution expressly provided that referendums on EU treaties were exempt from the requirement of clarity and precision.[171] This wording overturned the rulings of the Tribunal and made a treaty-related referendum possible. Such a referendum can be proposed by the Assembleia da República or as a

154   THE TRANSFORMATION OF EU TREATY MAKING

result of a citizens' initiative leading to a submission to the Assembly. Referendums can be held only on important matters of national interest as determined by the Assembly or the government through legislation or an international agreement.[172] The decision to call a referendum is up to the President of the Republic.[173] Despite these changes, the government has yet to propose the calling of a referendum on an EU treaty amendment.

Romania

Romania's constitution does not explicitly provide for treaty-related referendums, but they are possible nonetheless. Treaties that are contrary to the constitution cannot be ratified without a prior constitutional amendment[174] and a constitutional amendment requires a referendum.[175] It was in this context that Romanians went to the polls in 2003 to decide on a set of constitutional amendments in connection with EU accession. Treaties that are contrary to the constitution would require a similar constitutional referendum, although, to date, Romania's characteristically rigid constitution has remained unchanged in the face of EU treaty amendments.[176] The President of Romania has the constitutional authority to call a referendum to ask the people to express their will on matters of national interest.[177] Such a vote could, in principle, be called on a treaty, even though this has not happened to date.

Slovak Republic

Slovakia's constitution permits entry into a union of states by means of a constitutional law, which must be confirmed by a referendum.[178] It was on this basis that Slovakia held a referendum in 2003 on joining the EU. This member state has not held a treaty-related referendum to date and the constitution's provisions on treaty making do not explicitly provide for such a vote.[179] The constitution permits referendums on issues of public interest, except for matters concerning fundamental rights, freedoms, tax duties and national budgetary matters, with no reference to treaties in this list of prohibitions.[180] It falls to the President of the Slovak Republic to announce a referendum on the basis of a petition from at least 350,000 citizens or a resolution from the National Council of the Slovak Republic.[181] Referendum results that meet the required turnout and threshold are binding for at least three years,[182] after which time they can be derogated or abrogated by the National Council by means of a constitutional statute.[183]

Slovenia

Slovenia held a referendum in 1990 on whether to become an independent and sovereign state and by October 2017 had held twenty-two referendums on issues ranging from the laws governing the national archives to fertility treatment. Under the 1991 constitution, the National Assembly was empowered to call a referendum on any issue that is the subject of regulation by law.[184] A 2013 constitutional amendment prohibited the calling of such legislative referendums on laws concerning the approval of treaties.[185] However, under an earlier constitutional amendment, the National Assembly can call a referendum on treaties concerning the transfer of sovereign rights to international organisations prior to their ratification.[186] If a majority of voters vote in favour, then the referendum is passed. The outcome of the referendum is binding and a second referendum cannot be called after ratification. Kavčič suggests that when the National Assembly does not call for a referendum on the basis of Article 3a, it must call for a legislative referendum on the law ratifying the treaty when required to do so by 40,000 voters and that this constitutes an exception to the prohibition on referendums for international obligations.[187] Slovenia held a referendum on joining the EU (and the North Atlantic Treaty Organization [NATO]) in 2003. When these referendums were first called, they were consultative, but the 2003 constitutional amendment specified that the new Article 3a would also apply to these referendums thereby rendering them binding. Even though a petition to hold a referendum was lodged by a political party, it was rejected by the National Assembly. Similarly, a petition by voters to hold a referendum on Lisbon failed as there were not enough signatures supporting it. Hence the National Assembly did not invoke a referendum in relation to the European Constitution or the Lisbon Treaty. Referendums on EU treaties are thus possible rather than probable in Slovenia.

Spain

There is no explicit provision in the Spanish constitution for treaty-related referendums, but they are a possibility if treaties entail constitutional changes. Any constitutional revision necessitated by a treaty must be implemented before the treaty can be ratified.[188] In the case of

156   THE TRANSFORMATION OF EU TREATY MAKING

a total revision or certain categories of partial revision, a referendum must be held.[189] In other cases, the constitutional revision can be subject to a referendum if requested by one-tenth of the members of either chamber of the Cortes Generales.[190] As noted in Chapter 4, Spain has tended not to revise its constitution as a result of EU treaties, and where it has done so, as in the case of Maastricht, such revisions have been approved without recourse to a referendum.

'Political decisions of special importance' can be the subject of a consultative referendum in Spain if called by the King (this being a formal and symbolic power) or the President of the government and Congress.[191] This provision has been used in relation to treaties on two occasions. The first referendum addressed the question of whether Spain should remain a NATO member, which the country had acceded to four years earlier.[192] The second concerned the European Constitution. This referendum was not related to a constitutional amendment, the Constitutional Court having decided in 2004 that the European Constitution did not require changes to the Spanish constitution, but on the more general political question of whether voters approved the European Constitution.[193] Popular initiatives are allowed in Spain, but they cannot be used on matters concerning international affairs.[194] On this basis, it can be concluded that referendums on EU treaties have been a possibility since Spain joined the European Communities in 1986.

Sweden

Consultative referendums are possible under Sweden's Instrument of Government, and two such referendums were held on EU issues.[195] The government initially sought approval for Sweden's accession to the EU via the Riksdag, but, under pressure, it held a referendum.[196] In 2003 there was another referendum on whether Sweden should join the euro, the motion being defeated.[197] Since 1974, members of the Riksdag can also call a referendum on proposals concerning fundamental laws.[198] As such, treaties that entail constitutional amendments would, in principle, be open to a binding referendum. Under the Instrument of Government, a proposal for amending the fundamental law must be approved by the Riksdag twice after an intervening election unless deputies choose to approve such revisions by means of a single decision (see Chapter 4).[199] If the first of these routes to constitutional amendment is followed, it is possible for one-tenth of members of parliament to initiate a binding referendum after the first of the Riksdag's two votes provided one-third of members agree.[200] Such a vote has never been triggered. In practice, Sweden has not tended to amend its constitution in response to EU treaties, and it has shied away from binding referendums in favour of the consultative referendums.[201] Our judgement is that a referendum on an EU treaty is possible throughout the sample period.

United Kingdom

The United Kingdom's referendum vote to leave the EU in 2016 was arguably the most significant act of direct democracy in the history of the EU. That it came from a state with no great tradition of referendums made it all the more striking. True, the United Kingdom's recourse to referendums has increased, particularly at the subnational level in the context of devolution, but the 2016 EU vote was only the third nation-wide referendum ever held.[202] Two of these votes concerned EU membership, but none explicitly concerned treaty amendment, the 1975 referendum being premised on the more general question of staying in the European Community (Common Market) and the 2016 referendum concerned with whether the United Kingdom should remain a member of the EU.[203]

Under the United Kingdom's uncodified constitution, treaty making is a matter for the government under the Royal Prerogative and Parliament under prevailing constitutional norms (see Chapter 4).[204] Although these constitutional rules and norms are comparatively clear, the government faced pressure to hold a referendum on Maastricht. This pressure steadily increased with each successive treaty amendment until Tony Blair belatedly promised to put the European Constitution to the people. Having initially argued against a referendum on the grounds that the treaty did not represent a 'fundamental change to the British Constitution',[205] the Prime Minister changed his mind: 'Let the issue be put. Let the battle be joined', he told the House of Commons in 2004, promising to give voters a direct say on the new treaty.[206] The European Union Bill (2005) made good on this promise. Although the bill was shelved twice – temporarily after a general election was called and permanently after France and the Netherlands rejected the European Constitution – it confirmed that a treaty-related referendum was constitutionally possible if the government decided and parliament gave its assent.

Blair's successor Gordon Brown withstood pressure to hold a referendum on the Lisbon Treaty,[207] but opposition leader David Cameron insisted on the need for a public vote.[208] Cameron dropped his pledge

158   THE TRANSFORMATION OF EU TREATY MAKING

once the Lisbon Treaty had been ratified, but the Conservative Manifesto promised 'to make sure this shameful episode can never happen again'.[209] With the passage of the European Union Act (2011), after Cameron became Prime Minister, referendums on major EU treaty changes went from being probable to possible. This law set out three requirements before EU treaties can be ratified in the United Kingdom. The first is that an act of parliament must approve all new EU treaties.[210] The second requirement is that such treaties must meet either a referendum condition[211] or an exemption condition[212] or, in the case of treaties enacted under the simplified revision procedure, a significance condition.[213] The referendum condition necessitates that a pre-legislative referendum be held in which the majority of voters are in favour of the treaty. The exemption condition holds if the treaty does not fall within a detailed set of headings that, in general terms, cover changes that (1) extend the objectives, competences or powers of the Union; (2) impose new requirements, obligations or sanctions on the United Kingdom; or (3) remove member states' ability to apply the 'emergency brake' on decision making in certain policy domains. The significance condition, finally, holds where the treaty confers new powers on the EU to impose a requirement, obligation or sanction on the United Kingdom, but where the effects of that provision are not significant there is no need for a referendum. The third condition set out in this act requires a ministerial statement to be laid before parliament to justify a decision to invoke the exemption or significance conditions.[214]

The European Union (2011) Act was put into practice twice. The first concerned the ratification of the Article 136 TFEU amendment.[215] The second was to endorse both Croatia's accession to the EU and a set of legal guarantees offered to Ireland before that country re-ran a referendum on the Lisbon Treaty.[216] These treaty revisions met the conditions under which referendums are exempt.[217] Thus, the European Union Act (2011), though it made a treaty-related referendum probable, never triggered such a vote.

Conclusion

This chapter has explored the changing role of the people in EU treaty making over the period 1951–2016. There are different ways to classify referendums, with our approach following scholars such as Simmons and Lutz in concentrating on how likely a treaty-related referendum is under prevailing constitutional rules and norms. Judged in these terms,

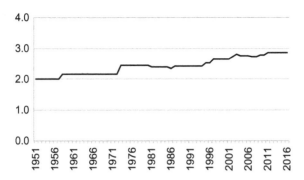

Figure 5.1 Referendums scale (average, 1951–2016).

the people have assumed a more prominent role in EU treaty making since 1951. Figure 5.1 shows that the average ratification index steadily increases from 2.0 in 1951 to 2.9 in 2016, meaning that referendums have gone from being improbable in the 'average' EU member state to being possible.

Referendums on EU treaties were improbable in the six founding member states of the European Coal and Steel Community when they ratified the Treaty of Paris. By 2016, referendums in relation to EU treaty amendments were possible in twenty of the EU's twenty-eight member states and probable in two. This left just six member states in which constitutional rules and norms rendered a public vote on treaties improbable. The accession of member states in which constitutional rules and norms favoured referendums only partly accounts for this shift. Rule and norm shifts that made referendums more likely occurred in eight member states after they joined the Union.

160 THE TRANSFORMATION OF EU TREATY MAKING

Appendix 5.1 Referendums Scales

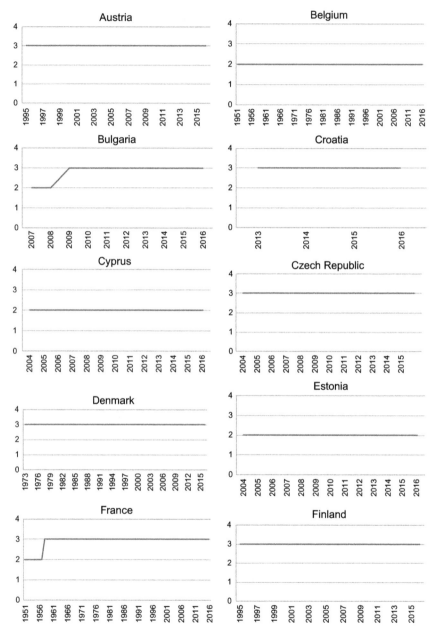

Figure 5.2 Referendums scales (by member state, 1951–2016).

THE RISE OF REFERENDUMS IN EU TREATY MAKING 161

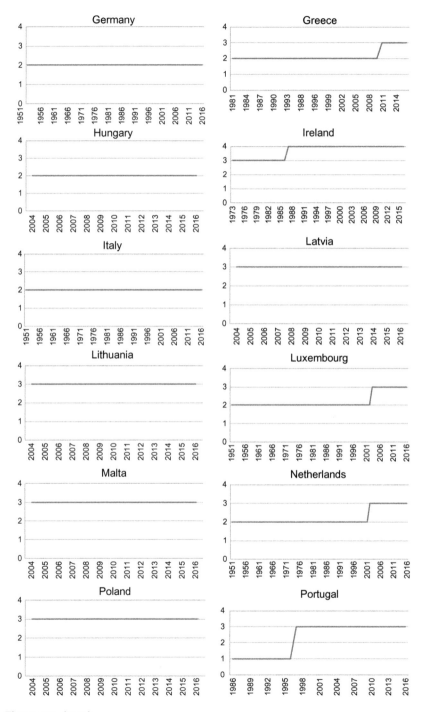

Figure 5.2 (*cont.*)

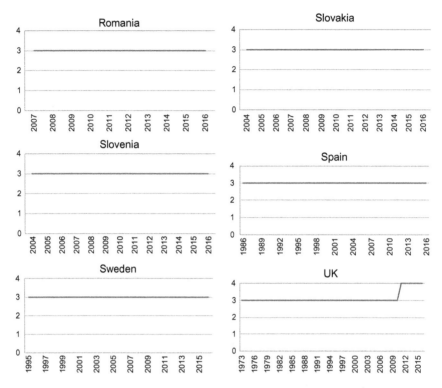

Figure 5.2 (cont.)

Notes

1 Morel (2012), p. 501.
2 Source: IDEA Direct Democracy Database: www.idea.int/data-tools/question-view/476.
3 Tierney (2013); Qvortrup (2014), p. 247.
4 Altman et al. (2014), appendix 1, excluding Swiss referendums.
5 Anckar (2014).
6 Tierney (2012a).
7 Referendums on national identity and political system account for 70 per cent of all referendums recorded by the Centre for Research on Direct Democracy, as compared with 5 per cent for referendums on foreign policy. Source: Centre for Research on Direct Democracy, data available at: www.c2d.ch.
8 Centre for Research on Direct Democracy, data available at: www.c2d.ch.

9 Centre for Research on Direct Democracy, data available at: www.c2d.ch.

10 Veenendaal (2016), pp. 31. See also Gerston (1989).

11 Authors' calculation based on Centre for Research on Direct Democracy data, available at: www.c2d.ch,

12 Smith (1976), p. 15.

13 Smith (1976), p. 9.

14 Smith (1976), p. 9. Legally, the referendum was essential to permit the state to become a member of the Communities. See Supreme Court of Ireland, *Crotty* v. *An Taoiseach* [1987] 1 IR 763 Finlay CJ at 767. As a legal requirement, then, that referendum (perhaps unlike later Irish referendums) could be classified as uncontrolled. Hence, politically there was no discretion as to whether or not to hold a referendum as the text of the constitution had to be changed to allow membership of an international body whose laws would take primacy over Irish law.

15 Hug (2003), p. 25.

16 Hug (2009), p. 259.

17 Mueller (1996), p. 179.

18 Mueller (1996), p. 9.

19 Closa (2013a), chapter 4.

20 Closa (2013a), p. 74.

21 Mendez et al. (2014), chapter 2.

22 Ulusoy (2008), p. 315, although the continuing functioning of the constitution since the break-up of the state in 1963 renders it a complex and unique constitutional context (Skoutaris 2011).

23 Tosi (2017).

24 UK Supreme Court, *R (Miller)* v. *Secretary of State for Exiting the EU* [2017] UKSC 5. See Hodson and Maher (2014).

25 Gerber and Hug (2001).

26 Majone (2009), pp. 17–18.

27 A case in point is France (Lutz 1994: p. 363).

28 Simmons (2009b), p. 383. For online appendix, see https://scholar.harvard.edu/files/bsimmons/files/APP_3.2_Ratification_rules.pdf.

29 Morel (2012).

30 Smith (1976), pp. 4–5.

31 Article 43, Austria Constitution of 1920 (reinstated in 1945 and amended to 2013).

32 Pelinka and Greiderer (1996), p. 23.

33 Article 49b, Austria Constitution of 1920 (reinstated in 1945 and amended to 2013).

34 Pfafferott (2013).

35 Article 41, Constitution; Pelinka and Greiderer (1996).

36 Sigalas (2015).

37 Strempel (2006).

38 Popelier and Lemmens (2015), p. 75.
39 Popelier and Lemmens (2015), p. 144.
40 Qvortrup (2005), p. 1.
41 Vandenbruwaene (2014), p. 30.
42 Bulgaria, Direct Citizen Participation in State and Local Government Act, No. 44/12.06.2009.
43 Articles 153–64, Constitution of the Republic of Bulgaria (1991, amended to 2015).
44 Tanchev and Belov (2008).
45 Article 84(5), Constitution of the Republic of Bulgaria (1991, amended to 2015).
46 Article 9(4), Direct Citizen Participation in State and Local Government Act (2009).
47 Article 10, Direct Citizen Participation in State and Local Government Act (2009).
48 Article 142, Constitution of the Republic of Croatia (1991, amended to 2010).
49 Article 87, Constitution of the Republic of Croatia (1991, amended to 2010); Butković (2017).
50 Article 87, Constitution of the Republic of Croatia (1991, amended to 2010).
51 Article 87, Constitution of the Republic of Croatia (1991, amended to 2010).
52 Cyprus, Law on Referendums 206/1989.
53 Law on the Practical Arrangements for the Conduct of the Referendum of the Greek Cypriot Community of 24 April 2004 (Law 74(I)/2004).
54 Article 10a, Constitution of the Czech Republic (1993, amended to 2013); Tichý and Dumbrovský (2018).
55 Czech Republic, Constitutional Act No. 515/2002 Sb.
56 EUbusiness.com (2005).
57 Harhoff (1983).
58 Section 20, the Constitutional Act of Denmark (1953).
59 Section 42(1), the Constitutional Act of Denmark (1953).
60 Section 42(6) the Constitutional Act of Denmark (1953).
61 Section 19, the Constitutional Act of Denmark (1953). See Due and Gulmann (1972).
62 Due and Gulmann (1972), p. 260.
63 Due and Gulmann (1972), p. 258.
64 See Section 19, the Constitutional Act of Denmark (1953); Laursen (2009), p. 5.
65 Petersen (1998), p. 4; Laursen (2009), p. 4.
66 Laursen (2009), p. 3.
67 Laursen (2009), pp. 8–9. The Supreme Court supported the decision not to hold a referendum. Supreme Court (Denmark), Case 199/2012, Decision of 20 February 2013; Olsen (2013).
68 §56, Constitution of the Estonian Republic (1992, amended to 2015).
69 §65(2), Constitution of the Estonian Republic (1992, amended to 2015).

70 §105, Constitution of the Estonian Republic (1992, amended to 2015).

71 §106, Constitution of the Estonian Republic (1992, amended to 2015).

72 §163, Constitution of the Estonian Republic (1992, amended to 2015).

73 Chs. 1 and XV of the Constitution (Ch. XV is about the procedures to amend the constitution); Besselink et al. (2014), p. 79.

74 Mendez, Mendez and Triga (2014), p. 55.

75 Besselink et al. (2014), p. 86.

76 Jaaskinen (1999), p. 408.

77 Section 53, Constitution of Finland (1999, amended to 2011).

78 Loughlin and Daftary (1999), p. 69.

79 Section 53, Constitution of Finland (1999, amended to 2011); Constitution of Finland Act 1112/2011.

80 Rosendahl (2016).

81 Section 95; Besselink et al. (2014), p. 82.

82 Articles 90 and 27, Constitution of the 4th Republic (1946).

83 Morel (1996), p. 70; Paris (2012), p. 12.

84 Article 31, Constitution of the 4th Republic (1946).

85 Article 89, Constitution of 4 October 1958 (amended to 2008).

86 Article 11, Constitution of 4 October 1958 (amended to 2008).

87 Morel (1996), p. 72.

88 Boyron (2012), p. 197.

89 Article 88(5), Constitution of 4 October 1958 (as amended in 2005).

90 Loi constitutionnelle n° 2008–724 du 23 juillet 2008, article 47, alinéa III.

91 Connolly (2004).

92 Böckenförde (2006).

93 Article 29, Basic Law of the Federal Republic of Germany (1949, amended to 2014).

94 Article 146, Basic Law of the Federal Republic of Germany (1949, amended to 2014).

95 Article 23, Basic Law of the Federal Republic of Germany (1949, amended to 2014).

96 Article 23 states that changes to the Basic Law resulting from an EU treaty will fall under Article 79.

97 Schuseil (2012).

98 Brown (2012).

99 German Federal Constitutional Court, Judgment of the Second Senate of 30 June 2009 – 2 BvE 2/08, para. 263.

100 Article 44(2), Constitution of Greece (1975, amended to 2008). Prior to a constitutional amendment in 1986, the President could call a referendum of this sort on their own initiative.

101 Contiades and Fotiadou (2015).

102 Clog (1987), pp. 138–9.

103 Mateo González (2006), p. 3.

104 Ungerer and Ziaka (2017).

105 Article 8(2), Fundamental Law of Hungary (2011, amended to 2013).

106 Constitutional Court of Hungary, Decisions Nos. 58/2004 (XII. 14) and 1/2006 (I. 30).

107 Article 8(3)(a), Fundamental Law of Hungary (2011, amended to 2013).

108 Article 8(3)(d), Fundamental Law of Hungary (2011, amended to 2013).

109 Act LXI of 2002 amending Article 79 of Act XX of 1949, the Constitution of the Republic of Hungary. Besselink et al. (2014), p. 127.

110 Constitutional Court of Hungary, Decision No. 61/2208 (on the Lisbon Treaty) and Decision no. 6/2005 (I. 13) of the National Election Commission (on the defunct treaty establishing an EU constitution); Mendez, Mendez and Triga (2014), p. 82.

111 Article 46, Constitution of Ireland (1937, amended to 2015).

112 The Common Market Defence Committee was an organised opposition group established in 1972 to campaign against Irish accession to the EEC (see Ferriter (2012: 377)).

113 See Crotty (1988) for an account of his opposition to European integration.

114 High Court (Ireland) *Crotty* v. *An Taoiseach* [1986] IEHC 3 (24 December 1986). Article 33(1) SEA: 'instruments of ratification will be deposited with the Government of the Italian Republic'.

115 High Court (Ireland) *Crotty* v. *An Taoiseach* [1987] IEHC 1 (12 Feb 1987).

116 Supreme Court of Ireland, *Crotty* v. *An Taoiseach* [1987] IR 713 (April 1987).

117 Finlay CJ, para. 6., Supreme Court of Ireland, *Crotty* v. *An Taoiseach* [1987] IR 713 (April 1987).

118 Laffan and O'Mahony (2008), p. 108.

119 On this point, see Hodson and Maher (2014), p. 651.

120 Article 29.4.9, which now reads: 'The State shall not adopt a decision taken by the European Council to establish a common defence pursuant to Article 42 of the Treaty on European Union where that common defence would include the State.'

121 There have been twenty referendums since 1974 but only three on constitutional issues. The most recent, in 2016, saw voters reject proposals for, inter alia, reforming the parliament.

122 Article 138, Constitution of the Italian Republic (1947, amended to 2012).

123 Article 75, Constitution of the Italian Republic (1947, amended to 2012).

124 Article 87(6), Constitution of the Italian Republic (1947, amended to 2012). In Italian, this is defined as 'un atto costituzionalmente dovuto' – that is to say, as a constitutionally required action. cf. Art. 15 and 34, legge n. 352/1970.

125 Article 75, Constitution of the Italian Republic (1947, amended to 2012).

126 Article 87(8), Constitution of the Italian Republic (1947, amended to 2012).

127 Article 11, Constitution of the Italian Republic (1947, amended to 2012).

128 Italy, Constitutional Law No. 2, 3 April 1989.

129 Article 72, Constitution of Latvia of 1922 (reinstated 1991, amended to 2014).
130 Article 68, Constitution of Latvia of 1922 (reinstated 1991, amended to 2014).
131 Article 79, Constitution of Latvia of 1922 (reinstated 1991, amended to 2014).
132 Article 77, Constitution of Latvia of 1922 (reinstated 1991, amended to 2014).
133 Article 79, Constitution of Latvia of 1922 (reinstated 1991, amended to 2014).
134 Article 9, Constitution of the Republic of Lithuania (1992, amended to 2006).
135 Article 148, Constitution of the Republic of Lithuania (1992, amended to 2006).
136 Jarukaitis (2010), p. 210.
137 Article 1(5), Law on Referendum, June 4, 2002. No. IX – 929 (as amended by 25 February 2003, No. IX – 1349).
138 Article 4, Law on Referendum, June 4, 2002. No. IX – 929 (as amended by 25 February 2003, No. IX – 1349).
139 Article 114, Constitution of Luxembourg (1868, as amended to 1948).
140 Article 49bis, the Constitution of Luxembourg (1868, as amended in 1956).
141 Loi du 19 décembre 2003 portant révision de l'article 114 de la Constitution, A116.
142 Loi du 19 décembre 2003 portant révision de l'article 114 de la Constitution. Article 114(3).
143 Dumont and Poirier (2006), p. 1189.
144 Gerkrath (2017).
145 Article 66(3), Constitution of Malta (1964, amended to 2014).
146 Tatham (2009), p. 266.
147 Article 65(1), Constitution of Malta (1964, amended to 2014).
148 Article 3(1), Referendum Act (1973).
149 Bonella (2003).
150 Article 14(1), Referendum Act (1973).
151 Article 13(2), Referendum Act (1973).
152 Besselink (2007), pp. 17–18.
153 (Temporary Referendum Act) Tijdelijke referendumwet, 16 July 2001.
154 Besselink (2007), p. 19.
155 (Consultative Referendum on the European Constitution Act) Wet raadplegend referendum Europese Grondwet, 27 January 2005.
156 See Nijeboer (2005).
157 Advisory Referendum Act (Wet raadgevend referendum), 1 July 2015.
158 The 2016 referendum on the Dutch Ukraine–European Union Association Agreement vote was the first use of this law (see Chapter 10 for more details). As this book went to print, the Dutch government was seeking to

168   THE TRANSFORMATION OF EU TREATY MAKING

revoke this law, with the lower house having voted for its repeal on 22 February 2018 (see Pieters 2018).

159 Article 90(3), Constitution of the Republic of Poland (1997, amended to 2009).

160 Article 125(2), Constitution of the Republic of Poland (1997, amended to 2009).

161 Article 125, Constitution of the Republic of Poland (1997, amended to 2009).

162 Article 235(6), Constitution of the Republic of Poland (1997, amended to 2009).

163 Frydrych (2004).

164 Article 118(2) Constitution of the Portuguese Republic (1976).

165 Article 118(3), Constitution of the Portuguese Republic (1976).

166 Article 164j, Constitution of the Portuguese Republic (1976).

167 Rodrigues (2013), p. 299.

168 Article 115(5), Portuguese Constitution (4th revision, 1997).

169 Portuguese Constitutional Court, Decision 531/98. A summary of the decision in English is available at: www.tribunalconstitucional.pt/tc/en/acordaos/19980531s.html.

170 Portuguese Constitutional Court, Decision 704/2004. A summary of the decision in English is available at: www.tribunalconstitucional.pt/tc/en/acordaos/20040704s.html. See generally Jerónimo (2003), p. 186.

171 Article 295, 7th Portuguese Constitution (7th revision, 2005).

172 Article 115(2) and (3), Portuguese Constitution (7th revision, 2005). There are exceptions to the scope of a referendum as well as the EU exception as to clarity.

173 Article 115(8) and (10).

174 Articles 11(3) and 147(3), Constitution of Romania (1991, amended to 2003).

175 Article 151(3), Constitution of Romania (1991, amended to 2003).

176 The 2003 constitutional amendment is the sole occasion on which Romania's constitution has been successfully amended since 1991.

177 Article 90, Constitution of Romania (1991, amended to 2003).

178 Articles 7(1) and 92(1), Constitution of the Slovak Republic (1992, amended to 2014).

179 See Articles 7 and 84, Constitution of the Slovak Republic (1992, amended to 2014).

180 Article 93(1), Constitution of the Slovak Republic (1992, amended to 2017).

181 Article 95, Constitution of the Slovak Republic (1992, amended to 2017).

182 Article 98, Constitution of the Slovak Republic (1992, amended to 2017).

183 Article 99, Constitution of the Slovak Republic (1992, amended to 2017).

184 Article 90, Constitution of the Republic of Slovenia (1991).

185 Article 90, Constitution of the Republic of Slovenia (1991, amended to 2013)

186 Article 3a, Constitution of the Republic of Slovenia (1991, amended to 2013)

187 Article 90(2); Kavčič (2014), p. 75.

188 Article 95(1), Spanish Constitution of 1978 (as amended to 2011).

189 Article 168 (1), Spanish Constitution of 1978 (as amended to 2011).

190 Article 167 (3), Spanish Constitution of 1978 (as amended to 2011).

191 Article 92, Spanish Constitution of 1978 (as amended up to 2011).

192 See Gooch (1986).

193 Constitutional Court of Spain, Declaración, DTC 1/2004, de 13 de diciembre).

194 Section 87, para. 3, Austria Constitution of 1920 (reinstated in 1945 and amended in 2013).

195 Chapter 8, Article 4 Instrument of Government (1974, amended to 2015). See Ruin (1996); Bernitz (2001), p. 912.

196 Ruin (1996), p. 177.

197 Widfeldt (2004).

198 Chapter 8, Article 15 (1974, amended to 2015).

199 Chapter 8, Articles 15 and 16 (1974, amended to 2015); Besselink et al. (2014), p. 259.

200 Chapter 8, Article 15 (1974, amended to 2015).

201 Bernitz (2001), p. 920.

202 Bogdanor (2009), chapter 7.

203 On the rules around referendum, see Part VII of the Political Parties, Elections and Referendums Act 2000; for an analysis of the UK and EU constitutional relationship, see generally UK Supreme Court, *R(Miller)* v. *Secretary of State* [2017] UKSC 5, p. 37.

204 UK Supreme Court, *R(Miller)* v. *Secretary of State* [2017] UKSC 5, p. 11.

205 Blair (2003).

206 Smith (2004).

207 Cowley and Stuart (2010), p. 138.

208 Evans (2008).

209 Conservative Party (2010), p. 113.

210 Sections 2(2) and 3(2), European Union Act (2011).

211 Sections 2(1b) and 3(1b), European Union Act (2011).

212 Sections 2(3) and 3(3), European Union Act (2011).

213 Section 3(4), European Union Act (2011).

214 Sections 2(1a) and 3(1a), European Union Act (2011).

215 European Union (Approval of Treaty Amendment Decision) Act (2012).

216 European Union (Croatian Accession and Irish Protocol) Act 2013.

217 European Union (Act), Section 4(4).

6 The Rise of Higher Courts in EU Treaty Making

Constitutional review is defined by David Robertson as 'a process by which one institution, commonly called a constitutional court, has the constitutional authority to decide whether statutes or other decrees created by the rule-making institutions identified by the constitution are valid given the terms of the constitution'.[1] Constitutional review is now a global phenomenon.[2] According to Ginsburg and Versteeg, as of 2011, 83 per cent of the world's constitutions permit some form of constitutional review compared with 38 per cent in 1951,[3] reflecting the increased judicalisation of politics worldwide.[4] The United States was among the first countries to permit constitutional review, this practice originating not from the language of the US constitution itself but from its interpretation by the US Supreme Court in *Marbury v. Madison*.[5] The American phenomenon whereby any court at any time in any case brought by any litigant may be called on to find a law unconstitutional is different from the much more constrained European model where constitutional review is usually in designated constitutional courts under particular conditions.[6]

Fewer countries give explicit authority to courts to decide on the constitutionality of treaties, although Mario Mendez includes more than thirty-two European, African and Latin American states that have such provisions.[7] One such case is Russia, where a federal Law on International Treaties allows the Constitutional Court, on a request from the President, the State Duma and the Supreme Court, among others, to review treaties that have not yet entered into force.[8] This law does not have the status of a constitution unlike the position in Afghanistan, where the government or courts can request the Supreme Court to examine international treaties or international covenants for their compliance with the constitution.[9] Many more countries allow prior

170

constitutional review of treaties either under general provisions on constitutional review or under prevailing constitutional norms. In Japan, for example, the Supreme Court has ruled that certain categories of international treaties can be reviewed even though no specific mention is made of such reviews in the constitution.[10]

The involvement of national courts in EU treaty making was once controversial but is now commonplace. Nowhere is this change more discernible than in Germany. In 1952, West Germany's Federal Constitutional Court was drawn into a dispute over the European Defence Community Treaty. Although the eventual failure of this treaty meant that its compatibility with the Basic Law was not ultimately reviewed, the incident was widely seen as an attempt to politicise the fledgling Federal Constitutional Court. Such was the sense of constitutional crisis over this affair that one contemporary commentator compared it to the Reich Constitutional Court's ruling on the Prussian coup of 1932.[11] And yet by the time it came to the Lisbon Treaty, the Federal Constitutional Court's involvement was widely accepted.[12] Germany is not unique in this respect, the Lisbon Treaty having faced judicial challenges in seven other member states: Austria, Belgium, the Czech Republic, France, Latvia, Poland and Slovenia.[13]

This chapter takes a closer look at the rise of courts at the consent stage of EU treaty making, producing the third of our ratification scales. Its focus is not on the substance of specific challenges against particular treaties but on the more general question of how constitutional reviews have become a feature of EU treaty making. The first section explores different ways of thinking about courts' involvement in treaty making before outlining the approach followed in this volume. This is followed by a detailed examination of changing constitutional rules and norms concerning the constitutional review of treaties in EU member states over the period 1951–2016.

Classifying the Role of Higher Courts

There is a rich recent literature in comparative law on constitutional review.[14] Ginsburg and Versteeg's work is the most empirically ambitious. The authors present a dataset of constitutional review for 204 countries spanning the period 1781–2011, which records all cases 'in which a constitution mandates a local court or court-like body to set aside or strike legislation for incompatibility with the national constitution'.[15] In a related study, Verdier and Versteeg identify those countries that provide for prior constitutional review of international treaties from a set of ninety states between 1815 and 2013.[16] Their findings show that the number of countries requiring such reviews has increased sharply since the early twentieth century, but they do not distinguish between the stringency of such reviews over time or across countries.

Among legal scholars working specifically on the EU, Maartje de Visser[17] and Monica Claes[18] offer the most comprehensive studies of constitutional review to date. De Visser presents in-depth case studies of constitutional review in Belgium, the Czech Republic, Finland, France, Germany, Hungary, Italy, the Netherlands, Poland, Spain and the United Kingdom, covering both the institutional design of higher courts in these countries and key characteristics of adjudication. These characteristics include the choice between centralisation and decentralisation in constitutional review, a priori and a posteriori review and concrete versus abstract review. This book offers a wealth of detail on comparative approaches to constitutional review, with its primary focus on understanding similarities and differences between national approaches. Claes in her path-breaking study analyses the influence of national courts on treaty making through case studies of constitutional review of EU treaties in Belgium Denmark, France, Germany, Ireland, Italy, the Netherlands, Spain and the United Kingdom. Courts' influence over treaty making, she notes, tends to be considerably greater under prior reviews than a posteriori ones, echoing Shapiro and Stone-Sweet's notion of the third chamber and highlighting the importance of when review occurs and on what basis.[19]

Political scientists have been more hesitant about analysing the role of courts in EU treaty making. In their study of the Maastricht Treaty, Hug and König, for example, observe that 'ratification processes were challenged in courts', but they say little about the nature of such challenges or explicitly incorporate them into their measure of ratification constraints.[20] The same is true of Beth Simmons's index of ratification constraints, although her hazard model of treaty ratification does control for the existence of a common law system. The rationale for doing so is that 'political resistance from the Bar or the Bench' against treaties is likely to be greater in common law systems, which rely on an organic, bottom-up development of law that sits uneasily with the imposition of top-down legal obligations through treaties.[21] Although Simmons presents evidence in support of this claim, her operationalisation of courts' roles sheds limited light on the nature of their involvement in treaty making.

The wider political science literature is of limited help here. Lijphart features judicial review among his patterns of democracy, but his taxonomy is not specifically concerned with the constitutional review of treaties.[22] Countries are distinguished in his approach between those that do not allow judicial review and those in which judicial reviews are weak, medium-strength or strong. Lijphart offers no criteria for measuring weakness and strength, relying instead on general references to the scholarly literature on judicial review. Within the EU literature, Closa's account of the role played by national courts in the EU is the most complete.[23] He classifies the role of courts along three dimensions: jurisdiction, timing and litigant. The first (jurisdiction) further distinguishes between ordinary jurisdiction in which courts can adjudicate on the constitutionality of laws, specialised jurisdiction, in which this role lies with a constitutional court, and ad hoc cases, where some other body, as in a parliamentary committee or Council of State, has this role. The second dimension (timing) distinguishes between instances in which courts adjudicate on the constitutionality of treaties before they are approved by parliament (prior review) or after (posteriori review). The third dimension (litigant) considers whether court challenges of treaties are triggered by legislatures, executives, presidents or citizens. Examining all treaty challenges before national courts from the European Coal and Steel Community Treaty to the Lisbon Treaty along three dimensions, Closa produces a detailed overview of court roles in EU treaty making. Pablo José Castillo Ortiz complements this study with the first book-length treatment of the judicial politics of EU treaty making.[24] Following Closa he examines all apex court cases challenging the ratification of EU treaties, exploring the circumstances that explain the courts' decisions (of which there were seventeen) on the merits. He uses legal doctrinal analysis (comparative constitutional law and EU law) as well as quantitative analysis and qualitative comparative analysis.

Our courts ratification scale assumes that constitutional review gives courts a more prominent role in treaty making compared with a situation in which no review is permissible, and that this prominence increases as standing encompasses a wider range of actors (Table 6.1). It assigns a score of 1 where prior constitutional review of courts is prohibited under prevailing constitutional norms. A score of 2 applies when the government or head of state can trigger a constitutional review, and a score of 3 is assigned when this power rests with the legislature or a body appointed by it. The highest score of 4 is reserved for instances in which citizens have standing to challenge the constitutionality of treaties prior to their ratification.

Table 6.1 Courts scale

No scope for ex-ante constitutional review	1
Executive can trigger ex-ante constitutional review	2
Parliament can trigger ex-ante constitutional review	3
Citizens can trigger ex-ante constitutional review	4

Evidently, this classification relies on a simplifying set of assumptions about the role played by national courts in EU treaty making. As in previous chapters we are interested in how constitutional rules and norms grant actors a greater or lesser role in EU treaty making. First, we assume that the level of a court does not have a bearing on this issue because constitutional courts, other higher courts and ad hoc constitutional committees can all have an impact on ratification, and if the treaty is somehow challenged in a lower court, there is likely to be an appeal to a higher court if the case has merit. Second, we allow for the possibility that advisory reviews can have a meaningful impact on treaty ratification when the constitutional norm (rather than just the rule) is that such advice is followed.[25] Third, we focus exclusively on prior constitutional reviews. Ex-post reviews are rare and, insofar as they concern the constitutionality of a treaty that has already been ratified, go beyond the scope of treaty making to that of treaty breaking.[26] Fourth, we treat the expansion of locus standi as increasing courts' role in the process of treaty making. The least inclusive form of review – to state the obvious – occurs where no actor can challenge the constitutionality of a treaty prior to its ratification. Challenges led by members of the legislature are more inclusive than those initiated by the executive. Treaties are negotiated in most cases by the executive branch and so a constitutional challenge launched by the executive branch is less likely to impede the ratification of the treaty.[27] A citizen-led challenge is the most inclusive of all since it maximises opportunities for individuals from outside the political sphere to impede the ratification of a treaty, although politicians, qua citizens, can opt to challenge the treaties via the courts.[28] We note the distinction between mandatory review where in effect constitutional review becomes part of the consent stage of treaty making and the uncertainty of loose standing rules whereby any citizen can challenge the treaty before the courts – allowing for issues that may not be predicted during negotiation to be constitutionally challenged.

This understanding of constitutional review treats courts as vehicles through which other actors seek to realise particular political (recast as legal) objectives. Whether courts respond to such challenges in ways that impede or expedite EU treaty making is a different question, which we return to in Chapter 8.[29]

Changing Rules and Norms in the EU-28

This section compares the evolution of courts' roles in EU treaty making in the EU-28 on the basis of the criteria outlined in the previous section. Appendix 6.1 graphs these scores from the year the member state joined the EU (or the European Communities) to 2016.

Austria

In Austria, the Administrative Supreme Court (*Verwaltungsgerichtshof*), the Supreme Court (*Oberster Gerichtshof*), an Administrative Court and any competent court can ask the Constitutional Court (*Verfassungsgerichtshof*) to decide on whether a federal law is unconstitutional.[30] The federal or Länder government(s) (in cooperation with the federal or Länder parliament(s)) can also ask the Constitutional Court for review. The Constitutional Court is authorised through this process to decide whether treaties are contrary to law,[31] and a posteriori review can be requested by individuals in such cases providing they can show a prima facie violation of constitutional law in relation to their personal rights that affect the plaintiff directly.[32] These provisions do not permit prior challenges of EU treaties, an interpretation that the Constitutional Court had previously upheld through its refusal to hear challenges against the European Constitution and Lisbon Treaty.[33] Thus, under prevailing constitutional rules and norms, prior constitutional review of EU treaties is not possible.

Belgium

Belgium is a state in which prior challenges of EU treaties by the executive, legislature or citizen are not permissible. Under Belgium's Constitution of 1831, acts and decisions by the executive were subject to judicial review but acts of parliament were not.[34] Since the approval of international agreements was subject to parliamentary approval under this constitution (see Chapter 4), the possibility of constitutional review

176   THE TRANSFORMATION OF EU TREATY MAKING

on treaties by the Court of Cassation was ruled out. In *Le Ski* (1971), the Court of Cassation ruled that it (and all other Belgian courts) had the power to review Belgian legislation for its compatibility with self-executing treaties, including Community treaties. The judgment said nothing about the review of the constitutionality of treaties per se.[35]

In 1983, a Court of Arbitration (*Cour d'arbitrage*) was created with the authority to review the constitutionality of, and to annul, parliamentary assents.[36] Whether this extended to acts of parliament concerning the approval of Community treaties was not clear at first, but in *Commune de Lanaken* (1991), the Court declared its authority to review the constitutionality of international agreements, the agreement in question concerning an international convention on taxation. Abstract constitutional review by the Court of Arbitration is indirect in that it is permissible only after an act has been approved and published in the *Moniteur belge/Belgisch Staatsblad*, thus ruling out the possibility of prior constitutional review of EU treaties.[37]

Under an organic law concerning the Constitutional Court (as the Court of Arbitration was renamed in 2007), actions for annulment against a government statute, decree or rule can be initiated by Belgium's Council of Ministers, by the government of a community or region, by the presidents of the legislative assemblies if instructed to do so by two-thirds of their members or 'by any natural or legal person with a justifiable interest'.[38] Thus the executive and legislative branches (subject to a two-thirds vote) can challenge the constitutionality of an EU treaty, as occurred in 1992 when the Council of State was asked for an advisory opinion on the Maastricht Treaty. For persons who are natural (individuals) or legal (companies), it is necessary to show the additional requirement of justifiable interest. In the *European School Case* (1994), parents sending their children to the European School challenged the compatibility of the school's legal statutes, which were set out in an international convention, with Belgium's constitution.[39] The parents lost but the Court of Arbitration accepted their standing. In 1994, the Court refused to consider a challenge by two individuals (a citizen and a local councilor) against the Maastricht Treaty's provisions regarding the rights of EU citizens to vote and stand in municipal elections, because of a lack of demonstrable justifiable interest specific to the plaintiffs – they still had the right to vote even if the franchise was being extended.[40] It had taken almost a year for the act of assent to appear in the *Moniteur belge/ Belgisch Staatsblad*, and by the time the case was brought, the treaty had entered into force. The court thus managed to avoid a difficult situation where the treaty would be in force but unconstitutional domestically.[41]

Three a posteriori challenges against the Lisbon Treaty were launched in Belgium. The third was ruled as inadmissible because the plaintiffs were in breach of the deadline for launching such a challenge,[42] but the Court allowed the first two, confirming that individuals could, in principle, have locus standi before the Constitutional Court in cases concerning the ratification of EU treaties.[43]

Belgium's Council of State (*Conseil d'État*) also features in EU treaty making. The government is required to ask this body for an opinion on all bills, including those that concern the approval of EU treaties, but it is neither required nor in many cases inclined to heed this advice.[44] In 1992, the Belgian government asked the Council of State to issue an advisory opinion on the constitutionality of the Maastricht Treaty prior to ratification. Although the Council advised that an amendment to Belgium's constitution was required prior to ratification, the government still proceeded with ratification and amended the constitution only after the treaty had been ratified.[45]

Bulgaria

Under Bulgaria's constitution, treaties that require a constitutional amendment cannot be ratified without the passage of such an amendment.[46] The state's Constitutional Court (the Конституционен съд на Република България) is responsible for ruling on the compatibility between international treaties and the constitution prior to the ratification of the former.[47] The President, the Council of Ministers, the Supreme Court of Cassation, the Supreme Administrative Court, the Prosecutor General and one-fifth of all members of the National Assembly can initiate such a review,[48] but citizens have no standing before the Constitutional Court.[49] At the time of writing, an EU treaty amendment had not faced a challenge before the Constitutional Court by one of these parties.

Croatia

Croatia's Constitutional Court (*Ustavni sud*) is empowered to decide on the conformity of laws with the constitution[50] and to repeal such laws that it finds to be unconstitutional.[51] However, no explicit mention is made in the constitution of the Court's power to decide on the compatibility of treaties with the constitution. Whether this prohibits the prior constitutional review of treaties is a matter of debate among legal scholars,[52] but the Court, in its case law, has ruled out such a role for

178   THE TRANSFORMATION OF EU TREATY MAKING

itself after adoption of the treaty.[53] Prior review is also not envisaged by the constitution. In U-I-672/2001, the Court rejected a challenge by a citizen against a treaty between Croatia and Bosnia and Herzegovina, and similarly in a later case concerning treaties with the Holy See it ruled that it was not competent to review validity of a ratified international treaty with the constitution.[54] Where citizens have sought to challenge international agreements by looking to the constitutionality of the implementing statutes, the Constitutional Court has decided it does have limited jurisdiction to review for formal deficiencies in the law only.[55] The use of a referendum to approve accession to the EU is seen as copper-fastening the constitutionality of the process surrounding accession.[56] On this basis, we judge that prior constitutional reviews of treaties are not possible in Croatia.

Cyprus

The Cypriot constitution provides for the possibility of the prior constitutional review of laws of the House of Representatives. Specifically, the President and Vice President of the Republic are empowered to ask the Supreme Court (*Ανώτατο Δικαστήριο*) to give its opinion on whether any law is repugnant to or inconsistent with the Constitution, prior to the promulgation of this law.[57] This opens the door to a prior constitutional review of treaties in cases where the ratification of a treaty requires approval by a law made by the House of Representatives.[58] A constitutional amendment that took effect in 2006 extended the scope for prior constitutional review to laws that may be repugnant to or inconsistent with EU law, but it eliminated the grounds for such an opinion in relation to treaties by recognising EU law as having supremacy over the constitution. According to this amendment, no provision in the constitution can annul laws, acts or measures taken by the Republic by reason of its obligations as an EU member state or directives or other binding measures of a legislative character taken by the EU.[59] In consequence, executive-led prior constitutional reviews of EU treaties were permissible prior to 2006, but there was no scope for constitutional review of any sort thereafter.

Czech Republic

Under the Czech constitution, the state's Constitutional Court (*Ústavní soud*) has jurisdiction to decide on a treaty's conformity with the constitutional order prior to the ratification of the agreement.[60] Where an authorised petition challenges the constitutionality of a treaty, the treaty may not be ratified prior to the Constitutional Court giving judgment.[61] This authorisation is given by the Constitutional Court Act (1993), which allows one of the chambers of the Parliament, at least 41 deputies, at least 17 senators (hence giving the opposition standing) and the President of the Republic to challenge the constitutionality of treaties before the Constitutional Court.[62] Should the Constitutional Court declare that a treaty is not in conformity with the constitution, that declaration would be an obstacle to ratification until the treaty and constitution were brought into conformity with each other.[63] Citizens do not have standing prior to ratification but can challenge the constitutionality of a treaty provision or a decision based on such a treaty through judicial review after ratification in connection with its application in a concrete case.

The Lisbon Treaty was the first occasion on which the Constitutional Court considered prior constitutional challenges against a EU treaty amendment.[64] The challenges have to be in relation to specific parts of the treaty and not the treaty per se. This allows for multiple challenges provided each petitioner comes with new arguments about different parts of the treaty. The Treaty was challenged twice before the courts, unsuccessfully invoking the constitution.[65] The first case in relation to the Lisbon Treaty was brought before the Constitutional Court by the Senate (agreed by a simple majority) in April 2008.[66] The submission questioned six particular elements of the Treaty, including the existence of the 'exclusive competencies of the European Union' and the 'flexibility clause'.[67] The ratification process was suspended while the treaty was before the Court,[68] which held an oral hearing live on television.[69] The Court unanimously found that the specific articles of the Lisbon Treaty cited in the Senate's petition were compatible with the Czech constitutional order.[70] The second submission to the Constitutional Court was made by seventeen Czech senators and centred on concerns as to whether the Lisbon Treaty formed the legal basis for the creation of a European 'super-state'.[71] On 3 November 2009 the Constitutional Court rejected the complaints against the Lisbon Treaty,[72] leaving the Czech President (who had joined the proceedings and argued through counsel) to ratify the treaty just a few hours after this ruling was handed down.[73]

Denmark

Constitutional review is permitted in Denmark but does not extend to the prior review of EU treaties. In *Grønberg* v. *Prime Minister* a private citizen challenged the constitutionality of Denmark's accession to the European Communities without an amendment to the Danish Constitution.[74] The Eastern High Court (*Østre Landsret*) ruled that this challenge was inadmissible, as Denmark's Treaty of Accession to the European Communities had not yet been adopted by the Parliament,[75] a decision that was upheld by the Supreme Court (*Højesteret*) three months later.[76] This established the constitutional norm that prior constitutional review of Community treaties was not permissible. Consistent with the norm was the government's decision to ratify the Maastricht Treaty in spite of a challenge by twelve citizens, who sought to block ratification on the grounds that this treaty was unconstitutional.[77] The Supreme Court did not rule on this case until 1998, by which time this attempted prior challenge had become a posteriori.[78] Contrary to the case law from the 1972 accession the Supreme Court declared the case admissible. A similar situation occurred with the ratification of the Lisbon Treaty, where a group of citizens challenged the legality of the treaty and lost in a posteriori case.[79]

Estonia

The role of Estonia's Supreme Court (*Riigikohus*) in the prior constitutional review of EU treaties arises not from the constitution but the Constitutional Review Court Procedure Act (2002). This act empowers the Supreme Court to adjudicate requests to verify the conformity of international agreements with the Constitution[80] before or after this agreement has entered into force.[81] In so doing, the Supreme Court can declare an international agreement to be in conflict with the Constitution.[82] While a constitutional amendment does not automatically follow, it would be required before the treaty can be applied.[83] The President of the Republic, the Chancellor of Justice, local government councils and the Riigikogu may submit requests to the Supreme Court.[84] The Chancellor of Justice is appointed by the legislature, the Riigikogu,[85] on a proposal from the President[86] but his or her independence is guaranteed under the constitution.[87] Citizens have unsuccessfully sought a role in the constitutional review of treaties. Private citizens launched nine challenges against Estonia's accession treaty, but the Supreme Court rejected all on procedural grounds.[88] Thus, we classify Estonia as a case in which the President, Chancellor of Justice, local government or the parliament can (albeit indirectly) initiate a prior constitutional review of EU treaties.

Finland

In overhauling its constitution in 2000, Finland gave power to courts to review the constitutionality of legislation after its enactment for the first time.[89] However, the power of prior abstract review continues to rest not with the courts but with parliament's Constitutional Law Committee (*perustuslakivaliokunta*), a quasi-judicial body established in 1906 that de Visser describes as 'the authoritative interpreter and ultimate guardian of the constitution'.[90] The committee's role was codified in Finland's new constitution, which instructs the committee to 'issue statements on the constitutionality of legislative proposals and other matters brought for its consideration'.[91] Under the parliament's rules of procedure, parliament, the speaker's council[92] or a relevant parliamentary committee[93] can refer a bill or other matters to the Constitutional Law Committee. The government can also trigger a review before the Constitutional Law Committee by stipulating that the bill concerning the passage of the treaty should be considered by this committee.[94] Major treaty changes are routinely referred to the Constitutional Law Committee, which decides whether the treaty is significant or not in relation to sovereignty. Decisions of the Constitutional Law Committee are binding on parliament.[95] On this basis, we think of Finland as a country in which constitutional review initiated by the executive and legislature is possible throughout the period under investigation.

France

Constitutional review did not take hold in France until the 1958 constitution entered into force.[96] Article 54 of this constitution allows the President of the Republic, the Prime Minister or the President of either assembly to request the Constitutional Council to assess whether an international obligation is unconstitutional.[97] Individuals do not have standing before the Constitutional Council, but the constitution was revised in 1992 to allow sixty deputies or senators – in addition to the officeholders named above – to call for the prior constitutional review of treaties.[98] This provision was first invoked by the Prime Minister in relation to the Budgetary Treaty (1970).[99] Since 1992, it has been routinely invoked for major treaty revisions, typically by the French President but not exclusively so. Two requests for constitutional review were made in relation to the Maastricht Treaty, one a joint request by the French President and Prime Minister[100] and the other by sixty senators.[101] If the Constitutional Council finds that a treaty is unconstitutional,

182 THE TRANSFORMATION OF EU TREATY MAKING

the treaty can be ratified only after amending the constitution.[102] With the exception of Nice, all majority EU treaties since Maastricht were adjudged to require constitutional amendment by the Constitutional Council.[103] On this basis, France can – since 1958 – be counted as a country in which prior constitutional review is possible. In relation to standing, the 1992 reform was significant since de facto it became possible for the opposition to refer a treaty to the Constitutional Council, with the involvement of the legislature in this aspect of EU treaty making more conspicuous from this point.

Germany

The Basic Law does not explicitly provide for the constitutional review of treaties, but the German Federal Constitutional Court (*Bundesverfassungsgericht*) has introduced – and gradually extended the scope for – legal challenges against EU treaties. Under the constitution, the Federal Government, a Land government or one-quarter of the members of the Bundestag can challenge the constitutionality of a federal law.[104] In 1952, the Court got embroiled in the political brouhaha surrounding the ratification of the European Defence Community Treaty.[105] One-third of the members of the Bundestag sought an injunction against ratification of the treaty. This was rejected on the basis that it was premature – review was possible only once there was legislation.[106] The Court did accept a request from the President of the Federal Republic of Germany to issue an advisory opinion on the agreement, but the President later withdrew this request under pressure from the government.[107] A petition seeking a declaration that ratification was possible by simple majority was rejected on procedural grounds. Once the treaties were ratified, but before they had been signed by the President, the MPs reactivated their challenge. This time, the Bundesverfassungsgericht simply delayed its opinion, with the matter ultimately resolved by the French rejection of the treaty. In 1992, four German members of the European Parliament and a former Commission official, Manfred Brunner, petitioned the Court to declare the Maastricht Treaty, which had been approved by the German Parliament alongside changes to the Basic Law, as unconstitutional.[108] The Court dismissed the petitions by the MEPs but agreed that Brunner had standing in relation to a specific claim regarding his rights as a citizen under German law.[109] Building on this precedent, German citizens launched a constitutional challenge against the Lisbon Treaty. The Bundesverfassungsgericht not only recognised their standing; it also upheld elements of their petition.[110] While the Court did not block the ratification of the Lisbon Treaty, it ruled that the accompanying law was unconstitutional, forcing the parliament to amend this law before the President of the Federal Republic agreed to sign the treaty.

Greece

Greece's constitution does not explicitly provide for constitutional review. However, judges have traditionally interpreted their responsibilities under this constitution as requiring them to review the constitutionality of laws.[111] This obligation extends to all civil and administrative courts, including Greece's Council of State (*Συμβούλιο της Επικρατείας*) and, if so convened, the Supreme Special Court (*Ανώτατο Ειδικό Δικαστήριο*) – echoing the expansive constitutional review jurisdiction found in the United States.[112] However, by convention, constitutional reviews have been limited to domestic statutes rather than international treaties, so Greek courts play no role in EU treaty making.[113] The Greek Council of State can examine the constitutionality of regulatory decrees, but its power of prior review does not extend to treaties.[114] On this basis, Greece is a member state in which there is no possibility of a constitutional review of EU treaties.

Hungary

Hungary's Fundamental Law authorises the Constitutional Court (*Magyarország Alkotmánybírósága*) to examine the constitutionality of acts not yet published,[115] but it does not explicitly provide for the prior constitutional review of treaties. The Act on the Constitutional Court clarifies matters by allowing the President of the Republic and, if the treaty is to be approved via decree, the government, to request a constitutional review of a treaty prior to its ratification.[116] Prior to 2012, citizens had the right to initiate proceedings of the Constitutional Court in the cases specified by law.[117] This right was significantly restricted under the new constitution,[118] although this did not make a difference to the constitutional review of treaties. Under Act XXXII of 1989 on the Constitutional Court, the right to challenge the constitutionality of treaties prior to their entry into force was restricted to the parliament, its standing committees, fifty members of parliament, the President of the Republic and the government.[119] Parliament continues to have the right to initiate such a review under Hungarian law.[120]

Ireland

The President of Ireland can refer certain categories of bill passed – or deemed to have been passed – by both houses of the Oireachtas to the Supreme Court to decide whether the bill in question is repugnant to the constitution.[121] The bill cannot be signed into law by the President until the Supreme Court has ruled on its constitutionality,[122] and bills that the Court judges to be unconstitutional cannot be signed at all.[123] If the bill is found to be constitutional, then it cannot be constitutionally challenged in court ever again, so this particular procedure is rarely invoked given the consequence of constitutional immunity. The Rules of the Superior Courts set out the procedure for individuals applying for leave for judicial review before the High Court.[124] The High Court will not grant leave unless the applicant is deemed to have sufficient interest in the case.[125] In the 1960s, the courts adopted a more expansive view of what constituted sufficient interest in such cases,[126] but it was not until the 1980s that the possibility of judicial review against Community treaties was established. As with constitutional norms concerning referendums, the *Crotty* case was the turning point.

The initial challenge against the ratification of the Single European Act by Raymond Crotty was rejected by the High Court as an undue interference in the lawful legislative function of parliament.[127] But, in a second challenge, Crotty won a temporary injunction against the ratification of the treaty. Grappling with the question of Crotty's standing, Barrington J., a High Court judge, concluded that the plaintiff clearly has a locus standi because his contention is that what is being done involves an amendment to the Constitution which should be submitted to a referendum, and that he, as a citizen, has the right to be consulted in such a referendum and that his right is being infringed.[128]

However, the same court (and judge) later ruled against making this injunction permanent. In so doing, it concluded that Crotty had no standing because the ratification of the Single European Act neither deprived him of the possibility of challenging the constitutionality of the treaty nor raised issues that immediately affected or threatened him.[129] The plaintiff successfully appealed against this ruling before the Supreme Court.[130] 'The Court is satisfied', concluded Finlay CJ, 'that in the particular circumstances of this case where the impugned legislation, namely the Act of 1986, will if made operative affect every citizen, the plaintiff has a locus standi to challenge the Act notwithstanding his failure to prove the threat of any special injury or prejudice to him, as distinct from any other citizen, arising from the Act'.[131] This broad interpretation of standing immediately made constitutional review more accessible for every voter, removing a procedural impediment by allowing access to the courts. That said, in recent years plaintiffs in such cases have turned out to be members of parliament,[132] and there is some suggestion that parliamentarians may have greater standing to bring some claims than ordinary citizens.[133] Nonetheless, there is still scope for any citizen to challenge before the courts the constitutionality of a statute ratifying revision of the EU Treaties.

Italy

The Italian Constitutional Court (*Corte costituzionale*) is empowered under the constitution to consider 'disputes concerning the constitutionality of laws and acts with the force of law adopted by state or regions'.[134] This allows the court to decide on the constitutionality of acts giving assent to treaties but only after they have been ratified by parliament.[135] In *San Michele*, for example, the court considered claims that elements of the European Coal and Steel Community Treaty were contrary to the Italian constitution, thirteen years after this agreement had been ratified.[136] As such, Italy is a member state in which there is no scope for prior constitutional review of treaties by the executive, legislature or citizens.

Latvia

Latvia's Constitutional Court (*Satversmes tiesa*) is entrusted with the authority to decide on the conformity of international agreements with the constitution.[137] Where the Court finds such an agreement to be non-compliant, it falls to the government to take forward constitutional amendments before the agreement can be ratified.[138] The Constitutional Court Law identifies a long list of officeholders who can petition the Constitutional Court, including the government, President and Saeima.[139] This guarantees the right of the government and parliament to challenge the constitutionality of treaties. Under the Constitutional Court Law persons whose fundamental rights have been infringed upon also can petition the Constitutional Court.

In 2003, the Court considered five petitions from individuals concerning the manner in which Latvia's constitution had been amended in connection with accession to the EU. The Saeima was not authorised to amend the constitution, these individuals claimed, without also

186 THE TRANSFORMATION OF EU TREATY MAKING

amending Articles 1 and 2, amendments that require the holding of a referendum.[140] The Constitutional Court rejected these petitions as being inadmissible because the individuals had not demonstrated that their fundamental rights, as guaranteed under the constitution, had been infringed.[141] This left open the question of whether individuals could challenge the constitutionality of a treaty until Case 2008-35-01, which heard a challenge by thirteen individuals against the ratification of the Lisbon Treaty. In its ruling, the Court accepted the individuals' challenge as admissible on the grounds that the Lisbon Treaty had a bearing on their rights to participate in the work of the state, as guaranteed under Article 101 of the constitution.[142] Although the Constitutional Court ultimately ruled that the Lisbon Treaty complied with Latvia's constitution, it established for, the first time, the right of citizens to participate in constitutional challenges concerning EU treaty making.

Lithuania

Under Lithuania's constitution, it falls to the Constitutional Court (*Konstitucinis Teismas*) to decide on whether international treaties to which Lithuania is a party are in conflict with the constitution.[143] Where a conflict is found, the treaty in question cannot be applied.[144] There are two possible forms of review: ex ante constitutional review, where an opinion is sought before ratification (this was done once as regards the ratification of the ECHR in 1995),[145] and ex post review of the law, which ratified a treaty (this has not been invoked to date). The constitution recognises the right of the President of the Republic and the Seimas to request a constitutional review of treaties before the Constitutional Court but not the right of individuals.[146] This situation is confirmed by the Law on the Constitutional Court, which prohibits the Court from considering petitions to investigate the compliance of a legal act with the constitution from an institution or person who does not have the right to apply to the Constitutional Court.[147] The Seimas attempted to amend the constitution in summer 2017 to introduce a right of constitutional complaint for individuals, but the measure did not receive enough support so this constitutional rule remains.

Luxembourg

There is no provision in Luxembourg for the prior constitutional review of EU treaties. Judicial or administrative courts can refer questions by parties concerning the constitutionality of specific laws to the Luxembourg

Constitutional Court (*Cour constitutionnelle*) by means of a preliminary opinion procedure,[148] but this takes the form of a concrete a posteriori review. The Constitutional Court is, moreover, explicitly prohibited from reviewing the constitutionality of laws concerning the approval of treaties.[149] Luxembourg's Council of State (*Conseil d'État*), formerly the country's highest administrative court but now an advisory body to the parliament, the Chamber of Deputies, is required to give an opinion on all proposed laws.[150] As such, the Council of State offers an advisory opinion on the constitutionality of laws approving EU treaties as a matter of course. Such opinions are non-binding, although they carry significant weight with the Chamber of Deputies.[151] In no case has the Chamber gone against the advice of the Council of State, although in all but one case the latter has advised that no constitutional reform was required. The exception was the Maastricht Treaty. In its opinion on this treaty, the Council of State advised that the treaty's provisions on voting rights for EU citizens required a constitutional amendment, although not necessarily before the Treaty had been ratified.[152] The Chamber of Deputies duly ratified the treaty and amended the constitution within the deadline set by the Council of State.[153] Although this illustrates the importance given to Council of State opinions under prevailing constitutional norms, such opinions do not give the courts a role in treaty making, as we define it.[154]

Malta

Malta's higher courts are invisible in EU treaty making. The Constitutional Court, a superior court, has the jurisdiction under Malta's constitution to hear appeals over certain aspects of electoral law, the enforcement of protective provisions and questions referred to it by other courts.[155] The Constitutional Court is also empowered to hear appeals under the European Conventions Act, which incorporates the European Convention on Human Rights into Maltese Law.[156] This jurisdiction leaves little room to challenge the constitutionality of treaty ratification before the Constitutional Court. The scope for prior review is further curtailed by the fact that laws passed by parliament are presumed by courts to be constitutional until proved otherwise by a plaintiff.[157]

The Netherlands

The Netherlands' constitution prohibits the country's courts from reviewing the constitutionality of both acts of parliament and treaties.[158] This rules out the possibility of both prior and a posteriori review of EU

188 THE TRANSFORMATION OF EU TREATY MAKING

treaties in the Netherlands. Under the constitution, the Council of State (*Raad van State*) must be consulted on proposals for the approval of treaties by the legislature, the States General, unless otherwise provided for by an act of parliament.[159] In offering an opinion, the Council of State can raise fundamental objections to a government bill and advise withdrawal. The government typically respects such opinions but is not obliged to do so and has on occasion ignored them. On this basis, and insofar as the Council of State when performing this advisory function is not a court to which the government, parliament or citizens can appeal, we classify the Netherlands as a country in which there is no significant form of constitutional review on the ratification of treaties.[160]

Poland

According to Poland's constitution, the President of the Republic may refer a treaty to the Constitutional Tribunal (*Trybunał Konstytucyjny*) before ratification with a request to adjudicate upon its conformity with the constitution.[161] Additionally, once ratified, the Constitutional Tribunal still has jurisdiction to adjudicate regarding the conformity to the constitution of international agreements and the statutes through which they are ratified.[162] Thus, both prior and a posteriori review of international treaties is possible in Poland. Prior review (i.e. before ratification) is possible only at the request of the President.[163] A posteriori review can be triggered by a range of actors, including the President of the Republic, the Marshals of the Sejm and Senate, the Prime Minister, fifty deputies and thirty senators.[164] The Treaty of Accession,[165] the Lisbon Treaty[166] and the Article 136 TFEU amendment[167] all faced prior reviews triggered by parliamentarians. In no case did Poland's Constitutional Tribunal hold these agreements to be unconstitutional.

Portugal

In Portugal, the Constitutional Court (*Tribunal Constitucional*) alone has the authority to decide on the constitutionality of a EU treaty prior to the ratification of this agreement. In the event of a referendum on such a treaty, the Constitutional Court is required to verify in advance the constitutionality of such a vote, as occurred when it ruled against the wording of a vote on the Amsterdam Treaty.[168] Citizens do not have standing before the Constitutional Court in this procedure. Under Portugal's constitution, the President of the Republic can ask the Constitutional Court 'to undertake a prior review of the constitutionality of the norms contained in laws and executive laws and international conventions'.[169] The President is also expressly authorised to request the Constitutional Court to consider the 'constitutionality of any norm contained in an international treaty' before he or she signs it.[170] As a result, only the President of the Republic can initiate a constitutional review when it comes to the approval of EU treaties in Portugal.

Romania

Romania's Constitutional Court (*Curtea Constituțională*) has the constitutional authority to pronounce on the constitutionality of treaties.[171] If a treaty is unconstitutional, a constitutional amendment is required before it can become law.[172] Conversely, if the Court finds a treaty to be constitutional, the constitutionality of this treaty cannot be challenged.[173] It falls to parliament to request a constitutional review of treaties at the behest of the President of the Chamber of Deputies, the President of the Senate, a parliamentary group or fifty deputies or twenty-five senators.[174] At the time of writing, there had been no constitutional challenges against a European amendment.

Slovak Republic

Slovakia's Constitutional Court (*Ústavný súd*) has the authority to decide on the conformity of treaties with the constitution and constitutional law, where such treaties require parliamentary approval.[175] Where the Constitutional Court decides that a treaty is not in conformity with the constitution, the treaty cannot be ratified.[176] The President or the government is authorised to request such a review,[177] but this did not stop a group of citizens affiliated to a conservative institute from challenging the proposed ratification of the European Constitution without recourse to a referendum before the Slovak Constitutional Court in 2005.[178] Their case hinged on the claim that their constitutional rights of participation in the administration of public affairs directly or by freely elected representatives[179] would be violated if a referendum was not held as the new European Constitution would create a union of states sufficiently different from the existing EU to require a referendum under Article 7(1) of the Slovak constitution. The Constitutional Court ultimately concluded that no referendum was required,[180] but in deciding to hear the case in July 2005 it confirmed the right of citizens to challenge the

190 THE TRANSFORMATION OF EU TREATY MAKING

constitutionality of treaties and halted the ratification of the treaty in the process.[181] On this basis, we consider citizen-led challenges against the ratification of EU treaties to be possible from 2005 onwards, where such treaties are viewed as infringing Article 7 of the constitution.

Slovenia

Slovenia's constitution explicitly allows for the prior constitutional reviews of treaties. Among the powers of the Constitutional Court (*Ustavno sodišče*) established by the constitution is the authority to decide on the conformity of treaties with the constitution.[182] It falls to the President of the Republic, the government or one-third of deputies of the National Assembly to initiate such a review in the process of ratifying a treaty.[183] The Constitutional Court exercised this power in relation to Slovenia's Accession Agreement, resulting in a constitutional amendment before the state could join the EU.[184] The Slovenian constitution also guarantees each citizen's right to appeal against the decisions of state authorities, where such decisions determine his or her rights, duties or legal instruments.[185] An individual can also lodge a constitutional complaint for violation of human rights and fundamental freedoms by statute (normally only after the exhaustion of other legal remedies).[186] A challenge to the Lisbon Treaty was brought to review the constitutionality of the law ratifying it by a group of citizens but was dismissed by the Constitutional Court due to a lack of standing as they could not show a direct interference with their legal interests.[187]

Spain

Spain's Constitutional Court (*Tribunal Constitucional de España*) is authorised under the constitution to review the constitutionality of international treaties after they have been signed but before they have been ratified.[188] This provision has been in place since the Constitution of 1978 was enacted even though the possibility of prior judicial review on other types of law was removed in 1985.[189] The government can request a prior review of treaties, as can either the Congress of Deputies or the Senate.[190] Should the Constitutional Court decide that a treaty is unconstitutional, then a constitutional amendment is required before the treaty can enter into force.[191] This provision has been used sparingly. Because of the special status of the EU in the Spanish constitution, an amending EU treaty could be unconstitutional only if it affects those provisions that impinge upon Spanish identity, viz. the fundamental social and democratic principles of the state, including fundamental rights.[192] Nonetheless, in 1992, the Spanish government petitioned the Constitutional Court to rule on the constitutionality of the Maastricht Treaty, with the Court deciding that the Spanish constitution must be amended to allow non-Spanish citizens to vote in municipal elections.[193] In 2004, the government asked the Constitutional Court to review the European Constitution. The court ruled in this case that no constitutional amendment was required.[194]

Sweden

In Sweden, any court can declare any provision to be in violation of fundamental law or another superior statute; however, where the provision has been approved by parliament or the government, it is set aside only if there has been a manifest error.[195] This implicitly excludes the prior review of EU treaties in the courts, this matter falling instead to the Council on Legislation (*Lagrådet*), the membership of which includes former judges from the Supreme Court and Supreme Administrative Court. The Council on Legislation's opinions are advisory, but they are, as a constitutional norm, adhered to by government. The government is not formally required to submit draft bills giving assent to treaties to the Council, but it typically does so for major treaties.[196] On this basis, we see scope for a prior constitutional review of EU treaties in Sweden, which can be activated by either the government or parliament under constitutional norms that have remained unchanged since the country joined the EU.

United Kingdom

When it comes to treaty making, the dominance of the executive and legislature (see Chapters 4 and 5) leaves little obvious room for the courts. But this did not stop citizens from seeking judicial review to challenge the ratification of EU treaties. The first legal challenge was before the United Kingdom had joined the EEC in 1973. In *Blackburn* v. *the Attorney General* (1971), a former member of parliament turned political campaigner argued that it was unlawful for the government to sign the Treaty of Rome on the grounds that this would entail an irrevocable loss of sovereignty. The case was dismissed on appeal with unusually short judgments. Stamp LJ offered a conservative view of what Courts could and should do in this domain. 'The Crown enters into treaties; Parliament enacts laws; and it is the duty of this Court in proper cases to interpret those laws where made', he noted, 'but it is no part of this Court's function or duty to make declarations in general terms regarding the powers of Parliament'.[197] Blackburn's challenge was, in other words, inadmissible.

Unequivocal though this judgment appeared to be, it was not the end of the matter. In 1993, William Rees Mogg, a crossbencher in the House of Lords who was opposed to European integration, applied for a judicial review against the ratification of the Maastricht Treaty.[198] Rees Mogg's case was that the Maastricht Treaty and specifically the Social Protocol had not lawfully been ratified by parliament. He also challenged the legality of Title V of the Maastricht Treaty as curtailing the government's prerogative powers in relation to foreign policy without changes to UK legislation, making explicit reference to the Irish case, *Crotty*.[199] Lloyd LJ ruled that parliamentary approval of the Maastricht Treaty encompassed the Social Protocol, that *Crotty* 'turned solely on the provisions of the Irish constitution' and that the Court had no jurisdiction to rule over the legality of Title V of the Maastricht Treaty precisely because it was an intergovernmental agreement that had not yet been ratified in UK law.[200] Crucially, however, Lloyd LJ ruled that Rees Mogg's standing was not in dispute, thus establishing the principle that individuals with 'sincere concern for constitutional issues' were permitted to seek a judicial review in such cases.[201]

A more ambitious challenge against treaty ratification by organised opponents of the EU is the case of *Wheeler* v. *The Prime Minister*.[202] Stuart Wheeler, an entrepreneur and later prominent member of the UK Independence Party, argued that the government acted unlawfully by promising a referendum on the European Constitution but failing to do so on the Lisbon Treaty. Richards LJ dismissed the case, inter alia, on the grounds that the government's commitment to hold a referendum on the European Constitution in no way implied an advance commitment to do likewise for future treaties. Even if such a promise had been made, he added, it was for parliament to hold the government to such a promise rather than the courts given the inherently political character of such a decision. In *Miller* the UK Supreme Court held that the United Kingdom could give notice to withdraw from the EU only on foot of statute, the European Union Referendum Act 2015 having been silent as to what was to happen if the referendum result was a vote to leave the EU.[203] Standing was addressed briefly in the Divisional Court with the court suggesting that virtually everyone in the United Kingdom and every British citizen would have standing, as withdrawal from the EU would affect their rights.[204] Given the breadth of standing and the controversy surrounding Brexit, further litigation is probable, but as it is not concerned

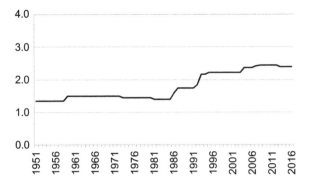

Figure 6.1 Courts scale (average, by member state, 1951–2016).

with EU treaty revision – the majority judgment in the Supreme Court noted that withdrawal is fundamentally different from variation in EU law arising out of treaty or legislative change[205] – it does not come within our ratification scale.

Conclusion

This chapter has explored the changing role of the courts in EU treaty making over the period 1951–2016. Our classification focuses on the question of standing, with the role of the courts increasing as the range of actors who can challenge the prior constitutionality of treaties expands from the executive branch to encompass a role for parliamentarians and ultimately citizens. Viewed in these terms, courts have assumed an altogether more prominent role in EU treaty making since the creation of the European Coal and Steel Community. Figure 6.1 shows the average courts scale across EU member states per year over this period. It increases from 1.3 in 1951 to 2.4 by 2016, suggesting that the 'average' EU member state has gone from a situation in which none can challenge the constitutionality of treaties to one in which legislatures can.

During the passage of the Treaty of Paris, prior constitutional review of treaties was not possible in five of the six founding member states. By 2016, there was scope for such a review in eighteen of the twenty-eight member states. In eleven of these jurisdictions, constitutional review could be triggered by parliaments. In five, citizens' standing had been established. Shifting rules and norms were observed in sixteen member states, with all but two of these cases resulting in a more prominent role for courts in EU treaty making.

Appendix 6.1 Courts Scales

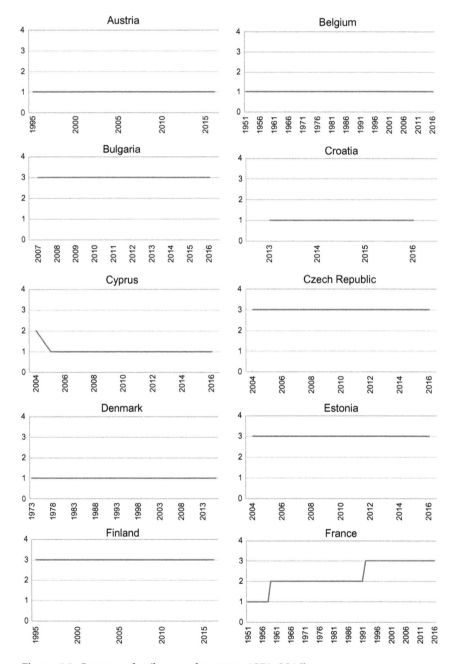

Figure 6.2 Courts scales (by member state, 1951–2016).

THE RISE OF HIGHER COURTS IN EU TREATY MAKING   195

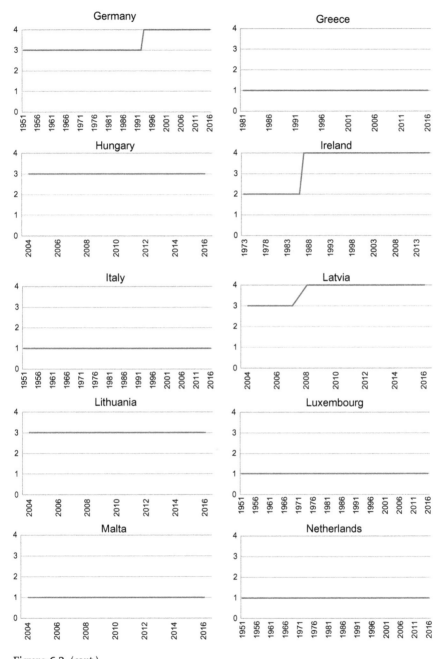

Figure 6.2 (cont.)

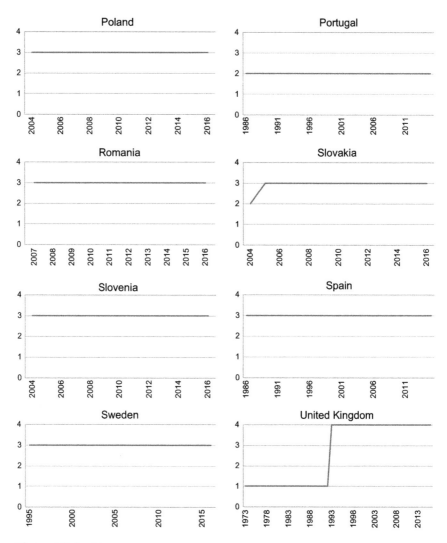

Figure 6.2 (cont.)

Notes

1 Robertson (2010), p. 5.
2 Shapiro and Stone Sweet (1994), p. 397.
3 Ginsburg and Versteeg (2014), p. 587.
4 Hirschl (2006), p. 721. See also Shapiro and Stone (1994).

5 US Supreme Court, *Marbury* v. *Madison*, 5 U.S. 137 (1803).

6 Shapiro and Stone Sweet (1994), p. 400.

7 Mendez (2017), p. 95n74.

8 Article 34, Russian Federal Law on International Treaties; Butler (1995), p. 1370.

9 Article 121, the Constitution of Afghanistan (2004); Schoiswohl (2006).

10 Goodman (2008), p. 247.

11 Loewenstein (1955), p. 806.

12 German Federal Constitutional Court, Judgment of the Second Senate of 30 June 2009 – 2 BvE 2/08.

13 Ortiz (2015), p. 8. See also Wendel (2011).

14 See also Mavčič (2013).

15 Ginsburg and Versteeg (2014), p. 600.

16 Verdier and Versteeg (2015).

17 De Visser (2013).

18 Claes (2006).

19 Claes (2006), p. 465.

20 Hug and König (2000), p. 94.

21 Simmons (2009a).

22 Lijphart (2012).

23 Closa (2013b).

24 Ortiz (2015).

25 On this general point, we agree with Closa (2013b), p. 103.

26 On treaty breaking, see Kuijper, Mathis and Morris-Sharma (2015).

27 On executives' motives for launching a constitutional treaty against a treaty that they negotiated, see Ortiz (2015), pp. 35–6.

28 Ortiz (2015), pp. 129–30.

29 For an in-depth study of this issue in relation to EU treaty making, see Ortiz (2015). On courts role in European constitutional politics more generally, see Shapiro and Stone (1994).

30 Article 140, Constitution of Austria, 1920 (reintroduced 1945, amended to 2013). The Court of Auditors can also apply to the constitutional court in certain cases; see Article 126a, Constitution of Austria.

31 Article 140a, Constitution of Austria, 1920 (reintroduced 1945, amended to 2013).

32 Constitutional Court (Austria), Case SV 2/08–3 et al. Treaty of Lisbon I, order of 30 September 2008; Austrian CC, Case SV 1/10–9 Treaty of Lisbon II, order of 12 June 2010. See Wendel (2011), p. 111.

33 Constitutional Court (Austria), Case G 62/05 Constitutional Treaty, decision of 18 June 2005. Constitutional Court (Austria), Case SV 2/08–3 et al. Treaty of Lisbon I, order of 30 September 2008 and Case SV 1/10–9 Treaty of Lisbon II, order of 12 June 2010. See Wendel (2011), p. 111.

34 Article 159, Constitution of Belgium (2012).

35 Court of Cassation (Belgium), *Etat belge* v. *Fromagerie Franco-Suisse 'Le Ski'*, 86 Journal des Tribunaux 461–71 (1971); *Michigan Law Review*, 72(1973–4), 118–28.

36 Bribosia (1997), p. 23.

37 Claes (2006), p. 218.

38 Section 1.3, Special Act of 6 January 1989 on the Constitutional Court of Belgium.

39 Court of Arbitration (Belgium), Judgment on Case 12/94, 3 February 1994.

40 Court of Arbitration (Belgium), Judgment on Case 76/94, 18 October 1994

41 Claes (2006) pp. 509–10.

42 Court of Arbitration (Belgium), Judgment on Case 156/09, 13 October 2009.

43 Court of Arbitration (Belgium), Judgment on Case 58/2009, 19-03-2009 and Judgment 125/2009, 16 July 2009.

44 de Visser (2013), p. 17.

45 See Arts (1993); Besselink et al. (2014), p. 201.

46 Article 85(4), Constitution of the Republic of Bulgaria (1991, amended to 2007).

47 Article 149(4), Constitution of the Republic of Bulgaria (1991, amended to 2007).

48 Article 150(1), Constitution of the Republic of Bulgaria (1991, amended to 2007).

49 Tanchev and Belov (2008).

50 Article 129, Constitution of the Republic of Croatia (1990, amended to 2010).

51 Article 131, Constitution of the Republic of Croatia (1990, amended to 2010).

52 See Božac and Carević (2015).

53 Constitutional Court of the Republic of Croatia, Case No. U-I-825/2001.

54 Constitutional Court of the Republic of Croatia, Case No. U-I-825/2001.

55 Constitutional Court of the Republic of Croatia, Cases U-I-1583/2000; U-I-559/2001 (decided only in 2010); U-I-2236/2017.

56 Čović (2012), p. 6.

57 Article 14(1), Constitution of the Republic of Cyprus (1960, amended to 2013). Although since the division of the island, there has been no Turkish Vice-President as required under the constitution.

58 Article 169(1), Constitution of the Republic of Cyprus (1960, amended to 2013).

59 Article 1 (a), Constitution of the Republic of Cyprus (1960, amended to 2013).

60 Article 97(2), Constitution of the Czech Republic (1993, amended to 2013).

61 Article 87 (2), Constitution of the Czech Republic (1993, amended to 2013); Tichý and Dumbrovský (2018).

62 §71a, Constitutional Court Act (1993).

63 Article 89 (3), Constitution of the Czech Republic (1993, amended to 2013).

64 Bříza (2009), p. 143.

65 Slosarcik, (2009); Tichý and Dumbrovský (2018), p. 12.

66 Decision of 26 November 2008, case No. Pl. ÚS 19/08 (published as No. 446/2008 Coll.)

67 Slosarcik (2009).

68 Miller (2009).

69 Bříza (2009), p. 144.

70 Constitutional Court of the Czech Republic, Case No. Pl ÚS 19/08 (published as No. 446/2008 Coll.). See Bříza (2009), p. 143.

71 Miller (2009), p. 8.

72 Constitutional Court of the Czech Republic, Case No. Pl US 29/09.

73 Miller (2009).

74 Supreme Court (Denmark), Decision, Case 321/1972, June 28, 1973. See Hinrichsen (1997), p. 572; Claes (2006), p. 490.

75 Eastern Provincial Court (Denmark), Judgment, 19 June 1972.

76 Supreme Court (Denmark), Judgment, Case I-195/1972, 27 September 1972.

77 Claes (2006), p. 490.

78 Supreme Court (Denmark), Case I-361/1997, Judgment of 6 April 1998, *Carlsen v. Rasmussen*.

79 Krunke (2014); Biering and Lehrer (2015); Olsen (2013).

80 §2, Constitutional Review Court Procedure Act (2002).

81 §6, Constitutional Review Court Procedure Act (2002).

82 §15(1), Constitutional Review Court Procedure Act (2002).

83 §15(3), Constitutional Review Court Procedure Act (2002).

84 §5–8, Constitutional Review Court Procedure Act (2002).

85 §65(6), Constitution of Estonia (1992, amended to 2015).

86 §78(11), Constitution of Estonia (1992, amended to 2015).

87 §139, Constitution of Estonia (1992, amended to 2015).

88 Albi (2007), pp. 51–2.

89 Section 106, Constitution of Finland (1999, amended to 2012).

90 de Visser (2013), p. 26.

91 Section 74, Constitution of Finland (1999, amended to 2012).

92 Section 32, Finnish Parliament's Rules of Procedure. The speaker, the deputy speakers and the committee chairpersons sit on this body.

93 Section 38, Finnish Parliament's Rules of Procedure.

94 de Visser (2013), p. 27.

95 Ojanen (2004), p. 205.

96 As Beardsley (1975: 189) notes, there were attempts to introduce constitutional review in France hitherto, but judges consistently refused to challenge the authority of lawmakers. See also Paris (2016).

97 Article 54, Constitution of 4 October 1958 (as amended in 2008).

98 Article 54, Constitution of 4 October 1958 (as amended in 1992).

99 French Constitutional Council, Décision no. 70–39 DC of 19 June 1970.

100 French Constitutional Council, Décision no. 92–308 DC of 9 April 1992.

101 French Constitutional Council, Décision no. 92–312 DC of 2 September 1992.

102 Article 54, French Constitution of 4 October 1958 (as amended in 2008).

103 Closa (2013a), p. 64.

104 Article 93(1) no. 2 Basic Law of the Federal Republic of Germany (1949). See also Sec. 13(6), sec. 76–79 Act on the Federal Constitutional Court (1951).

105 Collings (2015), p. 14. For this part, see McWhinney (1961–62), p. 13.

106 German Federal Constitutional Court, Case 1 BvG 396, Treaty of the European Defense Community, decision of 30 July 1952.

107 McWhinney (1961–62), p. 15.

108 *Manfred Brunner and Others* v. *The European Union Treaty* (Cases 2 BvR 2134/92 and 2159/92).

109 German Federal Constitutional Court, Case BVerfGE 89, 155, Treaty of Maastricht, decision of 12 October 1993.

110 German Federal Constitutional Court, Judgment of the Second Senate of 30 June 2009 – 2 BvE 2/08.

111 Articles 93(4) and 87(2), Constitution of Greece (amended to 2008). See Spiliotopoulos (1983), p. 47.

112 Greek Council of State, Decision 169/1893 of the AreiosPagosis described as the equivalent of Marbury and Madison for establishing constitutional review (see Panezi 2006).

113 Schermers (1983).

114 de Visser (2013), p. 13n.

115 Article 24 (2) (a), Fundamental Law of Hungary (2011, amended to 2013).

116 Section 23 (4), Act CLI of 2011 on the Constitutional Court.

117 Article 32/A, Act XX of 1949.

118 Article 6 (2) Fundamental Law. See de Visser (2013), p. 132.

119 Section 2 and 21.(1), Act XXXII of 1989 on the Constitutional Court. See also Hungarian Constitutional Court, Decision 4, 22 February 1997. Full text available at: http://hunconcourt.hu/uploads/sites/3/2017/11/en_0004_1997.pdf.

120 Section 32(1), Act CLI of 2011 on the Constitutional Court.

121 Article 26.1.1, Constitution of Ireland (1937, as amended to 2012).

122 Article 26.1.2, Constitution of Ireland (1937, as amended to 2012).

123 Article 26.1.3, Constitution of Ireland (1937, as amended to 2012).

124 Ireland, Rules of the Superior Courts, Order: 84, Judicial Review and orders affecting personal liberty. The Supreme Court is currently considering an appeal on how far the Order can validly regulate the substantive entitlement to seek judicial review; see *O'S* v. *Residential Institutions Redress Board* [2017] IESCDET 127.

125 Ireland, Rules of the Superior Courts, Order: 84, Judicial Review and orders affecting personal liberty.

126 Coakley and Gallagher (2004), pp. 86–7.

THE RISE OF HIGHER COURTS IN EU TREATY MAKING 201

127 High Court (Ireland) *Crotty* v. *An Taoiseach* [1986] IEHC 3 (24 December 1986).
128 High Court (Ireland) *Crotty* v. *An Taoiseach* [1986] IEHC 3 (24 December 1986, para. 31).
129 High Court (Ireland) *Crotty* v. *An Taoiseach* [1987] IEHC 1 (12 February 1987), para. 79.
130 Supreme Court of Ireland, *Crotty* v. *An Taoiseach* [1987] IR 713 (April 1987).
131 Supreme Court of Ireland, *Crotty* v. *An Taoiseach* [1987] IR 713 (April 1987), para. 3.
132 See Court of Justice of the EU, *Pringle* v. *Ireland* [2012] IESC 47 (plaintiff was a member of parliament); Supreme Court of Ireland, *Collins* v. *Minister for Finance* [2016] IESC 73 (plaintiff was member of parliament); Supreme Court of Ireland, *McKenna* v. *An Taoiseach* (No. 2) [1995] 2 IR 10 (SC) (plaintiff was a member of the European Parliament).
133 Compare in this regard Collins (ibid.) and *Hall* v. *Minister for Finance* [2013] 1 IR 620 (HC) and [2013] IESC 10.
134 Article 134, Constitution of the Italian Republic (2012).
135 Claes (2006), p. 622.
136 Italian Constitutional Court, *Acciaierie San Michele SpA (in liquidation)* v. *High Authority of the ECSC*, Case 9/65. Claes (2006), pp. 496–7.
137 Section 16(3), Constitutional Court Law.
138 Section 32(4), Constitutional Court Law.
139 Section 17, Constitutional Court Law.
140 Constitutional Court of Latvia, Case 119-123/2003.
141 Albi (2007), p. 55.
142 Constitutional Court of the Republic of Lithuania, Judgment on Behalf of the Republic of Latvia, 7 April 2009, Case No. 2008-35-01.
143 Article 105(3), Constitution of the Republic of Lithuania (1992, as amended to 2006); Jarukaitis (2010).
144 Article 107, Constitution of the Republic of Lithuania (1992, as amended to 2006).
145 Article 105, Constitution of the Republic of Lithuania (as amended); Jočienė (2007), p. 62.
146 Article 106, Constitution of the Republic of Lithuania (1992, as amended to 2006).
147 Article 69(1), Constitution of the Republic of Lithuania (1992, as amended to 2006).
148 Article 95, TER, 2, Constitution of Luxembourg (1868, as amended to 2009). This court will be abolished and a Supreme Court will be established if the constitutional reforms proposed are adopted in a referendum; see www.referendum.lu/fr/nouvelle-constitution/.
149 Article 95, TER, 2, Constitution of Luxembourg (1868, as amended to 2009).
150 Article 83bis, Constitution of Luxembourg (2009).

151 Besselink et al. (2014), p. 237.
152 Council of State (Luxembourg), Avis, 26.5.1992.
153 Gerkrath (2012), p. 247.
154 For an alternative view of Luxembourg's Council of State, see Thurner and Stoiber (2001), pp. 26–7.
155 Article 95, Constitution of Malta (1964, as amended to 2014).
156 Article 3(4) European Convention Act (1987).
157 Agius and Grosselfinger (1995), p. 391.
158 Article 120, Constitution of the Kingdom of the Netherlands (1815, as amended to 2008).
159 Article 73(1), Constitution of the Kingdom of the Netherlands (1815, as amended to 2008). See generally the Kingdom Act on the Approval and Publication of Treaties, 7 July 1994.
160 On this particular point, we agree with Closa (2013b), p. 103.
161 Article 133(2), Constitution of the Republic of Poland (1997, as amended to 2009).
162 Article 188(2), Constitution of the Republic of Poland (1997, as amended to 2009).
163 Article 133(2), Constitution of the Republic of Poland (1997, as amended to 2009).
164 Article 191(1), Constitution of the Republic of Poland (1997, as amended to 2009).
165 Polish Constitutional Tribunal, Decision Case K 18/04, 11 May 2005.
166 Polish Constitutional Tribunal, Decision, Case K 32/09, 24 November 2010.
167 Polish Constitutional Tribunal, Decision Case K 33/12, 26 June 2014.
168 Article 223f, Constitution of Portugal (2005, 7th Revision); Seabra (2003), p. 357.
169 Article 134g, Constitution of Portugal (2005, 7th Revision).
170 Article 278, Constitution of Portugal (2005, 7th Revision).
171 Article 146(b), Constitution of Romania (1991, amended to 2003).
172 Article 11(3) and Article 147(3), Constitution of Romania (1991, amended to 2003).
173 Article 147(3), Constitution of Romania (1991, amended to 2003).
174 Article 146(b), Constitution of Romania (1991, amended to 2003).
175 Article 125a(1), Constitution of the Slovak Republic (1992, as amended to 2014).
176 Article 125a(3), Constitution of the Slovak Republic (1992, as amended to 2014).
177 Article 125a(2), Constitution of the Slovak Republic (1992, as amended to 2014).
178 Slovak Constitutional Court, Case II. U.S. 171/05–175 Constitutional Treaty, decision of 27 February 2008.

179 Article 30(1), Constitution of the Slovak Republic (1992, as amended to 2017).

180 Slovak Constitutional Court, Case II. U.S. 171/05–175 Constitutional Treaty, decision of 27 February 2008.

181 Ortiz (2015), p. 100.

182 Article 160, Constitution of the Republic of Slovenia (1991, as amended to 2013); Sovdat (2013).

183 Article 160, Constitution of the Republic of Slovenia (1991, as amended to 2013).

184 Sovdat (2013), p. 900n.

185 Article 25, Constitution of the Republic of Slovenia (1991, as amended to 2013).

186 Article 160 Constitution of the Republic of Slovenia (1991, as amended to 2013).

187 Constitutional Court of the Republic of Slovenia, Case U-I-49/08 Treaty of Lisbon, Judgment of 15 October 2008.

188 Article 95(2), Spanish Constitution of 1978 (as amended up to 2011). Art. 2.1.e, Organic Law Constitutional Court, 2/1979, 3 October.

189 de Visser (2013), p. 107.

190 Article 95(2), Spanish Constitution of 1978 (as amended up to 2011). Art. 78 Organic Law Constitutional Court, 2/1979, 3 October.

191 Article 95(2), Spanish Constitution of 1978 (as amended up to 2011).

192 Article 93, Spanish Constitution of 1978 (as amended up to 2011). Besselink et al. (2014), p. 256.

193 Constitutional Court of Spain, Declaración DTC 1/1992, de 1 de julio. See Santacruz (1993).

194 Constitutional Court of Spain, Declaración DTC 1/2004, de 13 de diciembre.

195 Chapter 11, Article 14, Instrument of Government (1974, amended to 2015).

196 Instrument of Government, Chapter 8, Article 18 (1974, amended to 2015).

197 England and Wales Court of Appeal, *Blackburn* v. *Attorney-General* [1971] EWCA Civ J0510–2, [1971] 1 WLR 1037.

198 *R.* v. *Secretary of State for Foreign and Commonwealth Affairs ex p. Rees-Mogg*, Court of Appeal – Administrative Court, 30 July 1993, [1993] EWHC Admin 4.

199 Supreme Court of Ireland, *Crotty* v. *An Taoiseach* [1987] IR 713 (April 1987).

200 *R.* v. *Secretary of State for Foreign and Commonwealth Affairs ex p. Rees-Mogg*, Court of Appeal – Administrative Court, 30 July 1993, [1993] EWHC Admin 4.

201 England & Wales High Court (Administrative Court), *R.* v. *Secretary of State for Foreign and Commonwealth Affairs ex p. Rees-Mogg*, 30 July 1993, [1993] EWHC Admin 4.

202 England & Wales High Court (Administrative Court), *Wheeler*, v. *Office of the Prime Minister and Another*, [2008] EWHC 936 (Admin).

203 UK Supreme Court, *R(Miller)* v. *Secretary of State for Exiting the EU* [2017] UKSC 5.

204 England & Wales High Court, *R(Miller)* v. *Secretary of State for Exiting the European Union* [2016], EWHC 2768 (Admin) para. 7.

205 *R(Miller)* v. *Secretary of State for Exiting the EU* [2017] UKSC 5, para. 81.

7 Explaining the Transformation of EU Treaty Making

Parliaments, the people and courts – as the three preceding chapters have shown – have assumed a more prominent role in the consent stage of EU treaty making. Parliaments have always been part of the process through which member states give their consent to be bound to such treaties, but their prominence has increased over the period 1951–2016 as constitutional rules and norms in a number of member states shifted from simple majority voting towards either a qualified or super majority threshold and the number of chambers involved in treaty making have increased. Treaty-related referendums have also become more likely during this period. No member state is constitutionally compelled to hold a referendum on EU treaties, but a number of member states have introduced rules and norms that make such a vote possible or even probable in the event of a major EU treaty amendment. The role of higher courts in EU treaty making increased in a number of member states, especially as citizens acquired standing to challenge the ex-ante constitutionality of treaties.

The literature on treaty making tends to treat constitutional rules as an *explanans* rather than an *explanandum*. Beth Simmons offers a systematic overview of treaty ratification procedures, but her ratification index is an independent variable used to explain the rate of treaty ratification.[1] EU scholars share this interest in the consequences rather than the causes of treaty making rules and norms.[2] An exception is Carlos Closa, who theorises that national ratification procedures will exhibit path dependence over time and share similarities across member states.[3] The turn to referendums by several EU member states since the passage of the Single European Act certainly speaks to this point. Mendez, Mendez and Triga offer a qualitative analysis of treaty-related referendums as part of their broader study of EU referendums.[4] Using tabular analysis, they find that political elites typically called referendums on EU treaties because of constitutional considerations rather than partisan political calculations or legitimacy concerns.[5]

This chapter employs quantitative methods to test the two theoretical approaches at the core of this book. It asks whether the rise of parliaments, the people and courts in EU treaty making can be explained as an instance of hand tying in a two-level game or a response to the problems of trust facing the EU and its member states. As in other chapters, our approach draws inspiration from the comparative constitutionalism literature. Specifically, we are influenced by Gabriel L. Negretto's pathbreaking study of constitutional choice in Latin America, which uses regression analysis to test competing explanations for why constitutional framers in eighteen Latin American countries chose specific electoral and decision rules between 1900 and 2008.[6] Studies of constitutional amendment and rigidity by Carlos Closa[7] and Christer Karlsson[8] confirm the relevance of comparative constitutionalism for studying the EU and its member states, but our study is the first to apply such methods specifically to the changing constitutional rules and norms surrounding EU treaty making.

The remainder of this chapter is divided into five sections. The first two introduce our dependent and independent variables, respectively. The third section gives an overview of our data. The regression results are presented and discussed in the fourth section. The final section summarises the key findings of this chapter and the limitations of this approach.

Dependent Variables

The ratification scales derived in Chapters 4–6 are the dependent variables in this part of our study. They are, to be more precise, Likert scales that classify constitutional rules and norms according to the prominence they confer on parliaments, the people and courts in the consent stage of EU treaty making. As discussed in Chapter 1, we focus on constitutional rules and norms because the means through which EU member states give their consent to be bound by EU treaties cannot simply be 'read off' national constitutions. As the experience of Finland (Chapter 6) and Ireland (Chapter 5), among others, tells us, the process through which EU treaties are accepted depends not only on the procedures identified in constitutions but also on the approaches to treaty making that governments and other actors think of as appropriate. The comparison of

Table 7.1 Re-cap of ratification scales

Scale	Score
*Parliaments Scale**	
Chamber must be consulted	1
Approval by simple or absolute majority	2
Approval by 3/5 or 2/3 majority	3
Supermajority (greater than 2/3 majority)	4
Referendums Scale	
Referendums prohibited	1
Referendums improbable	2
Referendums possible	3
Referendums probable	4
Courts Scale	
No scope for ex-ante constitutional review	1
Executive can trigger ex-ante constitutional review	2
Parliament can trigger ex-ante constitutional review	3
Citizens can trigger ex-ante constitutional review	4

*Repeated for each parliamentary chamber involved in the consent stage.

constitutional rules and norms in Chapters 4–7 rests on a set of criteria that are reprised in Table 7.1.

The first of our three dependent variables, *Parliaments*, increases as the threshold for approving treaties and the number of parliamentary chambers involved increases. For each chamber, the lowest score is assigned for consultation, with a supermajority ranked above a three-fifths or two-thirds majority and the latter ranked above a simple majority requirement. Scores are added together for each parliamentary chamber involved in the consent stage. *Referendums* increases as the likelihood of

208   THE TRANSFORMATION OF EU TREATY MAKING

treaty-related referendums rises. The people are at their least prominent when referendums are prohibited under prevailing constitutional rules and norms, but this role increases, in turn, as rules and norms make referendums improbable, possible and probable. *Courts* increases as higher courts assume a more prominent role in the consent stage of treaty making. The lowest score is reserved for cases in which ex ante constitutional review of EU treaties is not permitted, and the highest for cases in which such reviews can be triggered by citizens. The intermediate options assume that a review triggered by the legislative branch gives courts a more prominent role than an executive-initiated review but a less prominent one than a review triggered by citizens.

The scores in the above exercise are ordered but the interval between them is unknown. While we are confident, for example, that rules and norms that render referendums probable should be ranked above ones that make referendums possible, we cannot be sure that the difference between these scores and others is identical. On this basis, we treat our ratification scales as ordinal rather than numerical variables, in consequence of which standard linear regression techniques are no longer valid.[9] This is because such techniques measure the effect of a one-unit change in independent variables on the dependent variables, a measurement that no longer makes sense when variables are ordinal.

Independent Variables

Having described the dependent variables in our study, we now consider which independent variables might explain variations in these ratification scales. As discussed in detail in Chapter 2, Robert Putnam's two-level game approach offers a ready-made explanation for the increasingly prominent role of parliaments, the people and courts in EU treaty making. Simply put, it sees national governments as tying their hands through tougher ratification procedures so as to drive a harder bargain in international negotiations. Putnam sees tying hands as a precarious strategy because of the possibility of involuntary defection. If a government were to restrict ratification procedures too much, he warns, negotiators could encounter deadlock.[10] Although Putnam thus recognises the pitfalls of hand tying, he does not specify in detail the conditions under which national governments will choose tighter ratification constraints.[11]

Robert Pahre has gone furthest among two-level game scholars in thinking through what these conditions might be.[12] His divided government model posits that hand tying will be credible – and therefore worth pursuing – only if the legislative majority's preferences differ significantly from those of the executive.[13] Otherwise, such constraints would confer no credible advantages in international negotiations. They would simply reinforce what executives already sought. Pahre's minority government model sees the lack of a majority in the legislature as a necessary condition for a government to adopt tighter ratification rules. When this condition does not hold, the model suggests, constraints would not be credible because the government could untie its hands just as easily as it had tied them.

Following Pahre,[14] we use political cleavages over the EU and the presence of significant anti-EU parties in parliament as a proxy for divided government. The divided government model does not expect member states in which there is elite and popular consensus in favour of the EU to choose tighter ratification rules because there is little to be gained from doing so. Conversely, member states in which Eurosceptic parties are strong and the public divided on the EU can credibly tie their hands and so are more likely to do so. *EU cleavage* measures the difference between the percentage of respondents who view EU membership as being beneficial for their country and those who do not. *Eurosceptic party* measures the vote share of Eurosceptic parties in national elections.

The minority government model, for Pahre, explains why the Danish Folketing has established strong parliamentary oversight of EU policy making whereas the UK parliament has not.[15] Although both parliaments are divided over European matters, only Denmark has a tradition of minority governments. Extending this logic to EU treaty making, we include *Minority*, a dummy variable that takes the value of one when a single or multiparty minority government is in power, among our independent variables.

The two-level legitimacy approach, as discussed in Chapter 2, takes as its point of departure the crisis of legitimacy facing the EU. Whereas national governments occupy a privileged position in treaty making in Putnam's two-level game, the two-level legitimacy approach sees this privilege as being under threat because of a loss of trust in the EU and those who govern it. To test this line of explanation, we include two measures of trust among our independent variables. *Trust in the EU* measures the percentage of respondents who tend to trust the EU. *Trust in government* measures the percentage of respondents who tend to trust national governments.

Treaty making is a complex area of policy making in which other explanatory factors are potentially at play. Constitutional rules and norms could reflect the degree of political, institutional and constitutional constraints in national polities, with actors in more constrained polities being less willing and able to amend treaty making rules and norms. Among our independent variables, we include Witold J. Henisz's POLCON variable, a measure of the feasibility of change in a member state's political institutions and the preferences of actors that inhabit them.[16] Population size and wealth are classic political economy cleavages in EU politics.[17] All other things being equal, we might expect larger and wealthier member states to have more to lose from treaty negotiations. Tom Ginsburg offers two reasons why this might be so.[18] First, larger states are more self-sufficient than smaller states and so the former are likely to prefer a smaller range of international agreements than the latter. Tying hands can help more powerful states to narrow the range of agreement that is up for negotiation. Second, larger states are less likely to comply with treaties than smaller states and so the former have a stronger incentive to tie their hands through more stringent treaty-making processes. For this reason, we include *GNIpc(ln)*, the natural log of gross national income per capita, and *POP(ln)*, the natural log of population, as independent variables.

EU member states have different legal traditions and these differences could have a bearing on the evolution of the constitutional rules and norms surrounding treaty making. A key issue in this respect is whether states are monist or dualist in nature. Monist states do not require legislation for treaties to enter into force in domestic law. The treaties are directly applicable and can be relied on by national courts. Dualist states require legislation for treaties to have effect domestically. Dualism can be understood as affording greater protection to parliamentary sovereignty by giving legislatures a gate-keeping role after ratification has taken place. This view raises the question of whether, in the absence of such protection, monist states are likely to give parliaments – and perhaps even the people and courts – a greater role in treaty making. However, even in monist states, only some treaties may be viewed as directly applicable and others may require legislation. Also, legislation may be required within both monist and dualist states but for different purposes. In monist states, the legislature may be required to approve the treaty before it can bind the state internationally. Thus, treaties may require legislation for them to be binding internationally on the state. Similarly, a dualist state will require legislation to incorporate the treaty in domestic law.[19] In view of this discussion, we include *Monist*, a dummy variable that takes the value of 1 when a member state has a monist legal system and 0 in other cases.

Data

The data are drawn from annual observations of EU member states between 1951 and 2016 (see Appendix 7.1 for a summary of data sources). We start with data for the six members that joined the European Coal and Steel Community in 1951 before adding additional states when they join the European Communities or, later, the EU. The result is an unbalanced panel that expands with each successive enlargement.

While data for our dependent variables run from 1951 (for the six founding members) to 2016 (see Chapters 4–6), data for our independent variables are not available until significantly later. The Comparative Politics Database includes data on minority governments from 1960. The Eurobarometer records annual data on trust in national government from 1993 and trust in the EU from 2003. The same source started asking respondents whether they viewed the EU as beneficial in 1983 but stopped in 2011. We construct vote shares of Eurosceptic parties using election data from the ParlGov database.[20] POLCON is available for all member states for the full sample period.[21] Data on population and gross national income per capita run from 1960 to 2016 and are taken from the European Commission's AMECO database and the World Bank's International Comparison Program database, respectively. We designate EU member states as monist or dualist following Andrea Ott's classification.[22] Table 7.2 presents the descriptive statistics for our dependent and independent variables on the basis of these data.

Regression Results

As we are dealing with ordinal dependent variables, the validity of the assumptions underpinning conventional linear regression techniques is, as noted above, open to question.[23] For this reason we estimate ordered probit models[24] to test for the relationship between each of our ratification scales, the independent variables suggested by the two-level game and two-level legitimacy approaches and our control variables. Because observations in our sample may be correlated across countries, usual measures of standard errors may not be meaningful in this setting, rendering the relationship between our dependent and independent

Table 7.2 Descriptive statistics: dependent and independent variables

Variable	Type	Observations	Mean	Standard deviation	Minimum	Maximum
Parliament	Ordinal	846	4	2.1	2	14
Referendum	Ordinal	846	2.6	0.6	1	4
Court	Ordinal	846	2	1.1	1	4
Eurosceptic	Numerical	846	4.3	6.3	0	29.2
Cleavage	Numerical	483	0.3	−0.4	−0.4	0.8
Minority	Dummy	792	0.2	0.4	0	1
Trust EU	Numerical	364	0.5	0.1	0.2	0.7
Trust in Government	Numerical	379	0.4	0.2	0.1	0.8
POLCON	Numerical	846	0.5	0.1	0.1	0.8
Population (ln)	Numerical	792	9.3	1.5	5.8	11.3
Gross national income (ln)	Numerical	782	10.2	0.5	8.8	11.6
Monist	Dummy	846	0.4	0.5	0	1

variables uncertain.[25] Accordingly, we use *standard* errors clustered by country. Table 7.3 shows our regression results for each of our three models, each one focusing on a different scale.

Model 1 provides no clear-cut support for the two-level game approach when it comes to explaining the role of parliaments in the consent stage of EU treaty making. Although an increase in the vote share of Eurosceptic parties is associated with a greater role for parliaments in the consent stage, the relationship between domestic cleavages over the EU and the parliamentary scale is the opposite to what is expected. The incidence of minority governments does not make a difference. The two-level legitimacy approach has greater explanatory power. Member states in which there are low levels of trust in national government, our findings suggest, are more likely to give their parliaments a greater role in treaty making. Trust in the EU makes little difference, however. Turning to control variables, wealthier member states are more likely to empower parliaments in the consent stage of treaty making, but the size of member states makes no difference. Whether a state is monist or dualist does not seem to matter and the same goes for political constraints.

Model 2 provides greater support for the two-level game approach. Minority governments are more likely to embrace constitutional rules and norms that favour referendums on EU treaties, a finding that is consistent, once again, with Pahre's predictions. The same holds for member states in which there are significant political cleavages over the EU and strong Eurosceptic parties. The regression results chime with the two-level legitimacy approach's concern for questions of political trust, although this time it is trust in the EU rather than trust in national government that has the expected impact. Member states in which there are low levels of trust in the EU are more likely to embrace treaty-related referendums. Smaller states are more likely to turn to referendums, but being a wealthier state or a monist or dualist one or having domestic political constraints makes no apparent difference.

Model 3 fits the court scale on our independent variables. A fall in the vote share of Eurosceptic parties is associated with a more prominent role for courts, which is the opposite of what the divided government model would predict. Domestic cleavages over the EU and the presence of a minority government make no difference. Consistent with the two-level legitimacy approach is the fact that member states with low levels of trust in the EU tend to give courts a greater role in treaty making.

214   THE TRANSFORMATION OF EU TREATY MAKING

Table 7.3 Determinants of ratification scales

Independent variables	Dependent variable: ratification scales		
	Model 1: Parliament	Model 2: Referendum	Model 3: Courts scale
Eurosceptic	0.043*	0.064*	−0.071**
	(0.025)	(0.033)	(0.031)
EU cleavage	−1.414*	3.128***	1.124
	(0.792)	(1.150)	(1.049)
Minority	0.097	0.668**	0.101
	(0.210)	(0.330)	(0.375)
Trust in EU	2.861	−6.877***	−5.535***
	(2.032)	(2.214)	(1.968)
Trust in government	−4.808***	−0.444	−1.474
	(1.173)	(2.248)	(2.024)
POLCON	−1.322	−2.202	1.880
	(1.909)	(1.761)	(1.337)
Population (ln)	0.205	−0.288*	−0.033
	(0.246)	(0.168)	(0.168)
Gross national income (ln)	1.363***	0.007	−0.717
	(0.447)	(0.511)	(0.536)
Monist	−0.575	0.452	0.990
	(0.363)	(0.625)	(0.647)
Wald Chi^2	49.400	38.33	83.13
Pseudo R^2	0.152	0.253	0.213
McKelvey & Zavoina R^2	0.405	0.489	0.481
N	229	229	229

Notes: Ordered probit regression. Numbers in parentheses are robust standard errors clustered by country.
*** $p < 0.01$, ** $p < 0.05$, * $p < 0.1$.

As in the case of referendums, trust in national governments has no discernible impact. Nor do population size, wealth or the nature of the legal system. Political constraints, as before, make no difference.

Estimated probabilities offer an alternative way to interpret these regression results. They show, for example, that the probability of a member state adopting constitutional rules and norms that make a referendum possible increases from 82 per cent to 92 per cent when trust in the EU falls from 50 per cent to 40 per cent, assuming all other variables are held constant. The probability of adopting a two-thirds or three-fifths majority threshold in two parliamentary chambers increases from 7 per cent to 15 per cent as trust in national government falls from 50 per cent to 40 per cent under the same assumptions. Similarly, as the difference between the percentage of respondents who view EU membership as being beneficial for their country and those that do not increases from 40 points to 50 points, the probability of adopting rules and norms that make a referendum possible increases from 89 per cent to 91 per cent.

Conclusion

This chapter has offered a large-N perspective on the puzzle at the heart of this book. It asked whether the variation in the role played by parliaments, the people and courts in the consent stage of EU treaty making can be explained by the two-level game and two-level legitimacy approaches. The most convincing evidence in favour of hand tying in a two-level game relates to referendums, with minority governments and those with strong Eurosceptic parties and domestic cleavages over the EU likely to embrace constitutional rules and norms that give the people a role in the consent stage of treaty making. Evidence in support of the two-level legitimacy approach is stronger. Member states with low levels of trust in national governments are more likely to empower parliaments in treaty making. Low levels of trust in the EU, meanwhile, are associated with rules and norms that make referendums more likely and foster a more prominent role for courts.

Important and informative though we think these findings are, they are subject to caveats. First, as predicted, other factors matter too when it comes to thinking about the transformation of EU treaty making. The size and economic weight of member states matters too in some cases. Second, studies of this sort are subject to data limitations, and ours is constrained by the availability of data on certain independent variables.

Finally, quantitative analysis of this sort is not designed as a substitute for qualitative analysis of the kind more commonly associated with this domain of study. Our findings shed light on the external validity of our theoretical explanations, but, as Negretto notes, such findings invite rather than override fine-grained analysis of the causal processes behind constitutional choice.

Appendix 7.1 Data Sources

Table 7.4 Data sources

Variable	Source
Cleavage	Eurobarometer
Court	Authors' own
Eurosceptic	Authors' own calculations based on Gottfried (2014) and ParlGov database
Gross national income (ln)	World Bank's International Comparison Program database
Minority	Comparative Politics Database
Monism	Ott (2008)
POLCON	Henisz (2017)
Parliament	Authors' own calculations
Population (ln)	European Commission's AMECO database
Referendum	Authors' own calculations
Trust in government	Eurobarometer
Trust in the EU	Eurobarometer

Notes

1 Simmons (2009b).
2 See, for example, Claes (2005), de Visser (2013) and Hug and König (2002).
3 Closa (2013a), p. 74.
4 Mendez, Mendez and Triga (2014).
5 Mendez, Mendez and Triga (2014), p. 98.
6 Negretto (2013).
7 Closa (2012).
8 Karlsson (2016).
9 Winship and Mare (1984).
10 Putnam (1988), p. 441.
11 Putnam (1988), p. 440.
12 Pahre (1997) focuses on legislative oversight of governments' role in EU policy making, but his model can be easily extended to the case of treaty making.

13 Pahre (1997), p. 148.
14 Pahre (1997), p. 152.
15 Pahre (1997), pp. 159–60.
16 See Henisz (2017).
17 See Bunse and Nicolaïdes (2012) and Schelkle (2012).
18 Ginsburg (2005), p. 750.
19 Sloss (2011).
20 Our designation of Eurosceptic parties is drawn, in part, from Gottfried (2014).
21 See Henisz (2017).
22 Ott (2008), p. 346.
23 Peel, Goode and Moutinho (1998), p. 75.
24 Greene (2012), pp. 827–30.
25 Cameron and Miller (2015).

PART III

The Practice of EU Treaty Making

8 How Changing Rules and Norms Have Shaped EU Treaty Making

Treaty making in the European Union (EU) has undoubtedly become more protracted as parliaments, the people and courts have acquired a more prominent role. The Treaty of Paris entered into force 463 days after it was signed. The Treaty of Lisbon took 720 days to enter into force and a further 926 days before a set of guarantees offered to Ireland following its initial rejection of this treaty took effect. But delay is not the same as deterrence; what matters more for our inquiry, as discussed in Chapter 2, is whether changing rules and norms constrain governments and how governments respond to these constraints. A key question in this context is whether the transformation of EU treaty making documented in early chapters has discouraged national governments from amending treaties. The second concerns how governments have responded to involuntary defection – the rejection by domestic constituents of agreements struck by governments in the international arena – or the risk thereof.

From a two-level game perspective, we would expect governments that find their hands too tightly bound to loosen such constraints. Were domestic constituents to reject a treaty that a government had supported, the latter's priority would be to find additional slack either by seeking other ways to gain domestic support for the agreement or by securing a similar agreement through other means. The two-level legitimacy approach, in contrast, would expect governments to take seriously the concerns over legitimacy that drove such constraints to begin with. We would, from this vantage point, expect governments to consider the possibility of voluntary concession, i.e. the abandonment by governments of a treaty because domestic constituents in one or more states had rejected the agreement.

Having explored in the preceding chapters how and why the rules and norms governing treaty making in the EU have changed over time, we now consider the consequences of this shift. In so doing, we focus on two central questions. First, have the changing rules and norms governing EU treaty ratification had any discernible impact on the rate of treaty amendment? Second, how have governments responded to the changing rules and norms in particular treaty-making episodes? To address the first of these questions we investigate the factors driving the rate of EU treaty amendment between 1952 and 2016. To address the second, this chapter how the EU responded to instances of involuntary defection and the risk thereof during this period. It presents evidence on how governments tackled ratification crises over the European Defence Community Treaty; the Maastricht, Nice and Lisbon treaties; and the European Constitution before considering their turn to international treaties during the euro crisis.

The Amendment Rate for EU Treaties

Donald Lutz was the first scholar to examine systematically the consequences of constitutional amendment procedures.[1] Two of his claims are particularly salient for our study of treaty making. The first is that more difficult amendment procedures lead to lower rates of constitutional amendment. The second is that low rates of amendments of long-lived constitutional arrangements encourage alternative means of constitutional change. Comparing constitutional amendment patterns across all US state constitutions, Lutz found that amendment procedures led by popular initiative were associated with lower success rates than those triggered by legislatures or special convention. Analysing national constitutions, he found that countries with more difficult amendment processes tend to have lower rates of amendment, with those requiring referendums recording the lowest rates of amendment.[2]

Lutz's research has inspired a sizable literature on constitutional amendment,[3] but there has been little systematic work of this sort on the effects of treaty amendment procedures on treaty amendment. Ken Conca comes closest in his study of global environmental governance, in which he records falling amendment rates for multilateral environmental accords between 1960 and 1992, but he offers no systematic explanation for this trend.[4] As regards EU treaty making, Carlos Closa posits that the dynamics of treaty amendment will mirror that of constitutional amendment, with the rate of treaty amendment falling as the number of veto players in treaty ratification increases.[5] In another study,

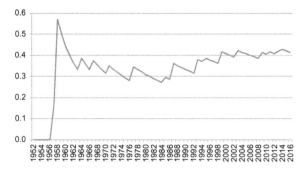

Figure 8.1 Treaty amendment rate (by treaty, 1952–2016).

Closa finds evidence that the rate of constitutional amendment in EU member states falls as the number of actors empowered increases, but he does not test this hypotheses in relation to treaty making.[6]

Following Lutz's definition, the treaty amendment rate can be defined as the total number of treaty amendments divided by the number of years since the treaty entered into force. Taking treaty making from Paris to the post-Lisbon period as a continuous process gives an average amendment rate of 0.42. Though not directly comparable, this puts the rate of EU treaty amendment well above what Lutz judges to be the low rate of amendment for the US constitution (0.13) but well below the relatively high rate for US state constitutions (1.23). Looking at EU treaty amendment rates on a year-by-year basis gives little indication that amendment rates have fallen as a result of more stringent ratification rules. Instead, it shows that amendment rates trended downwards between the late 1950s and mid-1980s before trending upwards thereafter (Figure 8.1). This picture fits with claims that the foundation of the European Communities in the 1950s gave way to a period of euro-sclerosis that the Single European Act brought to an end.[7]

Influential though Lutz's study of constitutional amendment is, his methodology has been criticised on a number of counts. Ferejohn argues that the tabular method favoured by Lutz fails to pick up on other factors that may have explanatory power, such as party organisation, constitutional traditions and political culture.[8] Ginsberg and Melton offer what is arguably the most sophisticated attempt to explore these factors.[9] These authors find evidence that amendment culture, defined as the frequency of amendment in the previous constitution, rather than the difficulty of current amendment processes predicts

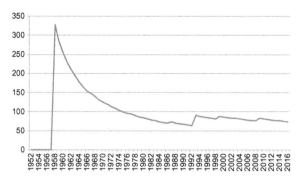

Figure 8.2 Treaty amendment rate (article by article, 1952–2016).

the contemporaneous rate of constitutional amendment. On this basis, Ginsberg and Melton conclude, 'constitutional designers have little influence over the observed flexibility of their product'.[10] Another criticism of Lutz is that he treats minor and major constitutional amendments as equal.[11] This point certainly applies to treaties, with the above calculations putting the act amending the Protocol on the Statute of the European Investment Bank (1993) on a par with the Maastricht Treaty (1992).

In view of these criticisms, we consider a more fine-grained analysis of treaty amendment since 1952 on an article-by-article basis. Identifying treaty articles is not a straightforward exercise, as such agreements include articles of their own as well as provisions amending existing articles. For the purpose of comparison, we count elements of EU treaty amendments that have their own CELEX number, a unique identifier used by EUR-Lex, the official website of European Union law. By this count the act amending the Protocol on the Statute of the European Investment Bank (1993) had six articles, whereas the Maastricht Treaty (1992) encompassed more than 1,000. The results of this exercise reveal a pattern of comprehensive treaty revisions followed by piecemeal ones, with the rate of amendment falling after the European Communities had been established (Figure 8.2). Whereas the period between the mid-1980s and the 2010s looks like a prolific one for treaty making when all amendments are treated as equal (Figure 8.1), the rate of amendment is steadily declining when changes in treaty articles are considered (Figure 8.2).

Although article-by-article analysis gives us a richer picture, it does not, by itself, allow us to make claims about what is driving treaty amendments. The lower rate of EU treaty amendment in the 1970s, for example, may reflect differences in the demand for treaty amendment among member states that have little to do with the stringency of treaty revision procedures. To address this issue, we regress amendment rates between 1952 and 2016 on the ratification scales derived in Chapter 7. These indexes are aggregated across countries to produce *Parliaments*, *Referendums* and *Courts*. As control variables, we include *Length(ln)*, which measures the natural log of the word count of EU treaties that are in force. This allows us to test a variation on Lutz's hypothesis that longer constitutions – or in this case treaties – will tend to be modified more because there is more to amend.[12] *GDP*, which measures the growth rate of real EU gross domestic product, offers a crude proxy for political economy factors that might encourage or deter member states from amending treaties. The first of these variables is based on the authors' own calculations and the second relies on data compiled by the Conference Board's Total Economy Database. Finally, we include *Prohibition*, a dummy variable that takes the value of 0 before 1958 and 1 thereafter. This variable picks up on the Treaty of Paris's prohibition on treaty amendments until five years after the establishment of the common market for coal.[13]

Since the dependent variables in our study are count variables, we employ negative binomial regression analysis.[14] Table 8.1 shows the regression results for two models, the first measuring the number of amendments in a given year and the second disaggregating treaty amendment into the number of articles involved. The results indicate that the rate of treaty amendment slows as the people assume a more prominent role in the consent stage of treaty making. This finding speaks to Liesbet Hooghe and Gary Mark's argument that referendum defeats cast long shadows on EU treaty making by contributing to a 'deep reluctance on the part of governments to hazard public debate on further integration'.[15] An increased role for parliaments does not affect the number of treaty-making episodes, our results suggest, but it is associated with a decline in amendment rates when measured on an article-by-article basis. Parliamentary involvement in EU treaty making, it would seem, is encouraging national governments to be more selective in their approach to treaty making. An increased role for higher courts is associated with an increase rather than a fall in treaty amendment. That courts do not deter treaty making could be linked to judges' willingness to question but not block treaty amendments (see later discussion). Turning to other variables, treaty amendment slows as the length of treaties increases. This runs contrary to Lutz's hypothesis

Table 8.1 Drivers of EU treaty amendment

Independent variables	Dependent variable: treaty amendment rates	
	Model 1: Amendment rate by number of amendments	Model 2: Amendment rate by number of articles
Parliament scale	0.000	−0.040***
	0.003	0.007
Referendum scale	−0.032***	−0.082***
	0.006	0.007
Courts scale	0.037***	0.140***
	0.008	0.007
Length (ln)	−0.085**	−0.145*
	0.043	0.007
GDP	0.001	0.004
	0.002	0.007
Prohibition	2.677***	8.874***
	0.922	0.007
Constant	−2.614	−1.421
	1.039	0.007
Wald Chi^2	98.45	170.97
Pseudo R^2	0.0417	0.2610
N	65	65

Notes: Negative binomial regression. Numbers in parentheses are robust standard errors.
*** $p < 0.01$, ** $p < 0.05$, * $p < 0.1$.

that longer constitutions provide more targets for amendment and suggests,[16] instead, that EU treaties are becoming more difficult to amend as their content becomes more unwieldy. Economic growth makes no difference to treaty making, but the Paris Treaty's prohibition on treaty making during the transitional phase of the European Coal and Steel Community did.

Ratification Crises

Instances of involuntary defection in relation to EU treaties are rare. Instances of voluntary concession are more exceptional still. The abandonment of the European Defence Community Treaty is the sole example of the Community abandoning a treaty after it had been rejected by domestic constituents, and, even so, it is not a clear-cut case. Signed in May 1952, this treaty had been ratified by Germany and the Benelux countries by the time the French National Assembly rejected it in August 1954. In fact, the National Assembly voted down not the treaty but a motion to debate it, although it was accepted by deputies on this basis that the treaty had been defeated. The foreign ministers of the Six made no serious attempt to untie their hands after this vote for two reasons. The first is that the question of how to re-arm Germany, a key motivation for the European Defence Community Treaty, was urgent. Rather than wait for the Six to find a solution, the five signatories of the Brussels Treaty (1948) – Belgium, France, Luxembourg, the Netherlands and the United Kingdom – agreed to modify this agreement to allow for the creation of a new Western European Union to which Germany and Italy would accede. The second reason is that Pierre Mendes France, President of the Council of Ministers, had sought unsuccessfully to reopen negotiations on the European Defence Community Treaty prior to its consideration by the French National Assembly. Neither the Assembly nor the foreign ministers of the Six endorsed Mendes France's proposed protocol. This left the government in an ambivalent position on the European Defence Community Treaty which it put to parliament without formally requesting its approval and without a mandate to renegotiate it. The rejection of the treaty was a defeat for the French government in one sense but a victory in another.[17]

One reason that involuntary defection is so rare in the EU is that national parliaments, in spite of their increased role in treaty making, tend to support treaty amendments. The troubled passage of the Maastricht Treaty before the British parliament was the closest the Community came to the parliamentary defeat of a treaty since 1954. The European Communities (Amendment) Act 1993, through which John Major's government sought to give legal effect to the Maastricht Treaty, won a large majority in the House of Commons at third reading, albeit after opponents of the treaty had tabled more than 600 amendments in an effort to derail ratification. MPs continued to table amendments even after the act received Royal Assent, with the government losing a vote concerning the treaty's Social Chapter. The day after its defeat, Major called a confidence vote on a revised resolution and won the support of MPs. This parliamentary siege of Maastricht, as David Baker, Andrew Gamble and Steve Ludlam call it, was spectacular but short lived.[18] Although there was no shortage of parliamentary dissent over subsequent treaty amendments in the United Kingdom and elsewhere, no legislature has since come as close to vetoing a treaty amendment.

Higher courts have shown a willingness to scrutinise EU treaties but with little appetite for precipitating involuntary defection. A possible exception in this regard is Ireland's Supreme Court, which, in the *Crotty* case, ruled that Title III of the Single European Act required an amendment to Ireland's constitution.[19] In so doing, the Court upheld an appeal against the approval of the Single European Act via legislation alone, thus necessitating a referendum before the treaty could be ratified. In all probability, however, the Court neither sought nor expected to jeopardise the ratification of the treaty through this ruling. The Single European Act was predictably backed by a sizable majority of Irish voters, and it was only after the Irish government chose to run referendums on major treaty amendments rather than face similar challenges that 'no' votes in treaty-related referendums occurred.[20] France's Constitutional Court also left its mark on EU treaty making, albeit it with less dramatic effects. By ruling that the Maastricht Treaty required a constitutional amendment and concluding likewise in relation to the Amsterdam and Lisbon treaties,[21] the Court raised the threshold for treaty amendments from a simple majority to a three-fifths majority requirement among the combined membership of the National Assembly and Senate.[22] The higher threshold did not endanger the approval of these treaties, however, with the more consequential 'petit oui' for Maastricht and the 'grand non' against the European Constitution arising from presidential decisions to hold referendums.[23]

Arguably the most influential judicial player in EU treaty making, Germany's Federal Constitutional Court has used this influence to guide future treaty makers rather than correct contemporaneous ones. In its October 1993 judgment on the Maastricht Treaty, the Court dismissed claims against the constitutionality of this treaty.[24] However, by arguing for the importance of building up 'the democratic bases of the Union ... in step with the integration process',[25] the Court signalled its expectations about the checks and balances necessitated by future treaty amendment.[26] The Court was more prescriptive still in its ruling on the Lisbon Treaty, which concluded, once again, that the agreement was constitutional, while signalling that future treaty amendments that 'crossed the threshold' from an association of sovereign states to a federal state would require a total revision of the Basic Law and hence a referendum.[27]

With the exception of the European Defence Community Treaty, it is the involvement of the people in EU treaty ratification that has given rise to involuntary defection. The first such instance occurred in June 1992 when voters in Denmark rejected the Maastricht Treaty by 50.7 per cent to 49.3 per cent. How did the EU member states react? Meeting in Oslo two days after the referendum, EC foreign ministers expressed their 'regret' over the vote, ruled out 'any reopening of the text signed in Maastricht' and signalled the determination of the Eleven, that is, all member states except Denmark, to move towards European Union.[28] There would be no 'attempt to meet the Danish objections', as Deirdre Curtin and Ronald Van Ooik put it; 'Denmark was to be isolated and perhaps even forced to leave the Community'.[29] A declaration adopted by the European Council in Birmingham in October showed some concern for legitimacy promising a 'Community close to its Citizens', and signaling a determination to 'respond to the concerns raised in the public debate'.[30] At odds with this message but consistent with the line taken by foreign ministers was the European Council's unshakeable commitment to the treaty amendments that had been rejected by Danish voters just four months before. The 'Community must develop together as Twelve', the European Council concluded, 'on the basis of the Maastricht Treaty, while respecting as the Treaty does, the identity and diversity of Member States'.[31]

The Danish government treaded more cautiously but it was no less keen to find some slack. By this point, the Danish Ministry of Foreign Affairs had responded with a White Paper, which explored 'outline solutions' to this impasse.[32] Among the options considered was reverting to the Treaty of Rome, but the report effectively ruled out voluntary concession of this sort. The 'cooperation provided for in the Maastricht Treaty', the government insisted, would continue because of the 'international, economic and political developments' that drove this treaty amendment.[33] Among the alternatives explored in the Danish government's White Paper was ratification of the Maastricht treaty after member states agreed to negotiate certain additions. This proposal was taken forward by most of the country's main political parties in the so-called national compromise,[34] which called on EU member states to offer Denmark 'exceptions' from EU cooperation on defence, justice and home affairs, citizenship, and Economic and Monetary Union before the government resubmitted the Maastricht Treaty for domestic approval. The national compromise was not, it is important to recognise, an instance of hand tying by the Danish government designed to extract further concessions from EU partners, which it has sought in the Maastricht Intergovernmental Conferences (IGCs) but failed to secure. It was, rather, a pact brokered between seven of the eight political parties in the Danish parliament designed to save a treaty on which they were originally divided. To the extent that concessions were extracted from this pact it was by the Socialistisk Folkeparti, an opposition party that had originally opposed the Maastricht treaty.[35] For the other parties to the national compromise, including the governing Konservative Folkeparti and Det Radikale Venstre, the national compromise was a pragmatic device rather than a point of leverage; it was, as Helle Krunke put it, the price to be paid for saving the Maastricht Treaty.[36]

The European Council endorsed the main thrust of the national compromise in Edinburgh in December 1992, but on the understanding that the text of the Maastricht Treaty would not be reopened.[37] The legal status of the Edinburgh Agreement is thus a matter of debate, with Krunke seeing it as both a 'ratification exception' attached by Denmark to the Maastricht Treaty and an international agreement between Denmark and its EU partners.[38] This was, Curtin and Van Ooik argue, an instance of treaty making within treaty making and a problematic one to boot. At Edinburgh, they note, the heads of state or government offered a deal to Denmark that was intended to be legally binding but offered their consent without recourse to ratification, an approach that was consistent with the Vienna Convention on the Law of Treaties but arguably at odds with the Community's approach to treaty making.[39] The deal was, moreover, an international agreement that impinged on the Community's legal order and the context in which the Maastricht treaty would be implemented but without amending the EU treaties.[40] Politically creative but constitutionally controversial,[41] the deal was sufficient to save the Maastricht Treaty, which won the backing of 56.7 per cent of Danish voters in a second referendum in May 1993.

To suggest that member states moved on from Maastricht without regard for legitimacy is not accurate. 'Within days of the Danish vote', writes Anthony Teasdale, 'Commission President Jacques Delors presented a secret memorandum to Foreign Ministers on ways in which the Community might concentrate its activities in a more limited range of important fields, repatriating competences in areas where EU legislation was seen as intrusive'.[42] The Birmingham Declaration's insistence that EU legislation should not interfere 'unnecessarily in the daily life of our citizens' diluted these radical plans but was nonetheless a sincere attempt by the UK presidency to court Eurosceptic voters in Denmark, not to mention those on the backbenches of the British Conservative Party.[43] In the longer term, the Danish vote also reshaped EU policymakers' plans for future treaty reform. At Maastricht, member states agreed that an IGC would be convened in 1996 to 'examine those provisions of this Treaty for which revision is provided',[44] the issues being largely technical in nature and concerning defence cooperation;[45] civil protection, energy and security;[46] and the hierarchy of Community acts.[47] When this IGC was finally convened, it was invited to grapple with an altogether more normative agenda. 'The Conference must make the Union more relevant to its citizens', agreed EU leaders in Madrid in June 1995,[48] echoing the Birmingham Declaration's calls to 'demonstrate to our citizens the benefits of the Community'.[49] Resonant too of the Birmingham Declaration was EU leaders' instruction at Madrid that the IGC address questions about subsidiarity, European value added and citizenship. In this sense, member states sought to address the concerns over the EU's legitimacy raised in relation to the Maastricht Treaty through a further round of treaty amendments.

The EU's response to Denmark's first Maastricht referendum, with its preference for untying hands while at the same time addressing concerns over EU legitimacy, informed future responses to involuntary defection. In June 2001, Ireland voted by a margin of 53.9 per cent to 46.1 per cent against the Nice Treaty, which had been supported by most parliamentary parties as well as a host of civil society groups. In a carbon copy of their remarks at Oslo nine years earlier, EU foreign ministers, meeting in Luxembourg four days after the Irish vote, expressed regret, ruled out renegotiation and reaffirmed their determination to ratify the Nice Treaty on schedule.[50] As in 1992, heads of state or government endorsed this approach at a summit in Göteborg later that month, offering to help the Irish government to find a way forward, taking into account the concerns reflected by this result, without reopening the text of the Nice Treaty. At no point did EU leaders entertain the possibility of voluntary concession. The Irish people remain 'deeply committed to the European Union and to the ratification of the Treaty of Nice', the European Council concluded, less than a fortnight after half a million Irish people had rejected the text.[51]

Turnout by Irish voters in June 2001, at 34.79 per cent, was low, although not exceptionally so for a vote to amend the Irish constitution.[52] Nonetheless, it provided a pretext for the Irish government to seek reassurances from the European Council before holding a second referendum. At the Seville European Council in June 2002, EU heads of state or government took 'cognisance' of a National Declaration presented by the Irish government in which it set out its commitment to EU foreign and security policy subject to Ireland's traditional policy of military neutrality.[53] A non-binding declaration on a non-binding declaration, the Seville agreement served 'primarily as a political signal to the Irish electorate',[54] which voted in October 2002 to approve the Nice Treaty by a wide margin on a much larger turnout.[55]

Ireland's ratification crisis over Nice mirrored the Danish crisis over Maastricht by emboldening rather than discouraging talk of further treaty changes. 'For me [the Irish referendum] is in every sense an extra incentive to get an ambitious declaration in Laeken', argued Belgium Prime Minister Guy Verhofstadt, who was tasked with laying the groundwork for the European Convention.[56] Although the Laeken Declaration made no explicit mention of the Irish vote, it conceded that some EU citizens saw the Union 'as a threat to their identity' and in need of 'better democratic scrutiny'.[57] Treaty amendments once again emerged as both the symptom and cure of the EU's legitimacy problems, with the European Council agreeing at Laeken to pursue a further round of revisions amendments designed to 'bring citizens, and primarily the young, closer to the European design and the European institutions'.[58]

The problem of involuntary defection in relation to the European Constitution was of a different order of magnitude.[59] By the time that French and Dutch voters rejected the treaty in mid-2005, ten of twenty-five member states had ratified the European Constitution.[60] Nine of these countries had done so via parliament with one, Spain, holding a referendum. Absent on this occasion was a commitment by all member states to press on with ratification. Some countries carried on, including Luxembourg, which approved the European Constitution in a referendum in July,[61] but the Czech Republic, Denmark, Ireland, Poland and Portugal soon cancelled planned referendums. That 'no' votes were predicted in some of these member states suggested that national governments were motivated by a desire to avoid involuntary defection.[62]

Faced with such divisions, voluntary concession over the European Constitution seemed inevitable. Instead, the European Council played for time, announcing a period of reflection involving citizens, civil society, social partners, national parliaments and political parties.[63] The result was a series of events aimed at civil society, including the Sound of Europe, a conference on European values, identity and culture organised by the Austrian presidency[64] and the European Commission's Plan D for Democracy.[65] Although these initiatives echoed the deliberative ideals of the European Convention, they were not exercises in treaty making. But by June 2006, tentative plans for treaty reform were beginning to emerge, with the European Council calling for extensive consultations with member states and the adoption of a declaration to mark fifty years of the Treaty of Rome. This declaration, signed by the Presidents (in office) of the European Parliament, Council of Ministers and European Commission in March 2007, agreed to place the Union on a 'renewed common basis' before the European Parliament elections in 2009.[66] To this end, the European Council agreed in June to 'move on' from the uncertainty over the EU's treaty reform process by opening an IGC to prepare a treaty.[67]

EU heads of state of government remained guarded at this point about the precise relationship between this treaty and the European Constitution. But a note prepared by EU foreign ministers made clear that those member states that had already ratified the European Constitution, while open to an 'alternative method of treaty change', insisted that 'the substance of the innovations agreed upon in the 2004 IGC' should be preserved.[68] Put another way, the European Constitution would be binned but much of its contents would be recycled.[69] Opinion is divided on the degree of political and legal overlap between the European Constitution and the Lisbon Treaty,[70] but the manner of their ratification differed significantly.[71] Whereas 10 countries had planned referendums on the European Constitution, all member states except Ireland committed themselves to approval via parliament. Nicolas Sarkozy was a prominent supporter of this shift, arguing in his successful campaign for the French presidency that a simpler treaty would not require a referendum.[72] Dutch Prime Minister Jan Pieter Balkenende concurred.[73]

In June 2008, Irish voters rejected the Lisbon Treaty by a margin of 53.4 per cent to 46.6 per cent. A familiar strategy of cutting slack followed. The question was not whether Ireland should vote again, argued Luxembourg Foreign Minister Jean Asselborn, but 'how can we prepare so that it can be won'.[74] A bespoke treaty amendment designed to address the concerns of the Irish people formed part of this plan. In December 2008, the Irish government committed itself to seek the ratification of the Lisbon Treaty in return for legal guarantees.[75]

In June 2009 the European Council adopted a decision on the concerns of the Irish people, covering abortion, family and education, taxation security and defence, alongside a declaration by the European Council concerning, inter alia, workers' rights and social policy and a national declaration by Ireland on military matters. For De Búrca, this deal was similar to the 1992 Edinburgh Declaration, which offered concessions to Denmark but without altering or amending the treaty under consideration.[76] But the European Council went further in 2009 than it did in 1992 by agreeing that the European Council's decision on the concerns of the Irish people would be incorporated into the treaties at the time of the next accession treaty.[77] No explicit guarantee had been offered to Denmark by the European Council in December 1992,[78] even though the Danish protocol would eventually be codified in the Amsterdam Treaty.[79] The European Council's willingness to pre-commit to treaty amendment in the Irish case followed Irish Prime Minister Brian Cowan's insistence on providing 'maximum legal reassurance to the Irish people' following an intense domestic debate over the legality of the concessions he sought.[80] In October 2009, Ireland duly voted in favour of the Lisbon Treaty at the second time of asking by a margin of 67.1 per cent to 32.9 per cent.[81] Three years later, the European Council convened an IGC on the Irish protocol, resulting in an amendment to the Lisbon Treaty, which entered into force in December 2014.[82] Thus EU leaders turned once again, albeit in a more modest way, to treaty amendment to address the legitimacy concerns raised by a previous round of treaty amendment.

The Turn to International Law Treaties

According to Glen S. Krutz and Jeffrey S. Peake, just 5.7 per cent of international agreements concluded by the United States between 1946 and 1999 were treaties negotiated by the President under Article II of the US Constitution,[83] which requires the advice and consent of the Senate expressed by means of a two-thirds majority vote.[84] Since the 1950s, presidents have turned increasingly to executive agreements, an instrument that allows international agreements to be struck with a reduced role for Congress or no role at all.[85] From a two-level game perspective, the rise of executive agreements in the United States can be understood as a case of untying hands in response to stringent treaty-making rules. Whereas some scholars warn against a potential abuse of power by the executive,[86] others claim that democratic oversight can be enhanced through the role played by the House of Representatives in some categories of executive agreement.[87] However, most commentators agree that executive agreements allow for the acceptance of treaties that the Senate would not agree to under the Constitution's formal provisions on treaty making.[88]

Can EU member states' recourse to international treaties be seen in similar terms? Agreements pre-dating EU membership are in principle honoured under Article 351 TFEU given the principle of *pacta sunt servanda*.[89] The Treaty of Rome using mandatory language required member states to enter into negotiations with each other in relation to specific fields,[90] leading to the Convention on the Mutual Recognition of Companies and Firms (1968)[91] and the Convention on Jurisdiction and the Enforcement of Judgments in Civil and Commercial Matters (1968).[92] More ambitious, and outside the parameters of the EU treaties, was the Schengen Agreement on the abolition of common border checks, signed in June 1985.[93] Recent international treaties include the European Stability Mechanism (ESM) Treaty,[94] which established a new European body to provide financial assistance to member states facing severe financing problems that threaten the stability of the eurozone, and the Fiscal Compact,[95] which encourages deeper economic policy coordination between member states in view of the euro crisis. Whereas the two Article 220 Conventions were signed by all the then member states, more recent international law agreements are agreed among a subset of EU member states. The Schengen Agreement was initially adopted by Belgium, France, Luxembourg, the Netherlands and West Germany. The ESM was agreed between the nineteen eurozone members, although it is open to all EU member states once they adopt the single currency. At the time of writing, all EU member states except the United Kingdom, Croatia and the Czech Republic were party to the Fiscal Compact.

International treaties are, Bruno de Witte argues, 'a curious legal phenomenon that fits oddly with the vision of the European Union as an autonomous legal order with its own legal instrument, its own system of decision-making, enforcement and judicial control'.[96] Traditionally, the choice of international over EU treaties offered a prelude to EU treaty making as well as a way to limit the powers entrusted to certain EU institutions.[97] Both explanations fit with the Schengen Agreement (1985), which reflected the willingness of Belgium, Luxembourg and the Netherlands to follow Franco-German efforts at border control and a long-standing reluctance by member states to countenance the Community method of policymaking in this domain.[98] Traditional explanations remain relevant for the latest generation of international treaties. In the case of the ESM Treaty, for example, an international law treaty suited the United Kingdom, which had sought to minimise its exposure to euro crisis funds, and eurozone members, which had sought to limit the European Commission's role in crisis resolution from the outset of the euro crisis.[99] In the case of the Fiscal Compact, EU heads of state or government met in December 2011 to consider the 'possibility of limited treaty changes' in response to the euro crisis. But after UK Prime Minister David Cameron tabled a set of proposals that other EU leaders refused to support, eurozone heads of state or government announced their intention to press ahead with an agreement among a subset of eurozone members to be codified in 'primary law'.[100]

EU member states' turn to international treaties is also consistent with the two-level game approach, which sees governments as seeking slack when the procedures governing treaty making become too tight. One advantage of international treaties is that they are not bound by the rules and norms governing EU treaty making, with the result that treaties can be negotiated in a tightly sealed intergovernmental setting. This makes it easier for governments to sidestep demands for the European Parliament to play a greater role. Had MEPs been involved in negotiations over the ESM Treaty or secondary legislation had been introduced instead, greater democratic oversight of the ESM would probably have resulted.[101] In other cases, international treaties allow member states to pursue closer cooperation where agreement within the EU has proved difficult, where EU institutions may have reservations about doing so and/or where the constraints of enhanced cooperation are not deemed desirable or possible.[102] The challenges of securing acceptable arrangements can be seen in the complexity of the European patent system, which has taken years to establish. In 2013, member states pressed ahead with plans to establish a European patent court by means of an international law treaty having modified the agreement to take account of the (negative) opinion of the EUCJ on an earlier version.[103] The Court has not yet been set up due to ratification problems including a constitutional challenge before the German constitutional court.[104]

The most significant advantage of international treaties from a two-level game perspective is that they potentially reduce the risk of involuntary defection. David Cameron's objections to the Fiscal Compact can be explained, in part, by a fear that an EU treaty amendment would trigger a ratification crisis at home. Whether a referendum on an EU fiscal compact would have been required under the European Union Act

(2011) is debatable, but pressure to hold such a vote was mounting nonetheless in advance of the December 2011 European Council.[105] Pushing other member states towards an international law treaty rather than an EU treaty amendment allowed the UK Prime Minister to avoid such domestic pressure, while, somewhat paradoxically, winning kudos at home for 'standing up to Brussels'.[106]

The Treaty of Paris provided for its own entry into force only after it had been ratified by 'all the Member States in accordance with their respective constitutional rules'[107] and established the same threshold for amendments to this treaty.[108] So it remains under the Lisbon Treaty. International treaties negotiated by EU member states have to comply with the norms of international treaties.[109] The Schengen Convention implementing the 1985 Agreement, for instance, was subject to the 'ratification, acceptance or approval' of its signatories.[110] The ESM Treaty was more radical still (in the EU context) in allowing for its own entry into force 'on the date when instruments of ratification, approval or acceptance have been deposited by signatories whose initial subscriptions represent no less than 90 per cent of the total subscriptions'.[111] For Fabbrini, this abandoning of the unanimity requirement for treaty making can be seen as a conscious attempt by member states to pre-empt the ratification failures witnessed at Maastricht, Nice and Lisbon.[112] In this sense, choosing international law treaty making over traditional modes of EU treaty making offered governments a variation on the strategy of cutting slack.

Some scholars see member states' departure from traditional modes of treaty making during the euro crisis as a product of the crisis itself. Conventional modes of treaty revision were impractical, Bruno de Witte suggests, in a fast-moving crisis that demanded a show of financial firepower that the EU's institutional framework could not provide.[113] The ESM Treaty entered into force eight months before the amendment to Article 136 TFEU took effect.[114] Had the ESM Treaty taken this long – or longer – member states' efforts to combat the euro crisis would have been significantly complicated. Negotiations over the Fiscal Compact also reflected concerns over the 'considerable rigidity' of the TFEU amendment process.[115] In a letter to Herman Van Rompuy, German Chancellor Angela Merkel and French President Nicolas Sarkozy openly considered alternatives to treaty change based on an agreement between all 'member states willing and able to do'.[116] Beukers, de Witte and Kilpatrick are of the view that the states accidentally stumbled into the conclusion of an international agreement with the ESM.[117] Kenneth Armstrong warns of consequences from such an approach, arguing that treaty making during the euro crisis 'was undertaken for purely political ends to send messages to nervous markets'.[118] Paul James Cardwell and Tamara Hervey share this view, describing treaty reform during the euro crisis as 'a parody of law – a form of "hyper legalism" where law is used simply to be seen to be "doing something"'.[119] Paul Craig puts it even more plainly when he describes Angela Merkel and Nicolas Sarkozy's decision to press ahead with the Fiscal Compact after traditional modes of treaty making failed as an exercise in face saving.[120]

There is also some evidence to suggest that EU leaders saw international treaties as easier to ratify in their own domestic arenas. In January 2012, Herman Van Rompuy floated the idea that the Fiscal Compact could be drafted in a way to obviate the need for either a referendum or parliamentary approval.[121] In point of fact, this proposal sought to transform the Fiscal Compact from an exercise in treaty making to one of legislation by activating a provision in the Treaty on the Functioning of the European Union that allows the Council to amend Protocol No. 12, which concerns the excessive deficit procedure, by means of a special legislative procedure.[122] Although Van Rompuy's trial balloon quickly burst, the idea that the Fiscal Compact would not necessitate approval via the usual channels persisted. Cyprus broke from EU treaty-making norms by approving this agreement by means of a government decree rather an act of the House of Representatives (see Chapter 4).[123] Ireland's break from EU treaty-making norms proved less successful. Having routinely put significant EU treaty amendments to a referendum since Maastricht, the Irish government initially refused to be drawn on whether the people would be offered a vote on the Fiscal Compact.[124] In the end, the government followed the Attorney General's advice that a referendum was required,[125] the treaty being approved by a margin of 60.3 per cent to 39.7 per cent.

The evidence presented in this section is consistent with the two-level game approach. International law treaties offered governments a way of circumventing EU treaty-making rules and norms in principle, if not always in practice. Does this mean that the normative considerations highlighted by the two-level legitimacy approach have simply been set aside? Not entirely so, as evidenced by governments' invitation to MEPs to participate in Eurogroup Working Group negotiations over the Fiscal Compact.[126] This indicates that the European Parliament could be gaining a foothold in international law treaty making over time, but the EU legislature's exclusion from negotiations over the ESM Treaty shows that parliamentary involvement is far from guaranteed,[127] as does the routine exclusion of national parliaments from the process through which EU member states form international law treaties.

EU policymakers' efforts to secure a fast-track ratification of the ESM Treaty and Fiscal Compact was understandable in the context of the euro crisis but it showed limited regard for legitimacy. The pressure placed on the Irish government not to hold a referendum was particularly problematic in this regard, challenging as it did prevailing constitutional norms in this member state concerning the ratification of EU treaties. Such pressure proved ineffective, however. Asked in January 2012 how he would respond if the government sought to ratify the Fiscal Compact without recourse to a public vote, the President of Ireland raised the possibility that he would not sign the bill giving effect to such a treaty.[128] This move significantly reduced the Irish government's room for manoeuvre over the ratification process, as did the prospect of a legal challenge by opposition parties. It ensured, in other words, that the norms surrounding EU treaty making extended to international treaties in spite of the government's hope of finding slack. Legal challenges against the ESM Treaty in Austria, Estonia, Germany, Ireland and Poland similarly confirmed that the role played by higher courts in EU treaty making would carry over into international law treaty making and perhaps even be enhanced.[129]

That the EU's turn to international treaties reflects governments' ambivalence about, rather than a disregard for, legitimacy is further reflected in motivations for such treaty making to begin with. The Schengen Agreement was welcomed by some, including Commission President Jacques Delors, as a laboratory for future EU treaty change, and so it proved to be with the eventual incorporation of the Schengen acquis in the Amsterdam Treaty.[130] The Fiscal Compact mandates that the necessary steps be taken with the aim of inclusion in the EU treaties following an assessment of the experience of implementation.[131] The Five Presidents' Report (2015), for instance, also argued for the integration into EU law of the Inter-governmental Agreement on the Single Resolution Fund and, eventually, the ESM Treaty, but member states showed little appetite at the time for opening treaties while existing arrangements appeared to be working and the euro crisis had yet to be resolved. The European Commission sees incorporation of the ESM in the EU treaty as only one possible step depending on the range of models chosen to strengthen EMU, explicitly noting that there could be an EU approach, an intergovernmental approach or a mixture of the two.[132]

Conclusion

How have national governments responded to the rise of the people, parliaments and courts in EU treaty making? By becoming more reticent about treaty amendment, while at the same time seeking to circumvent stricter EU treaty-making rules and norms when facing the risk of involuntary defection, this chapter concludes. Our findings show that the rate at which treaty articles are amended has slowed and that this decline was driven, in part, by changes to the rules and norms governing EU treaty making. As parliaments assume a greater role and the likelihood of treaty-related referendums increases, it was found, the rate of treaty amendment slowed. More stringent rules and norms increase the risk of involuntary defection, and governments, it was shown, have responded to this risk in two ways. First, faced with referendum votes against treaties, governments have consistently sought to rescue the agreement, either by rerunning the referendums after offering concessions – as with the ratification crises over Maastricht, Nice and Lisbon – or by salvaging much of the agreement in a new treaty – as in relation to the European Constitution. Second, EU member states turned to international law treaties as a way of minimising the risk of involuntary defections both by allowing fewer states to proceed in the negotiation of the treaty and by removing the unanimity requirement for adoption. Governments' preference for such treaties is linked in part to the opportunity they present to circumvent the rules and norms governing EU treaty making and EU law making. A concern to avoid a UK ratification crisis was a motivation behind the ESM Treaty and Fiscal Compact but did not preclude a challenge before the Court of Justice of the EU, albeit one expedited through both the Irish courts and Court of Justice of the EU, taking the extraordinarily short time of just over seven months.[133]

These findings chime with the two-level game approach, which expects governments to search for slack when their hands have been too tightly bound through ratification rules and norms. But they rest uneasily with the two-level legitimacy approach, with governments showing no preference for voluntary concession and limited regard for legitimacy when domestic constituents block treaty ratification. And yet the EU's increasing recourse to treaty change post-Maastricht was, it was noted, an attempt at recompense. The Amsterdam, Nice, and Lisbon treaties and the European Constitution were motivated, in part, by an attempt to address concerns over EU legitimacy raised by the preceding round of treaty amendment. The long battle to ratify the Lisbon Treaty

HOW CHANGING RULES AND NORMS HAVE SHAPED EU TREATY   241

broke this cycle but only partially so, as evidenced by governments' uneasy turn to treaties during the euro crisis. These agreements can be seen as a way to legitimate the EU's controversial response to the euro crisis, while avoiding the traditional EU levers of legitimation, although they were perhaps lucky to receive the imprimatur of the Court of Justice of the EU.

Notes

1 Lutz (1994).
2 Specifically, Lutz (1994: 358n) looked at amendment over 'the most recent period of constitutional stability exceeding 15 years' for each country.
3 See for example Rasch and Congleton (2006) and Dixon and Holden (2011).
4 Conca (2015).
5 Closa (2012).
6 Closa (2012).
7 Stone Sweet and Sandholtz (1997), p. 307.
8 Ferejohn (1997).
9 Ginsburg and Melton (2015). See also the study of constitutional mortality by Elkins, Ginsburg and Melton (2009).
10 Ginsberg and Melton (2015), p. 711.
11 Rasch and Congelton (2006), p. 545.
12 Lutz (1994), pp. 357–8.
13 Articles 85 and 96, Treaty Establishing the European Coal and Steel Community, 18 April 1951, 261 UNTS, 140 and The Convention on the Transitional Provisions provided for in Article 85 ECSC (full text available at: www.cvce.eu/en/obj/treaty_establishing_the_ecsc_convention_on_the_transitional_provi sions_paris_18_april_1951-en-b51c94eb-f52e-481c-a263-00ff65fad64a.html). The common market for coal was achieved in 1953 (Paxton, 1973: 41).
14 Greene (2012), pp. 846–7.
15 Hooghe and Marks (2009), p. 22.
16 Lutz (1994), pp. 357–8.
17 International Organization (1954).
18 Baker, Gamble, and Ludlam (1994).
19 Supreme Court of Ireland, *Crotty* v. *An Taoiseach* [1987] IR 713 (April 1987).
20 Hodson and Maher (2014).
21 French Constitutional Court, Decision 92–308 DC, Treaty on European Union; Decision 97–394 DC, Treaty of Amsterdam amending the Treaty on European Union, the Treaties establishing the European Communities and certain related instruments, Decision 2007–560 DC, Treaty of Lisbon amending the Treaty on European Union and the Treaty establishing the European Community.

22 See Chapter 4.
23 See Chapter 5.
24 German Federal Constitutional Court, Judgment of 12 October 1993, BVerfGE 89, 155.
25 German Federal Constitutional Court, Judgment of 12 October 1993, BVerfGE 89, 155.
26 Meessen (1993), p. 525.
27 German Federal Constitutional Court, Judgment of the Second Senate of 30 June 2009 – 2 BvE, 262–3.
28 General Affairs Council (1992).
29 van Ooik and Curtin (1994), p. 349.
30 European Council (1992a).
31 European Council (1992a).
32 Danish Ministry of Foreign Affairs (1992).
33 Danish Ministry of Foreign Affairs (1992), p. 192.
34 The Progress Group did not support the compromise (Svensson 1994: 72).
35 Krunke (2005), p. 342.
36 Krunke (2005), p. 343.
37 European Council (1992b).
38 Krunke (2005), pp. 350–1.
39 van Ooik and Curtin (1994), p. 354.
40 van Ooik and Curtin (1994), pp. 357–8.
41 van Ooik and Curtin (1994), p. 365.
42 Teasdale (1993), pp. 193–4.
43 Teasdale (1993), pp. 193–4.
44 Article N(2), Treaty on European Union, 7 February 1992, 1992 O.J. (C191) 1, 31 I.L.M. 253.
45 Article J.4, Treaty on European Union.
46 Declaration on civil protection, energy and security, Treaty on European Union.
47 Declaration on the hierarchy of Community Acts, Treaty on European Union.
48 European Council (1995).
49 European (Council (1992a).
50 General Affairs Council (2001).
51 Source: http://irelandelection.com/referendum.php?electype=6&elecid=201.
52 For example, the Sixteenth Amendment of the Constitution was enacted in 1996 after a referendum in which turn out was 29.23 per cent. Source: http://irelandelection.com/referendum.php?electype=6&elecid=194.
53 European Council (2002).
54 Gilland (2002).
55 Laffan and O'Mahony (2008), p. 108.
56 Reuters (2001).
57 European Council (2001).

58 European Council (2001).

59 Laursen (2008), sections II, V and VI.

60 Millns (2008)

61 Paris-Dobozy (2008), p. 510.

62 Financial Times (2005).

63 European Council (2005).

64 See www.eu2006.at/en/The_Council_Presidency/Conference_The_Sound_of_Europe/index.html.

65 European Commission (2005).

66 European Council (2007b).

67 European Council (2007c).

68 Council Presidency (2007), p. 3.

69 Walker (2008).

70 Open Europe (2008) estimates that the two treaties are 96 per cent similar, but Piris (2010: 6) argues that the differences between the two make the Lisbon Treaty a 'very different turning political point in the history of the European Union'.

71 Oppermann (2013b).

72 Traynor (2007).

73 Irish Times (2007).

74 Traynor and Watt (2008).

75 European Council (2008).

76 De Búrca (2009), p. 1484.

77 European Council (2009).

78 European Council (1992a).

79 Protocol (No. 5) on the Position of Denmark, Treaty of Amsterdam Amending the TEU, the Treaties Establishing the European Communities and Certain Related Acts, 2 October 1997, 1997 O.J. (C340) 1, 37 I.L.M. 253.

80 Taylor (2009).

81 Quinlan (2012)

82 Official Journal L 060, 02/03/2013 P. 0129–0139.

83 Krutz and Peake (2009), p. 2.

84 Article II, Section 2, US Constitution (1789, amended to 1992).

85 Congressional Research Service (2001), pp. 5–6 and 17.

86 Finch (1954).

87 Hathaway (2008).

88 Wirth (2016).

89 Article 351TFEU, Hofmann, Rowe and Türk (2011), p. 80.

90 Article 220, Treaty Establishing the European Economic Community (1957), also allowed double tax treaties between member states; Ward and McCormack (2001), p. 179. This provision was later repealed by the Lisbon Treaty.

91 Bulletin of the European Communities Supplement No. 2–1969, pp. 7–16.

92 Official Journal L 299, 31/12/1972, pp. 32–42; de Witte (2009).

93 For the Convention implementing the Agreement, see Official Journal L 239, 22/09/2000 pp. 19–62.

94 Text available at: www.esm.europa.eu/sites/default/files/20150203_-_esm_treaty_-_en.pdf.

95 Treaty on Stability, Coordination and Governance in the Economic and Monetary Union of 2 March 2012 – not published in the Official Journal. Full text available at: http://eur-lex.europa.eu/legal-content/EN/TXT/?uri=LEG ISSUM:1403_3.

96 de Witte (2009), pp. 272–3.

97 Dimopoulos (2015), pp. 288 and 295.

98 Zaiotti (2011), pp. 74–5.

99 Gocaj and Meunier (2013).

100 European Council (2011).

101 European Parliament (2013).

102 Beukers, de Witte and Kilpatrick (2017), p. 9.

103 Court of Justice of the EU, Opinion 1/09 of the Court (Full Court), 8 March 2011 (Opinion delivered pursuant to Article 218(11) TFEU – Draft agreement – Creation of a unified patent litigation system – European and Community Patents Court – Compatibility of the draft agreement with the Treaties), ECLI:EU:C:2011:123. See Jaeger (2012).

104 Richardson (2017).

105 Cash (2011).

106 Thompson (2011).

107 Article 99, Treaty Establishing the European Coal and Steel Community.

108 Article 96, Treaty Establishing the European Coal and Steel Community.

109 United Nations (2012), Section 3.

110 Article 139(1), Convention Implementing the Schengen Agreement of 14 June 1985 between the Governments of the States of the Benelux Economic Union, the Federal Republic of Germany and the French Republic, on the Gradual Abolition of Checks at their Common Borders, 19 June 1990. Official Journal L 239, 22/09/2000, pp. 19–62.

111 Article 48(1), Treaty Establishing the European Stability Mechanism, 2 February 2012. Text available at: www.esm.europa.eu/sites/default/files/20150203_-_esm_treaty_-_en.pdf.

112 Fabbrini (2016), p. 131.

113 Official Journal L 299, 31/12/1972, pp. 32–42; Bruno de Witte (2013), p. 4.

114 Borger (2015), p. 154.

115 de Witte (2011), p. 8.

116 Sarkozy and Merkel (2011).

117 Beukers, de Witte and Kilpatrick (2017).

118 Armstrong (2012).

119 Cardwell and Hervey (2015).

120 Craig (2012), p. 233.
121 Chaffin (2011).
122 Article 126(14), TFEU (consolidated version 2016), Official Journal C 202, 07.06.2016, pp. 1–405.
123 Pantazatou (2014), p. 38.
124 Cienski, Smyth and Spiegel (2012).
125 Stuart and McDonald (2012).
126 Armstrong (2012).
127 Héritier and Moury (2015).
128 Collins (2012).
129 Reestman (2017); Ginter (2013).
130 Zaiotti (2011), p. 39.
131 Article 16, Treaty on Stability, Coordination and Governance in the Economic and Monetary Union of 2 March 2012 – not published in the Official Journal. Full text available at: http://eur-lex.europa.eu/legal-content/EN/TXT/?uri=LEGISSUM:1403_3. European Commission (2017a), p. 4.
132 There is some caution also reflected in European Commission (2017b).
133 Case C-370/12, *Pringle* v. *Government of Ireland*, [2012], ECLI: EU:C:2012:756, paras. 24–27.

9 Eight Ideas for Reforming EU Treaty Making

The United Nations International Covenant on Human Rights 'would be more appropriately entitled as a Convenant on Human Slavery or subservience to government', argued US Senator John W. Bricker in 1951.[1] As these colourful remarks reflect, Bricker objected not only to the treaty in question but also to the idea of treaty making as a tool that can be exploited by the executive branch. A year later, Bricker proposed the first in a series of constitutional revisions to rein in the President's treaty-making powers.[2] The Bricker Amendment, as these proposals are known, was defeated, but it received considerable support from conservative politicians and pressure groups, including the Vigilant Women of the Bricker Amendment, which delivered a 500,000-strong petition to Washington, DC.[3] This outcry was a product of its time, but the 'ghost of Senator Bricker'[4] continues to haunt US treaty making. Although the 1972 Case-Zablocki Act[5] established congressional oversight of executive agreements, the use of such instruments in lieu of treaties is a matter of recurring debate.[6]

Treaties are no less contentious in the politics of European integration, but there is little appetite, among scholars at least, for imposing further checks and balances on treaty making. 'In the light of comparative constitutional law and the practice of international organisations, the general procedure for amending the treaties is particularly rigid', argued a high-level report on treaty amendment submitted by leading legal scholars to the European Commission in 2000.[7] Vivien Schmidt makes a similar point when she criticises current treaty-making rules and norms for allowing some member states 'to hold the others hostage, delaying the entry into vigour of treaties approved by the others and often watering down measures desired by large majorities in futile attempts to engineer compromise'.[8] Critical too is Carlos Closa, who argues that treaty revision procedures 'are too rigid and, hence, that national governments are increasingly tempted to channel reform via treaties outside the EU'.[9]

Concern for the rigidity of EU treaty making is understandable from a two-level game perspective. Tying hands can, Putnam conjectures, confer bargaining advantages in international diplomacy, but, if taken too far, 'negotiators would suddenly find themselves deadlocked, for the win sets no longer overlap at all'.[10] Seen in these terms, the case for greater flexibility in EU treaty is clear. Such flexibility would reduce the risk of involuntary defection witnessed in relation to treaty amendment from Maastricht to Lisbon. It would encourage governments to pursue future amendments as and when they are needed rather than if and when they can be ratified.

The evidence presented in Chapter 8 challenges the idea that EU treaty making is too rigid. Changing rules and norms concerning ratification are associated with falling treaty amendment rates, it was noted, but treaty making has by no means ground to a halt, not least as governments are willing and able to circumvent such constraints. From a two-level legitimacy perspective, there is, moreover, a risk to untying national governments' hands without understanding why they have been bound to begin with. This theoretical approach, as discussed in Chapter 2, sees national government's privileged position in treaty making as contested. The rise of parliaments, the people and courts in the negotiation and consent stages of EU treaty making are a response to, and reflection of, this contestation. As such, attempts to reassert national governments' privileged position could trigger a backlash. Before making treaties easier to amend, in other words, we should reflect on why treaty making has become more difficult.

This chapter critically examines the case for reforming EU treaty making, as viewed from the competing theoretical perspectives at the heart of this volume. The sections that follow debate, in turn, (1) the case for unanimity in treaty making, (2) the regulation of national referendums, (3) a pan-European referendum, (4) time locks on treaty reforms, (5) citizen-led treaty making, (6) judicial and parliamentary oversight, (7) a European Convention on the Law of Treaties and (8) allowing treaties to fail. Some of these ideas are familiar from the literature; others are offered in the interest of debate. Together, we hope they point the way towards a richer discussion of how Europe makes treaties and how it could make them differently.

Upholding the Unanimity Requirement

A perennial proposal concerning EU treaty making is to introduce majority voting, allowing the entry into force of a treaty without the backing of all member states. This idea owes a debt to the European Parliament's Draft Treaty on the European Union (1984), which broke from three decades of tradition by providing for its own entry into force if backed by a majority of member states representing two-thirds of the Community's population.[11] Penelope, Romano Prodi's 2003 ill-fated feasibility study on the European Constitution, offered a more provocative proposal still, arguing that the treaty should enter into force once five-sixths of member states had ratified it and that subsequent amendments would require approval by a reinforced majority.[12] Neither the Dooge Report nor the drafters of the Single European Act took up the European Parliament's proposal on majority voting. The drafters of the European Constitution, meanwhile, retained the unanimity requirement for both the ordinary and simplified revision procedures, as did the Lisbon Treaty.[13]

Among academic commentators, Fernando Mendez, Mario Mendez and Vasiliki Triga offer the most comprehensive treatment to date of this issue by setting out a number of 'models' that could serve as alternatives to the unanimity requirement in EU treaty making. One such model, inspired by the Draft Treaty on European Union, would allow a supermajority at both the negotiation and consent stages of treaty making, which the authors suggest could overcome 'the paralysis and stagnation' of treaty making in an enlarged Union.[14] Another, more innovative model would allow a subset of EU member states to conclude treaties within the EU's legal framework.[15] Enhanced constitutional reform, as Mendez, Mendez and Triga call it, would create serious questions about preserving the *acquis communautaire* and the EU internal market, the authors accept, although they envisage the empowerment of Community institutions through such treaties as helping to police such matters.[16]

Dropping the unanimity requirement at the consent stage of treaty making offers some advantages from a two-level game perspective. It ensures that states that do not ratify, accept or approve a treaty cannot derail this agreement. Consistent with this line of reasoning is Bruno de Witte's critique of EU treaty making for being too rigid; sooner or later, he argues, the EU 'will need to confront the "taboo" of the unanimity requirement for any kind of treaty amendment'.[17] For Closa, the unanimity requirement has resulted in EU treaty making becoming the antithesis of constitutional politics. The threat of vetoes from individual member states, he suggests, has pushed EU treaty negotiations into ever-more-detailed institutional reforms and compromises that are at odds with the general character of most national constitutions.[18]

Powerful though these arguments are, they rest uneasily with the evidence presented in this volume. Amendment rates have fallen as the likelihood of referendums has increased, but there is no sign, as Schmidt suggests, that EU treaty making is 'dead in its tracks'.[19] Had EU treaties been so hard to amend, it is hard to see how EU member states would have moved so rapidly from Maastricht to Amsterdam, from Amsterdam to Nice and from Nice to Lisbon via the European Constitution. Ratification crises might have discouraged governments from revising treaties after Lisbon but did not deter them entirely, as evidenced by the minimal but politically significant revision to Article 136 TFEU during the euro crisis allowing for the creation of the ESM.[20] Concerns over the 'rigidity of EU primary law', as de Witte acknowledges, rest uneasily with the 'constant trend to increase the volume of constitutional law' in the EU.[21]

The unanimity requirement is easier to defend from a two-level legitimacy perspective. 'Is it right', Hervé Bribosia asks, 'that the refusal of a few hundred thousand inhabitants should be allowed to block a reform desired by the representatives of five hundred million people?'[22] Where legitimacy is a primary consideration, the answer, we contend, is 'yes'. The consent to be bound is a defining principle of treaty making between sovereign states. In practice, new treaties do not typically enter into force unless the parties to it have expressed their consent to be bound.[23] The question of consent for treaty amendments is more intricate. Under the Vienna Convention on the Law of Treaties, an amendment to a multilateral treaty cannot bind a state that is party to the original treaty without that state having become a party to the amending agreement.[24] In practice, multilateral treaties often include standard amendment procedures that allow a qualified majority of parties to amend the existing treaties,[25] but states that oppose such amendments typically cannot be bound by such amendments against their will. Multilateral treaties sometimes include simplified amendment procedures, which in some cases allow for a majority of states to approve amendments that apply to all parties to the original agreement, whether they have given their consent to be bound by such changes or not or by allowing or compelling non-consenting states to withdraw from the treaty.[26]

Although the case against unanimity hinges on treaty making in other international organisations, majority voting is by no means the norm in such bodies. Amendments to the United Nations Charter, for example, can enter into force if ratified by two-thirds of members, but only if this majority includes all permanent members of the Security Council.[27] This gives the most powerful UN members an effective veto over amendments, a point that was challenged by smaller states when the UN Charter was agreed,[28] and which explains why formal amendments have been so rare since 1945.[29] The IMF's Articles of Agreement can be modified by three-fifths of the members, having 85 per cent of the total voting power, but the most sensitive aspects of the Fund's operation, such as a change to members' quotas, cannot be introduced without the consent of all. IMF members can withdraw from the Fund at any time, which may explain why amendments to the Articles of Agreement are infrequent.

Switching from unanimity to majority voting would be unlikely to enhance the EU's legitimacy and could even make matters worse. True, the threat of exclusion from the EU might encourage national parliaments or, in the case of referendums, voters to weigh more carefully the consequences of voting against specific treaties. However, such brinksmanship could backfire for the EU by turning a crisis over the ratification of a treaty into an existential one for the Union. Such concerns are more significant post-Brexit where the prospect of a member state withdrawing from the EU is real rather than imaginary and the costs to the Union from losing a member all too apparent. A switch from unanimity to majority voting could also harm the EU's legitimacy by causing the kind of fragmentation in EU law that such flexibility is designed to avoid. A situation in which some but not all member states adhere to a treaty, as Weiler and Modrall observed in their reflections on the Draft Treaty Establishing the European Union, could jeopardise the 'constitutionalisation of the European Community Treaties' by reconstruing them 'in international legal terms'.[30] This important point is overlooked by those who see majority voting in relation to EU treaty making as a step towards ever-closer union.

Regulating Referendums

'Perhaps it is time for an EU ban on referenda!' concluded a former EU adviser after Dutch voters rejected the EU-Ukraine Association Agreement in 2016.[31] A mischievous proposal this may have been, but the idea of untying hands in EU treaty making by regulating national referendums is taken seriously in popular and scholarly debates. Mendez, Mendez and Triga offer what is arguably the strongest argument for such limits. National referendums on EU treaties are effectively 'extra territorial' votes, they argue, because of the significant consequences generated by voters in one member state on the rest of the Union. Carlos Closa[32] makes a similar point when he argues that the rejection of a treaty generates negative externalities for other member states, as occurred in the Exchange Rate Mechanism crisis triggered by Denmark's 'no' vote against the Maastricht Treaty in 1992.[33]

An obvious limitation of such arguments is that the EU has no authority to determine the manner in which member states give their consent to be bound to treaties. Some scholars argue otherwise, such as Andreas Auer, who suggests that national voters are exceeding the limits of their power by being asked to decide on EU treaties, and Alfred Kellermann, who questions whether member states' willingness to hold referendums is compatible with the Treaty's 'duty of loyal cooperation'.[34] Such arguments are at odds with the Treaty on European Union's requirement that treaty amendments enter into force 'after being ratified by all the member states in accordance with their respective constitutional requirements'.[35] The Simplified Revision Procedure substitutes the word 'approved' for 'ratified' in this context, which hints at a less onerous expression of states' consent to be bound by such treaty amendments.[36] But, as Steve Peers notes, 'it is hard to see the difference between an "approval" and a "ratification" requirement, since the crucial element in either case is the need to satisfy the "respective constitutional requirements" of the Member States'.[37]

To date, the principle that states decide on such national constitutional requirements remains sacrosanct. Herman Van Rompuy's plan for a fast-track ratification of the Fiscal Compact is a rare example of EU policymakers' questioning this principle, but it was, as noted in Chapter 8, a short-lived one. Ireland was not the only member state that pushed back against Van Rompuy's plan. In Italy, opposition MPs criticised attempts to synchronise ratification with Germany, and the Italian government opted in the end to ratify the Fiscal Compact and Article 136 TFEU in tandem.[38] A similar merger took place in Greece, Italy, Malta, the Netherlands and Portugal, illustrating the resilience of national constitutional requirements in treaty making.[39] However problematic referendums might be as an instrument for deciding on EU treaties, their prohibition would be more troubling still from a two-level legitimacy perspective. A key theme of this book is that governments' willingness to consider referendums cannot be reduced to tactical considerations; it is an expression of, and response to, deep-seated concerns over the EU's legitimacy. European referendums are, as Stephen Tierney puts it, 'the people's last sigh'.[40] Richard Rose and Gabriela Borz present evidence that speaks to this point: those who lack confidence in EU decision making, are dissatisfied with EU democracy and dislike European integration are more likely to demand EU referendums.[41]

This is not to suggest that national constitutional traditions should not or do not evolve to limit referendums on EU treaties. In 2013, Slovenia enacted a constitutional amendment that prohibited so-called legislative referendums on EU treaties (see Chapter 5). This provision had not been used to trigger a referendum related to an EU treaty, although a public vote was called on the arbitration agreement between Slovenia and Croatia over a border dispute in 2010.[42] The 2013 constitutional amendment restricted the right to initiate legislative referendums to citizens only and prohibited its use in relation to laws concerning the rights of treaties.[43] The impetus for this reform came not from the EU but from a protracted domestic debate about the use of legislative referendums by parties and pressure groups to block reforms,[44] as in 2011, when four referendums against the economic policies of Prime Minister Borut Pahor brought the government down.

In December 2017, the Dutch government introduced a Draft Law to End the Advisory Referendum Law. This was an attempt to put 'the referendum genie back in its bottle', as one commentator put, following the popular vote against the Ukraine–European Union Association Agreement (Chapter 10).[45] Other examples of EU member states seeking to limit the scope of the people in EU treaty making are hard to find. Noticeable by its absence in the aftermath of *Crotty* was an attempt by the Irish government to recraft the Irish Constitution to circumvent the need for referendums on EU treaties.[46] New wording was finally introduced on the occasion of the second referendum on the Lisbon Treaty to affirm the country's 'commitment to the European Union within which the Member States of that Union work together to promote peace, shared values and the well-being of their peoples'.[47] However, Ireland's then Minister of Foreign Affairs, Micheál Martin, suggested this change was symbolic[48] and there is little prospect that it will make a material difference to how Ireland ratifies EU treaty amendments.[49]

Insofar as the regulation of referendums can be justified from a two-level legitimacy perspective it would be to limit the EU's tendency to overlook referendum results, as occurred in the re-run referendums over Maastricht, Nice and Lisbon and the willingness to salvage much of the European Constitution in spite of referendum votes against it. There are arguments in favour of second referendums. Sinnott, for example, finds a marked increase in both communication and understanding in Ireland's re-run referendum on the Nice Treaty.[50] But this practice is all too easily criticised, as Gráinne De Búrca notes, for failing 'to respect the outcome of legitimate constitutional processes and [undermining] the democratically expressed will of the people'. Stephen Tierney goes further by seeing second referendums as sending a clear message 'that national electorates will not be allowed to frustrate closer integration'.[51] Cormac Mac Amhlaigh makes a similar point, suggesting that repeat referendums run contrary to the democratic ideals on which the Union is based.[52]

Although the EU lacks the authority to regulate national ratification processes for the reasons discussed above, governments could agree unilaterally to respect the results of referendums before they are held, as senior politicians did before the Dutch European Constitution referendum. Political declarations of this sort are commonplace in relation to referendum results worldwide. In 2010, for example, campaigners on both sides of the South Sudanese independence referendum made a pledge to the UN Security Council to respect the results of the vote.[53]

A Pan-European Referendum

In 1952, Michel Debrés, a French member of the Ad Hoc Assembly, proposed a European referendum on the treaty concerning the European Political Community.[54] This proposal was influenced by Charles De Gaulle's call in 1949 for a referendum of 'free Europeans' on the future organisation of Europe. De Gaulle revived this idea in 1960 as part of his plan for a Union of States, arguing that a new intergovernmental policy community should be endorsed by a 'solemn European referendum'.[55] Altiero Spinelli called for a European referendum on a European constitution in 1964,[56] and his ideas were taken up four decades later by an unlikely coalition of Eurosceptics and Europhiles in the European Convention, who proposed a pan-European referendum on the European Constitution. A pan-European referendum has been championed by a number of public intellectuals, including Jürgen Habermas and Ulrich Beck, and politicians, among them Emmanuel Macron, who argued during his time as French economy minister for a 'true European referendum' on a new roadmap for Europe.[57] The Union of European

Federalists is among a number of pressure groups to have pushed for some time for European direct democracy.[58]

Among EU scholars, Richard Rose has made the case for such a vote. 'The most authoritative way to confirm the commitment of Europe's citizens to an ever closer Union', he suggests, 'is to put a treaty to a pan-European referendum in which all of Europe's citizens have the right to vote'.[59] Holding such a vote would not be popular with governments, he admits, but is the best means of securing popular commitment for the European project.[60] Francis Cheneval and Mónica Ferrin call for mandatory binding referendums to be held simultaneously in all EU member states.[61] Whereas most proponents of a pan-European referendum envisage a vote on a grand constitutional project, Cheneval and Ferrin turn this logic on its head. Partial treaty amendments are likely to be more accessible to voters, they argue, inasmuch as simplicity is a desirable property of direct democracy.

A pan-European referendum would be desirable in a two-level game only if it circumvented rather than compounded the risk of a ratification crisis. Such a vote could 'introduce intolerable constitutional rigidity', warn Mendez, Mendez and Triga, who conceive of a pan-European referendum as operating in conjunction with an end to the principle of unanimity.[62] It is for this reason that the idea of a pan-European referendum often resurfaces during ratification crises, as in 2006, when Austrian Prime Minister Wolfgang Schüssel proposed a European referendum on the stalled European Constitution. The European Constitution would enter into force, Schüssel argued, if approved by a majority of member states and voters. Rose's vision of a pan-European referendum preserves the unanimity requirement. As such, he is open to the possibility that such a vote could lead to a rejection rather than the approval of a treaty. Cheneval and Ferrin see a double majority requirement – whereby a majority of voters and a majority of member states decide the referendum outcome – as a more viable option.[63]

A pan-European referendum is often sold as a way of relegitimating the European project. In advocating such a vote on the European Constitution, Habermas saw the potential for a great debate among the people of Europe that would catalyse the European project. Beck and Grande are no less effusive when they champion a pan-European referendum as a way of strengthening European civil society and establishing a European public sphere.[64] Bellamy and Kröger are among several scholars to defend the idea of a pan-European referendum on grounds of fairness.[65] Between 72 per cent and 92 per cent of EU citizens have no chance to vote on a treaty, they note, an inequity that would be overcome if all voters had a chance to decide on treaty amendments.[66] Cheneval goes further by describing the situation whereby citizens in some member states have a direct say on treaties as a form of discrimination.[67]

The analysis presented in this book gives pause for thought on the case for a European referendum as a solution to the EU's legitimacy problems. First, it questions whether any citizens are truly prevented from voting on treaties. Referendums may be rare in some member states but they are prohibited in none. As discussed in Chapter 5, Portugal is the only member state to have prohibited a referendum in relation to EU treaty ratification, and it removed this constitutional rule in 1997. Second, calling a European referendum could aggravate problems of legitimacy by superseding national constitutional rules and norms. Referendums are unlikely in Germany and probable in Ireland, we contend, because of constitutional rules and norms in these member states. To refashion these rules and norms in the name of EU treaty making would be to transpose a European constitutional discourse on top of national ones in ways that could have unpredictable and unwelcome consequences. Such a move would cut across the current controversial kompetenz-kompetenz debates on the scope of EU law in light of core national constitutional values, in particular in the German Constitutional Court.[68] Although proponents of a pan-European referendum are quick to appeal to the idea of legitimacy, as we have seen, they appear to do so in the interests of legitimating a particular vision of European integration. Voters and member states that do not support this vision at a particular point in time are excluded. As in proposals for majority voting, the threat of exclusion could focus minds in referendum campaigns but could also turn a ratification crisis into one about the future of the EU. Third, proponents of pan-European referendums, for the most part, make strong assumptions about the quality of a European referendum campaign that is at odds with the national experience. As discussed above, national referendums on EU treaties often expose the limitations of referendums as legitimating devices. There is no guarantee that a European referendum would fare any better at a European level. Indeed, there are reasons to believe that a pan-European referendum run by pan-European parties with limited experience of referendums might fair even worse.

Time Locks on Treaty Reform

EU treaty making can be a self-reinforcing process. The rush to revise treaties in the 1990s and 2000s, we argued in Chapter 8, was a sincere, if somewhat contradictory, attempt to address the problems of legitimacy facing the EU. Governments reacted to legitimacy concerns raised by treaty ratification through another round of treaty amendment, which revealed further problems of legitimacy and so on.[69] Frequent treaty amendment may have been detrimental to the EU's legitimacy for this reason and because new treaty arrangements were given little time to bed down. A case in point is the Nice Treaty's provisions on qualified majority voting, which were in operation for less than two years before EU member states agreed, in the European Constitution, to revise them. While flexibility is a necessary and desirable feature of national constitutions, most, as Jan-Erik Lane notes, employ one or more mechanisms of constitutional inertia.[70] Such mechanisms can be problematic, Lane accepts, as when they contradict the democratic will of the people, but they can also bolster the legitimacy of constitutional law as a form of *lex superior*. The unanimity lock on EU treaty making serves as a powerful mechanism of constitutional inertia, but constitutional practices in EU member states and further afield point towards other possibilities. One is what Lane calls confirmation by a second decision. In Greece, MPs must back proposals on the need for constitutional amendment in two ballots held at least two months apart, with the decision on such revisions taken by MPs in the next parliament.[71] Intervening elections are also a feature of constitutional amendment in Belgium, Denmark, Estonia, Finland, Luxembourg, the Netherlands, Spain and Sweden.

Intervening elections would allow national parliaments to challenge their reputation (whether deserved or not) as a 'permissive rubber stamp' for European integration.[72] It would ensure a longer period of parliamentary debate before treaties can be ratified and give the people a powerful indirect say in the ratification process without necessarily resorting to a referendum. In effect it would provide a time delay. Greater involvement by national parliaments would not, of course, be a panacea. The rise of parliaments in EU treaty making may be linked to concerns over legitimacy, but national parliaments suffer from significant problems of legitimacy. In 2001, 51 per cent of EU citizens tended to trust their national parliaments. By 2015, this figure had fallen to 28 per cent.[73] Giving national parliaments an even greater say in EU treaty making is unlikely to reverse this trend, which is rooted in societal shifts that go well beyond EU affairs and, indeed, Europe.[74] It would, however, decelerate the process of EU treaty making.

Intervening elections could be seen as a recipe for political chaos in EU treaty making given the asynchronicity of national election calendars. For example, an EU treaty amendment approved in January 2017 would take up to five years before it could be approved by each national legislature either side of a scheduled election. From a two-level game perspective, this could increase the risk of involuntary defection, but this need not necessarily be the case. Whether European referendums are second-order events in which voters are motivated by domestic considerations rather than attitudes towards Europe is a matter of debate in the scholarly literature,[75] but such referendums certainly provide an opportunity for voters to give unpopular governments a bloody nose. In such circumstances, voters, as Gerald Schneider and Patricia Weitsman put it, 'choose between accepting an agreement on the basis of its merit and risk rewarding a government that has not successfully managed domestic politics, or rejecting the treaty, thereby punishing a popular government that negotiated and supported ratification of the agreement'.[76] A variation on this punishment trap, as Schneider and Weitsman call it, certainly seems to have played a role in some referendums on the European Constitution. In France, more than a quarter of voters who did not turn out were motivated by a desire to punish the government or President of the Republic, according to a Eurobarometer survey.[77] Among those who rejected the treaty, 18 per cent did so because they opposed the President, government or certain political parties.[78] Intervening elections would provide an opportunity to channel such frustration before referendum votes are held.

A simpler – and perhaps more workable – time lock would be to introduce a time limit between treaty amendments. Constitutional practice in EU member states, again, points towards reform ideas. In Greece, constitutional revisions are not permitted until five years after the previous round of revision is complete.[79] The Treaty of Paris included something similar. Amendments to the European Coal and Steel Community's founding treaty were not permitted until a five-year transition period had expired, and this provision appears to have had a noticeable impact on the rate of treaty amendment (see Chapter 8).[80] No such provision was included in later EU treaties. Time locks would, evidently, be undesirable from a two-level game perspective since they would impose yet another constraint on governments and, in so doing, unnecessarily complicate the task of treaty making. However, there is an argument for doing so in the future to address the instability and potential delegitimation of frequent, piecemeal revisions.

Citizen-Led Treaty Making

The issue of greater citizen involvement in treaty reform was discussed in the Convention on the Future of Europe but did not make it to the final treaty.[81] Instead, the Lisbon Treaty introduced, for the first time, a European Citizens' Initiative (ECI), which allows a group of not less than one million EU citizens to invite the Commission to submit legislation in a particular policy domain.[82] At the moment, such initiatives lead only to a Commission communication indicating how it proposes to address the matter raised, and the procedural barriers to successful submission are considerable.[83] Intended to allow citizens 'to make known and publicly exchange their views in all areas of Union action', the European Citizens' Initiative, Elizabeth Monaghan argues, offers 'a more radical understanding of the relationship between participation and democracy than has traditionally been found in the EU'.[84] The treaty does not explicitly foresee an initiative concerning treaty amendment, citizens being allowed only to invite the Commission to propose legal acts 'required for the purpose of implementing the Treaties'. However, Mendez, Mendez and Triga suggest that such limits be removed so as to allow treaty revision to be placed on the agenda by citizens.[85]

Involving citizens in EU treaty formation points towards benefits as well as risks from a two-level game perspective. On the plus side, it could potentially reduce the risk of involuntary defection by mobilising input from domestic constituents before the consent stage. On the minus side, the experience of citizen-led constitutional amendments in Central and Eastern Europe[86] and at the state level in the United States shows that such initiatives frequently fail to win popular and/or legislative backing.[87] Citizen initiatives could propose treaty amendments in new and less predictable directions. This may be positive or negative but it highlights the importance of how the initiatives are addressed once submitted, leaving control still with the EU institutions and the member states. Andrew Moravcsik is critical of participatory approaches to EU treaty making. However desirable it may be to involve citizens in EU decision making, it tends, he argues, to produce 'information-poor, institutionally unstructured, and unstable plebiscitary politics'.[88] The failure of the European Constitution was no accident, Moravcsik argues; it was 'doomed to failure'.[89]

There are several forms of citizen participation in constitutional reform (other than referendum) that could provide a model for citizen participation in EU treaty reform.[90] The mixed convention of citizens and parliamentarians is a form that was used in Ireland. There, a Constitutional Convention consisting of 100 members (66 were citizens selected at random by a polling company as a representative sample of the electorate) considered several reforms of the constitution including marriage equality, which was approved in a popular referendum in 2015.[91] A citizens' assembly consisting only of citizens is a form found more recently in Ireland where an assembly of 99 citizens recommended removal of the controversial right to life of the unborn provision in the constitution, going much further than had been expected, with a referendum in 2018.[92] Uniquely, a directly elected constituent convention pondered constitutional reform in Iceland after the financial crisis.[93] The six amendments put forward by the Convention were backed by voters in a non-binding referendum in 2012 before the Althingi, Iceland's parliament, refused to take changes forward.[94]

A number of EU member states, mainly but not exclusively the newer eastern European states, allow groups of citizens to put constitutional amendments directly to the people,[95] with Krunke suggesting this increase in citizen involvement is linked to accession to the EU.[96] For example, in Latvia, a group comprising not less than one-tenth of citizens eligible to vote can put forward a draft amendment for consideration by the Saeima, the country's parliament.[97] In Romania, at least 500,000 citizens with the right to vote from at least half of the country's counties can propose certain categories of constitutional amendment providing signatures are recorded in each of the counties and the Municipality of Bucharest.[98]

How helpful citizens' initiatives can be at enhancing the legitimacy of constitutional amendment is a matter of debate among scholars. The United States is an important test bed of direct democracy, with more than eighteen state constitutions allowing some form of constitutional amendment to be initiated by voters. The implementation of such provisions is problematic. Writing of Oregon's experience, Cody Hoesly concludes that a democratic revival through citizen-led constitutional change has given way to a situation in which 'professional direct democracy firms gather signatures and shop ballot titles while interest groups spend millions on advertising and political efforts'.[99] Recent attempts at citizen inclusion in Romanian constitutional reform have been labeled as government-driven, non-consensual and with populist overtones.[100] Contiades and Fotiadou suggest that two issues need to be addressed when considering direct citizen involvement in constitutional amendment (or in the case of EU treaty reform): first, the history of constitutional change to date and, second, the extent to which citizens are familiar with direct democracy. This is to ensure the traditional risks such as elite manipulation of referendums are not replicated while at the same time ensuring regulatory safeguards do not render the process so complex as to be of limited, if any, value.[101]

Viewed from a two-level legitimacy perspective, citizens' initiatives have the potential to give the people a new role in EU treaty making, but they would not constrain national governments as long as governments must agree to treaty amendments. An alternative approach would be to give citizens a right to block the initiation of treaty amendments. Power, as Peter Bachrach and Morton S. Baratz famously argued, has two faces: the power to take decisions and the power to limit the scope of decision making.[102] The second face, the power of non-decision making, rests squarely with national governments in relation to EU treaty making. A way of giving citizens a say over this second face of treaty-making power would be to hold periodic pan-European referendums on whether to amend EU treaties, for example, every five years. This proposal offers a variation on provisions for constitutional reform in a number of US states. The constitution of the State of Illinois, for example, requires that the electorate be asked at least every twenty years whether a Constitutional Convention should be convened.[103] To date, there have been just three state conventions since 1818, signaling citizens' preference for keeping wholesale constitutional reforms from the political agenda in spite of the many economic and political challenges facing this state.[104]

Judicial and Parliamentary Oversight

An advantage of EU treaty making – the two-level game approach suggests – is that governments can choose between alternative modes of treaty making so as to smooth negotiations and minimise the risk of involuntary defection. Circumventing the need for a convention, for instance, could make it easier for EU governments to reach agreement in sensitive policy domains. Reducing the scope for referendums or court challenges, likewise, could make it easier for member states to offer their consent to be bound. The two-level legitimacy approach warns that such game playing could rebound on governments. By restricting 'rightful membership' of EU treaty making, it suggests, governments could amplify concerns over trust and representation in the EU that drove changes to this domain to begin with.

Increasing the oversight of EU treaty making could be achieved through the Court of Justice of the EU or European Parliament. The *Pringle* case confirmed that the European Council's decision triggering the simplified revision procedure was justiciable, as it is for the Court to confirm the validity of decisions.[105] To ensure compliance with the requirements of that procedure, the Court looked to whether the revision fell within Part III of the TFEU and did not extend the competences of the EU, leading to a detailed (and arguably strained) analysis.[106] The Court noted that the legality of measures can be challenged under Article 263 TFEU, which has a strict two-month time limit. However, where it is not clear whether the applicant could bring such a direct annulment action (standing rules for individuals being more limited than those for institutions and member states), then a reference could be made from a national court. Hence ex post legal challenges via national courts of decisions under the simplified revision procedure are possible. Inviting the Court of Justice to give an opinion on treaty amendments after governments have reached agreement but before they launch the consent stage would pre-empt such legal challenges and the risk of unravelling treaty amendments at a very late stage and through a reference from a constitutional court, in particular the German Constitutional Court, which continues to be very active in this field and has at last made a reference to the Court of Justice of the EU.[107] Such a procedure would be similar to that found in Article 218(11) TFEU where the opinion of the Court can be sought in relation to draft international agreements.[108]

At odds with current practices though this proposal might appear, it is not so far removed from early visions of EU treaty making. Although the Treaty of Paris adopted a narrow intergovernmentalist vision of formal treaty amendment, it envisaged a significant role for the Common Assembly and the Court of Justice of the European Coal and Steel Community in informal modes of treaty making. An adaptation to 'the rules concerning the exercise by the High Authority of the powers which are conferred upon it' was permitted under certain conditions by this treaty but not before the Court considered 'all elements of law and fact' concerning these changes.[109] This was more than mere consultation. Treaty amendment could not be taken forward for approval unless the Court decided that the changes sought conformed to the Treaty's provision on informal treaty amendment.[110]

There are, to be sure, political and legal arguments against enhancing the Court's oversight role in EU treaty making. Politically, it could put the Court on a collision course with governments that had agreed on the manner, the substance and, perhaps, the urgency of treaty amendments. Legally, the independence of the Court would come under necessary scrutiny if it is both the arbiter of compliance with the treaties and able to prohibit amendment of the treaties.[111] This is why limiting review to the conditions set down for the exercise of the simplified revision procedure is important.

And yet courts are increasingly willing to challenge the means through which lawmakers amend constitutions. As Yaniv Roznai notes, such challenges depend on appeals to procedures and, where such procedures are absent, principles, as in the basic structure doctrine developed by Indian courts.[112] Halberstam suggests that expertise, voice and rights should inform the allocation of competence within constitutional systems as between the different branches of government, including the courts.[113] The *Pringle* case and an increased role for the Court of Justice of the EU in ensuring that treaty amendments are consistent with the treaties can be seen in this wider context of increased constitutional review.

Increasing the oversight function of the European Parliament in relation to the simplified revision procedure would be another way to police the rules and norms governing EU treaty making. The European Parliament plays such a role at present in relation to the ordinary revision procedure. If the European Council decides not to convene a convention under this procedure, it can do so only with the consent of the European Parliament, a provision that ensures that governments cannot exclude the EU legislator against its will from this mode of treaty making. The only such checks and balances in relation to the simplified revision procedure is that the European Council must consult the European Parliament before amending all or part of those provisions in the Treaty on the Functioning of the European Union that fall under this procedure.

In this book, we see the European Parliament's increasing role in EU treaty making as a product of its own ambitions and governments' efforts to address concerns over the EU's legitimacy. Whether the European Parliament can legitimate EU treaty making by so doing is a different question. The EU legislature, as the Union's only directed elected body, can make claims to legitimacy that other EU institutions cannot. And yet, like national parliaments, the European Parliament faces problems of legitimacy. According to the European Barometer, the percentage of people who tend to trust the European Parliament fell from 53 per cent in 1993 to 38 per cent in 2015. The European Parliament's new powers of oversight in relation to EU treaty making do not negate such normative challenges but neither should such challenges preclude such a role given the absence of ready-made alternatives.

A European Convention on the Law of Treaties

A common argument against making it more difficult to amend EU treaties is that further constraints would simply encourage national governments to make agreements outside the EU's legal framework.[114] It makes little sense to tie hands in a two-level game because the players, if they find their hands bound too tightly, can simply continue their game in an alternative, more amenable arena. The evidence presented in Chapter 8 certainly speaks to this point. As the rules and norms governing EU treaty making have become more restrictive, governments have turned to international treaties. The Fiscal Compact, in particular, was viewed by member states as a way of reducing the risk of involuntary defection, even if ratification proved more difficult than expected. From this perspective, any attempt to limit member states' international treaty-making power would be doubly counterproductive by reducing governments' room for maneouvre in both Level 1 and Level 2. An analogy can be drawn with the enhanced cooperation procedure, which is designed to allow a group of member states to integrate further in specific policy fields outside the exclusive competence of the EU without all states involved. The procedure is rarely used given the extent to which member state hands are tied.[115]

Scholarly opinion on EU member states signing international treaties with each other is divided. Consistent with the two-level legitimacy approach is Christian Joerges's view that agreements such as the Fiscal Compact circumvent and transform European law as part of a wider process that he calls delegalisation.[116] Nicole Scicluna agrees, criticising the Fiscal Compact for having 'a significant capacity to undermine the rule of law in the EU and, thereby, the integration project's legitimacy'.[117] Bruno de Witte disagrees along lines that are consistent with the two-level game approach. Treaties concluded under international rather than EU law 'are available in the toolbox of European cooperation', he argues, 'for the simple reason that the member states of the European Union are states'.[118]

Whether one is critical of, or pragmatic about, international treaties, they are by no means inevitable if governments find their hands bound too tightly by the rules and norms governing EU treaty making. European law already constrains its member states' treaty-making powers and it could do further. The early case law of the Court of Justice of the EU established that international agreements entered into by member states under international law prior to accession could not violate EU law[119] or affect or alter internal rules designed to achieve the objectives of an EU treaty.[120] Through its subsequent case law, the Court of Justice has narrowed the conditions under which member states can exercise their treaty-making powers not only in relation to third countries but also with each other. In *Defrenne*, the Court ruled that EU treaties can be modified only through the amendment procedure set out in the treaties and not via an international agreement.[121] *Pringle*, although it recognised member states' rights, in this case, to conclude treaties among themselves, made clear that this entitlement was not without limitations.[122] The European Stability Mechanism Treaty would not have been lawful, the Court indicated, if it had concerned an exclusive competence of the EU[123] or if it had disregarded member states' duty to comply with EU law.[124] Such constraints are also reflected in the Lisbon Treaty, which enshrined the EU's exclusive competence over the conclusion of international agreements provided for by EU legislation that are necessary for the exercise of EU internal competence or that may affect or alter the scope of common rules.[125] The same treaty removed earlier provisions that had encouraged member states to conclude international law treaties with each other in specific domains, notably foreign direct investment (see Chapter 8).[126] The shift in competence from the member states to the EU, while it imposes constraints, may be controversial in international law given the tension between the principle of *pacta sunt servanda* and the duty of sincere cooperation set out in the EU treaties.[127]

EU member states could choose to limit their own treaty-making powers yet further. One way forward would be to adopt a European Convention on the Law of EU Treaties that spells out more clearly the conditions under which member states can and cannot resort to international treaties. As things stand, the Vienna Convention on the Law of Treaties provides member states with a significant degree of discretion in how they pursue treaty amendments outside the scope of EU treaty-amendment procedures. In particular, it allows member states to depart from the EU's traditional unanimity requirement by making approval by two-thirds of states the default decision rule for the conclusion of an international treaty and allowing member states to adopt an alternative rule of their choosing.[128] The Vienna Convention also allows EU member states to express their consent to be bound to an international treaty by any means on which they agree, thus departing from the ratification and approval requirements that apply to EU treaties.

A European Convention could commit member states to ratify international treaties in accordance with the rules and norms that apply to EU treaty making. This would reduce governments' incentive to turn to international treaties as a way of reducing the ratification risk associated with EU treaties. The European Convention could also provide for the involvement of the European Parliament and national parliaments in international treaty making in ways that ensure some consistency with the ordinary and simplified revision procedures.

Allowing Treaties to Fail

Perhaps the most contentious question raised in this volume is whether treaties rejected by one or more member states should be allowed to fail. EU governments' aversion to doing so – as evidenced by their recalcitrant response to referendum votes against Maastricht, Nice, the European Constitution and Lisbon – is in line with the two-level game approach. International negotiations are typically not, Putnam notes, a contest over competing agreements but a choice between a particular agreement and the status quo.[129] The costs of non-agreement will be lower for some states than others, with the result that not all will approach negotiations with equal levels of enthusiasm.[130] Asymmetry of this sort is a common feature of EU treaty negotiations, Moravcsik finds, as in the IGC at Maastricht, which saw France give significant ground to Germany to overcome the latter's doubts about Economic and Monetary Union.[131] Once agreement is reached, however, governments will typically prefer ratification over non-ratification. Government preferences in this regard can and do change – not least because of elections – but diplomacy has sunk costs that negotiators are generally reluctant to forgo. Governments may even escalate the resources they devote to failing treaties, especially when they will be held personally responsible for such failure.[132]

Arguments from a two-level game perspective against allowing treaties to fail chimes with the views of some legal scholars about the norms and practice of treaty making. Under the Vienna Convention on the Law of Treaties, states must give their consent to be bound to a treaty, but they take on certain interim obligations at an earlier stage of the treaty-making process. Once a state signs a treaty, it is obliged not to defeat the object and purpose of the treaty until it makes clear its intention not to become a party to this agreement.[133] Typically, this provision is interpreted as prohibiting actions by states that run contrary to a treaty that has been signed but not yet ratified.[134] But some scholars suggest that it carries with it a moral obligation – and perhaps even a legal one – on states to ratify an agreement or, at any rate, to seek the successful ratification of an agreement, once it has been signed.[135]

From a two-level legitimacy perspective, the case for allowing treaties to fail is more complex. Abandoning an agreement could weigh heavily on the EU's legitimacy. EU leaders tend to stake their reputation, and that of the Union, on the successful negotiation and ratification of treaties. Partly for this reason, treaties are seen as a marker of integration, none more so than the Single European Act, an exercise of treaty making that, for some scholars, brought the 'dark ages' of European integration to an end.[136] Conversely, ratification crises over particular treaties can, as Mai Davis Cross shows, quickly spill over into generalised crises for the EU.[137]

Governments' desire to defend the EU's legitimacy – and their own – is understandable for these reasons. But such defensiveness forgoes opportunities to use the failure of treaties as a way of demonstrating to domestic constituents that their views are listened to in the process of treaty making. Research suggests that those who are on the losing side of elections over time tend to have lower levels of satisfaction with democracy.[138] Seen in these terms, persistent problems of trust in EU and national elites call for further opportunities for those who oppose European integration to be on the winning side. European Parliament elections should provide an opportunity for politics of this sort, but they suffer from low turnout and salience in a way that the process of ratification surrounding EU treaties does not.[139]

'What if European leaders had been bold enough to create European political union at Maastricht?' asks Josef Janning.[140] Compelling though this counterfactual question is, a more pertinent one from a two-level legitimacy perspective is: What if European leaders had allowed Maastricht to fail? The rejection of the Maastricht Treaty would almost certainly have prolonged the Exchange Rate Mechanism crisis and, with this, delayed plans for EMU. Would this delay have encouraged member states to be better prepared for the single currency than they proved to be in 1999? Would Euroscepticism have taken hold in the British Conservative Party as virulently as it did without a treaty to rebel against? Would EU governments have embarked on the continuous process of treaty reform that came to a head with the European Constitution?

Would enlargement have been slower? Such questions cannot be conclusively answered, but they bring into sharp relief governments' determination to press ahead with Maastricht regardless.

Among EU scholars, Richard Rose stands out for his willingness to see the failure of an EU treaty as an opportunity rather than a scenario to be avoided. Problematic though his proposal for a pan-European referendum is for the reasons discussed above, his presentation of it captures the logic of two-level legitimacy when he writes: 'If the outcome was positive, it would validate agreements arrived at in Brussels by showing that they were also agreeable to Europe's citizens. If a Treaty was rejected, it would show the need of the horizontal checks and balances operating within Brussels to be complemented by a vertical check in the hands of citizens.'[141]

Conclusion

Ideas are like 'switchmen', argued Max Weber.[142] The idea that EU treaty making is too rigid, one that dominates the literature, follows a track familiar to the theory of two-level games, with its concern that excessively constraining rules and norms are to be avoided for fear that they could jeopardise attempts by governments to codify agreements that they deem to be in their national interest. That such arguments resonate is reasonable given the high-profile ratification crises over treaties in the post-Maastricht period and EU member states' reticence about treaty amendment during the euro crisis. All other things being equal – the two-level game approach suggests – restricting the role played by parliaments, the people or courts in EU treaty making would reduce the risk of involuntary defection and so make it easier for EU member states to amend the treaties.

The two-level legitimacy approach points to another track. It makes little sense to seek slack, this approach warns, without understanding why governments' hands have been bound to begin with. The rise of parliaments, the people and courts in the negotiation and consent stages of EU treaty making cannot be reduced to brinksmanship between governments seeking bargaining advantage in European negotiations. It is the reflection, in part, of the problems of legitimacy facing the EU. As such, attempts to make treaty making more flexible by circumventing the role of parliaments, the people and courts could rebound on governments and the EU. If anything, the two-level legitimacy approach suggests, there is an argument for tying hands yet further.

268 THE TRANSFORMATION OF EU TREATY MAKING

This chapter has sought not to choose between these theoretical tracks but to switch between them in evaluating proposals for reforming EU treaty making. Doing so highlights not only the diplomatic advantages of making treaties more flexible – by allowing entry into force on the basis of a majority vote, regulating national referendums and holding a pan-European referendum – but also the potential of such measures to turn a ratification crisis into a deeper political drama for the Union. It weighs the normative case for time locks, limits on international treaty making, citizen-led treaty making and oversight mechanisms against the attendant risks of involuntary defection. It asks whether treaties should, on occasion, be allowed to fail, and what this would mean for the EU's contested credibility and legitimacy. Above all, it points towards a range of ideas for reforming EU treaty making, whether the aim is to push the accelerator on treaty making or apply the brake.

Notes

1 Bradley (2009), p. 136.
2 Dean (1953).
3 Richards (2006), p. 203.
4 Hathaway (2008), p. 1304.
5 The Case-Zablocki Act of 22 August 1972, 1 U.S.C. §112b. See Krutz and Peake (2009: 47) for further details.
6 Chinkin (1983) and Flietz (2017).
7 Ehlermann and Mény (2000), p. 9.
8 Schmidt (2009), pp. 26–7.
9 Closa (2014), p. 2.
10 Putnam (1988), p. 441.
11 The Draft Treaty Establishing the European Union (1984).
12 European Commission (2002), p. XII. Under this plan, subsequent amendments to Parts I and II of the European Constitution would require approval by five-sixths of member states; changes to Part III of the treaty would require ratification by three-quarters of member states.
13 A partial concession to Penelope, perhaps, is a referral mechanism included in the European Constitution, later preserved in the Lisbon Treaty. Under Article 48(5) of the Treaty on European Union, 'if, two years after the signature of a treaty amendment under the ordinary revision procedure, four-fifths of member states have ratified the agreement but one or more member states has encountered difficulties in doing so, the matter will be referred to the European Council'. This provision hints at the possibility that a member state might be encouraged to leave the Union if it fails to ratify a treaty, but it certainly does not require it.

14 Mendez, Mendez and Triga (2014), p. 203.

15 Mendez, Mendez and Triga (2014), p. 209.

16 Mendez, Mendez and Triga (2014), p. 209.

17 de Witte (2012), p. 127.

18 Closa (2011), p. 11.

19 Schmidt (2009), p. 25.

20 Note the EUCJ held that the amendment simply confirmed a pre-existing power of the member states, and hence ratification of the ESM Treaty did not require the decision amending Article 136TFEU to enter into force; see Court of Justice of the EU, C-370/12 *Pringle* v. *Government of Ireland* ECLI:EU: C:2012:756 paras. 183–5.

21 de Witte (2012), p. 127.

22 Bribosa (2009), p. 14.

23 Hollis (2012), p. 677.

24 Article 40, Vienna Convention on the Law of Treaties, 23 May 1969, 1115 UNTS, 331.

25 Hollis (2012), pp. 744–8.

26 Hollis (2012), p. 749.

27 Articles 108 and 109, United Nations, Charter of the United Nations, 24 October 1945, 1 UNTS XVI.

28 Jessup (1948), p. 144.

29 Willson (1996).

30 Weiler and Modrall (1985), p. 323.

31 Cameron (2016).

32 Closa (2014).

33 Closa (2014), p. 13.

34 Kellermann (2008), pp. 33–6.

35 Article 48(4), TFEU.

36 Article 48(6), TFEU.

37 Peers (2012), p. 36.

38 Dinmore (2012).

39 Maatsch (2016), p. 110.

40 Tierney (2012b).

41 Rose and Borz (2013).

42 Ribicic and Kaucic (2014), p. 21.

43 Article 90, Constitution of the Republic of Slovenia (2016).

44 Ribicic and Kaucic (2014).

45 Barber (2018).

46 Laffan and O'Mahony (2008), p. 109.

47 Article 29, 4, 2°, Constitution of Ireland (1937, amended to 2018).

48 Hodson and Maher (2014).

49 Barrett (2012), p. 25.

50 Sinnott (2003).

51 Tierney (2012a), p. 165.
52 Mac Amhlaigh (2009).
53 On how Dutch politicians responded to the referendum, see Closa (2013a), pp. 158; for Southern Sudan see Security Council Briefing on Sudan (2010).
54 Smith (1999), p. 51.
55 Teasdale (2016), p. 11.
56 Kaufmann (2012), p. 230.
57 Squires (2016).
58 See www.federalists.eu/uef/manifesto/.
59 Rose (2013), p. 154.
60 Rose (2013), p. 143.
61 Cheneval and Ferrin (2016).
62 Mendez, Mendez and Triga (2014), p. 221.
63 Cheneval and Ferrin (2016), p. 166.
64 Beck and Grande (2007), p. 230.
65 Bellamy and Kröger (2013).
66 Bellamy and Kröger (2013).
67 Cheneval (2007), p. 648.
68 Ortiz (2015), chapter 4.
69 Maher (2010).
70 Lane (1996), p. 114.
71 Article 110, Constitution of Greece (1975, amended to 2008).
72 Kiiver (2006), p. 4.
73 Source: Eurobarometer Interactive.
74 Rolef (2006).
75 See Hobolt (2005) and Glencross and Trechsel (2011).
76 Schneider and Weitsman (1996: 583) cited in Crum (2007: 63).
77 Eurobarometer (2005), p. 7.
78 Eurobarometer (2005), p. 17.
79 Article 110, Constitution of Greece (1975, amended to 2008).
80 Article 96, Treaty Establishing the European Coal and Steel Community, 18 April 1951, 261 UNTS, 140.
81 Krunke (2017).
82 Article 11, Consolidated version of the Treaty on the Functioning of the European Union (2007, amended to 2016), OJ, C 202, 7 June 2016.
83 European Commission (2015).
84 Monaghan (2012), pp. 291–2.
85 Mendez, Mendez and Triga (2014), p. 238.
86 Fruhstorfer and Hein (2016), p. 565.
87 Ellis (2002), p. 227n.
88 Moravcsik (2006), p. 227.
89 Moravcsik (2006), p. 221.
90 Renwick (2014), p. 8.

91 Farrell, Harris and Suiter (2017).

92 See https://www.citizensassembly.ie. The constitutional amendment in question was approved in that referendum.

93 The election to the assembly was overturned on procedural grounds by the Supreme Court and was reconstituted by the Parliament. See Renwick (2014), p. 60.

94 See Landemore (2015).

95 The full list is Albania, Croatia, Hungary, Latvia, Lithuania, Macedonia, Serbia, Slovakia, Slovenia and Ukraine; see Podolnjak (2015).

96 Krunke (2017).

97 Article 65, The Constitution of the Republic of Latvia (reinstated 1991, amended to 2014).

98 Articles 151–2, Constitution of Romania (1991, amended to 2003).

99 Hoesly (2005), p. 1193.

100 Blokker (2017).

101 Contiades and Fotiadou (2017), pp. 1–7.

102 Bachrach and Baratz (1962).

103 Article XIV, Section 1, Constitution of the State of Illinois (1970).

104 This is not to suggest that constitutional politics in Illinois is unproblematic. In 2008, nearly 70 per cent of voters rejected the calling of a constitution convention, but in the decade that followed the state experienced a severe fiscal crisis.

105 Case C-370/12, *Pringle* v. *Government of Ireland*, [2012], ECLI: EU:C:2012:756, para. 36.

106 Case C-370/12. para. 45. On strained analysis, see Craig (2013).

107 For the judgment of the Court of Justice of the EU in the case, see C-62/14 *Gauweiler* v. *Deutscher Bundestag*, ECLI:EU:C:2015:400.

108 See e.g. Court of Justice of the EU, Opinion 2/13 ECLI:EU:C:2014:2454.

109 Article 95, Treaty Establishing the European Coal and Steel Community.

110 Article 95, Treaty Establishing the European Coal and Steel Community.

111 On the issue generally, see Stanton Collett (2010).

112 Roznai (2017), p. 46.

113 Halberstam (2009).

114 de Witte (2013), p. 9.

115 Article 20 TEU; Articles 326–34 TFEU; Cantore (2011); Fabbrini (2013).

116 Joerges (2014).

117 Scicluna (2014).

118 de Witte (2013), p. 2.

119 Court of Justice of the EU, Case 10/61, *Commission* v. *Italy*, [1962] ECR 1, 23. Dimopoulos (2015), p. 206.

120 Court of Justice of the EU, Case 22/70, *Commission* v. *Council* (ERTA case) [1971] ECR 263 [22]

121 Case 43–75, *Gabrielle Defrenne* v. *Société anonyme belge de navigation aérienne Sabena*, [1976]. ECR 455 [58]. See Rosas (2010), p. 1319.

122 Case C-370/12, *Thomas Pringle* v. *Government of Ireland, Ireland and the Attorney General* [2012], ECLI: EU:C:2012:756 [68].

123 Court of Justice of the EU, Case C-370/12 [93].

124 Court of Justice of the EU, Case C-370/12 [69]

125 Article 3(2), Treaty on the Functioning of the European Union.

126 See Dimopoulos (2015), p. 290; Lavranos (2011).

127 Article 26, Vienna Convention on the Law of Treaties, and Article 4, Treaty on European Union, Official Journal of the European Union, C 202, 7 June 2016. Hofmann, Rowe and Türk (2011), pp. 70 and 80.

128 Article 9(2), Vienna Convention on the Law of Treaties.

129 Putnam (1988), p. 442.

130 Putnam (1988), p. 442.

131 Moravcsik (1998), pp. 440–7.

132 Staw (1976), p. 41.

133 Article 18, Vienna Convention on the Law of Treaties.

134 Jonas and Saunders (2010), p. 596.

135 Harley (1919).

136 Keohane and Hoffman (1991), p. 8.

137 Davis Cross (2017), pp. 108–59.

138 Banducci and Karp (2003).

139 Garry, Marsh and Sinnott (2005).

140 Janning (2014).

141 Rose (2013), p. 155.

142 Weber (1958), p. 280.

10 The Future of Treaty Making

The European Union (EU) is a test bed for treaty making. Treaties and amendments thereof have marked pivotal moments in European integration from the creation of the European Communities in the 1950s to euro crisis reforms in the 2010s. The manner in which the EU makes treaties has been transformed during this period. The Treaty of Paris, which created the first of the European Communities, was negotiated by national governments in a tightly sealed intergovernmental setting and approved by national parliaments on the basis of a simple majority vote. Six decades later, EU treaty making is a more crowded and contentious affair. The European Parliament is routinely involved in the initiation of treaties and their negotiation via intergovernmental conferences (IGCs). The Convention Method pioneered in the 2000s gives the European Parliament and national parliaments a more significant place still in the drafting of EU treaties. Member state parliaments have tightened their grip too on the consent stage, as the threshold for approving treaties has increased alongside the number of chambers involved. Today, major EU treaty amendment generally runs the gauntlet of referendums in one or more member state, and constitutional reviews of treaties before higher courts are now commonplace.

EU treaty making is often seen as a product of either political opportunism or constitutional necessity. Instead, we see the EU's changing approach to treaty making as being embedded in changing constitutional rules and norms that made specific approaches to treaty negotiation or ratification more, or less, likely. No member state is constitutionally required to hold a referendum on EU treaties, we contend, but constitutional rules and norms have shifted in several member states to make referendums on major EU treaties either possible or probable. A major contribution of this book has been to trace these changing rules and

273

norms between 1950 and 2016. This exercise showed how national governments, having tentatively deviated from the traditional IGC format in the 1950s, did so conclusively from the 1990s onwards (Chapter 3). It also showed, through a detailed analysis of constitutional developments in the EU's twenty-eight member states, when and how rules and norms shifted to allow a greater role for parliaments (Chapter 4), the people (Chapter 5) and courts (Chapter 6). Our ratification scales show that, on average, parliaments assumed a greater role in treaty making in the 1990s but relinquished this to some extent after the 2004 enlargement. The likelihood of referendums, in contrast, increased at various junctures, but especially after the mid-1990s. The role of higher courts, meanwhile, increased steadily from the late 1980s as parliaments and, especially citizens, acquired standing to challenge the constitutionality of treaties.

This book has considered two broad lines of explanation for this transformation of EU treaty making (Chapter 2). The first follows Robert Putnam's classic theory of two-level games in seeing national governments as tying their hands through treaty-making procedures to boost their bargaining position in treaty negotiations. The qualitative and quantitative evidence presented in this volume is consistent with this approach. Member states that are divided over the EU and those in which minority governments are more prevalent are, our results suggest, more likely to tie their hands through rules and norms that favour referendums (Chapter 7). This finding is in line with Robert Pahre's reworking of Putnam's two-level game approach. It also counts as a rare case of governments tying hands in international diplomacy rather than seeking to benefit from pre-existing constraints. Consistent too with the two-level game approach is how EU heads of state or government increased their grip on negotiations at the same time as giving the European Parliament and national parliaments a greater role. EU heads of state or government squared this circle, we concluded, by ensuring that their personal representatives are present in conventions and through a new simplified revision procedure, which allows the European Council to make small-scale but significant treaty amendments without recourse to either a convention or, indeed, an IGC (Chapter 3).

The second line of theoretical inquiry followed in this book is the two-level legitimacy approach. This approach sees the rise of new actors in EU treaty making as a response to problems of legitimacy facing the EU during this period. In particular, it considers the rise of parliaments, the people and courts to be a response to the problems of political trust facing the EU and member state governments during this period. The qualitative and quantitative evidence presented in this volume suggests that this transformation of EU treaty making is, indeed, driven by trust as well as tactics. Consistent with the two-level legitimacy approach is how national governments have incorporated parliaments into the negotiation stage of treaty making as problems of trust in the EU have intensified. Although the European Parliament's persistent claims for a presence in IGCs eventually bore fruit, the convention method, we argue, was driven by national governments seeking to reconnect with EU citizens. Turning to the consent stage, member states with low levels of trust in national governments are more likely to adopt constitutional rules and norms that give parliament a greater role in treaty making, our results suggests, whereas member states in which there are low levels of trust in the EU are likely to empower the people and courts (Chapter 7).

This book has sought to understand and explain not only the transformation of EU treaty making but also how member states have responded to it. The evidence we present indicates that changing constitutional rules are associated with declining rates of treaty making, while suggesting that reports of deadlock are overstated (Chapter 8). From a two-level game perspective, states have an incentive to circumvent or undo ratification constraints that risk involuntary defection, i.e. a situation in which states conclude treaties but are unable to ratify them. The two-level legitimacy approach warns against overlooking the reasons for why national governments' hands have been tied to begin with. Our analysis of how national governments responded to the risk of involuntary defection chimes with the first of these approaches (Chapter 8). A two-level game logic can be seen, in particular, in national governments' search for slack after referendum votes against treaties and in their increased recourse to international law agreements as EU treaty making became more complicated. Political expediency took precedence over procedural legitimacy in such cases, we conclude, although concerns over the latter were not entirely absent. EU treaty making became more inclusive with each successive ratification crisis, as national governments engaged in further rounds of treaty making to address the problems of political trust highlighted in previous rounds. The result, we conclude, was a pernicious cycle of treaty making that exposed rather than addressed the gap between EU elites and citizens.

A normative question explored in this book is whether EU treaty making should be more or less flexible (Chapter 9). The consensus in the literature, we noted, is that EU treaty making should become easier, with recurring reform ideas including a switch from unanimity to majority voting in EU treaty making, restrictions on national referendums and a pan-European referendum. Such ideas are consistent with the two-level game approach, which favours the untying of hands that have been too tightly bound. From a two-level legitimacy perspective, however, such reforms could accentuate the problems of trust facing the EU. To bring balance to this debate, we put forward a number of reform ideas for making EU treaty making more difficult, including a pledge to avoid second referendums, time locks on treaty reforms, citizen-led treaty making, judicial and parliamentary oversight of EU treaty making and limitations on EU member states' right to make international law treaties.

The End of EU Treaties?

In 2014, the *American Journal of International Law* held a debate that asked whether we are witnessing 'The End of Treaties'.[1] No respondent answered unequivocally in the affirmative, but Timothy Meyer went furthest with his suggestion that soft law and international legislation within multilateral organisations had eclipsed the treaty as a contract between sovereign states.[2] Far from lamenting this development, Meyer concluded that the traditional conception of treaties was no longer adequate in a world 'in which states are constantly negotiating the rules governing any given area of the law on a shifting geopolitical landscape'.[3] Joel P. Trachtman countered by arguing that reports of treaties' death are premature and unduly influenced by the ebbs and flows of multilateral negotiations in bodies such as the World Trade Organization. Treaties 'will grow in scope and complexity', he argued, because they offer benefits that are 'worth achieving'.[4] Taking stock of this debate, Duncan Hollis observed that one would be 'hard pressed to find an international law issue today where there is not some treaty that speaks, directly or indirectly, to the question'.[5]

Calling time on EU treaty making is a long-standing tradition, not least by national governments. In 1978, the European Council invited three politicians – Barend Biesheuvel, Edmund Dell and Robert Marjolin – to propose institutional reforms 'on the basis of and in compliance with the Treaties'.[6] 'This convoluted mandate was understood to mean', as Andrew Duff noted at the time, 'that the European Council was not contemplating any Treaty amendments'.[7] This view, Duff argues, reflected the reticence of heads of state or government towards Belgian

Prime Minister Leo Tindeman's modest proposals for treaty amendment in his report on European Union three years earlier. Soon after the Lisbon Treaty was signed, the European Council convened a high-level group led by former Spanish Prime Minister Felipe González 'to reflect on long-term challenges for the Union 'within the framework set out in the Lisbon Treaty'.[8] After two decades of troubled treaty making, there was, once again, little appetite for further amendment.

In spite of these and other pronouncements, moratoriums on EU treaty making rarely stick. Four years after it reviewed the Biesheuvel-Dell-Marjolin report, the European Council set in motion negotiations over the Single European Act. By the time the González Report was published, the European Council's seemingly sated appetite for treaty making had returned.[9] Within a few months, EU leaders had agreed to revise the Treaty on the Functioning of the European Union to make possible the establishment of the European Stability Mechanism.[10] In 2016, Jean-Claude Juncker predicted that 'there would be no treaty change' in the aftermath of Brexit.[11] And yet, just a year and a half later, the Commission president would describe treaty change as 'inevitable'.[12]

Future treaty change will not, in all likelihood, take its cue from the Commission. Aside from the Single European Act, the Commission has been, at best, a cautious champion of treaty reform. Even then, the EU executive took its lead from large member states in pushing forward plans to complete the single market.[13] Nor has the Commission been a vocal champion of new modes of treaty making, preferring instead to work behind the scenes in intergovernmental conferences (Chapter 3). The impetus for future treaty changes could come from the European Parliament, via its new right to initiate treaty negotiations. In December 2016, for example, MEP Guy Verhofstadt presented a report on future treaty amendments designed to strengthen foreign policy and fundamental rights and to enhance democracy, transparency and accountability. Reminiscent of Altiero Spinelli's Draft Treaty on European Union (see Chapter 3) was the report's call for future treaties to be adopted 'if not by an EU-wide referendum then after being ratified by a qualified majority of four-fifths of the Member States, having obtained the consent of Parliament'.[14]

The political impetus for changing the treaties ultimately depends on EU heads of state or government, without whom the ordinary and simplified revision procedures cannot be activated.[15] And even though any Member State government, the Commission, or the European Parliament can propose treaty amendments, it is for the European Council to decide to proceed.[16] EU heads of state or government remained divided at the time of writing over the desirability of treaty change. Amid uncertainty over Brexit and the relationship between eurozone and non-eurozone members, the EU's Rome Declaration soberly celebrated sixty years since the Treaties of Rome but remained silent about future treaty revisions.[17] This taboo on treaty reform had been broken, argued Emmanuel Macron in a press conference with German Chancellor Angela Merkel in May 2017. 'From a German perspective, it is possible to change the European treaties', responded Merkel.[18]

Macron's speech from the Pnyx – the birthplace of the Athenian assembly – in September 2017 was short on substance but strong on symbolism and suffused with concerns for how treaties are made. Rejecting clams that the treaties could not be amended while refusing to be drawn on whether they should be, the new French president called for an end to treaties 'negotiated sneakily behind closed doors in Paris, Brussels or Berlin'.[19] Instead, he proposed a series of democratic conventions to be held in Europe to 'build ... the foundations for an overhaul of Europe for the coming ten, fifteen years'.[20] Whether Macron's ideas for citizen-led treaty making – if that is what they amount to – will win the day remains to be seen. That such ideas are circulating nonetheless suggests that the transformation of EU treaty making is far from over.

Consentiflcation

A key question for future research is whether the increased role played by the people, parliaments and courts in EU treaty making is driven by or driving a wider battle over membership and conduct in EU policymaking. The transformation of EU treaty making, it could be argued, is symptomatic of national governments' attempt to 'treat' the EU's democratic deficit by empowering the European Parliament and, more recently, national parliaments.[21] We see tentative signs, however, that the transformation of EU treaty making is leaving its mark on EU policymaking more generally. Specifically, as the rules and norms governing the consent stage of EU treaty making have evolved, similar changes appear to be taking hold in other domains. We label this phenomenon 'consentification' to capture the EU's turn to new modes of consent as member state governments struggle to legitimate policy decisions given their own problems of legitimacy and those facing the Union. Such policies are neither politically nor legally on a par with EU treaties, but the former are approached and ratified as if they were treaties as governments seek consent for contentious decisions. The transformation of EU treaty making, we conjecture, has created new expectations about the role of the people, parliaments and/or the courts in the EU at a time when trust in political elites is at a premium.

Consentification can be seen, for example, in the controversy surrounding the Ukraine–European Union Association Agreement. The EU has negotiated agreements of this sort with third countries since 1961, but in April 2016, the Netherlands took the unprecedented step of putting the Ukraine–European Union Association Agreement to a referendum. The trigger for this vote came not from a government seeking tactical advantage but from NGOs who gathered 400,000 signatures for a petition to hold an advisory referendum against the act of parliament by which the Netherlands had ratified the agreement.[22] This was the first time that this member state's 2014 referendum law had been put into effect and it contained clear echoes of the 2005 referendum on the European Constitution (see Chapter 5) in both its form and result: 61 per cent of voters voted against the Association Agreement. EU leaders' response also followed standard operating procedures for EU treaties.[23] Faced with the prospect of involuntary defection, the heads of state or government acknowledged this result before seeking ways to circumvent it. Having secured certain reassurances from the European Council,[24] the Dutch government approved the agreement via parliamentary channels and without a second referendum before seeking to phase out this referendum law (see Chapter 9).

Another instance of consentification occurred in October 2016 when the Parliament of the Walloon Region withheld its consent for the EU-Canada Comprehensive Economic and Trade Agreement (CETA) shortly before this agreement was due to be signed.[25] At the same time, in Germany, citizen protestors placed multiple applications before the Federal Constitutional Court for a preliminary injunction to prevent the government from signing and concluding CETA. The Federal Constitutional Court did not grant the preliminary injunction and the Walloon parliament soon dropped its opposition, but the incident marked a new era for external treaty making.[26] 'Europe will never be able to negotiate trade treaties as it did before', according to Paul Magnette, Walloon minister-president and, as it happens, a scholar of EU treaty making.[27] Civil society campaigns to hold a referendum on the EU-US Transatlantic Trade and Investment Partnership in the Netherlands[28] suggests that he might be right.

Consentification is not limited to the EU's 'other treaties'. Greece's snap referendum in 2015 on negotiations with EU-IMF creditors is a case in point. This was a referendum about policy documents concerning economic reforms and debt sustainability in Greece submitted by the Commission, European Central Bank and IMF to the Eurogroup rather than a treaty. Nonetheless, these documents were treated with the symbolic solemnity of a treaty and subject to treaty-like ratification requirements.[29] Four years earlier, Prime Minister George Papandreou had called a referendum over the restructuring of this member state's debt. This would have been the first instance of direct democracy since the 1974 referendum on the Greek Republic, but, under pressure from EU partners and cabinet colleagues, Papandreou cancelled the vote. In 2015, Papandreou's successor, Alexis Tspiras, broke off negotiations over an extension to its existing loan agreement with the EU and IMF and put the terms of this technical discussion to a referendum. Questions remained over the constitutionality of such a vote since the constitution of Greece prohibits referendums on fiscal matters.[30] A legal challenge against the referendum by two citizens was rejected by the Council of State and the vote went ahead, resulting in a large majority against the terms that had been offered by Greece's international creditors.

The most consequential case of consentification to date concerns the United Kingdom. That the European Union Act (2011) made a referendum probable but not inevitable (Chapter 5) was a source of frustration for some British politicians. Had the Fiscal Compact been an EU treaty, it might just have triggered a referendum under this legislation, but Prime Minister David Cameron's refusal to support negotiations over such an agreement and eurozone members' determination to press ahead with an international law treaty ruled out this possibility. Although Cameron's 'veto' on EU treaty amendment was roundly cheered by members of the Conservative Party, the fact that no EU treaty materialised merely added to the pressure on the Prime Minister to hold a referendum. Cameron finally relented in January 2013, promising to seek a new settlement with the EU before holding an in-out referendum. The new settlement was not – as the Prime Minister had initially gambled on – part of a wider package of treaty reform driven by the euro crisis in which the United Kingdom could name its price.[31] Nor was it a standalone treaty designed to address UK concerns. And yet, through its negotiation and 'ratification' it was a sort of simulated treaty-making episode.

Further research is required to understand the extent and drivers of consentification. Having tied their hands in relation to EU treaty making, are national governments seeking similar tactical advantages elsewhere? Or does the challenge to national governments' privileged position extend to other areas of EU policymaking and so produce a more wide-spread empowerment of parliaments, the people and courts? Our working assumption is that both two-level game and two-level legitimacy logics are generally at play. Greece's 2015 referendum, for example, can be seen as a last-ditch attempt by Alexis Tsipras to boost his bargaining position in relation to the EU and IMF. The referendum may also have been designed to enhance the government's legitimacy at home among a public that was supportive of Syriza but deeply distrustful of both European and national elites. By late 2014, just 23 per cent of Greek citizens tended to trust the EU, according to the Eurobarometer.[32] The corresponding figure for trust in national government was 11 per cent.[33] The Netherlands' referendum on the Ukraine–European Union Association Agreement and the standoff over CETA offered few tactical advantages to governments. Instead, they reflected a concerted effort by citizens' groups to gain a foothold in external treaty making.[34] Such tactics were informed by the transformation of EU treaty making even though NGOs have, as we have seen, played a limited role in this domain.

David Cameron's in-out referendum can be seen as an attempt to strengthen the United Kingdom's hand in negotiations over a new settlement, as well, of course, as a cautionary tale about the dangers of involuntary defection when hands are bound too tightly. It also told the story of a member state in which the executive saw its formal authority over EU treaty making diminish as the legitimacy of EU and national elites was increasingly questioned. Why not leave the referendum decision for another day or another politician? The Prime Minister 'thought that public consent for UK membership on current terms was wafer thin', argues the United Kingdom's former Permanent Representative to the EU.[35] In retrospect, successive Prime Ministers' refusal to address these legitimacy concerns and/or call a referendum connected to the ratification of an EU treaty contributed to a referendum result with much graver consequences than a 'no' vote against the Maastricht, Amsterdam, Nice or Lisbon treaties.

Whether Brexit will deliver on leavers' promise to 'take back control' remains to be seen, but the manner of the United Kingdom's leaving has already illustrated the UK government's declining privilege in relation to treaty making. The Treaty on European Union gives any member state the right to withdraw from the EU in accordance with its own constitutional requirements.[36] Prime Minister Theresa May initially decided to do so under the royal prerogative and hence without parliamentary approval, but this decision was challenged by two citizens supported by various campaign groups in the High Court, which ruled that the rights granted under the European Communities Act (1972) could not be revoked without an act of parliament.[37] The British government unsuccessfully appealed this judgment before the Supreme Court and so was required to secure parliamentary approval for its decision to withdraw from the EU.[38] Even before this matter was settled, the government conceded that parliament would be allowed to vote on a withdrawal treaty.[39] Remainers welcomed this victory, while stepping up their calls for a referendum on this agreement.[40] The United Kingdom is leaving the EU, in other words, but both the motivation for, and manner of, its leaving are closely connected to the transformation of EU treaty making. Nor will the United Kingdom turn its back on treaty making once it leaves the EU. By one measure, the British government will need to negotiate at least 750 treaties with 168 states if it wishes to recover the agreements on trade, regulatory, nuclear and other issues that it will forgo by virtue of Brexit.[41]

Wider Implications

Amidst ongoing debates around the constitutionalisation of the EU, the idea of the EU as a sui generis entity becomes more embedded, even as political scientists and legal scholars also relate it to other forms of international cooperation and law.[42] Students of treaty making, insofar as they take an interest in the EU, tend to focus on the Union as a treaty maker on the world stage.[43] Duncan Hollis's seminal guide to treaty making dedicates a chapter to EU external treaties but says little about Europe's turbulent history of treaty amendment. The EU, as William Phelan notes, receives curiously little attention in Beth Simmons's work on human rights treaties.[44] Having begun this book by sketching the wider context for our research, we conclude by considering the wider significance of our findings.

EU treaty making, however self-contained it may appear, traces key themes and growing interdependence in the international system. From medieval times to the modern era, treaty making has been a site of struggle among those who seek the authority to speak and act on the international stage (Chapter 1). The EU was founded in a historical moment in which governments were the dominant force in treaty making and yet faced competition from other actors at home and abroad. The rise of parliaments in EU treaty making is consistent with the increased role of legislatures in this domain since the eighteenth century. Treaty-related referendums are not unknown outside the EU (Chapter 5). However, the shift in constitutional rules and norms recorded in this book make the EU an experiment in treaty making on a scale never before seen. The frequency with which higher courts in the EU are now drawn into challenges over the constitutionality of treaty making shows how far removed the Union is from treaty making tradition. As recently as 1946, J. Mervyn Jones wrote that 'Questions of form rarely arise in municipal courts', the implications being that treaty making was a matter for international rather than domestic constitutional law.[45]

Historical struggles over treaty making concern the negotiation as well as the consent stage, with international organisations and NGOs acquiring important new roles, especially after the Second World War (Chapter 1). Seen in this context, the EU is both radical and conservative. It is radical insofar as the role granted to the European Parliament in EU treaty making offers a degree of participation not matched by other international organisations. The UN's General Assembly may be a prolific treaty maker, but its principal achievement has been to bring states to the negotiating table rather than secure a seat alongside them. The European Parliament's role as an observer in EU treaty-making conferences and its empowerment alongside national parliaments through the Convention Method is altogether more significant. The EU is more conservative when it comes to the role of non-governmental actors in treaty making. The widespread involvement of NGOs is a signature of UN treaty making. Civil society observers were invited to the Convention on the Future of Europe, but NGOs were not directly involved in EU treaty making before or since (Chapter 3).

As well as containing echoes from history, treaty making within the EU contains hints about the future of the international system. That the EU still faces such a significant legitimacy crisis in spite of its comparatively inclusive approach to treaty making augurs badly for the rest of the world. It is tempting – and indeed partially justified – to blame EU elites for asking too much of treaties. The Maastricht Treaty was a major step forward for European integration that was ratified only after a protracted political crisis. Why then, future historians might ask, did EU member states follow it with a decade and a half of increasingly contentious treaty amendments? But the EU's problems run deeper than the rational miscalculations of governments. They reflect entrenched problems of trust in elites that are by no means germane to the EU. According to the Pew Research Centre, low trust in government is a worldwide phenomenon especially in advanced industrial democracies experiencing comparatively low rates of economic growth.[46] In the sixth wave of the World Values Survey, which covers the period 2010–2014, the percentage of respondents expressing a great deal or quite a lot of confidence in the UN was less than 50 per cent in forty-seven of the sixty states surveyed. Confidence levels were below 36 per cent in China, Russia and the United States, three states with a significant bearing on the future of the UN.

If this global trust deficit, as Peter Blair Henry calls it, continues, we expect three overlapping scenarios to unfold.[47] First, states might turn away from treaties and towards non-binding (soft law) instruments such as political declarations and memorandums of understanding that are easier to negotiate internationally and receive acceptance domestically. Second, they might turn against treaties entirely as either a response to or a way of evading problems of trust. Finally, they might turn to new actors as a way of legitimating treaty making. At the time of writing, the first and second scenarios are gaining ground. The rise of the Group of Twenty (G20) during the global financial crisis reflects states' growing appetite for soft law at a time when the International Monetary Fund's Articles of Agreement have proven difficult to amend.[48] US President Donald Trump's decision to withdraw from the Comprehensive and Progressive Agreement for Trans-Pacific Partnership (2016),[49] and from the Paris Agreement (2016)[50] and his threat to tear up the North American Free Trade Agreement (1994)[51] could be a sign that a new era of treaty breaking is under way. And yet such trends should not be exaggerated. The G20 shows no signs of eclipsing the UN, and, if anything, the former may have helped the latter's efforts on climate change.[52] To date, parties to treaties from which Trump has withdrawn (or threatened to withdraw from) have generally stood by such agreements.[53] For now, it looks as if treaty making will continue apace. Under this third scenario, governments that remain committed to treaty making will have to contend with problems of trust not only in Europe but worldwide. In consequence, the rise of parliaments, the people and courts in treaty making could become a global phenomenon and not just a European one.

Notes

1 Cumberland (2014).
2 Meyer (2014).

THE FUTURE OF TREATY MAKING   285

3 Meyer (2014).
4 Hollis (2014).
5 Hollis (2014).
6 Council of the European Union (1978).
7 Duff (1981), p. 237.
8 European Council (2007a), para. 9.
9 Phinnemore (2011), p. 2.
10 European Council (2011).
11 Zalan (2016).
12 Juncker (2017).
13 Moravcsik (1998), p. 359.
14 Verhofstadt (2016), para. 83.
15 Article 48, Treaty on European Union (1992, amended to 2016).
16 Under the ordinary revision procedure, proposals are submitted to the Council and the European Council before the latter decides whether to examine these proposals (Article 48(2) TEU). Under the simplified revision procedure, the European Council must decide whether to amend all or part of the provisions of Part Three of the Treaty on the Functioning of the European Union.
17 Karnitschnig and Eder (2017).
18 Samuel and Huggler (2017).
19 Macron (2017).
20 Macron (2017).
21 Rittberger (2012).
22 de Jong (2016). This followed the shooting down of a Malaysian civilian plane in Ukrainian airspace; most of the victims were Dutch.
23 Otjes (2016).
24 European Council (2016).
25 Van der Loo (2016).
26 German Federal Constitutional Court, Judgment of 13 October 2016, 2 BvR 1368/16, 2 BvE 3/16, 2 BvR 1823/16, 2 BvR 1482/16, 2 BvR 1444/16.
27 Magnette (2016). Magnette and Nicolaidis (2004).
28 See https://ttip-referendum.nl/.
29 The ratification was also symbolic insofar as these documents had been withdrawn by Greece's creditors by the time of the referendum.
30 Contiades and Fotiadou (2015).
31 Rogers (2017).
32 Source: http://ec.europa.eu/commfrontoffice/publicopinion/index.cfm/Chart/getChart/chartType/gridChart//themeKy/18/groupKy/97/savFile/187.
33 Source: http://ec.europa.eu/commfrontoffice/publicopinion/index.cfm/Chart/getChart/themeKy/18/groupKy/98/.
34 Hübner, Deman and Balik (2017).
35 Rogers (2017).

36 Article 50, Treaty on European Union (1992, amended to 2016).

37 *R (Miller)* v. *Secretary of State for Exiting the European Union* [2017] UKSC 5.

38 European Union (Notification of Withdrawal) Act (2017).

39 Mason and Asthana (2017).

40 Elgot (2017).

41 McClean (2017).

42 de Witte (1994); Curtin and Dekker (2010).

43 Cremona (2012).

44 Phelan (2012), p. 368.

45 Jones (1946), p. 57.

46 Pew Research Centre (2014).

47 Henry (2013).

48 Arner and Taylor (2009).

49 Presidential Memorandum Regarding Withdrawal of the United States from the Trans-Pacific Partnership Negotiations and Agreement, The White House Office of the Press Secretary, 23 January 2017.

50 Akhtar (2018).

51 Johnson (2017).

52 Kim and Chung (2012).

53 Deese (2017).

References

Abbott, K.W. (2008). Enriching rational choice institutionalism for the study of international law. *Illinois Law Review*, 2008(1), 5–46.

Ad Hoc Committee for Institutional Affairs (1985). Report to the European Council. 29–30 March.

Adam, S. and Mena Parras, F.J. (2014). The European Stability Mechanism through the legal meanderings of the Union's constitutionalism: Comment on Pringle. *European Law Review*, 38(6), 848–65.

Agius, C.A. and Grosselfinger, N.A. (1995). The Judiciary and Politics in Malta. In Tate, C.N. and Vallinder, T., eds., *The Global Expansion of Judicial Power*. New York, NY: New York University Press, pp. 381–402.

Akhtar, R. (2018). COP21 in Paris: Politics of Climate Change. In Akhtar, R. and Palagiano, C., eds., *Climate Change and Air Pollution: The Impact on Human Health in Developed and Developing Countries*. Berlin: Springer, pp. 41–6.

Albert, R. (2015). How unwritten constitutional norms change written constitutions. *Dublin University Law Journal*, 38(2), 387–418.

Albi, A. (2007). Selected EU judgments by CEE constitutional courts: Lessons on how (not) to amend constitutions? *Croatian Yearbook of European Law and Policy*, 3(3), 39–58.

Alen, A. and Peeters, P. (1998). *Federal Belgium within the International Legal Order: Theory and Practice*. Leiden: Martinus Nijhoff Publishers.

Alilonttinen, P. and Ruà, S. (2008). *Will the Åland Islands Become Finland's Greenland?* Helsinki: European Policy Institutes Network.

Alston, P. (1990). US ratification of the Covenant on Economic, Social and Cultural Rights: The need for an entirely new strategy. *American Journal of International Law*, 84(2), 365–93.

Altman, D., Donovan, T., Hill, R., Kersting, N., Morris, C., Kobori, M., White, S. and Qvortrup, M. (2014). Appendix A. In Qvortrup, M., ed., *Referendums around the World: The Continued Growth of Direct Democracy*. Basingstoke: Palgrave Macmillan, pp. 252–99.

Alvarez, J.E. (2005). *International Organizations as Law-Makers*. Oxford: Oxford University Press.

Anckar, D. (2014). Constitutional referendums in the countries of the world. *Journal of Politics and Law*, 7(1), 12–22.

288 REFERENCES

Anderson, C.J., Blais, A., Bowler, S., Donovan, T. and Listhaug, O. (2005). *Losers' Consent: Elections and Democratic Legitimacy*. Oxford: Oxford University Press.

Anderson, K. (2000). The Ottawa Convention Banning Landmines, the role of international non-governmental organizations and the idea of international civil society. *European Journal of International Law*, 11(1), 91–120.

Andó, B., Aquilina, K., Scerri-Diacono, J. and Zammit, D. (2012). Malta. In Palmer, V.V., ed., *Mixed Jurisdictions Worldwide: The Third Legal Family*, 2nd edition. Cambridge: Cambridge University Press, pp. 528–76.

Armingeon, K. and Ceka, B. (2014). The loss of trust in the European Union during the great recession since 2007: The role of heuristics from the national political system. *European Union Politics*, 15(1), 82–107.

Armstrong, K.A. (2012). Stability, coordination and governance: Was a treaty such a good idea? *EUtopia Law Blog*, 27 November.

Arner, D.W. and Taylor, M.W. (2009). The global financial crisis and the Financial Stability Board: Hardening the soft law of international financial regulation. *University of New South Wales Law Journal*, 32(2), 488–513.

Arts, D. (1993). Ratification processes of the Treaty on European Union: Belgium. *European Law Review*, 18(3), 228–3.

Athanassiou, P. (2009). Withdrawal and expulsion from the EU and EMU: Some reflections. *European Central Bank Reflection Papers*, 10.

Auel, K. (2013). De-parliamentarisation re-considered: Representation without corresponding communication'in EU affairs. Paper presented at 13th Biennial Conference of the European Union Studies Association, Baltimore, MD.

Bachrach, P. and Baratz, M.S. (1962). Two faces of power. *American Political Science Review*, 56(4), 947–52.

Bailer, S. and Schneider, G. (2006). Nash versus Schelling? The Importance of Constraints in Legislative Bargaining. In Thompson, T., ed., *The European Union Decides*. Cambridge: Cambridge University Press, pp. 153–57.

Baker, D., Gamble, A. and Ludlam, S. (1994). The parliamentary siege of Maastricht 1993: Conservative divisions and British ratification. *Parliamentary Affairs*, 47(1), 37–61.

Banducci, S.A. and Karp, J.A. (2003). How elections change the way citizens view the political system: Campaigns, media effects and electoral outcomes in comparative perspective. *British Journal of Political Science*, 33(3), 443–67.

Bang, G., Hovi, J. and Sprinz, D.F. (2012). US presidents and the failure to ratify multilateral environmental agreements. *Climate Policy*, 12(6), 755–63.

Barber, T. (2018). Why the Netherlands is rejecting referendums. *Financial Times*, 26 February.

Barrett, G. (2008). Creation's final laws: The impact of the Treaty of Lisbon on the 'final provisions' of earlier treaties. *Yearbook of European Law*, 27(1), 3–46.

  (2009). Building a Swiss chalet in an Irish legal landscape? Referendums on European Union treaties in Ireland and the impact of Supreme Court jurisprudence. *European Constitutional Law Review*, 5(1), 32–70.

  (2012). The constitutional location of Europe. UCD Working Papers in Law, Criminology & Socio-Legal Studies Research Paper, 06/2012.

REFERENCES   289

Bauer, P.C. and Fatke, M. (2014). Direct democracy and political trust: Enhancing trust, initiating distrust – or both? *Swiss Political Science Review*, 20(1), 49–69.

Beach, D. (2004). The unseen hand in treaty reform negotiations: The role and influence of the Council Secretariat. *Journal of European Public Policy*, 11(3), 408–39.

Beardsley, J. (1975). Constitutional review in France. *Supreme Court Review*, 20(3), 189–259.

Bebr, G. (1958). The relation of the European Coal and Steel Community Law to the law of the Member States: A peculiar legal symbiosis. *Columbia Law Review*, 58(6), 767–97.

Beck, U. and Grande, E. (2007). *Cosmopolitan Europe*. London: Polity.

Behrendt, C. (2013). The Process of Constitutional Amendment in Belgium. In Contiades, X., ed., *Engineering Constitutional Change: A Comparative Perspective on Europe, Canada and the USA*. London: Routledge, pp. 35–50.

Bellamy, R. and Kröger, S. (2013). Representation deficits and surpluses in EU policy-making. *Journal of European Integration*, 35(5), 477–97.

Bellamy, R. and Weale, A. (2015). Political legitimacy and European monetary union: Contracts, constitutionalism and the normative logic of two-level games. *Journal of European Public Policy*, 22(2), 257–74.

Bernitz, U. (2001). Sweden and the European Union: On Sweden's implementation and application of European law. *Common Market Law Review*, 38(4), 903–34.

Besselink, L.F. (2007). Constitutional referenda in the Netherlands: A debate in the margin. *Electronic Journal of Comparative Law*, 11(1).

Besselink, L.F.M. (2014). The Kingdom of the Netherlands. In Besselink, L.F.M., Bovend'Eert, P., Broeksteeg, H., de Lange, R. and Voermans, W., eds., *Constitutional Law of the EU Member States*. Alphen aan den Rijn: Kluwer, pp. 1187–241.

Besselink, L.F.M., Claes, M., Imamović, Š. and Reestman, J.H. (2014). National Constitutional Avenues for Further EU Integration. European Parliament, Directorate General for Internal Policies, Policy Department C: Citizens' Rights and Constitutional Affairs, Legal Affairs Committee, Constitutional Affairs Committee, PE 493.046 EN, Brussels.

Beukers, T., De Witte, B. and Kilpatrick, C. (2017). Constitutional Change through Euro-Crisis Law: Taking Stock, New Perspectives and Looking Ahead. In Beukers, T., De Witte, B. and Kilpatrick, C., eds., *Constitutional Change through Euro-Crisis Law*. Cambridge: Cambridge University Press, pp. 1–24.

Beyers, J. and Bursens, P. (2006). The European rescue of the federal state: How Europeanisation shapes the Belgian state. *West European Politics*, 29(5), 1057–78.

Biering, P. and Lehrer, S. (2015). To hold a referendum or not? *European Public Law*, 21(1), 169–91.

Blair, T. (2000). *Speech to the Polish Stock Exchange in Warsaw 6 October 2000*. London: Office of the Prime Minister.

(2001). Speech to the European Research Institute. *Guardian*, 23 November.

(2003). Speech in Warsaw. *The Guardian*, 30 May.

REFERENCES

Blanck, K. (2005). Austria: Between Size and Sanctions. In Laursen, F., ed., *The Treaty of Nice: Actor Preferences, Bargaining and Institutional Choice*. Leiden: Martijn Nijhoff, pp. 19–40.

Blokker, P. (2017). Constitutional Reform in Europe and Recourse to the People. In Contiades, X. and Fotiadu, A., eds., *Participatory Constitutional Change: The People as Amenders of the Constitution*. Abingdon: Routledge, pp. 31–51.

Böckenförde, M. (2006). Constitutional Referendum in Germany: Country Report. In Riedel, E.H. and Wolfrum, R., eds., *Recent Trends in German and European Constitutional Law*. Berlin: Springer-Verlag, pp. 107–25.

Bogdanor, V. (2009). *The New British Constitution*. London: Hart.

Bonella, J. (2003). Big majority favour EU constitution referendum. *Times of Malta*, 14 November.

Borger, V. (2015) The European Stability Mechanism: A Crisis Tool Operating at Two Junctures. In Haentjens, M. and Wessels B., eds., *Research Handbook on Crisis Management in the Banking Sector*. Cheltenham: Edward Elgar.

Bowler, S., Donovan, T. and Karp, J.A. (2007). Enraged or engaged? Preferences for direct citizen participation in affluent democracies. *Political Research Quarterly*, 60(3), 351–62.

Boyron, S. (2012). *The Constitution of France: A Contextual Analysis*. London: Bloomsbury.

Božac, I. and Carević, M. (2015). Judicial Application of International and EU Law in Croatia. In Rodin S. and Perišin, T., eds., *Judicial Application of International Law in Southeast Europe*. Berlin: Springer, pp. 135–63.

Bradley, C.A. (2007). Unratified treaties, domestic politics, and the U.S. Constitution. *Harvard International Law Journal*, 48(2), 307–36.

Bradley, M.P. (2009). The Ambiguities of Sovereignty: The United States and the Global Human Rights Cases of the 1940s and 1950s. In Howland, D. and White, L., eds., *The State of Sovereignty: Territories, Laws, Populations*. Bloomington, IN: Indiana University Press, pp. 124–48.

Braithwaite, J. (1998). Institutionalizing Distrust, Enculturating Trust. In Braithwaite, V. and Levi, M., eds., *Trust and Governance*. New York, NY: Russell Sage Foundation, p. 356.

Brand, R.A. (1994). External sovereignty and international law. *Fordham International Law Journal*, 18(5), 1685.

Bribosia, H. (1997). Report on Belgium. In Slaughter, A.-M., Stone Sweet, A. and Weiler, J.J.H., eds., *The European Court and National Courts: Doctrine and Jurisprudence*. Oxford: Hart, pp. 1–40.

(2009). *Revising the European Treaties: A plea in favour of abolishing the veto. Policy Paper No. 37*. Paris: Notre Europe.

Bříza, P. (2009). The Czech Republic: The constitutional court on the Lisbon treaty decision of 26 November 2008. *European Constitutional Law Review*, 5(1), 143–64.

Brölmann, C.M. (2011). International Organizations and Treaties: Contractual Freedom and Institutional Constraint. In Klabbers, J. and Wallendahl, A., eds., *Research Handbook on International Organizations*. Cheltenham: Edward Elgar, pp. 285–312.

Brooks, R.C. (1921). Swiss treaty initiative. *American Political Science Review*, 15(3), 423–5.

Brown, S. (2012). Risk, history shape German view on Europe referendum. *Reuters*, 24 July. Full text available at: http://uk.reuters.com/article/euro zone-germany-referendum-idUKL6E8INGNQ20120724.

Budden, P. (2002). Observations on the Single European Act and 'relaunch of Europe': A less 'intergovernmental' reading of the 1985 Intergovernmental Conference. *Journal of European Public Policy*, 9(1), 76–97.

Bunse, S. and Nicolaïdis, K. (2012). Large versus Small States: Anti-Hegemony and the Politics of Shared Leadership. In Jones, E., Menon, A. and Weatherill, S., eds., *The Oxford Handbook of the European Union*. Oxford: Oxford University Press, pp. 249–68.

Bunyan, J. and Fisher, H.H. (1961). *The Bolshevik Revolution, 1917–1918: Documents and Materials*. Stanford, CA: Stanford University Press.

Butković, H. (2017). The rise of direct democracy in Croatia: Balancing or challenging parliamentary representation?' *Croatian International Relations Review*, 23(77), 39–80.

Butler, D. and Ranney, A. (1994). *Referendums around the World: The Growing Use of Direct Democracy*. Washington, DC: American Enterprise Institute.

Butler, W.E. (1995). Russian federation: Federal law on international treaties. *International Legal Materials*, 34(5), 1370–92.

Cameron, A.C. and Miller, D.L. (2015). A practitioner's guide to cluster-robust inference. *Journal of Human Resources*, 50(2), 317–72.

Cameron, D. (2013). *EU speech at Bloomberg – 23 January 2013*. London: Office of the Prime Minister.

Cameron, F. (2016). Why we should ban referenda on EU policies. *Euractiv*, 4 April.

Cantore, C.M. (2011). We're one, but we're not the same: Enhanced cooperation and the tension between unity and asymmetry in the EU. *Perspectives on Federalism*, 3(3), E-1–21.

Cardozo, R. and Corbett, R. (1986). The Crocodile Initiative. In Lodge, J., ed., *European Union: The European Community in Search of a Future*. Houndmills: Macmillan, pp. 15–46.

Cardwell, P.J. and Hervey, T. (2015). The Roles of Law in a New Intergovernmentalist European Union. In Bickerton, C.J., Hodson, D. and Puetter, U., eds., *The New Intergovernmentalism: States and Supranational Actors in the Post-Maastricht Era*. Oxford: Oxford University Press, pp. 73–89.

Cash, B. (2011). Bill Cash MP presents bill for referendum on Eurozone fiscal union. Press release, 7 September. Full text available at: www.billcashmp.co.uk/

Castillo Ortiz, P.J. (2015). *EU Treaties and the Judicial Politics of National Courts: A Law and Politics Approach*. London: Routledge.

Cede, F. and Hafner, G. (1999). National treaty law and practice: Federal Republic of Austria. *Studies in Transnational Legal Policy*, 30(1), 1–32.

Chaffin, J. (2011). Van Rompuy draws up fast-track 'fiscal compact'. *Financial Times*, 7 December.

Cheneval, F. (2007). 'Caminante, no hay camino, se hace camino al andar': EU citizenship, direct democracy and treaty ratification. *European Law Journal*, 13(5), 647–63.

Cheneval, F. and Ferrin, M. (2016). *European Union and Direct Democracy: A Possible Combination?* Brussels: bEUcitizen.

Chinkin, C. (1983). The foreign affairs powers of the US President and the Iranian hostages agreement: Dames and Moore v. Regan. *International and Comparative Law Quarterly*, 32(3), 600–15.

Chirac, J. (1995). Discours de M. Jacques Chirac, Président de la République, à l'occasion de la réunion des Ambassadeurs. Palais de l'Elysée, Paris, 31 August.

   (2000). Address given by Jacques Chirac to the Bundestag entitled Our Europe. Full text available at: www.cvce.eu/en/obj/address_given_by_jacques_chirac_to_the_bundestag_entitled_our_europe_berlin_27_june_2000-en-6a747c46-88db-47ec-bc8c-55c8b161f4dc.html.

Chirac, J. and Schroeder, G. (2003). Contribution franco-allemande à la Convention européenne sur l'architecture institutionnelle de l'Union. Paris and Berlin, 15 January.

Christiansen, T. (2015). Institutionalist Dynamics behind the New Intergovernmentalism: The Continuous Process of EU Treaty Reform. In Bickerton, C.J., Hodson, D. and Puetter, U., eds., *The New Intergovernmentalism: States and Supranational Actors in the Post-Maastricht Era*. Oxford: Oxford University Press, pp. 90–107.

Christiansen, T. and Reh, C. (2009). *Constitutionalizing the European Union*, Basingstoke: Palgrave Macmillan.

Cienski, J., Smyth, J. and Spiegel, P. (2012). Sinn Fein legal threat hangs over fiscal deal. *Financial Times*, 20 January.

Claes, M. (2005). Constitutionalizing Europe at its source: The 'European clauses' in the national constitutions: Evolution and typology. *Yearbook of European Law*, 24(1), 81–125.

   (2006). *The National Courts' Mandate in the European Constitution*. London: Bloomsbury.

   (2007). The Europeanisation of national constitutions in the constitutionalisation of Europe: Some observations against the background of the constitutional experience of the EU-15. *Croatian Yearbook of European Law and Policy*, 3(3), 1–38.

Clark, I. (2005). *Legitimacy in International Society*. Oxford: Oxford University Press.

Clogg, R. (1987). *Parties and Elections in Greece: The Search for Legitimacy*, Durham, NC: Duke University Press.

Closa, C. (2011). Moving away from Unanimity: Ratification of the Treaty on Stability, Coordination and Governance in the Economic and Monetary Union. RECON Online Working Paper, 2011/38.

   (2012). Constitutional Rigidity and Procedures for Ratifying Constitutional Reforms in EU Member States. In Benz, A., and Knupling, F., eds., *Changing Federal Constitutions: Lessons from International Comparison*. Berlin: Verlag Barbara Budrich, pp. 281–310.

(2013a). *The Politics of Ratification of EU Treaties*. London: Routledge.

(2013b). National higher courts and the ratification of EU treaties. *West European Politics*, 36(1), 97–121.

(2014). Between a rock and a hard place: the future of EU treaty revisions. SIEPS European Policy Analysis (2014:2epa).

Coakley, J. and Gallagher, M. (2004). *Politics in the Republic of Ireland*. London: Routledge.

Collings, J. (2015). *Democracy's Guardians: A History of the German Federal Constitutional Court, 1951–2001*. Oxford: Oxford University Press.

Collins, S. (2012). Higgins's remarks on treaty alarm Ministers. *Irish Times*, 25 February.

Conca, K. (2015). *An Unfinished Foundation: The United Nations and Global Environmental Governance*. Oxford: Oxford University Press.

Congressional Research Service (2001). *Treaties and Other International Agreements: The Role of the United States Senate*. Washington, DC: Library of Congress.

Connolly, K. (2004) Germany ponders a return to banned plebiscites. The Telegraph, 20 October.

Conservative Party (2010). *Invitation to Join the Government of Britain: The Conservative Manifesto 2010*. London: Conservative Party.

Consultative Assembly of the Council of Europe (1952). *Resolution 14 Adopted on 30 May 1952 by the Consultative Assembly of the Council of Europe Concerning the Most Appropriate Means of Drafting the Statute of the European Political Community*. Communication, Doc. 40, 15 September.

Contiades, X. and Fotiadou, A. (2015). The Greek Referendum: Unconstitutional and Undemocratic. Constitutional Change through Euro Crisis Law: A Multi-Level Legal Analysis of Economic and Monetary Union, European University Institute Department of Law, 7 July.

(2017). Introduction: Participatory Constitutional Change. In Contiades, X. and Fotiadou, A., eds., *Participatory Constitutional Change: The People as Amenders of the Constitution*. London: Routledge, pp. 1–6.

Corbett, R. (1998). *The European Parliament's Role in Closer EU Integration*, Basingstoke: Palgrave.

COSAC Secretariat (2014). *COSAC: Historical Development*. Full text available at: www.panue.eu/wp-content/uploads/2013/11/History-of-COSAC-MARCH-2013-EN-1.pdf.

Council of the European Union (1978). Conclusions of the Presidency of the European Council. Brussels, 5 December.

(2002). Seville European Council Presidency Conclusions. Brussels, 21-11 June.

Council Presidency (2007). Pursuing the treaty reform process. Council of the European Union 10659/07.

Čović, A. (2012). Croatia's EU accession referendum. Referendum Briefing No. 1, European Parties Elections and Referendums Network, 22 January.

Cowley, P. and Stuart, M. (2010). Where has all the trouble gone? British intra-party parliamentary divisions during the Lisbon ratification. *British Politics*, 5(2), 133–48.

Craig, P., (2012). The Stability, Coordination and Governance Treaty: Principle, politics and pragmatism. *European Law Review*, 37(3), 231–48.

(2013). Pringle: Legal reasoning, text, purpose and teleology. *Maastricht Journal of European and Comparative Law*, 20(1), 3–11.

(2014). Economic governance and the euro crisis. Oxford Legal Studies, Research Paper No. 30/2014.

Crawford, J. (2012). *Brownlie's Principles of Public International Law*. Oxford: Oxford University Press.

Cremona, M. (2012). Who Can Make Treaties? The European Union. In Hollis, D.B., ed., *Oxford Guide to Treaties*. Oxford: Oxford University Press, pp. 93–124.

Crespy, A. and Schmidt, V. (2014). The clash of titans: France, Germany and the discursive double game of EMU reform. *Journal of European Public Policy*, 21(8), 1085–101.

Cross, M.K.D. (2017). *The Politics of Crisis in Europe*. New York, NY: Cambridge University Press.

Crotty, R.D. (1988). *A Radical's Response*. Dublin: Poolbeg Press.

Croxton, D. (2013). *Westphalia: The Last Christian Peace*. Basingstoke: Palgrave.

Crum, B. (2007). Party stances in the referendums on the EU constitution: Causes and consequences of competition and collusion. *European Union Politics*, 8(1), 61–82.

Cumberland, E. (2014). The end of treaties? An online agora. *AJIL Unbound*, www.asil.org/blogs/end-treaties-online-agora.

Curtin, D. and Dekker, I. (2010). The European Union from Maastricht to Lisbon. Institutional and Legal Unity Out of the Shadows. In Craig, P. and De Búrca, G., eds., *The Evolution of EU Law*, 2nd edition. Oxford: Oxford University Press, pp. 155–86.

Daimer, S. (2006). Latvia and the Constitution: A Pragmatic 'Yes'. In König, T. and Hug, S., eds., *Policy-Making Processes and the European Constitution: A Comparative Study of Member States and Accession Countries*. London: Routledge, pp. 144–51.

Dalton, R.J. (2005). The social transformation of trust in government. *International Review of Sociology*, 15(1), 133–54.

Danish Ministry of Foreign Affairs (1992). White Paper on Denmark and the Maastricht Treaty, SN 4364/92.

De Becker, A. (2011). Belgium: The state and the sub-state entities are equal, but is the state sometimes still more equal than the others? In Panara, C., ed., *The Role of the Regions in EU Governance*. Berlin: Springer Science & Business Media, pp. 251–74.

de Búrca, G. (2009). If at first you don't succeed: Vote, vote again: Analyzing the second referendum phenomenon in EU treaty change. *Fordham International Law Journal*, 33(5), 1472–8.

de Jong, S. (2016). Why the Dutch referendum on Ukraine is a joke. *EU Observer*, 4 April.

De Schoutheete, P. and Wallace, H.S. (2002). *The European Council*. Notre Europe Paris Research and European Issues, 19. Paris: Notre Europe.

de Visser, M. (2013). *Constitutional Review in Europe: A Comparative Analysis*. London: Bloomsbury.

de Witte, B. (1994). Rules of change in international law: How special is the European Community? *Netherlands Yearbook of International Law*, 25(1994), 299–333.

(2004). *The National Constitutional Dimension of European Treaty Revision*. Groningen: Europa Law Publishing.

(2009). International law as a tool for the European Union. *European Constitutional Law Review*, 5(2), 265–83.

(2011). The European Treaty Amendment for the creation of a financial stability mechanism. Swedish Institute for European Policy Studies, *European Policy Analysis* 6, 1–8.

(2012). Treaty Revision after Lisbon. In Ripley, S., Biondi, A. and Eeckhout, P., eds., *EU Law after Lisbon*. Oxford: Oxford University Press.

(2013). Using international law in the euro crisis. Centre for European Studies, University of Oslo, Working Paper, No. 4.

de Witte, B. and Beukers, T. (2013). Court of Justice approves the creation of the European Stability Mechanism outside the EU legal order: Pringle. *Common Market Law Review*, 50(3), 805.

Dean, A.H. (1953). The Bricker Amendment and authority over foreign affairs. *Foreign Affairs*, 32(1), 1–19.

Deese, B. (2017). Paris isn't burning: Why the climate agreement will survive Trump. *Foreign Affairs*, 96(4), 83.

Dehousse, R. (2006). The unmaking of a constitution: Lessons from the European referenda. *Constellations*, 13(2), 151–64.

Dicey, A.V. (2013 [1889]). *The Law of the Constitution*. Oxford: Oxford University Press.

Dimitrakopoulos, D.G. and Kassim, H. (2005). Inside the European Commission: preference formation and the Convention on the Future of Europe. *Comparative European Politics*, 3(2), 180–203.

Dimopoulos, A. (2015). Taming the conclusion of Inter Se Agreements between EU member states: The role of the duty of loyalty. *Yearbook of European Law*, 34(1), 286–318.

Dinmore, G. (2012). Monti challenged over fiscal compact. *Financial Times*, 7 May.

Division of International Law of the Carnegie Endowment for International Peace (1920). *The Proceedings of the Hague Peace Conferences*. Oxford: Oxford University Press.

Dixon, R. and Holden, R. (2011). Constitutional amendment rules: The denominator problem. University of Chicago, Public Law Working Paper, No. 346.

Duchhardt, H. (2004). Peace Treaties from Westphalia to the Revolutionary Era. In Lesaffer, R., ed., *Peace Treaties and International Law in European History: From the Late Middle Ages to World War One*. Cambridge: Cambridge University Press, pp. 45–58.

Due, O. and Gulmann, C. (1972). Constitutional implications of the Danish accession to the European Communities. *Common Market Law Review*, 9(3), 256.

REFERENCES

Duff, A. (1981). The report of the three wise men. *Journal of Common Market Studies*, 19(3), 237–54.

(2005). *The Struggle for Europe's Constitution*. London: Federal Trust for Education & Research.

Dumbrovsky, T. (2014). *Constitutional Change through Crisis Law: Czech Republic*. Fiesole: European University Institute.

Dumont, P. and Poirier, P. (2006). Luxembourg. *European Journal of Political Research*, 45(7–8), 1182–97.

Dyck, J.J. (2009). Initiated distrust: Direct democracy and trust in government. *American Politics Research*, 37(4), 539–68.

Dyson, K. and Featherstone, K. (1999). *The Road to Maastricht: Negotiating Economic and Monetary Union*. Oxford: Oxford University Press.

Economist (2012). Internet regulation: A digital cold war? The internet seems to be an even more divisive than capitalist-or-communist ideology. *The Economist*, Babbage Blog (14 December).

Edelenbos, J. and Eshuis, J. (2012). The interplay between trust and control in governance processes: A conceptual and empirical investigation. *Administration & Society*, 44(6), 647–74.

Ehlermann, C.-D. and Meny, Y. (2000). *Reforming the Treaties' Amendment Procedures*. Fiesole: Robert Schuman Centre for Advanced Studies.

Elgot, J. (2017). Lib Dems call for second EU referendum in December 2018. *The Guardian*, 20 December.

Elias, O. (2012). Who Can Make Treaties? International Organization. In Hollis, D.B., ed., *Oxford Guide to Treaties*. Oxford: Oxford University Press, pp. 73–92.

Elkins, Z., Ginsburg, T. and Melton, J. (2009). *The Endurance of National Constitutions*. Cambridge: Cambridge University Press.

Ellis, R.J. (2002). *Democratic Delusions: The Initiative Process in America*. Lawrence, KS: University Press of Kansas.

Emilianides, A. (2014). Cyprus: Everything Changes and Nothing Remains the Same. In Farran, S., Örücü, E. and Donlan, S.P., eds., *A Study of Mixed Legal Systems: Endangered, Entrenched or Blended*. Farnham: Ashgate, pp. 213–40.

Engström, V. (2010). How to tame the elusive: Lessons from the revision of the EU Flexibility Clause. *International Organizations Law Review*, 7(2), 343–73.

EPRS (2014). The road to the 1984 Spinelli Report. Full text available at: https://epthinktank.eu/2014/02/03/the-road-to-the-1984-spinelli-report/.

EUbusiness.com (2005). Czech referendum on EU constitution 'impossible' for now: PM Paroubek. *EUbusiness.com*, 26 May.

Euractiv (2001). France and Germany agree on a European Constitution. *Euroactiv*, 26 November.

Eurobarometer (2005). *The European Constitution: Post-Referendum Survey in France*. Brussels: Eurobarometer.

(2016). *Standard Eurobarometer 86 Autumn*. Brussels: Eurobarometer.

European Commission (2001). *European Governance: A White Paper*, COM(2001) 428.

(2002). *Feasibility Study: Contribution to a Preliminary Draft Constitution of the European Union*. Working Document 4 December 2002.

(2005). *Communication from the Commission to the Council, the European Parliament, the European Economic and Social Committee and the Committee of the Regions: The Commission's contribution to the period of reflection and beyond: Plan-D for Democracy, Dialogue and Debate*, COM(2005) 494 final Brussels: European Commission.

(2015). *Report from the Commission to the European Parliament and the Council: Report on the application of Regulation (EU) No. 211/2011 on the citizens' initiative*, COM (2015) 145 final.

(2017a). *The Fiscal Compact: Taking Stock*, C(2017) 1200 final.

(2017b). *Reflection Paper on the Deepening of the Economic and Monetary Union*. Brussels: European Commission.

European Council (1990). *Special Meeting of the European Council Dublin 28 April 1990*, SN 46/3/90.

(1992a). *Conclusions of the Presidency (16 October 1992)*, SN 343/1/92.

(1992b). *Conclusions of the Presidency (11–12 December)*, SN 456/92.

(1994). *Conclusions of the Corfu European Council*, SN 100/94.

(1995). *Presidency Conclusions (15 and 16 December)*, SN 400/95.

(2001). *Laeken Declaration on the Future of the European Union*, SN 300/1/01 REV 1.

(2002). *Conclusions of the Presidency, (21–22 June 2002)*, 13463/02.

(2005). *Declaration by the Heads of State or Government of the Member States of the European Union on the Ratification of the Treaty Establishing a Constitution for Europe*, SN 117/05.

(2007a). *Presidency Conclusions: Brussels European Council – 14 December 2017*, ST 16616 2007 INIT.

(2007b). *Declaration on the Occasion of the 50th Anniversary of the Signature of the Treaties of Rome*. Available at: http://europa.eu/50/docs/berlin_declaration_en.pdf.

(2007c). *Brussels European Council of 21–22 June*, SN 11177/1/07

(2008). *Presidency Conclusions (11 and 12 December)*, SN 17271/1/08 REV 1.

(2009). *Presidency Conclusions (18–19 June)*, SN 11225/2/09.

(2011). *Presidency Conclusions (25 January)*, EUCO 139/1/11.

(2016). *European Council Meeting (15 December 2016) – Conclusions*, ST 34 2016.

European Law Blog (2012). Pringle – The Unconstitutional Constitutional Amendment Conundrum. *European Law Blog*, 6 December.

European Parliament (1987). *European Parliament Resolution on the Single European Act A2–169/86*.

(2000). *GC: Nicole Fontaine Happy with Extremely Productive Discussions on Ep Proposals*, press release, 22 May.

(2011). *Explanation of votes – Wednesday, 23 March 2011*, PV 23/03/2011 – 13.1.

(2013). *European Parliament resolution of 12 June 2013 on strengthening European democracy in the future EMU*, 2013/2672(RSP).

Evans, P.B. (1993). Building an Integrative Approach to International and Domestic Politics: Reflections and Projections. In Putnam, R.D., Evans, P.B. and Jacobson, H.K., eds., *Double-Edged Diplomacy: International Bargaining and Domestic Politics*. Berkeley, CA: University of California Press, pp. 397–430.

Evans, P.B., Jacobson, H.K. and Putnam, R.D. (1993). *Double-Edged Diplomacy: International Bargaining and Domestic Politics*. Berkeley, CA: University of California Press.

Evans, S. (2008). Consigning its past to history? David Cameron and the conservative party. *Parliamentary Affairs*, 61(2), 291–314.

Fabbrini, F. (2013). Enhanced cooperation under scrutiny: Revisiting the law and practice of multi-speed integration in light of the first involvement of the EU judiciary. *Legal Issues of Economic Integration*, 40(3), 197.

(2016) *Economic Governance in Europe: Comparative Paradoxes and Institutional Challenges*. Oxford: Oxford University Press.

Farrell, D.M., Harris, C. and Suiter, J. (2017). Bringing People into the Heart of Constitutional Design: The Irish Constitutional Convention of 2012–14. In Contiades, X. and Fotiadou, A., eds., *Participatory Constitutional Change: The People as Amenders of the Constitution*. Abingdon: Routledge, pp. 120–35.

Farrell, H. and Knight, J. (2003). Trust, institutions, and institutional change: Industrial districts and the social capital hypothesis. *Politics & Society*, 31(4), 537–66.

Faure, G.O. (2012). *Unfinished Business: Why International Negotiations Fail*. Athens, GA: University of Georgia Press.

Ferejohn, J. (1997). The politics of imperfection: The amendment of constitutions. *Law & Social Inquiry*, 22(2), 501–30.

Ferriter, D. (2012). *Ambiguous Republic: Ireland in the 1970s*. London: Profile Books.

Financial Times (2005). EU constitution faces oblivion, according to polls. *Financial Times*, 3 June.

Finch, G.A. (1954). The need to restrain the treaty-making power of the United States within constitutional limits. *The American Journal of International Law*, 48(1), 57–82.

Finke, D. (2009). Domestic politics and European treaty reform understanding the dynamics of governmental position-taking. *European Union Politics*, 10(4), 482–506.

Finke, D. and König, T. (2009). Why risk popular ratification failure? A comparative analysis of the choice of the ratification instrument in the 25 Member States of the EU. *Constitutional Political Economy*, 20(3–4), 341–65.

Fitzhardinge, L. (1968). Hughes, Borden, and dominion representation at the Paris Peace Conference. *Canadian Historical Review*, 49(2), 160–9.

Fitzmaurice, M. (2005). Consent to be bound: Anything new under the sun? *Nordic Journal of International Law*, 74(3–4), 483.

Flietz, F. (2017). Trump will withdraw from the Paris Agreement: Good. *National Review*, 31 May.

Follesdal, A. and Hix, S. (2006). Why there is a democratic deficit in the EU: A response to Majone and Moravcsik. *Journal of Common Market Studies*, 44(3), 533–62.

Fontanelli, F. and Martinico, G. (2008). Cooperative antagonists: The Italian Constitutional Court and the preliminary reference: Are we dealing with a turning point? Eric Stein Working Paper, No. 5/2008.

Foster, N. (2013). *Austrian Legal System and Laws*. London: Routledge.

Franklin, M., Marsh, M. and McLaren, L. (1994). Uncorking the bottle: Popular opposition to European unification in the wake of Maastricht. *Journal of Common Market Studies*, 32(4), 455–72.

Fredriksson, P.G. and Gaston, N. (2000). Ratification of the 1992 climate change convention: What determines legislative delay? *Public Choice*, 104(3), 345–68.

Fruhstorfer, A. and Hein, M. (2016). From Post Socialist Transition to the Reform of Political Systems. In Fruhstorfer, A. and Hein, M., eds., *Constitutional Politics in Central and Eastern Europe: From Post-Socialist Transition to the Reform of Political Systems*. Berlin: Springer, pp. 547–75.

Frydrych, M. (2004). Poland ready for referendum on Constitution. *EU Observer*, 25 March.

Fursdon, E. (1980). *The European Defence Community: A History*. London: Palgrave Macmillan UK.

Garry, J., Marsh, M. and Sinnott, R. (2005). 'Second-order' versus 'issue-voting' effects in EU referendums: Evidence from the Irish nice treaty referendums. *European Union Politics*, 6(2), 201–21.

General Affairs Council (1992). *EC Foreign Ministers Meeting*, Oslo, 4 June 1992.

(2001). *2356th Council Meeting General Affairs*, Luxembourg, 11–12 June 2001, 9398/01 (Presse 226).

Gerber, E.R. and Hug, S. (2001). Legislative Response to Direct Legislation. In Mendelsohn, M. and Parkin, A., eds., *Referendum Democracy*. Berlin: Springer, pp. 88–108.

Gerkrath, J. (2012). Constitutional Amendment in Luxembourg. In Contiades, X., ed., *Engineering Constitutional Change*. London: Routledge, pp. 229–55.

(2016). Luxembourg: The Constitution of Luxembourg in the Context of EU and International Law as 'Higher Law'. In Albi, A. and Bardutzky, S., eds., *The Role of National Constitutions in European and Global Governance*. The Hague: T.M.C. Asser Press.

(2017). The Sudden Eagerness to Consult the Luxemburgish People on Constitutional Change. In Contiades, X. and Foitadou, A., eds., *Participatory Constitutional Change: The People as Amenders of the Constitution*. Abingdon, Oxon, UK: Routledge, pp. 139–55.

Gerston, L.N. (1989). Policymaking by referendum in Palau: Grassroots democracy or political paralysis? *Asian Affairs: An American Review*, 16(4), 175–85.

Gilland, K. (2002). Ireland's Second Referendum on the Treaty of Nice. Referendum Briefing No. 1, October 2002.

Ginsburg, T. (2005). Locking in democracy: Constitutions, commitment, and international law. *New York University Journal of International Law and Politics*, 38, 707–60.

Ginsburg, T. and Melton, J. (2015). Does the constitutional amendment rule matter at all? Amendment cultures and the challenges of measuring amendment difficulty. *International Journal of Constitutional Law*, 13(3), 686–713.

Ginsburg, T. and Versteeg, M. (2014). Why do countries adopt constitutional review? *Journal of Law, Economics, & Organization*, 30(3), 587–622.

Ginter, C. (2013). Constitutionality of the European Stability Mechanism in Estonia: Applying proportionality to sovereignty. *European Constitutional Law Review*, 9(2), 335–54.

Glencross, A. and Trechsel, A. (2011). First or second order referendums? Understanding the votes on the EU Constitutional Treaty in four EU Member States. *West European Politics*, 34(4), 755–72.

Glockner, I. and Rittberger, B. (2012). The European Coal and Steel Community (ECSC) and European Defence Community (EDS) Treaties. In Laursen, F., ed., *Designing the European Union: From Paris to Lisbon*. Basingstoke: Palgrave, pp. 16–47.

Gocaj, L. and Meunier, S. (2013). Time will tell: The EFSF, the ESM, and the euro crisis. *Journal of European Integration*, 35(3), 239–53.

Gooch, A. (1986). A surrealistic referendum: Spain and NATO. *Government and Opposition*, 21(3), 300–16.

Goodman, C.F. (2008). *The Rule of Law in Japan: A Comparative Analysis*. Alphen aan den Rijn: Kluwer Law International.

Gottfried, G. (2014). Continental drift: Understanding the growth of Euroscepticism. *IPPR*, 8 October.

Gouveia, J.B. (2011). *Constitutional Law in Portugal*. Dordrecht: Kluwer Law International.

Granat, K. (2014). *Constitutional Change through Euro Crisis Law: Poland*. Fiesole: European University Institute.

(2015). Approval of Article 136 TFEU Amendment in Poland: The perspective of the Constitutional Court on Eurozone crisis law. *European Public Law*, 21(1), 33–46.

Grant, T. (2012). Who Can Make Treaties? Other Subjects of International Law. In Hollis, D.B., ed., *Oxford Guide to Treaties*. Oxford: Oxford University Press, pp. 125–49.

Gray, M. and Stubb, A. (2001). Keynote article: The Treaty of Nice – Negotiating a poisoned chalice? *JCMS: Journal of Common Market Studies*, 39(s1), 5–23.

Greene, W.H. (2012). *Econometric Analysis: International Edition*. London: Pearson Education.

Grey, T.C. (1979). Constitutionalism: An Analytic Framework. In Pennnock, J.R. and Chapman, J.W., eds., *Constitutionalism: Nomos XX*. New York, NY: New York University Press, pp. 189–209.

Griffiths, R.T. (2000). *Europe's First Constitution: The European Political Community, 1952–1954*. Dordrecht: Springer/Federal Trust.

Grosser, A. (2009). The Federal Constitutional Court's Lisbon Case: Germany's Sonderweg – An outsider's perspective. *German Law Journal*, 10(8), 1263.

Gunlicks, A. (2003). *The Länder and German Federalism*. Manchester: Manchester University Press.

Gurrea Martens, A.M. (2005). Portugal: The Fight against the Big Ones. In Laursen, F., ed., *The Treaty of Nice: Actor Preferences, Bargaining and Institutional Choice*. Leiden: Brill, pp. 247–62.

Hagemann, S. (2007). *The EU Reform Treaty: Easier Signed than Ratified?* European Policy Centre Policy Brief, 1–9.

Haggenmacher, P. (1991). Some hints on the European origins of legislative participation in the treaty-making function. *Chicago Kent Law Review*. 67, 313–39.

Halberstam, D. (2009). Constitutional Heterarchy: The Centrality of Conflict in the European Union and the United States. In Dunoff, J.L. and Trachtman, J.P., eds., *Ruling the World? Constitutionalism, International Law and Global Governance*. Cambridge: Cambridge University Press, pp. 326–55.

Halberstam, M. (1997). United States ratification of the Convention on the Elimination of All Forms of Discrimination against Women. *George Washington Journal of International Law and Economics*, 31(2), 49–96.

Hamilton, A. (2010 [1788]). The treaty-making power of the executive: Federalist No. 75. *Independent Journal*, 26 March.

Hardin, R. (1998). Trust in Government. In Braithwaite, V. and Levi, M., eds., *Trust and Governance*. New York, NY: Russell Sage Foundation, pp. 9–27.

Hardman, I. (2012). Ministerial aides push Cameron on EU. *The Spectator*, 2 July.

Harhoff, F. (1983). Greenland's withdrawal from the European Communities. *Common Market Law Review*, 20(1), 13.

Harley, J.E. (1919). The obligation to ratify treaties. *American Journal of International Law*, 13(3), 389–405.

Harrington, J. (2006). Scrutiny and approval: The role for Westminster-style parliaments in treaty-making. *International & Comparative Law Quarterly*, 55(1), 121–60.

Hathaway, O.A. (2008). Treaties' end: The past, present, and future of international lawmaking in the United States. *Yale Law Journal*, 117(7), 1236–372.

  (2009). Presidential power over international law: Restoring the balance. *The Yale Law Journal*, 119(2), 140–268.

Hayes-Renshaw, F. and Wallace, H. (2006). *The Council of Ministers*, 2nd edition. Basingstoke, Hampshire: Palgrave Macmillan.

Henisz, W.J. (2017). *The Political Constraint Index (POLCON) Dataset*. See https://mgmt.wharton.upenn.edu/faculty/heniszpolcon/polcondataset/.

Henry, P.B. (2013). The global trust deficit. *Project Syndicate*, 1 July.

Hepburn, E. (2014). Forging autonomy in a unitary state: The Åland Islands in Finland. *Comparative European Politics*, 12(4–5), 468–87.

Héritier, A. and Moury, C. (2015). *The European Parliament as a Driving Force of Constitutionalisation: Study Commissioned by the Policy Department for Citizen's Rights and Constitutional Affairs at the Request of the AFCO Committee*. Brussels: European Parliament.

Herron, E.S. and Randazzo, K.A. (2003). The relationship between independence and judicial review in post-communist courts. *Journal of Politics*, 65(2), 422–38.

Hinrichsen, N.R. (1997). The constitutional objection to European Union Membership: A challenge for the Danish Supreme Court. *Boston University International Law Journal*, 15(1), 571.

Hirschl, R. (2006). The new constitutionalism and the judicialization of pure politics worldwide. *Fordham Law Review*, 75(2), 721.

  (2014). *Comparative Matters: The Renaissance of Comparative Constitutional Law*. Oxford: Oxford University Press.

REFERENCES

Hix, S. (2002). Constitutional agenda-setting through discretion in rule interpretation: Why the European Parliament won at Amsterdam. *British Journal of Political Science*, 32(2), 259–80.

Hobolt, S.B. (2005). When Europe matters: The impact of political information on voting behaviour in EU referendums. *Journal of Elections, Public Opinion & Parties*, 15(1), 85–109.

Hodson, D. and Maher, I. (2002). Economic and monetary union: Balancing credibility and legitimacy in an asymmetric policy-mix. *Journal of European Public Policy*, 9(3), 391–407.

(2014). British brinkmanship and Gaelic games: EU treaty ratification in the UK and Ireland from a two level game perspective. *The British Journal of Politics & International Relations*, 16(4), 645–61.

Hoesly, C. (2005). Reforming direct democracy: Lessons from Oregon. *California Law Review*, 93(4), 1191–248.

Hoffman, A.M. (2002). A conceptualization of trust in international relations. *European Journal of International Relations*, 8(3), 375–401.

Hoffmann, L. (2002). The Convention on the Future of Europe: Thoughts on the convention-model. *Jean Monnet Working Papers*, 11(2).

Hoffmeister, F. (2007). Constitutional implications of EU membership: A view from the Commission. *Croatian Yearbook of European Law and Policy*, 3(3), 59–97.

Hofmann, H.C., Rowe, G.C. and Türk, A.H. (2011). *Administrative Law and Policy of the European Union*. Oxford: Oxford University Press.

Hollis, D.B. (2005). Why state consent still matters: Non-state actors, treaties, and the changing sources of international law. *Berkeley Journal of International Law*, 23, 137.

(2012). *The Oxford Guide to Treaties*. Oxford: Oxford University Press.

(2014). The end of treaties? The end of history? *Opinio Juris*, 29 April.

Hooghe, L. and Marks, G. (2009). A postfunctionalist theory of European integration: From permissive consensus to constraining dissensus. *British Journal of Political Science*, 39(1), 1–23.

House of Commons Information Office (2010). *Treaties*, House of Commons Factsheet Procedure Series 14.

House of Commons Library (1996). *Towards the IGC: Approaching Turin*, Research Paper 96/41.

(2003). *The draft Treaty establishing a European Constitution: Technical and Constitutional Issues in Parts I and IV*, Research Paper 03/60.

Hübner, K., Deman, A.-S. and Balik, T. (2017). EU and trade policy-making: The contentious case of CETA. *Journal of European Integration*, 39(7), 843–57.

Hug, S. (2003). *Voices of Europe: Citizens, Referendums, and European Integration*. Boulder, CO: Rowman & Littlefield.

(2009). Some thoughts about referendums, representative democracy, and separation of powers. *Constitutional Political Economy*, 20(3–4), 251.

Hug, S. and König, T. (2002). In view of ratification: Governmental preferences and domestic constraints at the Amsterdam Intergovernmental Conference. *International Organization*, 56(2), 447–76.

Hug, S. and Schulz, T. (2007). Referendums in the EU's constitution building process. *The Review of International Organizations*, 2(2), 177–218.

Hunter, B. (1991). Luxembourg: Grand-Duché de Luxembourg. In Hunter, B., ed., *The Statesman's Year-Book: Statistical and Historical Annual of the States of the World for the Year 1991–1992*. Berlin: Springer, pp. 820–3.

Hyde, S.D. (2011). Catch us if you can: Election monitoring and international norm diffusion. *American Journal of Political Science*, 55(2), 356–69.

Hyland, R. (1993). Pacta sunt servanda: A meditation. *Virginia Journal of International Law*, 34, 405.

International Organization (1954). European Defence Community. *International Organization*, 8(4), 599–601.

Irish Times (2007). Dutch government rules out EU vote. *Irish Times*, 21 September.

Jaaskinen, N. (1999). The application of Community Law in Finland: 1995–1998. *Common Market Law Review*, 36(2), 407–41.

Jacobsen, J.K. (1996). Are all politics domestic? Perspectives on the integration of comparative politics and international relations theories. *Comparative Politics*, 29(1), 93–115.

Jaeger, T. (2012). Back to square one? An assessment of the latest proposals for a patent and court for the internal market and possible alternatives. *IIC – International Review of Intellectual Property and Competition Law*, 43(3), 286–303.

Janning, J. (2014). Thinking Big: What If EU Leaders Had Been Bold Enough to Create European Political Union at Maastricht? In Parkes, R. and Möller, A., eds., *'What If the EU . . .?' An Exercise in Counterfactual Thinking to Address Current Dilemmas*. Berlin: Deutschen Gesellschaft für Auswärtige Politik, pp. 31–7.

Jarukaitis, I. (2010). Lithuania's Membership in the European Union and Application of EU Law at National Level. In Lazowski, A., ed., *The Application of EU Law in the New Member States: Brave New World*. The Hague: Asser, pp. 209–42.

Jennings, I. (1967). *The Law and the Constitution*. London: University of London Press.

Jennings, M.K. (1998). Political Trust and the Roots of Devolution. In Braithwaite, V. and Levi, M., eds., *Trust and Governance*. New York, NY: Russell Sage Foundation, pp. 218–44.

Jerónimo, P. (2003). Adoption and Entry into Force of the Constitution for Europe. In Ziller, J., ed., *Europeanisation of Constitutional Law in the Light of the Constitution for Europe*. Paris: Editions L'Harmattan, pp. 173–204.

Jessup, P.C. (1948). *A Modern Law of Nations: An Introduction*. New York, NY: Macmillan.

Jha, S.K. (2006). *Final Act of WTO: Abuse of Treaty-Making Power*. New Delhi: Centre for Study of Global Trade System and Development.

Jočienė, D. (2007). The European Convention on Human Rights in the Lithuanian legal system: Interaction between the European Court of Human Rights and the Lithuanian courts. *Teisė*.

Joerges, C. (2014). Law and politics in Europe's crisis: On the history of the impact of an unfortunate configuration. *Constellations*, 21(2), 249–61.

304 REFERENCES

Johnson, J.W. (2017). The art of breaking the deal: What President Trump can and can't do about NAFTA. *C.D. Howe Institute Commentary*, 46.

Jonas, D.S. and Saunders, T.N. (2010). The object and purpose of a treaty: Three interpretive methods. *Vanderbilt Journal of Transnational Law*, 43(3), 565–609.

Jones, J.M. (1946). *Full Powers and Ratification: A Study in the Development of Treaty-Making Procedure*. Cambridge: Cambridge University Press.

Juncker, J.-C. (2017). *State of the Union Address 2017*. Brussels: European Commission.

Kaelberer, M. (2003). Knowledge, power and monetary bargaining: Central bankers and the creation of monetary union in Europe. *Journal of European Public Policy*, 10(3), 365–79.

Karlsson, C. (2016). Explaining constitutional change: Making sense of cross-national variation among European Union member states. *Journal of European Public Policy*, 23(2), 255–75.

Karnitschnig, M. and Eder, F. (2017). Europe's elite put on grand show of unity in Rome. *Politico Europe*, 25 March.

Kaufmann, B. (2012). Transnational 'Babystep': The European Citizens' Initiative. In Setälä, M. and Schiller, T., eds., *Citizens' Initiatives in Europe: Procedures and Consequences of Agenda-Setting by Citizens*. Basingstoke: Palgrave Macmillan, pp. 228–42.

Kavčič, I. (2014). Ustavne omejitve in prepovedi zakonodajnega referenduma. *Zbornik znanstvenih razprav*, 74(2014), 59–92.

Kellermann, A.E. (2008). The Irish referendum on the Lisbon Treaty. *Amicus Curiae*, 2008(75), 33–6.

Keck, M.E. and Sikkink, K. (1998). *Activists beyond Borders: Advocacy Networks in International Politics*. Ithaca, NY: Cornell University Press.

Keohane, R.O. and Hoffmann, S. (1991). *The New European Community: Decisionmaking and Institutional Change*. Boulder, CO: Westview Press.

Kerrouche, E. (2006). The French Assemblée nationale: The case of a weak legislature? *The Journal of Legislative Studies*, 12(3–4), 336–65.

Kiiver, P. (2006). *The National Parliaments in the European Union: A Critical View on EU Constitution-Building*. The Hague: Kluwer Law International.

Kilbourne, S. (1996). US failure to ratify the UN Convention on the Rights of the Child: Playing politics with children's rights. *Transnational Law & Contemporary Problems*, 6(2), 437–41.

Kim, J.A. and Chung, S.-Y. (2012). The role of the G20 in governing the climate change regime. *International Environmental Agreements: Politics, Law and Economics*, 12(4), 361–74.

Knudsen, T. and Jakobsen, U. (2003). The Danish Path to Democracy. Paper for the 2nd ECPR General Conference, Marburg, 18–21 September 2003

Kohn, M. (2008). *Trust: Self-Interest and the Common Good*. Oxford: Oxford University Press.

König, T. and Finke, D. (2007). Reforming the equilibrium? Veto players and policy change in the European constitution-building process. *The Review of International Organizations*, 2(2), 153–76.

König, T. and Hug, S. (2000). Ratifying Maastricht parliamentary votes on international treaties and theoretical solution concepts. *European Union Politics*, 1(1), 93–124.

Konig, T. and Slapin, J. (2004). Bringing parliaments back in: The sources of power in the European treaty negotiations. *Journal of Theoretical Politics*, 16(3), 357–94.

König, T. and Slapin, J.B. (2006). From unanimity to consensus: An analysis of the negotiations at the EU's Constitutional Convention. *World Politics*, 58(3), 413–45.

Korontzis, G. (2012). Making the Treaty. In Hollis, D.B., ed., *The Oxford Guide to Treaties*, Oxford: Oxford University Press, p. 185.

Kovziridze, T. (2008). *Hierarchy and Interdependence in Multi-Level Structures: Foreign and European Relations of Belgian, German and Austrian Federated Entities*. Brussels: ASP/VUBPRESS/UPA.

Krunke, H. (2005). From Maastricht to Edinburgh: The Danish solution. *European Constitutional Law Review*, 1(3), 339–56.

  (2014). The Danish Lisbon Judgment–Danish Supreme Court, Case 199/2012, Judgment of 20 February 2013. *European Constitutional Law Review*, 10(3), 542–70.

  (2017). Sovereignty, Constitutional Identity, Direct Democracy? Direct Democracy as a National Strategy for Upholding the Nation State in EU Integration. In Contiades, X. and Fotiadou, A., eds., *Participatory Constitutional Change: The People as Amenders of the Constitution*. Abingdon: Routledge, pp. 191–208.

Krutz, G.S. and Peake, J.S. (2009). *Treaty Politics and the Rise of Executive Agreements: International Commitments in a System of Shared Powers*. Ann Arbor, MI: University of Michigan Press.

Kuijper, P.J., Mathis, J.H. and Morris-Sharma, N.Y. (2015). *From Treaty-Making to Treaty-Breaking: Models for ASEAN External Trade Agreements*. Cambridge: Cambridge University Press.

Kumlin, S. and Haugsgjerd, A. (2017). The Welfare State and Political Trust: Bringing Performance Back In. In Zmerli, S. and van der Meer, T.W.G., eds., *Handbook on Political Trust*. Cheltenham: Edward Elgar, pp. 285–301.

Kumm, M. (1999). Who is the final arbiter of constitutionality in Europe: Three conceptions of the relationship between the German Federal Constitutional Court and the European Court of Justice. *Common Market Law Review*, 36(2), 351.

Kumm, M. and Comella, V.F. (2005). The primacy clause of the constitutional treaty and the future of constitutional conflict in the European Union. *International Journal of Constitutional Law*, 3, 473.

Laffan, B. and O'Mahony, J. (2008). *Ireland and the European Union*. Basingstoke: Palgrave Macmillan.

Landemore, H. (2015). Inclusive constitution-making: The Icelandic experiment. *Journal of Political Philosophy*, 23(2), 166–91.

Lane, J.-E. (1996). *Constitutions and Political Theory*. Manchester: Manchester University Press.

306 REFERENCES

Larson, D.W. (1997). Trust and missed opportunities in international relations. *Political Psychology*, 18(3), 701–34.

Laursen, F. (1994). *The Ratification of the Maastricht Treaty: Issues, Debates, and Future Implications*. Alphen aan den Rijn: Kluwer Law International.

(2002). *The Amsterdam Treaty*. Odense: Odense University Press.

(2005a). *The Treaty of Nice: Actor Preferences, Bargaining and Institutional Choice*. Leiden: Brill.

(2005b). The role of national parliamentary committees in European scrutiny: Reflections based on the Danish case. *The Journal of Legislative Studies*, 11(3–4), 412–27.

(2006). Denmark: The Battle to Avoid a Referendum. In Laursen, F., ed., *The Treaty of Nice: Actor Preferences, Bargaining and Institutional Choice*. Leiden: Martinus Nijhoff Publishers, pp. 57–82.

(2008). *The Rise and Fall of the EU's Constitutional Treaty*. Leiden: Martinus Nijhoff Publishers.

(2009). Denmark and the ratification of the Lisbon Treaty. How a referendum was avoided. Dalhousie EUCE Occasional Paper 7.

(2012a). *The EU's Lisbon Treaty: Institutional Choices and Implementation*. Farnham: Ashgate Publishing.

(2012b). *Designing the European Union: From Paris to Lisbon*. Basingstoke: Palgrave Macmillan.

(2012c). Introduction: On the Study of EU Treaties and Treaty Reforms. In Laursen, F., ed., *Designing the European Union: From Paris to Lisbon*. Basingstoke, Hampshire: Palgrave Macmillan UK, pp. 1–15.

Laursen, F. and Vanhoonacker, S. (1992). *The Intergovernmental Conference on Political Union: Institutional Reforms, New Policies and International Identity of the European Community*. Leiden: Brill.

Lavranos, N. (2011). Member states' bits: Lost in transition? Unpublished paper, Centro de Estudios Políticos y Constitucionales.

Lesaffer, R. (2000). The medieval canon law of contract and early modern treaty law. *Journal of the History of International Law*, 2(2), 178–98.

(2004). Peace Treaties from Lodi to Westphalia. In Lesaffer, R., ed., *Peace Treaties and International Law in European History: From the Late Middle Ages to World War One*. Cambridge: Cambridge University Press, pp. 9–44.

Leucht, B. (2010). Expertise and the Creation of a Constitutional Order for Core Europe: Transatlantic Policy Networks in the Schuman Plan Negotiations. In Kaiser, W., Leucht, B. and Gehler, M., eds., *Transnational Networks in Regional Integration: Governing Europe 1945–83*. Basingstoke: Palgrave Macmillan UK, pp. 18–37.

Levenotoglu, B. and Tarar, A. (2005). Prenegotiation public commitment in domestic and international bargaining. *American Political Science Review*, 99(3), 419–33.

Levi, M. (1998). A State of Trust. In Braithwaite, V. and Levi, M., eds., *Trust and Governance*. New York, NY: Russell Sage Foundation, pp. 77–101.

Levi, M. and Stoker, L. (2000). Political trust and trustworthiness. *Annual Review of Political Science*, 3(1), 475–507.

Levin, R.Z. and Chen, P. (2012). Rethinking the Constitution–treaty relationship. *International Journal of Constitutional Law*, 10(1), 242–60.

Lewis, J. (2017). Coreper: National Interests and the Logic of Appropriateness. In Hodson, D. and Peterson, J., eds., *The Institutions of the European Union*, 4th edition. Oxford: Oxford University Press, pp. 334–56.

Lijphart, A. (2012). *Patterns of Democracy: Government Forms and Performance in Thirty-Six Countries*. New Haven, CT: Yale University Press.

Lobel, J. (1985). The limits of constitutional power: Conflicts between foreign policy and international law. *Virginia Law Review*, 71(7), 1071–180.

Locke, J. (2016 [1689]). *Second Treatise of Government and a Letter Concerning Toleration*. Oxford: Oxford University Press.

Lodge, H.C. (1925). *The Senate and the League of Nation*. New York, NY: Charles Scribner's Sons.

Lodge, J. (1984). European Union and the first elected European Parliament: The Spinelli Initiative. *Journal of Common Market Studies*, 22(4), 377–402.

Loewenstein, K. (1955). The Bonn Constitution and the European Defense Community Treaties: A study in judicial frustration. *The Yale Law Journal*, 64(6), 805–39.

Lorenz, A. (2005). How to measure constitutional rigidity: Four concepts and two alternatives. *Journal of Theoretical Politics*, 17(3), 339–61.

Loth, W., Wallace, W. and Wessels, W. (1998). *Walter Hallstein: The Forgotten European?* Hampshire, UK: Palgrave Macmillan.

Loughlin, J. and Daftary, F. (1999). Insular regions and European integration: Corsica and the Åland Islands compared. European Centre for Minority Issues Report #5.

Louis, J.-V. (1995). *The Community Legal Order*, 2nd edition. Brussels: Office for Official Publications of the European Communities.

Luchaire, F. (1991). The participation of Parliament in the elaboration and application of treaties. *Chicago Kent Law Review*, 67, 341.

Luhmann, N. (1979). *Trust and Power*. London: John Willey & Sons.

Lutz, D.S. (1994). Toward a theory of constitutional amendment. *American Political Science Review*, 88(2), 355–70.

Maatsch, A. (2016). *Parliaments and the Economic Governance of the European Union: Talking Shops or Deliberative Bodies?* London: Taylor & Francis.

Mac Amhlaigh, C. (2009). Revolt by referendum? In search of a European constitutional narrative. *European Law Journal*, 15(4), 552–63.

Macron, E. (2017). Discours du Président de la République, Emmanuel Macron, à la Pnyx, Athens, 7 September. Full text available at: www.elysee.fr/declarations/article/discours-du-president-de-la-republique-emmanuel-macron-a-la-pnyx-athenes-le-jeudi-7-septembre-201/.

Magnette, P. (2016). Wallonia blocked a harmful EU trade deal – But we don't share Trump's dreams. *The Guardian*, 14 November.

REFERENCES

Magnette, P. and Nicolaidis, K. (2004). The European Convention: Bargaining in the shadow of rhetoric. *West European Politics*, 27(3), 381–404.

Maher, I. (2006). Economic governance: Hybridity, accountability and control. *Columbia Journal of European Law*, 13(3), 679.

(2010). Trust and EU law and governance. *Cambridge Yearbook of European Legal Studies*, 12, 283–311.

Mahne, K.P. (2012). A unitary patent and Unified Patent Court for the European Union: An analysis of Europe's long standing attempt to create a supranational patent system. *Journal of the Patent and Trademark Office Society*, 94(2), 162–91.

Mair, P. (1997). *Party System Change: Approaches and Interpretations*. Oxford: Oxford University Press.

(2013). *Ruling the Void: The Hollowing of Western Democracy*. London: Verso Books.

Majone, G. (2009). The 'referendum threat', the rationally ignorant voter, and the political culture of the EU. University College Dublin Law Research Paper, 4.

Malley, R. and Agha, H. (2001). Camp David: The tragedy of errors. *New York Review of Books*, 48(13), 59–65.

Mance, H. (2016). Britain has had enough of experts, says Gove. *Financial Times*, 3 June.

Marek, D. and Baun, M. (2010). *The Czech Republic and the European Union*. London: Routledge.

Martinico, G. and Pollicino, O. (2012). *The Interaction between Europe's Legal Systems: Judicial Dialogue and the Creation of Supranational Laws*. Cheltenham: Edward Elgar Publishing.

Mason, R. and Asthana, A. (2017). May to put Brexit deal to MPs' vote before it goes to European parliament. *The Guardian*, 7 February.

Mateo González, G. (2006). *Domestic Politics and Referendums on the Constitutional Treaty*. Fiesole: Robert Schuman Centre for Advanced Studies, European University Institute.

Maurer, A. (2002). The European Parliament: Win-Sets of a Less Invited Guest. In Laursen, F., ed., *The Amsterdam Treaty: National Preference Formation, Interstate Bargaining and Outcome*. Odense: University Press of Southern Denmark, pp. 405–50.

(2003). Less bargaining, more deliberation: The convention method for enhancing EU democracy. *Internationale Politik und Gesellschaft*, 2003(1), 167–91.

Mavčič, A. (2013). *Constitutional Review*, 2nd edition. Lake Mary: Vandeplas Publishing.

McClean, P. (2017). After Brexit: The UK will need to renegotiate at least 759 treaties. *Financial Times*, 30 May.

McGowan, L. (2010). *The Antitrust Revolution in Europe: Exploring the European Commission's Cartel Policy*. Cheltenham: Edward Elgar Publishing.

McNair, B.A.D.M. (1961). *The Law of Treaties*. Oxford: Oxford University Press.

McWhinney, E. (1961). Judicial restraint and the West German Constitutional Court. *Harvard Law Review*, 75(1), 5–38.

Meessen, K.M. (1993). Hedging European integration: The Maastricht Judgment of the Federal Constitutional Court of Germany. *Fordham International Law Journal*, 17, 511.

Mendez, F., Mendez, M. and Triga, V. (2014). *Referendums and the European Union: A Comparative Inquiry*. Cambridge: Cambridge University Press.

Mendez, M. (2017). Constitutional review of treaties: Lessons for comparative constitutional design and practice. *International Journal of Constitutional Law*, 15(1), 84–109.

Meron, T. (1995). The authority to make treaties in the late Middle Ages. *American Journal of International Law*, 89(1), 1–20.

Meyer, T. (2014). Collective decision-making in international governance. *AJIL Unbound*. Full text available at: www.asil.org/blogs/collective-decision-making-international-governance-agora-end-treaties.

Miller, V. (2003). The Convention on the Future of Europe: Proposals for a European Constitution. House of Commons Library Research Paper, 03/23.

(2009). The Lisbon Treaty: Ratification by the Czech Republic. House of Commons Library, International Affairs and Defence Section, SN05214.

Miller, V., Dodd, T. and Watson, F.M. (1995). *Towards the IGC: Enter the Reflection Group*. London: House of Commons Library.

Millns, S. (2008). Constitution for Europe. In Cane, P. and Conaghan, J., eds., *The New Oxford Companion to Law*. Oxford: Oxford University Press.

Milner, H.V. (1997). *Interests, Institutions, and Information: Domestic Politics and International Relations*. Princeton, NJ: Princeton University Press.

Milner, H.V. and Rosendorff, B.P. (1997). Democratic politics and international trade negotiations: Elections and divided government as constraints on trade liberalization. *Journal of Conflict Resolution*, 41(1), 117–46.

Mo, J. (1995). Domestic institutions and international bargaining: The role of agent veto in two-level games. *American Political Science Review*, 89(4), 914–24.

Monaghan, E. (2012). Assessing participation and democracy in the EU: The case of the European Citizens' Initiative. *Perspectives on European Politics and Society*, 13(3), 285–98.

Moravcsik, A. (1991). Negotiating the Single European Act: National interests and conventional statecraft in the European Community. *International Organization*, 45(1), 19–56.

(1993a). Armaments among Allies: European Weapons Collaboration, 1975–1985. In Evans, P.B., Jacobson, H.K. and Putnam, R.D., eds., *Double-Edged Diplomacy: International Bargaining and Domestic Politics*. Berkeley, CA: University of California Press, pp. 128–67.

(1993b). Preferences and power in the European Community: A liberal inter-governmentalist approach. *Journal of Common Market Studies*, 31(4), 473–524.

(1994). Why the European Community strengthens the state: Domestic politics and international cooperation. CES Working Paper, 52.

(1998). *The Choice for Europe: Social Purpose and State Power from Messina to Maastricht*. Ithaca, NY: Cornell University Press.

310 REFERENCES

(1999). 'Is something rotten in the state of Denmark?' Constructivism and European integration. *Journal of European Public Policy*, 6(4), 669–81.

(2002). Reassessing legitimacy in the European Union. *Journal of Common Market Studies*, 40(4), 603–24.

(2006). What can we learn from the collapse of the European constitutional project? *Politische Vierteljahresschrift*, 47(2), 219–41.

(2008). The myth of Europe's 'democratic deficit'. *Intereconomics*, 43(6), 331–40.

Morel, L. (1996). France: Towards a Less Controversial Use of the Referendum? In Uleri, P.V. and Gallagher, M., eds., *The Referendum Experience in Europe*. Basingstoke: Macmillan, pp. 66–85.

(2012). Referendums. In Rosenfeld, M. and Sajó, A., eds., *The Oxford Handbook of Comparative Constitutional Law*. Oxford: Oxford University Press, pp. 501–28.

Mueller, D.C. (1996). *Constitutional Democracy*. Oxford: Oxford University Press.

Muñoz, J. (2017). Political Trust and Multilevel Government. In Zmerli, S. and van der Meer, T.W.G., eds., *Handbook on Political Trust*. Cheltenham: Edward Elgar, pp. 69–88.

Muñoz, J., Torcal, M. and Bonet, E. (2011). Institutional trust and multilevel government in the European Union: Congruence or compensation? *European Union Politics*, 12(4), 551–74.

Negretto, G.L. (2013). *Making Constitutions: Presidents, Parties, and Institutional Choice in Latin America*. Cambridge: Cambridge University Press.

Neumann, I.B. (2012). *At Home with the Diplomats: Inside a European Foreign Ministry*. Ithaca, NY: Cornell University Press.

Nielsen, J.B. (2013). Denmark. In Cook, B.A., ed., *Europe since 1945: An Encyclopaedia*. Abingdon: Routledge, p. 57.

Nijeboer, A. (2005). The Dutch referendum. *European Constitutional Law Review*, 1(3), 393–405.

Norman, P. (2003). *The Accidental Constitution: The Story of the European Convention*. Brussels: Eurocomment.

Norris, P. (1997). Representation and the democratic deficit. *European Journal of Political Research*, 32(2), 273–82.

(2017). The Conceptual Framework of Political Support. In Zmerli, S. and van der Meer, T.W.G., eds., *Handbook on Political Trust*. Cheltenham: Edward Elgar, pp. 19–32.

Norton, P. (1996). *National Parliaments and the European Union*. Hove: Psychology Press.

Ojanen, T. (2004). EU law and the response of the Constitutional Law Committee of the Finnish Parliament. *Scandinavian Studies in Law: Public Law*. Full text available at: www.scandinavianlaw.se/pdf/52-12.pdf, pp. 531–64.

Olsen, H.P. (2013). The Danish Supreme Court's decision on the constitutionality of Denmark's ratification of the Lisbon Treaty. *Common Market Law Review*, 50 (5), 1489–503.

O'Neill, M. (2008). *The Struggle for the European Constitution: A Past and Future History*. London: Routledge.

O'Neill, O. (2002). *A Question of Trust: The BBC Reith Lectures 2002*. Cambridge: Cambridge University Press.

Open Europe (2008). *A Guide to the Constitutional Treaty*, 2nd edition. London: Open Europe.

Oppermann, K. (2013a). The politics of avoiding referendums on the Treaty of Lisbon. *Journal of European Integration*, 35(1), 73–89.

(2013b). The politics of discretionary government commitments to European integration referendums. *Journal of European Public Policy*, 20(5), 684–701.

Ortiz, P.J.C. (2015). *EU Treaties and the Judicial Politics of National Courts: A Law and Politics Approach*. London: Routledge.

Osiander, A. (2001). Sovereignty, international relations, and the Westphalian myth. *International Organization*, 55(2), 251–87.

Otjes, S. (2016). Is a Nexit now on the cards? What the UK's referendum means for the Netherlands. *LSE European Politics and Policy (EUROPP) Blog*, 28 June.

Ott, A. (2008). Multilevel Regulations Reviewed by Multilevel Jurisdictions: The ECJ, the National Courts and the ECtHR. In Føllesdal, A., Wessel, R.A. and Wouters, J., eds., *Multilevel Regulation and the EU: The Interplay between Global, European, and National Normative Processes*. Leiden: Brill, pp. 345–66.

Pahre, R. (1997). Endogenous domestic institutions in two-level games and parliamentary oversight of the European Union. *Journal of Conflict Resolution*, 41(1), 147–74.

Panezi, M. (2006). *A Description of the Structure of the Hellenic Republic, the Greek Legal System, and Legal Research*. Hauser Global Law School Program, New York University School of Law, April.

Pantazatou, P. (2014). *Constitutional Change through Euro Crisis Law*. Fiesole: European University Institute.

Paris, M.-L. (2012). Popular Sovereignty and the Use of the Referendum: Comparative Perspectives with Reference to France. In Carolan, E., ed., *The Constitution of Ireland: Perspectives and Prospects*. Dublin: Bloomsbury Professional, p. 279.

(2016). The French System of Rights-Based Review: From Exceptionalism to Parochial Constitutionalism. In Paris, M.-L. and Bell, J., eds, *Rights-Based Constitutional Review: Constitutional Courts in a Changing Landscape*. Camberley: Edward Elgar, pp. 302–45.

Paris-Dobozy, M.-L. (2008). The Implications of the 'No' Vote in France: Making the Most of a Wasted Opportunity. In Laursen, F., ed., *The Rise and Fall of the EU's Constitutional Treaty*. Leiden: Brill, pp. 497–524.

Park, S. (2006). Theorizing norm diffusion within international organizations. *International Politics*, 43(3), 342–61.

Pasha-Robinson, L. (2017). Emmanuel Macron and Angela Merkel agree changing EU treaties 'no longer a taboo'. *The Independent*, 15 January.

Paxton, J. (ed.) (1973). *The Statesman's Year-Book 1973–74*. London: Macmillan.

Peake, J.S., Krutz, G.S. and Hughes, T. (2012). President Obama, the senate, and the polarized politics of treaty making. *Social Science Quarterly*, 93(5), 1295–315.

REFERENCES

Peel, M.J., Goode, M.M. and Moutinho, L.A. (1998). Estimating consumer satisfaction: OLS versus ordered probability models. *International Journal of Commerce and Management*, 8(2), 75–93.

Peers, S. (2012). The future of EU treaty amendments. *Yearbook of European Law*, 31(1), 17–111.

Pelinka, A. and Greiderer, S. (1996). Austria: The Referendum as an Instrument of Internationalisation. In Uleri, P.V. and Gallagher, M., eds., *The Referendum Experience in Europe*. Berlin: Springer, pp. 20–32.

Pergantis, V. (2017). *The Paradigm of State Consent in the Law of Treaties Challenges and Perspectives*. Cheltenham: Edward Elgar.

Petersen, N. (1998). The Danish referendum on the Treaty of Amsterdam Europas? *ZEI-Zentrum Fur Europaische Ingegrationsforschung*, ZEI Discussion paper C-17 1998.

Peterson, G. (1945). II. Political inequality at the Congress of Vienna. *Political Science Quarterly*, 60(4), 532–54.

Petrovcic, U. (2015). *Constitutional Change through Euro Crisis Law: Slovenia*. Firenze: EUI Law Department.

Pettit, P. (1998). Republican Theory and Political Trust. In Braithwaite, V. and Levi, M., eds., *Trust and Governance*. New York, NY: Russell Sage Foundation.

Pew Research Center (2014). *Faith and Skepticism about Trade, Foreign Investment*. Full text available at: www.pewglobal.org/2014/09/16/faith-and-skepticism-about-trade-foreign-investment/.

Pfafferott, C. (2013). People's consultation in Austria on military service. *Democracy International Blog*, 16 January.

Pharr, S.J. and Putnam, R.D. (2000). *Disaffected Democracies: What's Troubling the Trilateral Countries?* Princeton, NJ: Princeton University Press.

Phelan, W. (2012). What is sui generis about the European Union? Costly international cooperation in a self-contained regime. *International Studies Review*, 14(3), 367–85.

Phinnemore, D. (2011) Treaty change after Lisbon: Is there no end in sight? Exchanging Ideas on Europe 2011, UACES 41st Annual Conference, Robinson College.

Pieters, J., (2018). Dutch Parliament agrees to abolish referendum. NLTIMES.NL, 23 February.

Pinder, J. (2010). Federal Democracy in a Federal Europe. In Burgess, M. and Gagnon, A.-G., eds., *Federal Democracies*. London: Routledge, pp. 178–201.

Piodi, F. (2007). Towards a single parliament: The influence of the ECSC Common Assembly on the Treaties of Rome. European Parliament DG dor the Presidency, Archive and Documentation Centre.

Piris, J.-C. (2010). *The Lisbon Treaty: A Legal and Political Analysis*. Cambridge: Cambridge University Press.

Podolnjak, R. (2015). Constitutional reforms of citizen-initiated referendum: Causes of different outcomes in Slovenia and Croatia. *Journal for Constitutional Theory and Philosophy of Law*, 26(2015), 129–49.

Pollack, M.A. (1999). Delegation, agency and agenda setting in the Treaty of Amsterdam. *European Integration Online Papers (EIoP)*, 3(6).

(2001). International relations theory and European integration. *Journal of Common Market Studies*, 39(2), 221–44.

(2006). Rational Choice and EU Politics. In Jørgensen, K.E., Pollack, M.A. and Rosamond, B., eds., *The Sage Handbook of European Union Politics*. London: Sage, pp. 31–56.

Ponsonby, A. (1928). *Falsehood in War Time: Containing an Assortment of Lies Circulated throughout the Nations during the Great War*. London: Garland.

Popelier, P. and Lemmens, K. (2015). *The Constitution of Belgium: A Contextual Analysis*. Basingstroke, Hampshire, UK: Bloomsbury Publishing.

President of European Council (2003). *Report from the Presidency of the Convention to the President of the European Council*, CONV 851/03.

Priebus, S. (2016). Hungary. In Fruhstorfer, A. and Hein, M., eds., *Constitutional Politics in Central and Eastern Europe: From Post-Socialist*. Berlin: Springer, pp. 101–43.

Prodi, R. (2000). *Address Given by Romano Prodi (Strasbourg, 3 October 2000)*. Brussels: European Commission.

(2001). *Speech by Romano Prodi, President of the European Commission Meeting with the National Parliaments*, SPEECH/01/128.

Puetter, U. (2012). Europe's deliberative intergovernmentalism: The role of the Council and European Council in EU economic governance. *Journal of European Public Policy*, 19(2), 161–78.

Putnam, R.D. (1988). Diplomacy and domestic politics: The logic of two-level games. *International Organization*, 42(3), 427–60.

Quinlan, S. (2012). The Lisbon experience in Ireland: 'No' in 2008 but 'Yes' in 2009 – How and why? *Irish Political Studies*, 27(1), 139–53.

Qvortrup, M. (2005). *A Comparative Study of Referendums: Government by the People*. Manchester: Manchester University Press.

(2006). The three referendums on the European constitution treaty in 2005. *The Political Quarterly*, 77(1), 89–97.

(2014). *Referendums around the World: The Continued Growth of Direct Democracy*. Basingstoke: Palgrave Macmillan.

(2016). Europe has a referendum addiction. *Foreign Policy*, 21 June.

Ranjan, P. (2009). Treaties on trade and investment and the Indian legal regime: Should we mind the gap? *Australian Journal of Asian Law*, 11(1), 56–8.

Rasch, B.E. and Congleton, R. (2006). Amendment Procedures and Constitutional Stability. In Congleton, R.D. and Swedenborg, A.B., eds., *Democratic Constitutional Design and Public Policy: Analysis and Evidence*. Cambridge, MA: MIT Press, pp. 372–401.

Rasnača, Z. (2013). *Constitutional Change through Euro Crisis Law: Latvia*. Fiesole: European University Institute.

Raustiala, K. (2012). The Role of NGOs in Treaty-Making. In Hollis, D.B., ed., *The Oxford Guide to Treaties*. Oxford: Oxford University Press, pp. 150–75.

Reestman, J.-H. (2017). Legitimacy through Adjudication: The ESM Treaty and the Fiscal Compact before the National Courts. In Beukers, T., de Witte, B. and

REFERENCES

Kilpatrick, C., eds., *Constitutional Change through Euro-Crisis Law*. Cambridge: Cambridge University Press, pp. 243–78.

Renwick, A. (2014). *After the Referendum: Options for a Constitutional Convention*. London: The Constitution Society.

Reuters (2001). No vote shows need for closer EU, Belgian PM. *Irish Times*, 10 June.

(2012). Eurosceptic Czech president says won't sign ESM treaty. *Reuters Business News*, 7 December.

Ribicic, C. and Kaucic, I. (2014). Constitutional limits of legislative referendum: The case of Slovenia. *Lex Localis*, 12(4), 899–928.

Richards, N. (2006). The Bricker Amendment and Congress's failure to check the inflation of the executive's foreign affairs powers, 1951–1954. *California Law Review*, 94(1), 175–213.

Richardson, M. (2017). Unified Patent Court: The end of the beginning or the beginning of the end? *Lexecology*, 2 November.

Risso, L. (2004). The (Forgotten) European political community 1952–1954. Research student conference on European foreign policy, LSE 2–3 July 2004.

Rittberger, B. (2012). Institutionalizing representative democracy in the European Union: The case of the European Parliament. *JCMS: Journal of Common Market Studies*, 50(s1), 18–37.

Robertson, D. (2010). *The Judge as Political Theorist: Contemporary Constitutional Review*. Princeton, NJ: Princeton University Press.

Rodrigues, A.F.G. (2013). *The Referendum in the Portuguese Constitutional Experience*. Leiden: Leiden University Press.

Rogers, I. (2017). Lecture to Hertford College, Oxford, by UK's former EU ambassador. *Politico*, 24 November.

Rolef, S.H. (2006). *Public Trust in Parliament: A Comparative Study*. Jerusalem: The Knesset Information Division.

Rosas, A. (2010). The status in EU law of international agreements concluded by EU Member States. *Fordham International Law Journal*, 34, 1304.

Rose, R. (2013). *Representing Europeans: A Pragmatic Approach*. Oxford: Oxford University Press.

Rose, R. and Borz, G. (2013). What determines demand for European Union referendums? *Journal of European Integration*, 35(5), 619–33.

Rosendahl, J. (2016). Finnish parliament, pressured by weak economy, debates euro exit. *Reuters 3 Minute Read*, 28 April.

Roznai, Y. (2017). *Unconstitutional Constitutional Amendments: The Limits of Amendment Powers*. Oxford: Oxford University Press.

Ruin, O. (1996). Sweden: The Referendum as an Instrument for Defusing Political Issues. In Gallagher, M. and Uleri, P.V., eds., *The Referendum Experience in Europe*. Berlin: Springer, pp. 171–84.

Ruokola, K. (2007). The Åland Islands to also decide on the EU reform agreement. Permanent Representative of Finland to the EU, News, 23 October.

Saalfeld, T. (1995). The German houses of parliament and European legislation. *The Journal of Legislative Studies*, 1(3), 12–34.

Sabel, R. (2006). *Procedure at International Conferences: A Study of the Rules of Procedure at the UN and at Inter-Governmental Conferences.* Cambridge: Cambridge University Press.

Samuel, H. and Huggler, J. (2017). Emmanuel Macron and Angela Merkel pledge to draw up 'common road map' for Europe. *The Telegraph*, 15 May.

Sandler, T. (2004). *Global Collective Action.* Cambridge: Cambridge University Press.

Santacruz, M.A. (1993). Spain. *European Law Review*, 18(3), 247–8.

Sarkozy, N. and Merkel, A. (2011). French and German leaders outline proposals ahead of EU talks: Joint letter from Nicolas Sarkozy, President of the Republic, and Angela Merkel, Chancellor of Germany, to Herman Van Rompuy, President of the European Council, Paris, 7 December 2011.

Saunders, R. (2016). How an army of 'Mr Europes' helped win the 1975 referendum for the CBI. *LSE Brexit Blog*, 2 February.

Savage, D. and Weale, A. (2009). Political representation and the normative logic of two-level games. *European Political Science Review*, 1(1), 63–81.

Saxena, R. (2007). Treaty-making powers: A case for 'federalisation' and 'parliamentarisation'. *Economic and Political Weekly*, 42(1), 24–8.

Scharpf, F.W. (1999). *Governing in Europe: Effective and Democratic?* Oxford: Oxford University Press.

   (2003). Problem-solving effectiveness and democratic accountability in the EU. MPIfG Working Paper 03/1, February.

Schelkle, W. (2012). Rich versus Poor. In Jones, E., Menon, A. and Weatherill, S., eds., *The Oxford Handbook of the European Union.* Oxford: Oxford University Press, pp. 278–91.

Schelling, T.C. (1980). *The Strategy of Conflict.* Cambridge, MA: Harvard University Press.

Schermers, H.G. (1983). *Judicial Protection in the European Union.* London: Kluwer Law International.

Schmidt, V.A. (2009). Re-envisioning the European Union: Identity, democracy, economy. *Journal of Common Market Studies*, 47(s1), 17–42.

Schneider, G. and Weitsman, P.A. (1996). The punishment trap: Integration referendums as popularity contests. *Comparative Political Studies*, 28(4), 582–607.

Schoiswohl, M. (2006). The new Afghanistan constitution and international law: A love–hate affair. *International Journal of Constitutional Law*, 4, 664.

Schoppa, L.J. (1993). Two-level games and bargaining outcomes: Why gaiatsu succeeds in Japan in some cases but not others. *International Organization*, 47(3), 353–86.

Schuseil, P. (2012). Germany may be heading towards a referendum on further European integration. *Europp European Politics and Policy*, 28 August.

Schütze, R. (2015). EU Competences: Existence and Exercises. In Arnull, A. and Chalmers, D., eds., *The Oxford Handbook of European Union Law.* Oxford: Oxford University Press, pp. 75–102.

Scicluna, N. (2014). Politicization without democratization: How the Eurozone crisis is transforming EU law and politics. *International Journal of Constitutional Law*, 12(3), 545–71.

REFERENCES

Scott, J.B. (1924). Ratification of treaties in Great Britain. *The American Journal of International Law*, 18(2), 296–8.

Seabra, M.J. (2003). Portugal: One Way to Europeanisation. In Wessels, W., Maurer, A. and Mittag, J., eds., *Fifteen into One?: The European Union and Its Member States*. Manchester: Manchester University Press, pp. 355–68.

Secretariat of the Constitutional Committee (1953). *Information and Documents on the Constitutional Committee 1952–3*. Paris: Quai Anatole France.

Secretariat of the European Convention (2002). *Speeches delivered at the inaugural meeting of the Convention on 28 February 2002* CONV 4/02.

Shapiro, M. and Stone, A. (1994). The new constitutional politics of Europe. *Comparative Political Studies*, 26(4), 397–420.

Shaw, J. (2003). What's in a convention?: Process and substance in the project of European Constitution-Building. Report for Reihe Politikwissenschaft/Institut für Höhere Studien, Vienna.

Shaw, M. (2014) *International Law*, 7th edition. Cambridge: Cambridge University Press.

Sigalas, E. (2015). Austria: After Brexit and Grexit, could Auxit be next? *LSE EUROPP Blog*, 21 October.

Simmons, B.A. (2009a). *Mobilizing for Human Rights: International Law in Domestic Politics*. Cambridge: Cambridge University Press.

   (2009b). Appendix 3.2: Ratification rules. See https://scholar.harvard.edu/files/bsimmons/files/APP_3.2_Ratification_rules.pdf.

Sinnott, R. (2003). Attitudes and behaviour of the Irish electorate in the second referendum on the Treaty of Nice. Institute for the Study of Social Change, University College Dublin.

Skoutaris, N. (2011). *The Cyprus Issue: The Four Freedoms in a Member State under Siege*. London: Bloomsbury Publishing.

Slosarcik, I. (2009). The Treaty of Lisbon and the Czech Constitutional Court: Act II. CEPS Policy Brief 197/27.

Sloss, D. (2011). Domestic Application of Treaties. In Hollis, D.B., ed., *Oxford Guide to Treaties*. Oxford: Oxford University Press, pp. 367–95.

Slovenian Ministry of Foreign Affairs (2016). *Sklepanje Mednarodnih Pogodb in Drugih Mednarodnih Aktov – Priročnik*. Ljubljana: Slovenian Ministry of Foreign Affairs.

Smith, G. (1976). The functional properties of referendums. *European Journal of Political Research*, 4(1), 1–23.

Smith, J. (1999). *Europe's Elected Parliament*. Sheffield: Sheffield Academic Press
   (2004). Let battle be joined on Europe, says Blair. *The Independent*, 19 April.

Smith, M.P. (1996). Democratic legitimacy in the European Union: Fulfilling the institutional logic. *The Journal of Legislative Studies*, 2(4), 283–301.

Soares, M. (1998). *The Ocean: Our Future*. Cambridge: Cambridge University Press.

Sovdat, J. (2013). The Constitutional Court of the Republic of Slovenia and European Union law. *Hrvatska i komparativna javna uprava*, 13(3), 895–929.

Spiliotopoulos, E. (1983). Judicial review of legislative acts in Greece. *Temple Law Review*, 56, 463–71.

Spinelli, A. (1978). Reflections on the institutional crisis in the European community. *West European Politics*, 1(1), 77–88.

Spyropoulos, P.K. and Fortsakis, T. (2009). *Constitutional Law in Greece*. Alphen aan den Rijn: Kluwer Law International.

Squires, N. (2016). France's Macron wants EU-wide referendum, far-left slams Hollande 'nervousness'. *Telegraph*, 25 June.

Stanton Collett, T. (2010). Judicial independence and accountability in an age of unconstitutional constitutional amendments. *Loyola University Chicago Law Journal*, 41, 327.

Staw, Barry M. (1976). Knee-deep in the big muddy: A study of escalating commitment to a chosen course of action. *Organizational Behavior and Human Performance*, 16(1), 27–44.

Steiger, H. (2004). Peace Treaties from Westphalia to the Revolutionary Era. In Lesaffer, R., ed., *Peace Treaties and International Law in European History: From the Late Middle Ages to World War One*. Cambridge: Cambridge University Press, pp. 59–99.

Sternberg, C. (2013). *The Struggle for EU Legitimacy: Public Contestation, 1950–2005*. Berlin: Springer.

Stewart, H. and McDonald, H. (2012). Ireland set for referendum on eurozone fiscal treaty. *The Guardian*, 28 February.

Strempel, P. (2006). Austria's ratification – A more than silent yes. *The New Federalist*, 13 April.

Stuart, G. (2003). *The Making of Europe's Constitution*. London: Fabian Society.

Sutton, M. (1993). France and the Maastricht design. *The World Today*, 49(1), 4–8.

Svensson, P. (1994). The Danish Yes to Maastricht and Edinburgh: The EC Referendum of May 1993. *Scandinavian Political Studies*, 17(1), 69–82.

Sweet, A.S. and Sandholtz, W. (1997). European integration and supranational governance. *Journal of European Public Policy*, 4(3), 297–317.

Tanchev, E. and Belov, M. (2008). Constitutional gradualism: Adapting to EU membership and improving the judiciary in the Bulgarian Constitution. *European Public Law*, 14(1), 3–19.

Tarar, A. (2005). Constituencies and preferences in international bargaining. *Journal of Conflict Resolution*, 49(3), 383–407.

Tatham, A.F. (2009). *Enlargement of the European Union*. Alphen aan den Rijn: Kluwer Law International.

Taylor, S. (2009). Cowen wants Lisbon guarantees in protocol. *European Voice*, 19 June.

Teasdale, A.L. (1993). Subsidiarity in post-Maastricht Europe. *The Political Quarterly*, 64(2), 187–97.

  (2016). The Fouchet Plan: De Gaulle's intergovernmental design for Europe. LEQS Paper No. 117.

Templeman, L. (1991). Treaty-making and the British Parliament. *Chicago Kent Law Review*, 67, 459.

Thomassen, J., Andeweg, R. and van Ham, C. (2017). Political Trust and the Decline of Legitimacy Debate: A Theoretical and Empirical Investigation into

REFERENCES

Their Interrelationship. In Zmerli, S. and van der Meer, T.W.G., eds., *Handbook on Political Trust*. Cheltenham: Edward Elgar, pp. 509–28.

Thompson, G. (2011). *The European Financial Stabilisation Mechanism (EFSM)*, House of Commons Library SN/EP/5973.

Thompson, H. (1996). *The British Conservative Government and the European Exchange Rate Mechanism, 1979–1994*. London: Psychology Press.

Thurner, P.W. and Stoiber, M. (2001). Comparing ratification processes within EU member states: The identification of real veto players. MZES Working Papers, No. 27.

Tichý, L. and Dumbrovský, T. (2018). EU Integration and the Czech Constitution: Assertive Judiciary and Baffled Administration. In Griller, S., Claes, M. and Papadopoulou, L., eds., *Member States' Constitutions and EU Integration*. Oxford: Oxford University Press.

Tierney, S. (2012a). *Constitutional Referendums: The Theory and Practice of Republican Deliberation*. Oxford: Oxford University Press.

  (2012b). The people's last sigh: Referendums and European integration. *European Public Law*, 18(4), 683–700.

  (2013). Whose political constitution? Citizens and referendums. *German Law Journal*, 14(12), 2185–96.

Torcal, M. (2017). Political Trust in Western and Southern Europe. In Zmerli, S. and van der Meer, T.W.G., eds., *Handbook on Political Trust*. Cheltenham: Edward Elgar, pp. 418–39.

Tosi, D.E. (2017). The Use of Referendums on European Topics in the Integration Process of the European Union. In Contiades, X. and Fotiadou, A., eds., *Participatory Constitutional Change: The People as Amenders of the Constitution*. Abingdon: Routledge, pp. 173–90.

Tovey, A. (2015). CBI attacked as 'voice of Brussels' by anti-EU campaigners. *The Telegraph*, 9 November.

Traynor, I. (2007). Sarkozy calls for simplified treaty to end EU impasse. *The Guardian*, 2 May.

Traynor, I. and Watt, N. (2008). Lisbon treaty: Pressure on Ireland for second vote. *Guardian*, 19 June.

Trigona, A.S. (2012). A sham ratification. *Times of Malta*, 10 July.

Ulusoy, K. (2008). The Europeanization of Turkey and its impact on the Cyprus problem. *Journal of Southern Europe and the Balkans*, 10(3), 309–29.

Ungerer, J. and Ziaka, L. (2017). Reflections on the Greek capital controls: How the rescue of the national economy justifies restricting private business. *Legal Issues of Economic Integration*, 44(2), 135–49.

United Nations (2012). *Treaty Handbook*. New York, NY: Treaty Section of the Office of Legal Affairs, United Nations.

  (2015). *Seventy Years of Multilateral Treaty Making at the United Nations*. New York, NY: UN Headquarters.

Van der Loo, G. (2016). CETA's signature: 38 statements, a joint interpretative instrument and an uncertain future. *CEPS Commentary*, 31 October.

REFERENCES 319

van der Meer, T.W.G. (2017). Democratic Input, Macroeconomic Ouptput and Political Trust. In Zmerli, S. and van der Meer, T.W.G., eds., *Handbook on Political Trust*. Cheltenham: Edward Elgar, pp. 270–84.

van Dijk, P. and Tahzib, B.G. (1991). Parliamentary participation in the treaty-making process of the Netherlands. *Chicago Kent Law Review*, 67, 413.

Van Elsuwege, P. (2008). *From Soviet Republics to EU Member States: A Legal and Political Assessment of the Baltic States' Accession to the EU*. Leiden: Brill.

Van Malleghem, P.-A. (2013). Pringle: A paradigm shift in the European Union's Monetary Constitution. *German Law Journal*, 14(1), 141.

van Ooik, R. and Curtin, D. (1994). *Denmark and the Edinburgh Summit: Maastricht without Tears*. London: Wiley Chancery Law, pp. 349–65.

Vandenbruwaene, W. (2014). *Constitutional Change through Euro Crisis Law: Belgium*. Fiesole: Europen University Institute.

Vatsov, M. (2015). *Constitutional Change through Crisis Law: Bulgaria*. Firenze: EUI.

Veenendaal, W.P. (2016). How democracy functions without parties: The Republic of Palau. *Party Politics*, 22(1), 27–36.

Verdier, P.-H. and Versteeg, M. (2015). International law in national legal systems: An empirical investigation. *American Journal of International Law*, 109(3), 514–33.

Verhofstadt, G. (2016). *Report on Possible Evolutions of and Adjustments to the Current Institutional Set-up of the European Union*, European Parliament, PE 585.741v02–00.

Vick, B.E. (2014). *The Congress of Vienna: Power and Politics after Napoleon*. Cambridge, MA: Harvard University Press.

Vitâ, V. (2014). *Constitutional Change through Crisis Law: Romania*. Fiesole: European University Institute.

Vollrath, H. (2004). The Kiss of Peace. In Lesaffer, R., ed., *Peace Treaties and International Law in European History: From the Late Middle Ages to World War One*. Cambridge: Cambridge University Press, pp. 162–83.

Waldron, J. (2006). Are constitutional norms legal norms? *Fordham Law Review*, 75(3), 1697.

Walker, N. (2008). Not the European Constitution. *Maastricht Journal of European and Comparative Law*, 15(1), 135–41.

Waluchow, Wil (2009). Four Concepts of Validity: Reflections on Inclusive and Exclusive Positivism. In Adler, M. and K.E. Himma, K.E., eds., *The Rule of Recognition and the US Constitution*. Oxford: Oxford University Press, pp. 123–44.

Ward, J. and McCormack, B. (2001). Tax Treaty Interpretation in Ireland. In Lang, M., ed., *Tax Treaty Interpretation*. The Hague: Kluwer, pp. 171–94.

Warren, M.E. (1999). Introduction. In Warren, M.E., ed., *Democracy and Trust*. Cambridge: Cambridge University Press, pp. 1–21.

  (2018). Trust and Democracy. In Uslaner, E.M., ed., *The Oxford Handbook of Social and Political Trust*. Oxford: Oxford University Press,

Watt, N. (2012). David Cameron says Britain will get vote on leaving EU, but not yet. *The Guardian*, 2 July.

Weatherford, M.S. (1992). Measuring political legitimacy. *American Political Science Review*, 86(1), 149–66.

Weber, M. (1958). *From Max Weber: Essays in Sociology*, edited by Hans Heinrich Gerth and C. Wright Mills. New York, NY: Oxford University Press.

Weiler, J. (1997). Legitimacy and Democracy of Union Governance. In Edwards, G. and Pijpers, A., eds., *The Politics of European Treaty Reform: The 1996 Intergovernmental Conference and Beyond*. London: Pinter.

Weiler, J.H. and Modrall, J. (1985). Institutional reform: Consensus or majority? *European Law Review*, 10(5), 316–33.

Wendel, M. (2011). Lisbon before the courts: Comparative perspectives. *European Constitutional Law Review*, 7(1), 96–137.

Westlake, M. (1995). The European Parliament, the national parliaments and the 1996 Intergovernmental Conference. *The Political Quarterly*, 66(1), 59–73.

Widfeldt, A. (2004). Elite collusion and public defiance: Sweden's euro referendum in 2003. *West European Politics*, 27(3), 503–17.

Wiener, A. (2006). Conflictive Meanings: Constitutional Norms in Three Political Arenas. In Falke, J., Liebert, U. and Maurer, A., eds., *Postnational Constitutionalisation in the Enlarged Europe*. Baden-Baden: NOMOS, pp. 197–216.

(2007). Contested meanings of norms: A research framework. *Comparative European Politics*, 5(1), 1–17.

Wildhaber, L. (1971). *Treaty-Making Power and Constitution: An International and Comparative Study*. Basel: Helbing and Lichtenhahn.

Willson, C.L. (1996). Changing the charter: The United Nations prepares for the twenty-first century. *American Journal of International Law*, 90(1), 115–26.

Wilson, W. (1918). *Address of the President of the United States, Delivered at a Joint Session of the Two Houses of Congress, January 8, 1918*. Washington, DC: Government Printing Office.

Winship, C. and Mare, R.D. (1984). Regression models with ordinal variables. *American Sociological Review*, 49, 512–25.

Wirth, D.A. (2016). Is the Paris Agreement on Climate Change a legitimate exercise of the executive agreement power? *Lawfare Blog*, 29 August.

Zaiotti, R. (2011). *Cultures of Border Control: Schengen and the Evolution of European Frontiers*. Chicago, IL: University of Chicago Press.

Zalan, E. (2016). Leaders rule out treaty change to reform EU. *EU Observer*, Brussels, 29 June.

Závecz, G. (2017). Post-Communist Societies of Central and Eastern Europe. In Zmerli, S. and van der Meer, T.W.G., eds., *Handbook on Political Trust*. Cheltenham: Edward Elgar, pp. 440–60.

Zmerli, S. and van der Meer, T.W.G. (2017). The Deeply Rooted Concern with Political Trust. In Zmerli, S. and van der Meer, T.W.G., eds., *Handbook on Political Trust*. Cheltenham: Edward Elgar, pp. 1–18.

Zwolski, K. (2009). Euthanasia, gay marriages and sovereignty: Polish ratification of the Lisbon Treaty. *Journal of Contemporary European Research*, 5(3), 489–97.

Index

accountability, 41. *See also* governments, EU accountability to; responsibility
democratic, 40–1
trust and, 46
two-level games and, 39
Ad Hoc Assembly, 58–9, 75
Adam, Stanislas, 69
Adenauer, Konrad, 58
Afghanistan, 170
Åland convention, 9
Åland Islands, 101, 143
American Peace Society, 7
Amsterdam Treaty, 11
Denmark and, 11
European Parliament and, 38, 67
negotiation stage and, 61, 67
ratification constraints and, 37
Schengen Agreement and, 239
Andeweg, Rudy, 42–3
Armstrong, Kenneth, 237–8
Article 136 amendment, 64–5, 78–9
Czech Republic and, 98
ESM Treaty and, 249
EU Court of Justice and, 65, 69
Poland and, 112
Asselborn, Jean, 233
Assembly of the Council of Europe, 71
Assizes
European Parliament and, 74
Mitterrand and, 75–6
parliaments and, 60
Auer, Andreas, 251
Austria
constitutional amendments and, 91, 137
constitutional review and, 175, 197
executives and, 90–1
parliaments and, 90–1, 137–8, 175
referendums and, 91, 137–8

Bachrach, Peter, 260
Baker, David, 228

Balkenende, Jan Pieter, 233
Bang, Guri, 48
Baratz, Morton S., 260
Barnier, Michele, 76
Bebr, Gerhard, 88
Beck, Ulrich, 254
Belgium, 8
CETA and, 279, 281
constitutional amendments and, 93
constitutional review and, 175–7
executives and, 92, 175–6
Maastricht Treaty and, 176–7
parliaments and, 92–3, 175–6, 279
parliaments, subnational, and, 4, 92–3
referendums and, 138
Treaty of Lisbon and, 177
Bellamy, Richard, 39, 51, 254–5
Beukers, Thomas, 237
Biesheuvel-Dell-Marjolin report, 276–7
Birmingham Declaration, 231
Blackburn v. the Attorney General, 191–2
Blair, Tony, 61, 157
European Convention and, 77–8
Borz, Gabriela, 252
Braithwaite, John, 47
Brazil, 133
Brexit, 4–5, 11, 157, 192
Bribosia, Hervé, 249
Bricker Amendment, 246
Bricker, John W., 246
Brown, Gordon, 157
Bulgaria, 124
constitutional amendments and, 93–4, 139, 177
constitutional review and, 177
executives and, 177
parliaments and, 93–4, 139, 177
referendums and, 139
De Búrca, Gráinne, 234, 253
Butler, David, 46

322 INDEX

Cameron, David, 4–5, 35, 157–8, 236–7, 280–1
Cardwell, Paul James, 238
Carter, Jimmy, 34–5
Case-Zablocki Act, 246
CETA. *See* EU-Canada Comprehensive Economic and Trade Agreement
Cheneval, Francis, 254–5
chief negotiators, 69
Chirac, Jacques, 79–80
  Convention Method and, 77
  European Parliament and, 76
Christiansen, Thomas, 4, 13, 68
citizen-led treaty making, 258–60, 278
  ECI as, 258
  European Constitution and, 258
  pan-European referendum and, 260
  two-level games and, 258
citizens, constitutional review and, 174, 205
  Belgium and, 176
  Croatia and, 178
  Czech Republic and, 179
  Denmark and, 179–80
  Estonia and, 180
  Germany and, 182–3
  Hungary and, 183
  Ireland and, 184–5
  Latvia and, 186
  Lithuania and, 186
  Portugal and, 188
  Slovenia and, 189–90
  UK and, 191–2
citizens' initiatives
  constitutional amendments and, 258–60
  legitimacy and, 259–60
  two-level legitimacy and, 260
Claes, Monica, 12–13, 172
Clark, I., 42
Cleveland, Grover, 9
Closa, Carlos, 13, 173, 205, 246–7
  parliaments and, 88
  referendums and, 135, 251
  treaty amendments and, 88, 206, 222–3
  unanimity requirement and, 248–9
Common Market Defence Committee, 147, 166
comparative constitutionalism, 15–16, 206
Conca, Ken, 222
concession
  two-level legitimacy and, 49–50, 221
  voluntary, 49, 221
conclusion stage, 2
Conference of Parliamentary Committees for Union Affairs of Parliaments of the European Union (COSAC), 74
Congress of Europe, 10
Congress of Vienna, 7

consent stage, 2–3, 8, 13–14, 19, 205–16.
  See also ratification
  courts and, 170–93
  parliaments and, 8, 87–119, 275
  referendums and, 133–59
  two-level games and, 213
  two-level legitimacy and, 213
consentification, 278–82
  Brexit and, 280–2
  CETA and, 279
  Greek snap referendum and, 279–81
  legitimacy and, 278–9
  Ukraine–European Union Association Agreement and, 279
constitutional amendments, 88–9. *See also* treaty amendments, European Constitution and
  Austria and, 91, 137
  Belgium and, 93
  Bulgaria and, 93–4, 139, 177
  citizens' initiatives and, 258–60
  constitutional inertia and, 256
  Croatia and, 94–5, 139
  Cyprus and, 95–6
  Denmark and, 98–9
  Estonia and, 99, 142, 180
  Finland and, 100, 142–3
  France and, 102, 182, 228
  Germany and, 103–4
  Greece and, 104–5, 256–7
  Hungary and, 105–6
  Iceland and, 259
  Illinois and, 260, 271
  Ireland and, 106–7, 147–8, 163, 259
  Italy and, 107, 148–9
  Latvia and, 108, 149, 185–6, 259
  Lithuania and, 108–9, 150
  Lutz on, 222–4, 241
  Luxembourg and, 109–10, 150–1, 187
  Malta and, 111, 151
  Netherlands and, 111–12
  Oregon and, 259
  Portugal and, 114
  Romania and, 114–15, 154, 168, 189, 259
  Slovak Republic and, 115
  Slovenia and, 116
  Spain and, 116–17, 155–6, 190–1
  Sweden and, 117, 156–7
  UK and, 118
  US and, 222–3, 259–60
constitutional requirements, domestic, 6
constitutional review, 9, 12–13, 170–93.
  See also citizens, constitutional review and
  Afghanistan and, 170
  Austria and, 175, 197
  Belgium and, 175–7

Bulgaria and, 177
Croatia and, 177–8
Cyprus and, 178
Czech Republic and, 178–9
Denmark and, 179–80
Estonia and, 180
executives and, 174
  Belgium and, 175–6
  Bulgaria and, 177
  Cyprus and, 178
  Estonia and, 180
  Finland and, 181
  France and, 181
  Germany and, 182–3
  Hungary and, 183
  Ireland and, 184
  Latvia and, 185
  Lithuania and, 186
  Poland and, 188
  Portugal and, 188–9
  Slovak Republic and, 189
Finland and, 181
France and, 181–2, 199, 228
Germany and, 171, 182–3, 228–9
Greece and, 183
Hungary and, 183
Ireland and, 184–5, 200
Italy and, 185
Japan and, 171
Latvia and, 185–6
Lithuania and, 186
Luxembourg and, 186–7
Malta and, 187
Netherlands and, 187–8
parliaments and, 175–7, 179–83, 185–9, 191
Poland and, 188
Portugal and, 188–9
Romania and, 189
Russia and, 170
Slovak Republic and, 189–90
Slovenia and, 190
Spain and, 190–1
Sweden and, 191
UK and, 191–2
US and, 170
constitutional rules and norms, 14–16, 19–20, 273–4
contestation and, 14
pan-European referendum and, 255
parliaments and, 89–132
referendums and, 136–60
Wiener on, 14
contestation, constitutional rules and norms and, 14
Contiades, Xenophon, 259–60
control, trust and, 46

Convention Method, 79–83
Chirac and, 77
employment of, 64, 78
European Commission and, 73–4
European Constitution and, 57, 63–4, 80
European Parliament and, 79, 273, 283
heads of state or government and, 69
IGCs and, 63
parliaments and, 67, 78–9, 273
ratification constraints and, 39
treaty amendments and, 78–9
Treaty of Lisbon and, 64, 70
two-level games and, 35
Convention on the Future of Europe. *See* European Convention
Convention Responsible for Drafting the Charter of Fundamental Rights, 62
Coreper, 69–70
COSAC. *See* Conference of Parliamentary Committees for Union Affairs of Parliaments of the European Union
courts, 4, 9, 205, 208, 274, 283. *See also* constitutional review; EU Court of Justice; US Supreme Court
Claes on, 12–13
classification of, 171–5, 193–204
consent stage and, 170–93
Denmark and, 164
Germany and, 279
Hug and König on, 172
involuntary defection and, 228
Ireland and, 147–8, 228
judicial oversight by, 261–2
Luxembourg and, 201
negotiation stage and, 57
Simmons on, 172
treaty amendments and, 225, 228–9, 273
Treaty of Lisbon and, 79
trust and, 18, 45–6, 52, 213–15
UK and, 281–2
Covenant of the League of Nations, 8
Cowan, Brian, 234
Craig, Paul, 238
Crespy, Amadine, 39–40
Croatia
constitutional amendments and, 94–5, 139
constitutional review and, 177–8
executives and, 96–8, 139
parliaments and, 94–5, 139
referendums and, 94–5, 139, 178
Crocodile Club, 72
Cross, Mai Davis, 266
Crotty case, 147–8, 163, 166, 184–5, 192, 228
Curtin, Deirdre, 229–30
Cyprus, 163, 198, 238
constitutional amendments and, 95–6

INDEX

Cyprus, (cont.)
constitutional review and, 178
executives and, 95–6, 178
parliaments and, 95–6, 140
referendums and, 135, 140
Czech Republic
Article 136 amendment and, 98
constitutional review and, 178–9
executives and, 96
parliaments and, 96–8, 140, 179
referendums and, 97, 140
Treaty of Lisbon and, 97–8, 179

Debrés, Michel, 253
Defrenne case, 264
deliberative methods
European Convention and, 67–8
governments and, 67–8
heads of state or government and, 67–8
Delors, Jacques, 73
democratic accountability, 40–1
Denmark, 45
Amsterdam Treaty and, 11
constitutional amendments and, 98–9
constitutional review and, 179–80
courts and, 164
Maastricht Treaty and, 75, 141, 180,
229–31
parliaments and, 80, 98–9, 141, 209, 230
referendums and, 4, 11, 75, 98, 140–2,
164, 229–31
Single European Act and, 141
Treaty of Lisbon and, 180
Dicey, A.V., 14
distrust, 46
divided government, tying hands, strategy
of, and, 208–9
domestic law, 2–3
Draft Treaty on European Union, 72, 277
Draft Treaty on the European Union, 248
Duff, Andrew, 63, 276–7

early modern period, treaty making in, 6–7
ECB. *See* European Central Bank
ECI. *See* European Citizens' Initiative
Economic and Social Council (ECOSOC), 11
economic crises, trust and, 44–5
ECOSOC. *See* Economic and Social Council
ECSC Common Assembly. *See* European
Coal and Steel Community Common
Assembly
EDC Treaty. *See* European Defence
Community Treaty
Edinburgh Agreement, 230
enhanced cooperation procedure, 263
ESM Treaty. *See* European Stability
Mechanism Treaty

Estonia
constitutional amendments and, 99, 142,
180
constitutional review and, 180
executives and, 180
parliaments and, 99, 180
referendums and, 142
EU. *See* European Union
EU Charter of Fundamental Rights, 105
EU cleavage, 209
EU Court of Justice
Article 136 amendment and, 65, 69
ESM Treaty and, 240, 264, 269
Fiscal Compact and, 240
international law treaties and, 264
judicial oversight by, 261–2
negotiation stage and, 68–9
simplified revision procedure and, 65,
261
Westendorp Group and, 68–9
EU policy expertise, of European
Parliament, 66
EU treaties
end of, 276–8
list of, 21
EU treaty making reform, 246–72, 275–6
citizen-led treaty making and, 258–60,
278
European Commission and, 277
European Convention on the law of
treaties and, 264–5
European Council and, 276–7
European Parliament and, 277
heads of state or government and, 277–8
judicial oversight and, 261–2
pan-European referendum and, 253–5,
267
parliamentary oversight and, 262–3
referendum regulation and, 250–3
time locks and, 255–7
treaty failure and, 265–7
unanimity requirement and, 248–50,
256
EU-Canada Comprehensive Economic and
Trade Agreement (CETA), 279
Belgium and, 279, 281
Germany and, 279
euro crisis, 39–40, 236–45
simplified revision procedure and, 12
trust and, 44–5
Euroatom Treaty, 59
European Central Bank (ECB), 60–1
European Citizens' Initiative (ECI), 258
European Coal and Steel Community, 109
European Coal and Steel Community
Common Assembly (ECSC Common
Assembly), 58–9, 71

European Coal and Steel Community
  Treaty, 111, 257
European Commission
  Convention Method and, 73–4
  ESM Treaty and, 239
  EU treaty making reform and, 277
  IGCs and, 73–4
  Treaties of Rome and, 73
European Constitution, 3, 42, 111, 232–3,
  243
  citizen-led treaty making and, 258
  Convention Method and, 57, 63–4, 80
  France and, 257
  legitimacy and, 76–7
  pan-European referendum and, 254
  referendums and, 4, 37, 135–6, 152–3,
    157, 192, 232
  treaty amendments and, 268
  UK and, 192
  unanimity requirement and, 248
European Convention (Convention on the
  Future of Europe), 62–3. *See also*
  Convention Method
  Blair on, 77–8
  deliberative methods and, 67–8
  European Parliament and, 63
  heads of state or government and, 62–3
  IGCs and, 39
  Nice Treaty and, 77
  pan-European referendum and, 253
  parliaments and, 62–3, 66
  untying hands, strategy of, and, 39
European Convention on the law of treaties,
  264–5
European Council, 19, 231, 262
  Biesheuvel-Dell-Marjolin report and,
    276–7
  EU treaty making reform and, 276–7
  González Report and, 277
  legitimacy and, 75, 83, 229
  Seville Agreement and, 232
  treaty amendments and, 285
  Treaty of Lisbon and, 63–4, 234
European Defence Community Treaty
  (EDC Treaty), 58, 71, 75
  France and, 227
  Germany and, 171, 182
  rejection of, 227
European Parliament, 59–64, 79, 283
  Amsterdam Treaty and, 38, 67
  Assizes and, 74
  Chirac on, 76
  Convention Method and, 79, 273, 283
  EU policy expertise of, 66
  EU treaty making reform and, 277
  European Convention and, 63
  governments and, 73–4

IGCs and, 61
international law treaties and, 238–9
legitimacy and, 262–3, 266
parliamentary oversight by, 262–3
simplified revision procedure and, 262
Spinelli on, 72
European patent system, 236
European Stability Mechanism Treaty
  (ESM Treaty), 235–9, 277
  Article 136 amendment and, 249
  EU Court of Justice and, 240, 264, 269
  European Commission and, 239
  UK and, 236
Evans, Peter, 37
executive power, 2–3, 246
executives. *See also* constitutional review,
  executives and; ratification,
  executives and
  Austria and, 90–1
  Belgium and, 92, 175–6
  Bulgaria and, 177
  Croatia and, 96–8, 139
  Cyprus and, 95–6, 178
  Czech Republic and, 96
  Estonia and, 180
  Finland and, 181
  France and, 102, 181
  Germany and, 182–3
  Greece and, 104
  Hungary and, 183
  international agreements and, 234–5
  Ireland and, 184
  Italy and, 148
  Latvia and, 185
  legitimacy and, 40
  Lithuania and, 186
  Poland and, 112–13, 188
  Portugal and, 113–14, 154, 188–9
  referendums and, 139, 148, 154, 156
  Romania and, 114, 154
  Slovak Republic and, 154, 189
  Spain and, 116, 156
experts
  negotiation stage and, 68
  Spaak Committee and, 68
  Westendorp Group and, 68

Fabbrini, Federico, 237
Federal Constitutional Court (Germany), 4
federative power, 2–3
Ferejohn, John, 223
Ferrin, Mónica, 254
Finke, Daniel, 37
Finland
  Åland Islands and, 101, 143
  constitutional amendments and, 100,
    142–3

326   INDEX

Finland (cont.)
 constitutional review and, 181
 executives and, 181
 parliaments and, 99–101, 181
 referendums and, 100, 142–3
Fiscal Compact, 235–9, 251
 EU Court of Justice and, 240
 involuntary defection and, 263
 legitimacy and, 263
 UK and, 280
Fischer, Joscka, 76–7
FitzGerald, Garrett, 106
Five Presidents' Report, 239
France, 9, 40–1
 constitutional amendments and, 102,
  182, 228
 constitutional review and, 181–2, 199,
  228
 EDC Treaty and, 227
 European Constitution and, 257
 executives and, 102, 181
 Maastricht Treaty and, 228
 parliaments and, 5, 66, 76, 101–2, 181,
  227
 referendums and, 101–2, 143–4, 228, 257
France, Pierre Mendes, 227
French Constitution, 8
full powers, ratification and, 6

G20. See Group of Twenty
Gamble, Andrew, 228
De Gasperi, Alcide, 75
De Gaulle, Charles, 253
Germany
 CETA and, 279
 constitutional amendments and, 103–4
 constitutional review and, 171, 182–3,
  228–9
 courts and, 279
 EDC Treaty and, 171, 182
 executives and, 182–3
 Federal Constitutional Court in, 4
 Maastricht Treaty and, 103–4, 182, 228
 parliaments and, 103–4, 182–3
 referendums and, 144–5
 Treaty of Lisbon and, 171, 182–3, 228–9
Ginsburg, Tom, 16, 170–1, 210, 223–4
González Report, 277
governments, 57, 59. See also minority
  governments
 deliberative methods and, 67–8
 EU accountability to, 41
 EU treaty making complicated by, 17
 European Parliament and, 73–4
 trust and, 45
 two-level games and, 40
 two-level legitimacy and, 49

Grande, Edgar, 254
Gray, Mark, 61
Greece, 44
 constitutional amendments and, 104–5,
  256–7
 constitutional review and, 183
 executives and, 104
 parliaments and, 104–5
 referendums and, 145–6, 279–81
Greenland, referendums and, 141
Group of Twenty (G20), 284

Habermas, Jürgen, 254
Hague Peace Conferences, 7
Halberstam, Daniel, 262
Hallstein, Walter, 58
Hamilton, Alexander, 3
Hathaway, Oona, 3
Haugsgjerd, Atle, 44–5
heads of state or government, 79
 Convention Method and, 69
 deliberative methods and, 67–8
 EU treaty making reform and, 277–8
 European Convention and, 62–3
 negotiation stage and, 61, 67
 parliaments and, 71–83, 274
 Putnam and, 82
 representatives of, 69–70
 Treaty of Lisbon and, 64
 two-level games and, 69–70
Henisz, Witold J., 210
Henry, Peter Blair, 284
Hervey, Tamara, 238
Hix, Simon, 66
Hoesly, Cody, 259
Hoffman, Arron, 43
Hollis, Duncan, 276, 282
Hooghe, Liesbet, 225
Hovi, Jon, 48
Hug, Simon, 15, 37, 88, 90
 courts and, 172
 referendums and, 134–5
Hungary
 constitutional amendments and, 105–6
 constitutional review and, 183
 executives and, 183
 parliaments and, 105–6, 183
 referendums and, 146
 Treaty of Lisbon and, 105–6
Hurd, Douglas, 70

ICBL. See International Campaign to Ban
  Landmines
Iceland, 259
ICJ. See International Court of Justice
IGCs. See intergovernmental conferences
ILC. See International Law Commission

Illinois, 260, 271
IMF. *See* International Monetary Fund
India, 87
intergovernmental conferences (IGCs), 3–4, 19, 65
    Convention Method and, 63
    European Commission and, 73–4
    European Convention and, 39
    European Parliament and, 61
    Maastricht Treaty and, 61
    Spinelli on, 72
    Treaty of Lisbon and, 19
    Treaty of Paris and, 58
international agreements
    executives and, 234–5
    United States Constitution and, 234–5
    untying hands, strategy of, and, 234
International Campaign to Ban Landmines (ICBL), 11
International Court of Justice (ICJ), 10
International Law Commission (ILC), 9
international law treaties, 234–40, 263–5
    EU Court of Justice and, 264
    European Parliament and, 238–9
    legitimacy and, 238–9
    Treaty of Lisbon and, 264
    two-level games and, 236–8
    two-level legitimacy and, 238–9, 275
    de Witte on, 263
International Monetary Fund (IMF), 2, 250
intervening elections
    involuntary defection and, 257
    treaty amendments and, 256–7
interwar period, treaty making in, 7–8
involuntary defection, 221, 240, 275
    courts and, 228
    Fiscal Compact and, 263
    intervening elections and, 257
    parliaments and, 227–8
    referendums and, 229–34
    tying hands, strategy of, and, 48, 208
    untying hands, strategy of, and, 17
Ireland
    Common Market Defence Committee in, 147, 166
    constitutional amendments and, 106–7, 147–8, 163, 259
    constitutional review and, 184–5, 200
    courts and, 147–8, 228
    Crotty case and, 147–8, 163, 166, 184–5, 228
    executives and, 184
    Nice Treaty and, 231–2
    parliaments and, 106–7, 185
    referendums and, 14, 107, 134, 137, 147–8, 163, 166, 231–2, 238–9, 252

Single European Act and, 147–8, 184–5, 228
    Treaty of Lisbon and, 233–4
Irish constitution, 14
Italy
    constitutional amendments and, 107, 148–9
    constitutional review and, 185
    executives and, 148
    parliaments and, 107, 148–9
    referendums and, 148–9, 166

Jacobsen, John Kurt, 49
Janning, Josef, 266
Japan, 171
Joerges, Christian, 263
Jones, J. Mervyn, 283
judicial oversight, 261–2
Juncker, Jean-Claude, 277
justification, two-level games and, 39–40

Kaczyński, Jaroslaw, 113
Kaczyński, Lech, 112–13
Karlsson, Christer, 206
Kellermann, Alfred, 251
Kilpatrick, Claire, 237
Kirk-Reay Report, 72
Klaus, Vaclav, 97–8
König, Thomas, 15, 37–9, 88, 90, 172
Krunke, Helle, 230, 259
Krutz, Glen S., 234
Kumlin, Staffan, 44–5
Kwasniewski, Aleksander, 152

Laeken Declaration, 73, 232
Lane, Jan-Erik, 256
Latvia
    constitutional amendments and, 108, 149, 185–6, 259
    constitutional review and, 185–6
    executives and, 185
    parliaments and, 107–8, 149, 185–6
    referendums and, 108, 149
    Treaty of Lisbon and, 186
Laursen, Finn, 13
League of Nations, 8–9
legislative hurdles, parliaments and, 88–90
legitimacy, 42. *See also* trust; two-level legitimacy
    citizens' initiatives and, 259–60
    consentification and, 278–9
    democratic accountability and, 40–1
    European Constitution and, 76–7
    European Council and, 75, 83, 229
    European Parliament and, 262–3, 266
    executives and, 40
    Fiscal Compact and, 263
    international law treaties and, 238–9

INDEX

legitimacy, (cont.)
  Maastricht Treaty and, 230–1, 266–7
  1990s crisis of, 75
  pan-European referendum and, 254–5
  parliaments and, 256
  privilege and, 44, 209
  treaty amendments and, 240–1, 255–6
Leopold III (King), 138
Leventoglu, Bahar, 37
de Ligne (Prince), 7
Lijphart, A., 173
Lithuania
  constitutional amendments and, 108–9,
    150
  constitutional review and, 186
  executives and, 186
  parliaments and, 108–9
  referendums and, 108, 150
Locke, John, 2–3
Ludlam, Steve, 228
Lutz, Donald, 16, 89, 136, 222–4, 241
Luxembourg, 8
  constitutional amendments and, 109–10,
    150–1, 187
  constitutional review and, 186–7
  courts and, 201
  European Coal and Steel Community and,
    109
  Maastricht Treaty and, 187
  parliaments and, 109–10, 150–1, 187
  referendums and, 109, 150–1

Maastricht Treaty, 12–13, 283
  Belgium and, 176–7
  Birmingham Declaration and, 231
  Denmark and, 75, 141, 180, 229–31
  ECB and, 60–1
  Edinburgh Agreement and, 230
  EU established by, 3
  France and, 228
  Germany and, 103–4, 182, 228
  IGCs and, 61
  legitimacy and, 230–1, 266–7
  Luxembourg and, 187
  national compromise and, 229–30
  negotiation stage and, 61, 66
  parliaments and, 60
  referendums and, 4, 41, 75
  treaty amendments and, 224
  UK and, 192, 227–8
Mac Amhlaigh, Cormac, 253
Macron, Emmanuel, 253, 278
Magnette, Paul, 39, 68, 279
Mair, Peter, 44, 52
Major, John, 227–8
majority voting. *See* unanimity requirement
Makarios II (Archbishop of Cyprus), 140

Malta
  constitutional amendments and, 111, 151
  constitutional review and, 187
  parliaments and, 110–11, 151
  referendums and, 151
  Treaty of Paris and, 110
María Aznar, José, 67–8
Marks, Gary, 225
Martin, Micheál, 252
Maurer, Andreas, 67
May, Theresa, 281–2
medieval period, treaty making in, 5–6, 35
Melton, James, 223–4
Mena Parras, Francisco Javier, 69
Mendez, Fernando, 13, 135–6, 205–6, 248,
    251
  ECI and, 258
  pan-European referendum and, 254
Mendez, Mario, 9, 13, 135–6, 170, 205–6,
    248, 251
  ECI and, 258
  pan-European referendum and, 254
Merkel, Angela, 39–40, 237, 278
Messina Conference, 59
Meyer, Timothy, 276
Miller, Leszek, 152
Milner, Helen, 36
minority governments, 209, 213
mistrust, 46
Mitterrand, François, 75–6, 79–80, 102
Mo, Jongryn, 36–8
Mogg, William Rees, 192
Monaghan, Elizabeth, 258
Monnet, Jean, 58
Moravcsik, Andrew, 17, 36, 40–2, 258, 265
Morel, Laurence, 133

national compromise, Maastricht Treaty
    and, 229–30
negotiation stage, 2, 13, 19, 57–83
  Amsterdam Treaty and, 61, 67
  courts and, 57
  EU Court of Justice and, 68–9
  experts and, 68
  heads of state or government and, 61, 67
  Maastricht Treaty and, 61, 66
  parliaments and, 57, 66–7, 74–5, 275
  Peace of Westphalia and, 6–7
  referendums and, 57
  trust and, 43–4
  two-level games and, 36, 66–70
  two-level legitimacy and, 70–9
  win sets and, 34
Negretto, Gabriel L., 16, 206, 216
Netherlands
  constitutional amendments and, 111–12
  constitutional review and, 187–8

European Coal and Steel Community
  Treaty and, 111
  parliaments and, 111–12
  referendums and, 135–7, 151–2, 167, 270,
    279, 281
  Ukraine–European Union Association
    Agreement and, 279, 281
New Zealand, 133
NGOs. *See* non-governmental actors
Nice Treaty, 61, 77
  European Convention and, 77
  Ireland and, 231–2
  Seville Agreement and, 232
Nicholas II (Tsar), 7
Nicolaïdis, Kalypso, 39, 68
19th century, treaty making in, 7
non-governmental actors (NGOs), 1–2, 7,
    283
  ratification and, 66
  UN and, 1–2, 10–11
non-ratification, 8
  allowing, 265–7
  US and, 47–8
Norton, Phillip, 88
Nothomb, Charles-Ferdinand, 74

oaths, treaty making, medieval period, and, 6
Obama, Barack, 3
Opperman, Kai, 35
Oregon, constitutional amendments and, 259
Ortiz, Pablo José Castillo, 173
Ottawa Treaty, 11

pacta sunt servanda, 1
Pahre, Robert, 217
  ratification constraints and, 38
  two-level games and, 16, 274
  tying hands, strategy of, and, 208–9
Palau, referendums and, 133
Panama Canal Treaty, 34–5
pan-European referendum, 253–5, 267
  citizen-led treaty making and, 260
  constitutional rules and norms and, 255
  European Constitution and, 254
  European Convention and, 253
  legitimacy and, 254–5
  Mendez, F., Mendez, M., and Triga on, 254
  two-level games and, 254
  unanimity requirement and, 254
Papandreou, George, 280
Paris Agreement, 3
Paris Climate Change Conference, 1–2
Paris Peace Conference, 7–8, 69
parliamentary oversight, 262–3
parliaments, 3–4, 59–65, 205, 207, 274,
    282–3. *See also* European Parliament
  Ad Hoc Assembly and, 59

Assizes and, 60
Austria and, 90–1, 137–8, 175
Belgium and, 4, 92–3, 175–6, 279
Bulgaria and, 93–4, 139, 177
classifications of, 88–90, 118–32
Closa on, 88
consent stage and, 8, 87–119, 275
constitutional review and, 175–7, 179–83,
    185–9, 191
constitutional rules and norms and,
    89–132
Convention Method and, 67, 78–9, 273
COSAC and, 74
Croatia and, 94–5, 139
Cyprus and, 95–6, 140
Czech Republic and, 96–8, 140, 179
Denmark and, 80, 98–9, 141, 209, 230
ECSC Common Assembly and, 71
Estonia and, 99, 180
European Convention and, 62–3, 66
Finland and, 99–101, 181
France and, 5, 66, 76, 101–2, 181, 227
Germany and, 103–4, 182–3
Greece and, 104–5
heads of state or government and, 71–83,
    274
Hungary and, 105–6, 183
India and, 87
involuntary defection and, 227–8
Ireland and, 106–7, 185
Italy and, 107, 148–9
Latvia and, 107–8, 149, 185–6
legislative hurdles and, 88–90
legitimacy and, 256
Lithuania and, 108–9
Luxembourg and, 109–10, 150–1, 187
Maastricht Treaty and, 60
Malta and, 110–11, 151
negotiation stage and, 57, 66–7, 74–5, 275
Netherlands and, 111–12
pivot positions and, 88
Poland and, 112–13, 152, 188
Portugal and, 113–14, 153–4
ratification constraints and, 88, 90
Romania and, 114–15, 189
Slovak Republic and, 115
Slovenia and, 115–16, 155
Spain and, 116–17, 156
states, monist *vs.* dualist, and, 210–11
subnational and, 4, 92–3
Sweden and, 117, 156–7, 191
treaty amendments and, 225, 227–8, 256
treaty making, medieval period, and, 5
Treaty of Lisbon and, 63–4, 233
Treaty of Paris and, 119
trust and, 18, 213, 215, 275
two-level games and, 37–9, 66, 213

330   INDEX

parliaments, (cont.)
  two-level legitimacy and, 79–80
  UK and, 8, 117–18, 157–8, 209, 227–8
passerelle clauses, Treaty of Lisbon and, 32
Peace of Münster, 6
Peace of Westphalia, 6–7
Peake, Jeffrey S., 234
Peers, Steve, 251
Penelope (draft treaty), 74, 248
the people. *See* referendums
Peterson, Genevieve, 7
Pharr, Susan J., 46–7
Phelan, William, 282
Piris, Jean-Claude, 243
pivot positions, parliaments and, 88
Plan D for Democracy, 233
Poland
  Article 136 amendment and, 112
  constitutional review and, 188
  executives and, 112–13, 188
  parliaments and, 112–13, 152, 188
  referendums and, 112–13, 152–3
Pollack, Mark, 67
Ponsonby, Arthur, 117–18
population size, 210
Portugal
  constitutional amendments and, 114
  constitutional review and, 188–9
  executives and, 113–14, 154, 188–9
  parliaments and, 113–14, 153–4
  referendums and, 153–4, 168, 188, 255
power, 1
Pringle case, 65, 261, 264
privilege, legitimacy and, 44, 209
Prodi, Romano, 66, 73, 248
public statements, two-level games and,
  37
Putnam, Robert, 265
  on chief negotiators, 69
  heads of state or government and, 82
  ratification and, 40
  trust and, 46–7
  two-level games and, 17, 19, 36, 38, 40,
  50
  tying hands, strategy of, and, 34–5, 208,
  247, 274

Qvortrup, Matt, 35, 138

Ranney, Austin, 46
ratification, 13, 205, 207, 214. *See also*
  consent stage
  constitutional requirements, domestic,
  and, 6
  executives and
    Austria and, 90–1
    Belgium and, 92

Cyprus and, 95–6
Czech Republic and, 96
France and, 102
Greece and, 104
Poland and, 112–13
Portugal and, 113–14
Romania and, 114
Spain and, 116
full powers and, 6
NGOs and, 66
non-, 8, 47–8, 265–7
Putnam on, 40
trust and, 44
untying hands, strategy of, and, 20
ratification constraints
  Amsterdam Treaty and, 37
  Convention Method and, 39
  as endogenous, 37–8
  as exogenous, 37–8
  Pahre on, 38
  parliaments and, 88, 90
  tying hands, strategy of, and, 36–9
ratification crises, 47–9, 266
  treaty amendments and, 227–34
  trust and, 44
  tying hands, strategy of, and, 48–50
Raustiala, Kal, 66
referendums, 162, 205–8, 273–4, 283
  Austria and, 91, 137–8
  Belgium and, 138
  Brazil and, 133
  Bulgaria and, 139
  classifications of, 134–7, 158–9
  Closa on, 135, 251
  consent stage and, 133–59
  constitutional rules and norms and,
  136–60
  Croatia and, 94–5, 139, 178
  Cyprus and, 135, 140
  Czech Republic and, 97, 140
  Denmark and, 4, 11, 75, 98, 140–2, 164,
  229–31
  Estonia and, 142
  European Constitution and, 4, 37, 135–6,
  152–3, 157, 192, 232
  executives and, 139, 148, 154, 156
  Finland and, 100, 142–3
  France and, 101–2, 143–4, 228, 257
  Germany and, 144–5
  Greece and, 145–6, 279–81
  Greenland and, 141
  Hug on, 134–5
  Hungary and, 146
  involuntary defection and, 229–34
  Ireland and, 14, 107, 134, 137, 147–8,
  163, 166, 231–2, 238–9, 252
  Italy and, 148–9, 166

Latvia and, 108, 149
Lithuania and, 108, 150
Luxembourg and, 109, 150–1
Maastricht Treaty and, 4, 41, 75
Malta and, 151
negotiation stage and, 57
Netherlands and, 135–7, 151–2, 167, 270, 279, 281
New Zealand and, 133
Palau and, 133
pan-European referendum as, 253–5
Poland and, 112–13, 152–3
Portugal and, 153–4, 168, 188, 255
regulation of, 250–3
re-runs of, 252–3
Romania and, 114, 154
Simmons on, 136
Slovak Republic and, 154–5, 189–90
Slovenia and, 116, 155, 252
South Sudan and, 253
Spain and, 155–6
Sweden and, 156–7
Switzerland and, 8, 133
treaty amendments and, 225, 240, 273
Treaty of Lisbon and, 157–8
treaty-making, interwar period, and, 8
trust and, 18, 46–7, 213, 215
two-level legitimacy and, 251–3
tying hands, strategy of, and, 35, 215, 274
UK and, 4–5, 134, 157–8, 280–1
Reflection Group. *See* Westendorp Group
regulation, of referendums, 250–3
Reh, Christine, 13, 68
responsibility, two-level games and, 39. *See also* accountability
revision procedures, 11–12, 268, 285. *See also* simplified revision procedure
Robertson, David, 170
Romania
constitutional amendments and, 114–15, 154, 168, 189, 259
constitutional review and, 189
executives and, 114, 154
parliaments and, 114–15, 189
referendums and, 114, 154
Rome Statute, 2, 10
Rose, Richard, 252, 254, 267
Roznai, Yaniv, 262
Russia, 170

Sarkozy, Nicolas, 39–40, 233, 237
Savage, Deborah, 39, 51
Sceberras Trigona, Alex, 111
Scharpf, Fritz W., 43
Schelling, Thomas, 34–5
Schengen Agreement, 235, 239

Schengen Convention, 237
Schmidt, Vivien, 39–40, 246, 249
Schneider, Gerald, 257
Schulz, Tobias, 37
Schuman Plan Conference, 58
Schüssel, Wolfgang, 254
Scicluna, Nicole, 263
Seville Agreement, 232
Simmons, Beth, 15, 48, 87–9, 205, 282
courts and, 172
referendums and, 136
simplified revision procedure, 70, 78–9, 251, 274, 285
EU Court of Justice and, 65, 261
euro crisis and, 12
European Parliament and, 262
Single European Act, 60–1, 266
Denmark and, 141
Ireland and, 147–8, 184–5, 228
Sinnott, Richard, 253
Slapin, Jonathan, 38–9
Slovak Republic
constitutional amendments and, 115
constitutional review and, 189–90
executives and, 154, 189
parliaments and, 115
referendums and, 154–5, 189–90
Slovenia
constitutional amendments and, 116
constitutional review and, 190
parliaments and, 115–16, 155
referendums and, 116, 155, 252
Smith, Gordon, 134, 137
social contract theory, 51
Sound of Europe, 233
South Sudan, 253
Spaak Committee, 68
Spaak, Paul Henri, 59
Spain
constitutional amendments and, 116–17, 155–6, 190–1
constitutional review and, 190–1
executives and, 116, 156
parliaments and, 116–17, 156
referendums and, 155–6
Spinelli, Altiero, 72, 253, 277
European Parliament and, 72
IGCs and, 72
Sprinz, Detlef F., 48
state sovereignty, 2, 12
states
dualist, 210–11
monist, 210–11
wealth of, 210
Statute of the European Investment Bank, 224
Strategy of Conflict (Schelling), 34

INDEX

Stubb, Alexander, 61
Sweden
  constitutional amendments and, 117,
    156–7
  constitutional review and, 191
  parliaments and, 117, 156–7, 191
  referendums and, 156–7
Switzerland, 8, 133

tactics, treaty amendments and, 18
Tarar, Ahmer, 36–7
Teasdale, Anthony, 230–1
Thatcher, Margaret, 70
Tierney, Stephen, 252–3
time locks, 255–7
Tindeman, Leo, 276–7
Torrijos, Omar, 34–5
Trachtman, Joel P., 276
treaties, allowing failure of, 265–7
Treaties of Rome, 59, 73
treaty amendments, 3–5, 18, 30. *See also*
    Article 136 amendment;
    constitutional amendments
  Closa on, 88, 206, 222–3
  Convention Method and, 78–9
  courts and, 225, 228–9, 273
  European Constitution and, 268
  European Council and, 285
  IMF Articles of Agreement and, 250
  intervening elections and, 256–7
  legitimacy and, 240–1, 255–6
  Maastricht Treaty and, 224
  parliaments and, 225, 227–8, 256
  rate of, 222–6, 240, 256
  ratification crises and, 227–34
  referendums and, 225, 240, 273
  revision procedures and, 11–12
  Statute of the European Investment Bank
    and, 224
  tactics and, 18
  treaties, length of, and, 225–6
  Treaty of Lisbon and, 32, 63–4, 70
  Treaty of Paris and, 225–6, 257, 261
  United Nations Charter and, 250
  de Witte on, 12
treaty making, 7. *See also* citizen-led treaty
    making; consent stage; EU treaty
    making; negotiation stage
  in early modern period, 6–7
  history of, 5–11
  in interwar period, 7–8
  in medieval period, 5–6, 35
  participatory approaches to, 3–4
  rigidity of, 246–7, 267, 275–6
Treaty of Amiens, 110
Treaty of Bern, 9
Treaty of Canterbury, 5

Treaty of Elbing, 8
Treaty of Frankfurt, 8
Treaty of Lisbon, 11–12, 221, 233–4, 243,
  277
  Belgium and, 177
  Convention Method and, 64, 70
  courts and, 79
  Czech Republic and, 97–8, 179
  Denmark and, 180
  ECI introduced by, 258
  European Council and, 63–4, 234
  Germany and, 171, 182–3, 228–9
  heads of state or government and,
    64
  Hungary and, 105–6
  IGCs and, 19
  international law treaties and, 264
  Ireland and, 233–4
  Latvia and, 186
  parliaments and, 63–4, 233
  passerelle clauses of, 32
  referendums and, 157–8
  treaty amendments and, 32, 63–4, 70
  unanimity requirement and, 248
Treaty of Paris, 3–4, 7, 57, 221, 237, 273
  IGCs and, 58
  Malta and, 110
  parliaments and, 119
  treaty amendments and, 225–6, 257,
    261
Treaty of Rome, 235
  UK and, 191–2
Treaty on European Union, 281
Triga, Vasiliki, 13, 135–6, 205–6, 248,
  251
  ECI and, 258
  pan-European referendum and, 254
Trotsky, Leon, 8
Trump, Donald, 284
trust, 16–18, 43–6, 209, 283–4
  accountability and, 46
  control and, 46
  courts and, 18, 45–6, 52, 213–15
  distrust and, 46
  economic crises and, 44–5
  euro crisis and, 44–5
  forms of, 43
  governments and, 45
  Mair on, 52
  mistrust and, 46
  negotiation stage and, 43–4
  parliaments and, 18, 213, 215, 275
  Putnam on, 46–7
  ratification and, 44
  ratification crises and, 44
  referendums and, 18, 46–7, 213, 215
  as relational, 43

Schelling on, 35
two-level legitimacy and, 35, 42–7, 215, 274–5
Tspiras, Alexis, 280–1
Tusk, Donald, 113
two-level games, 213, 260, 275
  accountability and, 39
  citizen-led treaty making and, 258
  consent stage and, 213
  Convention Method and, 35
  governments and, 40
  heads of state or government and, 69–70
  international law treaties and, 236–8
  justification and, 39–40
  negotiation stage and, 36, 66–70
  normative perspectives on, 39–42
  Pahre on, 16, 274
  pan-European referendum and, 254
  parliaments and, 37–9, 66, 213
  public statements and, 37
  Putnam on, 17, 19, 36, 38, 40, 50
  responsibility and, 39
  time locks and, 257
  treaty failure, allowing, and, 265–6
  tying hands, strategy of, and, 34–9, 49–50, 221, 263, 267, 274
  unanimity requirement and, 248–9
two-level legitimacy, 17–19, 42–7, 260, 275
  citizens' initiatives and, 260
  consent stage and, 213
  governments and, 49
  international law treaties and, 238–9, 275
  negotiation stage and, 70–9
  parliaments and, 79–80
  referendums and, 251–3
  treaty failure, allowing, and, 266–7
  trust and, 35, 42–7, 215, 274–5
  tying hands, strategy of, and, 267
  unanimity requirement and, 249
  untying hands, strategy of, and, 247
  voluntary concession and, 49, 221
tying hands, strategy of, 17. See also untying hands, strategy of
  divided government and, 208–9
  involuntary defection and, 48, 208
  Pahre on, 208–9
  Putnam on, 34–5, 208, 247, 274
  ratification constraints and, 36–9
  ratification crises and, 48–50
  referendums and, 35, 215, 274
  two-level games and, 34–9, 49–50, 221, 263, 267, 274
  two-level legitimacy and, 267

UK. See United Kingdom
Ukraine–European Union Association Agreement, 279, 281

UN. See United Nations
UN Framework Convention on Climate Change, 1
UN General Assembly, 283
unanimity requirement, 248–50, 256
  Closa on, 248–9
  European Constitution and, 248
  pan-European referendum and, 254
  Treaty of Lisbon and, 248
  two-level games and, 248–9
  two-level legitimacy and, 249
United Kingdom (UK), 71
  Blackburn v. the Attorney General and, 191–2
  Brexit and, 4–5, 11, 157, 192
  constitutional amendments and, 118
  constitutional review and, 191–2
  courts and, 281–2
  Crotty case and, 192
  ESM Treaty and, 236
  European Constitution and, 192
  Fiscal Compact and, 280
  Maastricht Treaty and, 192, 227–8
  parliaments and, 8, 117–18, 157–8, 209, 227–8
  referendums and, 4–5, 134, 157–8, 280–1
  Treaty of Rome and, 191–2
  Wheeler v. The Prime Minister and, 192
United Nations (UN), 1–2, 9–11
United Nations Charter, 9, 31, 250
United Nations International Covenant on Human Rights, 246
United States (US)
  constitutional amendments and, 222–3, 259–60
  constitutional review and, 170
  non-ratification and, 47–8
United States Constitution, 8, 222–3, 234–5
untying hands, strategy of
  European Convention and, 39
  international agreements and, 234
  involuntary defection and, 17
  ratification and, 20
  two-level legitimacy and, 247
US. See United States
US Supreme Court, 9

Van Rompuy, Herman, 238, 251
Verdier, P.-H., 171–2
Verhofstadt, Guy, 77, 138, 232, 277
Versteeg, Mila, 16, 170–2
Vienna Convention on the Law of Treaties, 2, 10, 31, 249, 264–6
de Visser, Maartje, 172, 181

Waldron, Jeremy, 15
Weale, Albert, 39, 51

334 INDEX

Weber, Max, 267
Weiler, Joseph H., 250
Westendorp Group
  EU Court of Justice and, 68–9
  experts and, 68
Wheeler v. The Prime Minister, 192
WHO. *See* World Health Organization
de Wicquefort, Abraham, 8
Wiener, Antje, 14

Wilson, Harold, 134
Wilson, Woodrow, 8, 69
win sets, 34, 36–7
de Witte, Bruno, 235, 237, 248–9
  international law treaties and,
    263
  state sovereignty and, 12
  treaty amendments and, 12
World Health Organization (WHO), 10